ANCI
TRADITIO   Y

TRANSLATED BY

A BOARD OF SCHOLARS

AND EDITED BY

Prof. J.L. SHASTRI

VOLUME 12

ANCIENT INDIAN TRADITION AND MYTHOLOGY SERIES

[PURĀṆAS IN TRANSLATION]

VOLUMES

ŚIVA 1-4

LIṄGA 5-6

BHĀGAVATA 7-11

GARUḌA 12-14

NĀRADA 15-19

KŪRMA 20-21

BRAHMĀṆḌA 22-26

AGNI 27-30

VARĀHA 31-32

BRAHMA 33-36

VĀYU 37-38

VOLUMES UNDER PREPARATION

BHAVIṢYA

BRAHMAVAIVARTA

DEVĪBHĀGAVATA

KĀLIKĀ

MĀRKAṆḌEYA

MATSYA

PADMA

SKANDA

VĀMANA

VIṢṆU

VIṢṆUDHARMOTTARA

THE

GARUḌA PURĀṆA

TRANSLATED AND ANNOTATED BY

A BOARD OF SCHOLARS

PART I

MOTILAL BANARSIDASS PUBLISHERS
PRIVATE LIMITED
DELHI

First Edition: Delhi, 1978
Reprinted: Delhi, 1990

ISBN: 81-208-0344-2

Also available at :

MOTILAL BANARSIDASS
Bungalow Road, Jawahar Nagar, Delhi 110 007
Chowk, Varanasi 221 001
Ashok Rajpath, Patna 800 004
24 Race Course Road, Bangalore 560 001
120 Royapettah High Road, Mylapore, Madras 600 004

UNESCO COLLECTION OF REPRESENTATIVE WORKS—Indian Series.
This book has been accepted in the Indian Translation Series of the UNESCO Collection of Representative Works jointly sponsored by the United Nations Educational, Scientific and Cultural Organization (UNESCO) and the Government of India.

PRINTED IN INDIA
BY JAINENDRA PRAKASH JAIN AT SHRI JAINENDRA PRESS, A-45 NARAINA INDUSTRIAL AREA, PHASE I, NEW DELHI 110 028 AND PUBLISHED BY NARENDRA PRAKASH JAIN FOR MOTILAL BANARSIDASS PUBLISHERS PVT. LTD., BUNGALOW ROAD, JAWAHAR NAGAR, DELHI 110 007

PUBLISHER'S NOTE

The purest gems lie hidden in the bottom of the ocean or in the depth of rocks. One has to dive into the ocean or delve into the rocks to find them out. Similarly, truth lies concealed in the language which with the passage of time has become obsolete. Man has to learn that language before he discovers that truth.

But he has neither the means nor the leisure to embark on that course. We have, therefore, planned to help him acquire knowledge by an easier course. We have started the series of *Ancient Indian Tradition and Mythology* in English Translation. Our goal is to universalize knowledge through the most popular international medium of expression. The publication of the Purāṇas in English translation is a step towards that goal.

PREFACE

The present Volume contains the *Garuḍa Purāṇa* Part I (chapters 1-146) in English translation. It is the twelfth in the series of fifty Volumes on *Ancient Indian Tradition and Mythology.*

The project of the series was envisaged and financed in 1970 by late Lala Sunderlal Jain, the Veteran enterprizer in the field of Oriental Publication and the leading partner Messrs Motilal Banarsidass. Hitherto twelve Volumes of the Series, including the present one, (that is, four Vols. of the *Śiva Purāṇa*, two Vols. of the *Liṅga Purāṇa*, five Vols. of the *Bhāgavata Purāṇa* and one Vol. of the *Garuḍa Purāṇa*) have been published and released for sale.

The *Garuḍa Purāṇa* is normally classified as a Vaiṣṇava Purāṇa, but, in fact, this Purāṇa is non-sectarian and cosmopolitan in character. Its encyclopedic nature is reflected in the treatment of multifarious or miscellaneous subjects such as Medicine, Astrology, Palmistry, Metrics, in addition to the legitimate topics of a Purāṇa. This variety of topics needed elucidation—a task which could not be accomplished by a mere translation. Hence the provision has been made for the footnotes. Further, to help the reader understand the background of the subject matter, an introduction has been added to this Volume. A list of Abbreviations is also prefixed for the convenience of the reader.

Acknowledgment of Obligations

It is our pleasant duty to put on record our sincere gratitude to Dr. S. K. Chatterjee, Dr. V. Raghavan, Dr. R. N. Dandekar, Shri K.R. Kripalani and the authorities of the UNESCO for their kind encouragement and valuable help which render this work more useful to scholars than it would otherwise have been. We must also thank Shri T. V. Parameswar Iyer for his valuable spade-work which lightened our labour especially in the initial stage.

Editor

CONTENTS

ABBREVIATIONS		xiii
INTRODUCTION		xv-xxxv
PART I		
Chapters		Pages
1	Incarnations of Viṣṇu	1
2	Tradition of Garuḍa Purāṇa	6
3	Statement of Contents	14
4	Beginning of Creation	15
5	Creation of Progenitors	19
6	Description of families	23
7	Worship of the sun, etc.	29
8	Worship of Viṣṇu and Vajranābha maṇḍala	31
9	Viṣṇu-dīkṣā	33
10	Worship of Lakṣmī	34
11	Nava-vyūha worship of Viṣṇu	35
12	Order of worship	39
13	Viṣṇupañjarastotra	41
14	Meditation	42
15	Viṣṇu-sahasra-nāma-stotra	44
16	Contemplation of Hari and Sun-worship	72
17	Sun-Worship	74
18	Worship of Amṛteśa Mṛtyuñjaya	75
19	Prāṇeśvarī Vidyā	78
20	Mantras for removing poison	81
21	Worship of Pañca-vaktra Śiva	83
22-23	Worship of Śiva	84-86
24	Worship of Tripurā	93
25	Adoration of Āsana	94
26	Assignment of limbs over the body	95
27	Mantras to cure snake-bite	97
28	Worship of Gopāla	97
29	Trailokya-mohinī	100
30	Worship of Śrīdhara	101
31	Worship of Viṣṇu	104
32	Worship of Pañca-tattvas	108

33	Worship of Sudarśana	112
34	Worship of Hayagrīva	114
35	Worship of Gāyatrī	119
36	Method of performing Sandhyā	120
37	Gāyatrī kalpa	122
38	Worship of Durgā	123
39	Worship of the Sun	126
40	Worship of Maheśvara	129
41	Mantras to obtain Women	132
42	Pavitrāropaṇa of Śiva	133
43	Pavitrāropaṇa of Viṣṇu	136
44	Contemplation of Brahman or Viṣṇu's form	140
45	Characteristics of Śālagrāma	142
46	Vāstu-pūjā	146
47	Characteristics of Palaces	150
48	Installation of idols	153
49	Four Varṇas and āśramas	163
50	Daily routine for the aspirant	167
51	Charity	175
52	Prāyaścitta	178
53	Eight nidhis	181
54-57	Bhuvana-kośa	182-190
58	Description of the planets	191
59-62	Astrology	194-201
63-65	Physiognomy	203-205
66	Astrology	218
67	Svarodaya or Pavana-vijaya	220
68	On the test of Gems—Diamond	224
69	On the test of Gems—Pearls	228
70	On the test of Gems—Ruby	232
71	On the test of Gems—Emerald	236
72	On the test of Gems—Sapphire	238
73	On the test of Gems—Lapis Lazuli	240
74	On the test of Gems—Topaz	242
75	On the test of Gems—Karketana	242
76	On the test of Gems—Bhīṣmamaṇi	243
77	On the test of Gems—Pulaka	244
78	On the test of Gems—Blood stone	245
79	On the test of Gems—Crystal	246

80	On the test of Gems—Coral	246
81	Sacred Places	247
82-86	Greatness of Gayā	251-265
87	Fourteen Manus	268
88-90	Story of Ruci	272, 275, 282
91	Worship of Hari	282
92	Meditation on Viṣṇu	284
93-106	Teachings of Yājñavalkya	286
107	Teachings of Parāśara	323
108-115	Bṛhaspati-nīti-Sāra	327-365
116-137	Sacred Rites (Vratas)	365-397
138	The Solar Dynasty	398
139	The Lunar Dynasty	402
140	Genealogy of the Pauravas	407
141	Genealogy of the Pauravas and others	409
142	Greatness of Sītā	410
143	The Story of Rāma	413
144	Incarnation of Kṛṣṇa	416
145	The Story of the Mahābhārata	417
146	Description of Diseases	421

ABBREVIATIONS

CDHM	A Classical Dictionary of Hindu Mythology : John Dawson (Routledge and Kegan Paul Ltd, London : 1968)
CSL	A Companion to Sanskrit Literature : S.C. Banerji (Motilal Banarasidass, Delhi, 1971)
GPEA	Garuḍa Purāṇa—Eka Adhyayana : A.B. Avasthi (Kailash Prakashan Lucknow, 1968)
GVDB	Glossary of Vegetable Drugs in Bṛhat trayī : K.C. Chamekar (Chawkhamba Sanskrit Series, Varanasi, 1972)
MBHK	Mahābhārata Kośa (Parts I, II) : Ram Kumar Rai (Chawkhamba Sanskrit Series Varanasi 1964, 1966)
MS	Maitrāyaṇī Saṁhitā
PE	Purāṇic Encyclopedia : (English Version) Vettam Mani (Motilal Banarsidass, Delhi 1975)
PK	Paurāṇika Kośa : R.P. Sharma (Gyan mandala Ltd. Varanasi, Saṁvat 2028)
SED	A Sanskrit-English Dictionary : Monier Williams (Motilal Banarsidass, Delhi, 1974)
SKD	Śabdakalpadruma (Motilal Banarsidass, Delhi, 1964)
SSED	The Students' Sanskrit-English Dictionary V.S. Apte (Motilal Banarsidass, Delhi 1973)
VC	A Vedic Concordance : Maurice Bloomfield (Motilal Banarsidass, Delhi, 1964)
VINS	Vedic Index of Names and Subjects (Vols. I, II) Macdonell & Keith, 1967)
VN	Vanauṣadhi Nidarśikā : R. S. Sinha (Hindi Samiti, Sūchanā Vibhāga, Lucknow 1969)

INTRODUCTION

THE PURĀṆA—DEFINITION

As a class of literature the Purāṇa deals with ancient Indian religion, philosophy, history, geography, sociology, politics and other subjects and supplies the material for the study of various branches of knowledge and ancient wisdom.

The Purāṇa has been defined as *Pañcalakṣaṇa*[1] and is supposed to contain five topics: (i) Creation (*sarga*), (ii) Dissolution and Re-creation (*pratisarga*), (iii) Genealogy (*vaṁśa*), (iv) Periods of time with Manu as the primal ancestor (*manvantara*) and (iv) History of Royal dynasties both solar and lunar (*vaṁśānucarita*). But this definition is inadequate. For, the texts that have come to us under the title 'Purāṇa' contain either something more or something less than the five characteristics. This fact was noticed by the Purāṇic redactors themselves who later on adopted a *daśalakṣaṇa*[2] definition that suited the Purāṇic text.

But this too is not a standard definition. For, the Purāṇas contain aspects that are not covered by any of the ten characteristics. Besides, some of the characteristics covered by this definition are not found in certain Purāṇas.

In fact, the Purāṇa as a class represents different phases or aspects of Indian life in diverse ages. It is not possible, therefore, to adopt a standard definition for the class of literary composition that contains heterogeneous phases or aspects.

1 For details see Kirfel : *Das Purāṇa Pañcalakṣaṇa*; also *Brahmāṇḍa* 1. 1. 37-38; *Vāyu* 4. 10-11; *Matsya* 53, 65; *Kūrma* 1. 1. 12; *Garuḍa* 1. 223. 14; *Vārāha* 2. 4.; *Vāmana* 1. 1. 41; *Bhaviṣya* 1. 2. 4-5.

Amarasiṁha, the famous lexicographer (600 A. D.), also includes the pañcalakṣaṇa definition in his lexicon *Nāmaliṅgānuśāsana*, popularly known as *Amarakośa*.

2 For the daśalakṣaṇa definition, see *Bhāgavata Purāṇa* (xii 7. 9-10).

सर्गोऽस्याथ विसर्गश्च वृत्तिरक्षान्तराणि च ।
वंशो वंशानुचरितं संख्या हेतुरपाश्रयः ।।
दशभिर्लक्षणैर्युक्तं पुराणं तद्विदो विदुः ।
केचित्पञ्चविधं ब्रह्मन् महदल्पव्यवस्थया ।।

Moreover, a definition formed on the numerical basis of points cannot be perfect.[1]

We can, however, describe the Purāṇa as a class of literature that deals with the legends of gods, asuras, sages and kings of ancient times, contains abstracts of works in arts, sciences, medicine, grammar, dramaturgy, music, astrology and other subjects, affords insight into different phases and aspects of Hinduism—its mythology, idol-worship, theism, pantheism, love of God, philosophy, superstition, festivals and ceremonies.[2] In brief, the Purāṇas constitute a popular encyclopedia of ancient and medieval Hinduism in all its traits—religious, philosophical, historical, personal, social and political.[3]

ORIGIN AND DEVELOPMENT

The term Purāṇa connotes simply an old narrative[4] or the record of old events.[5] Ancient writers[6] derived the term as (i) पुरा भवम् (ii) पुरा नीयते (iii) पुरा अनति. According to Skanda[7] and Matsya[8] Purāṇas and the Mahābhāṣya[9] of Patañjali, there was at first a single work of literature called Purāṇa or Purāṇa-Saṁhitā. But when the process of interpolation started with the rise of sectarianism in India, the Purāṇa assumed a massive form. Each sect built up a structure of its doctrines around the nucleus of ancient material. The original Purāṇa underwent different forms and shaped itself into Vaiṣṇava, Śaiva and Brāhma Purāṇas.

CLASSIFICATION

The Purāṇa is divided into two classes : (i) Mahā-Purāṇa

1 Dr. Pusalker : *Studies in the Epics and Purāṇas*, Intro.
2 Winternitz : *HIL*. I. 529.
3 *Encyclopaedia of Religion and Ethics*, Vol X., p, 448.
4 Vāyu 1. 123.
5 Matsya 53-63.
6 Ibid. 1. 203; *ŚKD* under Purāṇa.
7 Skanda, Revā Māhātmya 1. 23, 30.
8 Matsya 53.4. पुराणमेकमेवासीदस्मिन् कल्पान्तरे नृप
9 Patañjali : *Mahābhāṣya*, Āhnika I.

(ii) Upa-Purāṇa.[1] Each class consists of eighteen Purāṇas.[2] Thus the numbeı of the Purāṇas is thirtysix.

The Mahā-Purāṇas are classified mainly into three categories—Vaiṣṇava, Brāhma and Śaiva in proportion as they accord preferential treatment to Viṣṇu, Brahmā and Śiva. The Purāṇas glorifying Viṣṇu are styled as Sāttvika, those glorifying Brahmā as Rājasa and those glorifying Agni and Śiva as Tāmasa.[3] According to this description the eighteen Mahā-purāṇas can be classified into Sāttvika, Rājasa and Tāmasa as under:

Sāttvika: Bhāgavata, Viṣṇu, Garuḍa, Matsya, Kūrma, Vāyu.
Rājasa: Skanda, Padma, Vāmana, Vārāha, Agni, Bhaviṣya.
Tāmasa: Brahmāṇḍa, Liṅga, Brahmavaivarta, Mārkaṇḍeya, Brahma, Āditya.

It is remarkable to note that in the list of Tāmasa Purāṇas the Garuḍa Purāṇa mentions Āditya Purāṇa instead of Nārada.[4]

The Purāṇas are not unanimous on this division. For instance, among the Śāttvika Purāṇas, the Padma Purāṇa[5] omits Matsya, Kūrma and Vāyu which are replaced by Nārada, Padma and Vārāha, retains only the Bhāgavata, Viṣṇu and Garuḍa of the Garuḍa list. Among the Rājasa Purāṇas the Padma Purāṇa retains only the Vāmana Purāṇa but leaves out

1 For details see R. C. Hazra : *Studies in the Upapurāṇas*, 2 Vols.

2 Bhāgavata XII. 7. 22-24; Garuḍa I. 223, 15-20.

3 Mārkaṇḍeya P. 53. 68-69.

सात्त्विकेषु पुराणेषु माहात्म्यमधिकं हरेः ।
राजसेषु च माहात्म्यमधिकं ब्रह्मणो विदुः ॥
तद्वदग्नेश्च माहात्म्यं तामसेषु शिवस्य च ।
सङ्कीर्णेषु सरस्वत्याः पितृणां च निगद्यते ॥

4 GP III. 1. 55

5 Padma P. Uttarakhaṇḍa 263. 81-84.

मात्स्यं कौर्म्यं तथा लैङ्गं शैवं स्कान्दं तथैव च ।
आग्नेयं च षडेतानि तामसानि निबोध मे ॥
वैष्णवं नारदीयं च तथा भागवतं शुभम् ।
गारुडं च तथा पद्मं वाराहं शुभदर्शने
सात्त्विकानि पुराणानि विज्ञेयानि शुभानि वै ॥
ब्रह्माण्डं ब्रह्मवैवर्तं मार्कण्डेयं तथैव च ।
भविष्यं वामनं ब्राह्मं राजसानि निबोध मे ॥

Skanda, Padma, Vārāha and Agni from the Rājasa list which are replaced by Brahmāṇḍa, Brahma, Brahmavaivarta, Mārkaṇḍeya and Bhaviṣya. Among the Tāmasa Purāṇas Padma Purāṇa retains only the Liṅga Purāṇa but omits Brahmāṇḍa, Brahma-Vaivarta, Brahma, Mārkaṇḍeya and Āditya of the Garuḍa list. Instead, it includes Matsya, Kūrma, Śiva, Skanda and Agni. Thus we find that there is confusion in this kind of classification which becomes more complicated by the statement of Skanda Purāṇa[1] which assigns ten Purāṇas to Śiva, four to Brahmā, two each to Devī and Viṣṇu.

Yet another kind of classification is recorded in the Devī bhāgavata[2] which names the mahā-Purāṇas by their initial letters except the Garuḍa which it mentions by the full name.

NUMBER OF THE PURĀṆAS

According to the Viṣṇupurāṇa,[3] the sage Kṛṣṇa Dvaipāyana Vyāsa compiled a Purāṇasaṁhitā from the various ancient episodes and imparted it to his disciple Romaharṣaṇa. The latter composed his own Purāṇasaṁhitā and among his disciples Kāśyapa (=Akṛtavraṇa), Sāvarṇi and Śāṁśapāyana composed their own. These four were the original Purāṇasaṁhitās. This was the first stage.

The Vāyupurāṇa specifies the number of the Purāṇas as ten. This represents the second stage in the development of the Purāṇas. The traditional number eighteen is the final stage.

1. Skanda P. Kedāra Khaṇḍa 1:
अष्टादश पुराणेषु दशभिर्गीयते शिवः ।
चतुर्भिर्भगवान् ब्रह्मा द्वाभ्यां देवी तथा हरिः ॥

2. Devi Bhāgavata 1. 3.
मद्वयं भद्वयं चैव ब्रत्रयं वचतुष्टयम् ।
नालिपाग्निपुराणानि. कूस्कं गारुडमेव च ॥

3. Viṣṇu P. III. 6.15.
आख्यानैश्चाप्युपाख्यानैर्गाथाभिः कल्पशुद्धिभिः ।
पुराणसंहितां चक्रे पुराणार्थविशारदः ॥
प्रख्यातो व्यासशिष्योऽभूत्सूतो वै रोमहर्षणः ।
पुराणसंहितां तस्मै ददौ व्यासो महामतिः ॥
सुमतिश्चाग्निवर्चाश्च मित्रायुश्शांशपायनः ।
अकृतव्रणसावर्णिष्षट् शिष्यास्तस्य चाभवन् ॥
काश्यपः संहिताकर्ता सावर्णिश्शांशपायनः ।
रोमहर्षणिकी चान्या तिसृणां मूलसंहिता ॥
चतुष्टयेन भेदेन संहितानामिदं मुने ॥

The traditional list as given by most of the Purāṇas comprises the following :

(1) Brahma, (2) Padma, (3) Viṣṇu, (4) Vāyu (or Śiva), (5) Bhāgavata, (6) Nāradīya, (7) Mārkaṇḍeya, (8) Agni, (9) Bhaviṣya, (10) Brahma-vaivarta, (11) Liṅga, (12) Vārāha, (13) Skanda, (14) Vāmana, (15) Kūrma, (16) Matsya, (17) Garuḍa, (18) Brahmāṇḍa.

The Purāṇic scholars are agreed upon the authenticity of the Purāṇas. But in regard to Vāyu or Śiva there is a difference of opinion. Majority of the Purāṇas include Śiva Purāṇa in the list while a few others substitute Vāyu for Śiva.[1]

GARUḌA PURĀṆA : THE NOMENCLATURE

The Purāṇas themselves discuss their nomenclature.[2] So far as the Garuḍa Purāṇa is concerned it is so called because the speaker of this Purāṇa is Garuḍa himself.

On the evidence of the Bhāgavata Purāṇa[3] the Garuḍa Purāṇa was also called Sauparṇa. The Vāyu Purāṇa calls it Vainateya, Alberuni[4] as Tārkhya. Ballāla, the author of Dāna-sāgara, mentions Tārkṣya in the list of Mahā-Purāṇas. In the nibandha-granthas, the terms Tārkṣya, Vainateya, Sauparṇa are often used which according to Sanskrit lexicons are synonyms of Garuḍa.

But the quotations made under the names Tārkṣya, Vainateya or Sauparṇa are not found in the extant Garuḍa. It is not certain whether these quotations existed in the old text of the Garuḍa Purāṇa which, later on, suffered change in the hands of redactors or whether they belonged to a Purāṇa that was quite different from the extant text called Garuḍa.

The Purāṇa is called Garuḍa because the original speaker is Garuḍa who narrates it to Kaśyapa. The latter narrates it to Vyāsa and Vyāsa to Śiva.

ARRANGEMENT

The Garuḍa Purāṇa in Veṅkaṭeśvara Edition, on which

1. For details, see introduction to Śiva Purāṇa, Part I Eng. Trans.
2. Śiva Purāṇa, Umā Saṁhitā 44. 125-135.
3. Bhāgavata Purāṇa XII. 13. 8.
4. Alberuni : Indica I. p. 130.

the present translation is based, consists of three parts (kāṇḍas): (i) *ācāra* or *karma*, (ii) *preta* or *dharma* (iii) *Brahma* or *mokṣa.*

Ācāra Kāṇḍa is known as pūrva khaṇḍa (Section I), Preta as uttara khaṇḍa (Section II), Brahma kāṇḍa as Mokṣa-kāṇḍa (Section III).

The ācāra kāṇḍa is called *karma kāṇḍa* because it deals with Karman. The preta kāṇḍa is called *dharma kāṇḍa* because it concerns religion. The Brahma kāṇḍa is called *Mokṣa kāṇḍa* because it leads to salvation. Thus

1. *ācāra* (= *karma*) *kāṇḍa*[1] Pūrvakhaṇḍa
2. *preta* (= *dharma*) *kāṇḍa*[2] Uttarakhaṇḍa
3. *Brahma* (= *mokṣa*) *kāṇḍa*[3] Uttarakhaṇḍa

The three Sections (*khaṇḍas*) are distinct and differ widely from one another in form as also in content. The number of chapters in the Sections is not uniform. For instance, the ācāra-kāṇḍa consists of chapters 1-240, pretakāṇḍa of 1-49 and Brahmakāṇḍa of 1-29. But in spite of this difference, the three Sections together constitute the *Garuḍa Purāṇa*. This threefold division is recognized in the *Garuḍa Purāṇa*[4] itself.

GENERAL CHARACTER OF THE KĀṆḌAS

Ācāra-kāṇḍa

As previously remarked, the GP. consists of three kāṇḍas: (i) Ācāra (ii) Dharma and (iii) Brahma. *Ācāra* (*karma*) *kāṇḍa* consists of 240 chapters, is the biggest of the three kāṇḍas in dimension. Of these 14 deal with the five principal characteristics of the Purāṇas, 48 with the medicine, 53 with the

1. Colophon of ācārakāṇḍa Ch I reads : इति गारुडे महापुराणे पूर्वखण्डे प्रथमांशाख्ये कर्मकाण्डे एतत्पुराणप्रवृत्तिहेतुनिरूपणं नाम प्रथमोऽध्यायः । The colophons of the other chapters of this khaṇḍa read आचारकाण्डे instead of कर्मकाण्डे ।

2. Colophon of the pretakāṇḍa (Uttara Khaṇḍa) Ch. I reads : इति श्रीगारुडे महापुराणे उत्तरखण्डे द्वितीयांशाख्ये धर्मकाण्डे प्रथमोऽध्यायः । The Colophons of the other Chapters of this Khaṇḍa read प्रेतखण्डे or प्रेतकाण्डे or प्रेतकल्पे ।

3 Colophon of the Brahmakāṇḍa (Uttara Khaṇḍa) Chapter I reads : इति श्रीगारुडे महापुराणे सूतशौनकसंवादे उत्तरखण्डे तृतीयांशे ब्रह्मकाण्डे प्रथमोऽध्याय: ।

4. Vide Brahmakāṇḍa Ch. I Verses 47-48 :
आद्यांशं वै कर्मकाण्डं वदन्ति
द्वितीयांशं धर्मकाण्डं तमाहुः ।
तृतीयांशं ब्रह्मकाण्डं वदन्ति
तेषां मध्ये त्वन्तिमोऽयं वरिष्ठः ॥

worship of deities, 61 with the Dharmaśāstra matter, 8 with morals, 13 with lapidary science, and 43 with miscellaneous topics, such as astrology, physiognomy, etc.

Dharma-(Preta-) kāṇḍa

Dharma- (Preta-) kāṇḍa deals with the subject of death, metempsychosis, karman and release from karman. It throws light on the omens of death, the path to Yama, the fate of the pretas, the torments of hells and the pretas as causes of omens and dreams. It describes rites to be performed at the time of death, funeral rites, ancestor worship and special funeral rites for the Satī. There are legends of the pretas, describing the causes of their wretched existence which recall the Buddhist legends recorded in Petavatthu.

Brahma-kāṇḍa

Available only in Veṅkaṭeśvara edition, this section contains a dialogue between lord Kṛṣṇa and Garuḍa on the supremacy of Viṣṇu, the nature and forms of gods, description of Veṅkaṭeśvara shrine at Tirupati and other Tīrthas (chs 23-27). It criticises the doctrines of Upādhi, Māyā, Avidyā, and upholds the doctrine of Madhva's dvaita school.[1]

GENERAL CHARACTERISTICS OF THE PURĀṆA APPLIED TO THE GARUḌA PURĀṆA

The Garuḍa Purāṇa gives more attention to extraneous subjects than to subjects that fall under the legitimate lakṣaṇa of Purāṇa. For instance, of the 240 chapters in the Pūrva-Khaṇḍa, 14 chapters deal with the Pañcalakṣaṇa. Section I, Chs 4-5 deal with the primary and secondary creation (*sarga-prati-sarga*). Section I, ch. 6 deals with the genealogies of gods and sages (*vaṁśa*). Section I, chs 87-90 with the ages of Manus (*manvantara*). Section I, chs. 138-141 deal with the genealogy of kings (*Rāja-vaṁśa*). The history of Royal dynasties is treated in a very condensed form and interspersed with the genealogies of Royal dynasties (Section I, chs 138-141). The subject of creation and dissolution is taken up again in section I chapters 54-58 and 224 respectively.

1. For detail GP.—A Study by N. Gaṅgādharan, pp. 1-109—All India Kashirāj Trust, Varanasi.

(i) *Creation* (*sarga*)[1]

The supreme god Viṣṇu assumes the form of Brahmā, and as Brahmā, he begins the process of creation. As Viṣṇu, he protects the world. As Rudra, he destroys the universe.[2]

Though devoid of attributes, he has an inherent Energy which manifests itself in the form of three principles—Sattva, Rajas and Tamas which are responsible for creation, maintenance and dissolution of the universe.

Accordingly, the supreme lord in the form of Brahmā creates the cosmic egg consisting of 24 principles. The cosmic egg is insentient at first but when the lord in the form of Brahmā pervades it, it goes in motion. Thus different kinds of creation are evolved out of it.

Creation is classified into 3 categories : (i) Primary, (ii) Secondary and Primary-Secondary. The three categories are arranged as follows: (Vide GP. I. 4)

Primary प्राकृत	Secondary वैकृत	Primary-Secondary
(1) महत्सर्ग = विरूप	(4) मुख्यसर्ग	प्राकृत-वैकृत
(Intellect and Ego)	insentient	कौमार
	objects (स्थावर)	mind-born sons
(2) भूतसर्ग = पञ्चतन्मात्रा	(5) तिर्यक् स्रोतस्	of Brahmā
(Five subtle elements)	animals	
(3) ऐन्द्रियक सर्ग	(6) देवसर्ग	
Five organs of action	Divine Beings	
Five organs of knowledge	(7) अर्वाक् स्रोतस्	
Manas	मानुष	
	human beings	
This threefold creation is	(8) अनुग्रह सर्ग	
called *prākṛta*.	sentient beings	
	This five-fold	This single creat-
	creation is called	ion is called
	Vaikṛta.	*Prākṛta-Vaikṛta*.

1. Bhāgavata Purāṇa XII. 7.11 :
अव्याकृतगुणक्षोभान्महतस्त्रिवृतोऽहमः ।
भूतमात्रेन्द्रियार्थानां सम्भवः सर्ग उच्यते ॥
2. GP. I.124.3, 6
ब्रह्मा भूत्वाऽसृजद्विष्णुर्जगत्पाति हरिः स्वयम् ।
रुद्ररूपी च कल्पान्ते जगत्संहरतेऽखिलम् ॥
cf. GP.I.4. 11-12.

According to the Purāṇas, the ninefold creation refused to proceed on the work of creation. Brahmā divided himself into two—One half in the form of a woman and the other half in the form of a man. In that half form of a woman he created a couple—Svāyambhuva Manu and Śatarūpā who began the work of creation.

(ii) *Re-creation after Dissolution* (*pratisarga*)[1]

The creation of the universe is not a permanent feature, for all creations end in dissolution which in turn give place to re-creation. The description of this process constitutes one of the five main features of a mahā-Purāṇa.

The process of dissolution is complicated. For, several dissolutions occur before the universe is completely dissolved. As the Purāṇas relate, a creation lasts for a day of Brahmā equal to the age of fourteen manvantaras. At the end of each manvantara, there occurs a dissolution. Thus a day of Brahmā contains fourteen dissolutions.

In like manner, during the life of the creator, several creations and dissolutions take place. Then occurs a complete dissolution when the creator has completed his life-time. The elements are dissolved and merged into the body of the creator. The creator takes rest for some time and then starts the process of re-creating the universe. In this way, we have a series of dissolutions and re-creations succeeding each other.

(iii) *Genealogies* (*vaṁśa*)

The Garuḍa Purāṇa deals with the Genealogies of kings in Ācāra kāṇḍa (chapters 138-141). The Purāṇa follows the Vāyu tradition as regards the solar dynasty, from Vaivasvata Manu onwards and the common tradition regarding the other dynasties. It omits several historical dynasties which the other Purāṇas describe.

1. Bhāgavata Purāṇa XII. 7.12.
पुरुषानुगृहीतानामेतेषां वासनामयः ।
विसर्गोऽयं समाहारो बीजाद् बीजं चराचरम्

Sons of Vaivasvata Manu and their Successors[1]

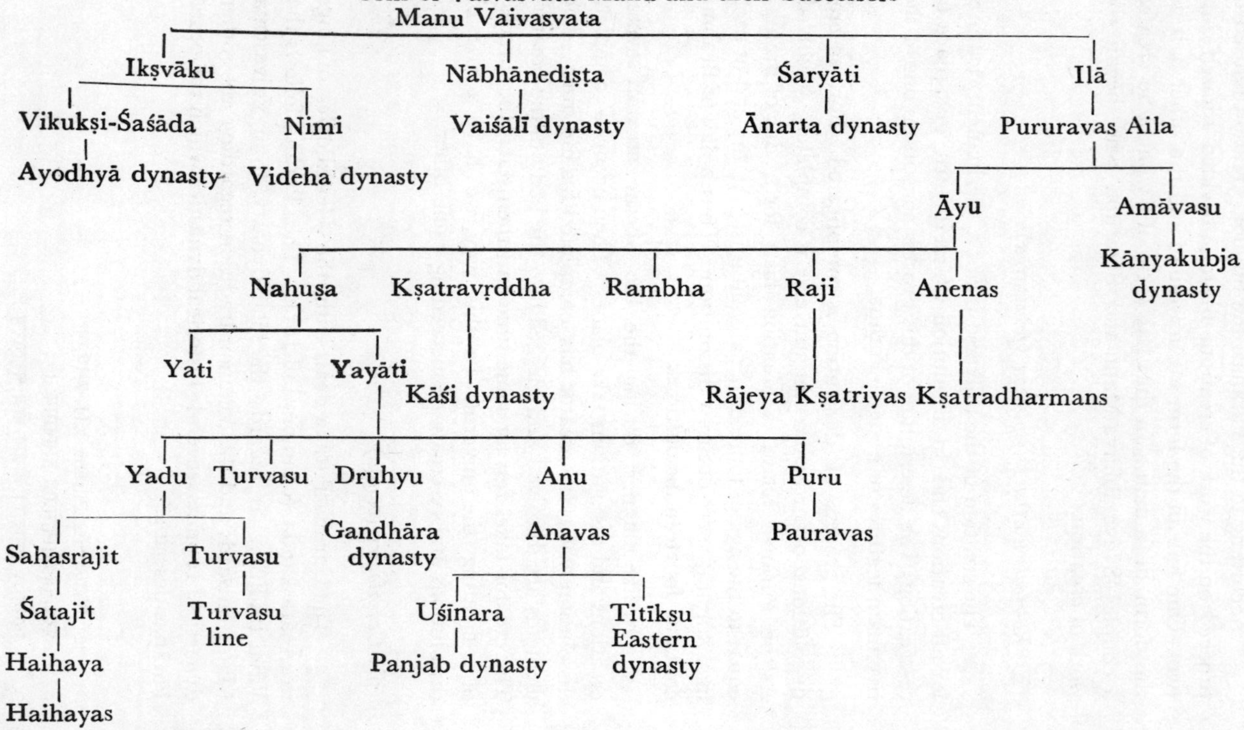

1. GP. I. 138.1 ff.

The Garuḍa Purāṇa deals with the dynasties of Kośala, Kāśī and Vaiśālī. The Videha dynasty descended from Nimi, son of Ikṣvāku. The Garuḍa Purāṇa confuses the dynasties of Ayodhyā and Videha, omitting certain kings from the line of Videha and adding these to the line of Vikukṣi, the originator of Ayodhyā line. Among the Magadha kings the Purāṇa mentions Bārhadrathas[1] who lived in pre-Bimbisāra age. In this context, the Purāṇa records that the Bārhadrathas will be succeeded by impious and Śūdra kings.[2]

The Bārhadrathas of Magadha were the successors of the Bṛhadbala dynasty which descended from the Solar race of Ikṣvāku.[3] According to the Garuḍa Purāṇa, Śuddhodana of Kapilavastu, father of Gautama Buddha, and the son of Śākya was Aikṣvākava.[4] This is confirmed by Mahāvastu which states that Śuddhodana belonged to Ikṣvāku dynasty. He was succeeded by Bahula (=Rāhula).[5] Rāhula's son was Prasenajit (=Senajit) and his son Kṣudraka.[6]

1. GP. 1. 141. 9ff.
जरासन्धः सहदेवः सोमापिश्च श्रुतश्रवाः
अयुतायुर्निरमित्रः सुक्षत्रो बहुकर्मकः ॥
श्रुतञ्जयः सेनजिच्च भूरिश्चैव शुचिस्तथा ।
क्षेम्यश्च सुव्रतो धर्मः श्मश्रुलो दृढसेनकः ॥
सुमतिः सुबलो नीतः सत्यजिद्विश्वजित्तथा ।
इषुञ्जयश्च इत्येते नृपा बार्हद्रथाः स्मृताः ॥
2. Ibid. 1. 141. 12.
अधार्मिष्ठाश्च शूद्राश्च भविष्यन्ति नृपास्ततः ।
3. Ibid. 1. 141. 5-8.
बृहद्बलास्तु कथ्यन्ते नृपाश्चेक्ष्वाकुवंशजाः ॥
बृहद्बलादुरुक्षयो वत्सव्यूहस्ततः परः ।
वत्सव्यूहात्ततः सूर्यः सहदेवस्तदात्मजः ॥
बृहदश्वो भानुरथः प्रतीच्यश्च प्रतीतकः ।
मनुदेवः सुनक्षत्रः किन्नरश्चान्तरिक्षकः ॥
सुपर्णः कृतजिच्चैव बृहद्भ्राजश्च धार्मिकः ।
कृतञ्जयो धनञ्जयः सञ्जयः शाक्य एव च ॥
शुद्धोदनो बाहुलश्च सेनजित्क्षुद्रकस्तथा ।
सुमित्रः कुडवश्चातः सुमित्रान्मागधाञ्छृणु ॥
4. Viṣṇu Purāṇa 4. 22.8.
5. GP. 1. 141. 8; Viṣṇu Purāṇa 4. 22.8.
6. Ibid.

Vaiśāli Dynasty

Vaiśāli dynasty descended from Manu's son Nābhānediṣṭa. This dynasty is recorded in seven Purāṇas, but only four lists of this Purāṇa are complete : those in the Vāyu, Viṣṇu, Bhāgavata and Garuḍa. The dynasty derived its name from king Viśāla who founded Viśālā or Vaiśālī as his capital.

(iv) *History of Royal Dynasties* (*vaṁśānucarita*)

The Garuḍa Purāṇa is not bothered about the history of royal dynasties. It treats the subject in a very condensed form. For instance, it does not take up the narrative of king Śaśāda though it mentions why the king was called by that name.[1] The history of Paraśurāma, the son of Jamadagni is recorded only in two verses.[2] The history of Rāma, the son of Daśaratha, which is longer, is recorded in eight verses.[3] The story of Rāma is taken up again but the entire account is condensed in fifty-one verses.[4] The history of Vṛṣṇi vaṁśa in the context of lord Kṛṣṇa is treated in eleven verses[5] and that of the Pāṇḍavas in thirtynine.[6] We find that the historical account (vaṁśānucaritam) in the Garuḍa Purāṇa is meagre and succinct but is still useful for comparison and sometimes for elucidating the older accounts.

(v) *The Ages of Manus* (*manvantaras*)

The time durations become manifest as manvantara, yuga, saṁvatsara and other relatively bigger and smaller units in the rotating wheel of time. The Purāṇas mention fourteen manvantaras in order.

1	Svāyambhuva	2	Svārociṣa
3	Uttama	4	Tāmasa
5	Raivata	6	Cākṣuṣa
7	Vaivasvata	8	Sāvarṇi

1. GP. I. 138. 19. शशादः शशभक्षणात् ।
2. Ibid. I. 142. 8-9.
3. Ibid. I. 142. 10-17.
4. Ibid. I. 143. 1-51.
5. Ibid. I. 144. 1-11.
6. Ibid. I. 145. 1-39.

9 Dakṣa Sāvarṇi
10 Dharmaputra
11 Rudraputra
12 Raucya
13 Bhautya

The fourteen manvantaras derive their names from fourteen successive progenitors and sovereigns of the earth. Svāyambhuva manvantara is the first and is known after Svāyambhuva Manu who produced the ten prajāpatis and is so called because he sprang from Svayambhu, the self-existent Brahman.

Each manvantara comprises 4,3200 human years or 1/14th day of Brahmā. A complete set of fourteen manvantaras makes up one whole day of Brahmā. Each of the fourteen manvantaras is presided over by its own Manu, god, seers and kings. This scheme of creation and dissolution repeats itself from one age of Manu to another and is described in all the mahā-Purāṇas. The Garuḍa Purāṇa is no exception to the rule. Garuḍa Purāṇa[1] mentions the fourteen Manus, their sons, seers, deities, lords of deities and asuras slain by Viṣṇu who incarnates himself in each of the fourteen manvantaras.

DATE OF COMPOSITION

The Garuḍa Purāṇa is a compilation of an encyclopaedic nature. The study of the text reveals different stages of production.[2] In view of the additions and redactions during different periods of time it iṣ difficult to fix the date of the Purāṇa as a whole.[3]

However, on the basis of internal and external evidence, we can suggest only probable dates for each section separately.

(i) *Dharma section*

The earliest reference to this Purāṇa is made by Halāyudha in his *Brāhmaṇa-sarvasva*. According to P. V. Kane, Halāyudha lived in the latter half of the 12th century A.D.

1. Garuḍa P. 1. 87. 1-62; Bhāgavata P. XII. 7. 15.

2. For example, in the enumeration of contents of the Garuḍa Purāṇa (GP. I.3.1-9) there is no mention of the topics dealt with in the Uttara-khaṇḍa.

3. R. C. Hazra: Studies in the Purāṇic Records on Hindu Rites and Customs, pp. 141-145.

Hemādri (1260-1270 A.D.) quotes from the Garuḍa Purāṇa in his *Caturvarga-cintāmaṇi*, Dāna and Vrata khaṇḍas.

The Mithilā pandits Vidyāpati (1360-1448) and Vācaspati Miśra (1425-1490 A.D.) recognize the authority of the Garuḍa Purāṇa. They draw upon it in their works Gaṅgāvākyāvali and Tīrthacintāmaṇi respectively.

Govindānanda quotes from the Garuḍa Purāṇa in his *Śrāddhakaumudī*, *Varṣakriyākaumudī* and *Śuddhikaumudī* ; Raghunandana in his *Smṛtitattva*, Kamalākara in his *Nirṇayasindhu*, Gopālabhaṭṭa in his *Haribhaktivilāsa* and Rūpagosvāmin in his *Haribhaktirasāmṛtasindhu*.

The citations from the Garuḍa Purāṇa in the Nibandha texts provide a further clue to date the Dharma section in the Garuḍa Purāṇa. A tenth century date has been proposed by Dr. Hazra on the basis of the Smṛti chapters in the Pūrvakhaṇḍa.

Dr. Kane holds the same view. On the strength of verses borrowed from Yājñavalkya and Parāśara smṛtis in the Dharma section of the Garuḍa Purāṇa he comes to the conclusion that this section cannot be carlier than the sixth century A.D.

Grammar

In the chapters on Grammar the Garuḍa Purāṇa omits reference to Pāṇini. We know from other sources that the study of Pāṇini was discontinued in the early part of the Christian era and the place of Pāṇini was taken over by Kātyāyana and other grammarians. The Grammatical chapters of Kātyāyana in the Garuḍa Purāṇa were most probably composed in the third century A.D.

Alaṁkāra

The portion on the alaṅkāras in the Garuḍa Purāṇa is older than the fifth century A.D., for the Garuḍa Purāṇa does not refer to any work on the alaṅkāras by name or to any writer, though there were works on rhetorics in that period.

Medicine

The preliminary chapters of the *Aṣṭāṅgahṛdaya* of Vāgbhaṭa agree with the chapters on medicine in the Garuḍa

Purāṇa. Vāgbhaṭa flourished between the 7th and the 8th century A.D. Thus the medicinal chapters in the Garuḍa Purāṇa could not have been written before the 8th or the 9th century A.D.

Polity, Ethics

A verse of the Bṛhaspati Saṁhitā of the Garuḍa Purāṇa occurs among the introductory verses of Bāṇa's Kādambarī.[1] Bāṇa lived in the seventh century A.D. A considerable period of time be allowed for the verse to gain popularity. Thus the Nīti portion of the Garuḍa Purāṇa cannot be earlier than the 8th or the 9th century A.D. Moreover, a number of references depict the helpless condition of the country during the foreign rule.[2] This in itself is sufficient to establish a very late date for this section of the Purāṇa.

Geography

The Garuḍa Purāṇa (1.55.6) reads

पूर्वे किराता यस्यास्ते पश्चिमे यवनाः स्थिताः ।
अन्ध्रा दक्षिणतो यस्य तुरुष्काश्चापि चोत्तरे ।।

And the Garuḍa Purāṇa (I.55.17) reads

पश्चिमे सैन्धवा म्लेच्छा नास्तिका यवनास्तथा ।

According to D.C. Sircar, the Turuṣkas and Andhras mentioned in the above verse are no other than the Turkish Musalmans and the Kākatīyas respectively. The Mlecchas of Sindhu deśa refer to the occupation of Sindh by the Muslim conquerors. This portion might have been added when the country was overrun by Muslim invaders from Central Asia.

1. GP. I. 112. 16; cf. Kādambarī, Introductory Verse 11
अकारणाविष्कृतकोपधारिणः
खलाद् भयं कस्य न नाम जायते ।
विषं महाहेर्विषमस्य दुर्वचः
सुदुस्सहं सन्निपतेत्सदा मुखे ।।
2. GP. I. 108. 7:
कालो हि दुरतिक्रमः ।
Ibid. I. 115. 3
धन्यास्ते ये न पश्यन्ति देशभङ्गं कुलक्षयम् ।।
Ibid. I. 115. 4
कुराज्ये नास्ति जीवितम्
Ibid. I. 108. 6
कालेन रिपुणा सन्धिः काले मित्रेण विग्रहः ।
कार्यकारणमाश्रित्य कालं क्षिपति पण्डितः ।।

Thus the sections on Geography in the Garuḍa Purāṇa could not have been written earlier than the 13th century A.D.

Lapidary section

Varāhamihira in his *Bṛhatsaṁhitā* mentions 22 gems but the Garuḍa Purāṇa treats of only 12. This portion is therefore not later than Varāhamihira (550 A.D).

A comparison between the Garuḍa Purāṇa and the Agni Purāṇa shows that the former was modelled upon the latter. The Garuḍa Purāṇa can be dated in the tenth century A.D.

The Garuḍa Purāṇa quotes verses from those portions of the Kūrma Purāṇa which were added by the Pāśupatas between 700-800 A.D.

Vāgbhaṭa, the author of the *aṣṭāṅga-hṛdaya-saṁhitā* lived between the 8th and the 9th century A.D. The Garuḍa Purāṇa cannot be earlier than about the middle of the 9th century A.D. It is highly probable that the extant Garuḍa Purāṇa was compiled between 850-1000 A.D.

LOCALITY

The three Kāṇḍas into which the extant Garuḍa Purāṇa is divided are distinct works. Each Kāṇḍa has a fresh beginning and might have been produced at different locality and later on put together.

Ācārakāṇḍa

The Nibandha writers of Mithilā quote verses from the ācārakāṇḍa of Garuḍa Purāṇa in their dharma śāstras. On this basis Dr Hazra remarks that the ācārakāṇḍa might have been produced in Mithila.

Pretakāṇḍa

The Kāṇḍa, as previously stated, is a later addition. The internal evidence does not help us to assign this kāṇḍa to any particular locality.

Brahmakāṇḍa

This Kāṇḍa deals with the greatness of Tirupati and other Vaiṣṇavite sacred places, Śrīraṅga, Kañci, etc., and sacred rivers such as Kāverī, Bhīmā, Narmadā, Svarṇamukhī and hills such as Śrīmuṣṭa, Śrīśaila, etc. and describes waterfalls in the hills. As these sacred places, rivers and hills are in the South, this Kāṇḍa might have been written in South India.

But the foregoing data is conjectural. In the absence of adequate evidence it is not possible to declare the place of origin or compilation of the whole Purāṇa.

AUTHENTICITY OF THE PRESENT TEXT

There have been additions to the Purāṇas from time to time and Garuḍa Purāṇa is no exception. Taking the Pūrva-Khaṇḍa at first, we find that chs 141-145 deal with the incarnations of Viṣṇu and in connection with them narrate the stories of the *Rāmāyaṇa*, *Mahābhārata* and *Harivaṁśa*, none of which has been referred to in the synopsis of contents stated in the Garuḍa Purāṇa I. 3. The number of incarnations named in the chapters 141-145 is only ten and here Vāmana is replaced by Dhanvantari. This number is not in agreement with that given in ch. I where 21 incarnations are named. Again in ch. 202 the number of Viṣṇu's incarnations is seventeen[1] and among them there are four names, viz., Rāma, Hayagrīva, Makaradhvaja and Nāga which are not found in ch. I. These varying lists of incarnations cannot be ascribed to one hand. Hence these chapters cannot but be spurious.

So far about the Pūrvakhaṇḍa. But the Uttarakhaṇḍa is decidedly a later addition. For, in the verses which are cited from the GP. in *Madanapārijāta*, *Smṛtitattva* and *Haribhakti vilāsa*, Garuḍa has been addressed as "khaga" "pakṣīndra" and these verses are not found in this khaṇḍa. Hence, the spurious character of this khaṇḍa is undeniable.

GARUḌA PURĀṆA—A VAIṢṆAVA PURĀṆA

The Garuḍa Purāṇa is ranked among the Vaiṣṇava Purāṇas, for it glorifies Viṣṇu by his various names and in his various forms. In this respect, it follows the Pañcarātra School of *Vaiṣṇava sampradāya* which eulogises Viṣṇu frequently by his names Hari and Nārāyaṇa. But the Pañcarātra āgamas speak

1. Hazra: Purāṇic Records P. 144, refers to Vaṅga Edition.

of four Vyūhas while the Garuḍa Purāṇa mentions nine.[1] The Garuḍa Purāṇa (Section 1, Chapter 12, Verses 13-14) introduces nine forms of Viṣṇu: (1) Sudarśana, (2) Hari, (3) Acyuta, (4) Trivikrama, (5) Vāsudeva, (6) Pradyumna, (7) Saṁkarṣaṇa, (8) Aniruddha and (9) Anantaka. But elsewhere[2], it mentions five forms: (i) Vāsudeva, (ii) Saṁkarṣaṇa, (iii) Pradyumna, (iv) Aniruddha and (v) Nārāyaṇa.

As a Vaiṣṇava Purāṇa, the Garuḍa Purāṇa gives prominent place to Viṣṇu, describing his various forms which Viṣṇu assumed for the protection of the Vedic dharma and the destruction of daitya cult.[3] This section mentions twelve incarnations viz. (1) Matsya, (2) Kūrma, (3) Dhanvantari[4], (4) Mohinī (5) Vārāha, (6) Narasiṁha, (7) Paraśurāma, (8) Rāma Dāśarathi, (9) Balarāma Vāsudeva, (10) Kṛṣṇa Vāsudeva, (11) Buddha, (12) Kalki. This list omits Vāmana. In I. 86. 10-12, the Garuḍa Purāṇa mentions 11 incarnations of Viṣṇu. It omits Dhanvantari and Mohinī but includes Vāmana. The Garuḍa Purāṇa (I.86.10-11) mentions ten avatāras, viz. (1) Matsya, (2) Kūrma, (3) Varāha, (4) Narasiṁha, (5) Vāmana, (6) Paraśurāma, (7) Rāma, (8) Kṛṣṇa, (9) Buddha and (10) Kalki. The Garuḍa Purāṇa (1. 3. 14-34) mentions 22 incarnations of Viṣṇu, viz. (1) Kumāra (2) Varāha, (3) Nārada, (4) Nara-Nārāyaṇa (5) Kapila, (6) Datta, (7) Yajña, (8) Urukrama (Ṛṣabha), (9) Pṛthu, (10)

1. GP. I. 11. 1.
   नवव्यूहार्चनं वक्ष्ये यदुक्तं कश्यपाय हि ।
2. Ibid. 1.32.3-6
   एक एवाव्ययः शान्तः परमात्मा सनातनः ॥
   वासुदेवो ध्रुवः शुद्धः सर्वव्यापी निरञ्जनः ।
   स एव मायया देव पञ्चधा संस्थितो हरिः ॥
   लोकानुग्रहकृद् विष्णुः सर्वदुष्टविनाशनः ।
   वासुदेवस्वरूपेण तथा सङ्कर्षणेन च ॥
   तथा प्रद्युम्नरूपेणानिरुद्धाख्येन च स्थितः ।
   नारायणस्वरूपेण पञ्चधा ह्यद्वयः स्थितः ॥
3. Ibid. 1. 142. 1.
   वंशादीन्पालयामास ह्यवतीर्णो हरिः प्रभुः ।
   दैत्यधर्मस्य नाशार्थं वेदधर्मादिगुप्तये ॥
4. Ibid. 1. 175. 1 mentions Dhanvantari as Viṣṇu:
   एवं धन्वन्तरिर्विष्णुः सुश्रुतादीनुवाच ह ।

Matsya, (11) Kūrma, (12) Dhanvantari, (13) Mohinī, (14) Narasiṁha, (15) Vāmana, (16) Paraśurāma, (17) Vyāsa, (18) Rāma Dāśarathi, (19) Balarāma, (20) Kṛṣṇa, (21) Buddha, (22) Kalki. The Garuḍa Purāṇa verses (I. 1. 13-34) that describe the avatāras of Viṣṇu are Verbatim found in the Bhāgavata Purāṇa (I.3. 6-26). The Garuḍa Purāṇa (1. 196. 6-13) mentions twenty-eight incarnations which include all incarnations of other lists.

Among the deities glorified in this Purāṇa Viṣṇu holds the supreme position. The Garuḍa Purāṇa (I. 227 ff)deals with Viṣṇubhakti. In I. 233. Sage Mārkaṇḍeya glorifies Viṣṇu by his names: Dāmodara, Adhokṣaja, Varāha, Vāmana, Viṣṇu, Narasiṁha, Janārdana, Mādhava, Puruṣa, Lokanātha, Sahasraśiras, Deva, Mahāyoga, Yajñayoni and Viśvarūpa. Besides, the Garuḍa Purāṇa (I.15) records one thousand names of Viṣṇu as the Supreme Being and mentions his attributes. In all these places the influence of Bhāgavata cult is distinctly visible.

Still this Purāṇa cannot be deemed as sectarian. For, as the study reveals, this Purāṇa deals with the worship of other deities too, though it devotes greater attention to Viṣṇu as the Supreme Being. For instance, we find the mode of worship of Śiva (I. 22-23), the mode of worship of Sūrya as a form of Viṣṇu (I. 17, 39), the mode of worship of Durgā (I. 38) and others.

Next to Viṣṇu, Śiva holds a prominent place. His worship, his Vratas such as Śiva-rātri, building his temple, installation of his image are described in several chapters. Among the Śaivite deities we find references to Vināyaka, Skanda, Viśākha, Durgā and Seven Mothers (sapta-mātṛkās):

Next to Śiva come Brahmā, Indra, Sūrya, Agni, Candra and Vāyu.

Thus we find that though the Purāṇa describes Viṣṇu as the Supreme Being, identical with Brahman, it does not omit the worship of other deities, though no other deity receives more attention than Viṣṇu. The eulogy of Śiva, Dvrgā, Skanda,

Gaṇeśa and other deities in an otherwise Vaiṣṇava Purāṇa is the strongst testimony that this Purāṇa attempts to remain non-sectarian in character. The other deities are Viṣṇu's attendants. The concept of Viṣṇu as Brahma annihilates all objects in the universe to the concept of formless, non-dual entity which is designated as an indivisible all-pervading Brahman.[1]

Though other deities receive equally an honourable treatment, yet portions of this Purāṇa are decidedly pro-Vaiṣṇavite.[2] The last Section, Brahma, is evidently pro-Vaiṣṇava. It cannot tolerate the non-devotees of Viṣṇu. It is very hard upon non-Vaiṣṇavites. It shows extreme rigidity in its preference for Viṣṇu over other gods.

In between the sectarian and non-sectarian character of the Purāṇa there is a marked tendency to uphold the non-dual nature of the supreme deity 'Viṣṇu' who can be realized by knowledge and not by worship (*kriyā*).[3] In Ch. 226 the supreme lord is considered to be limitless, impersonal, non-dual, infinite and formless. The Purāṇa refers to the identity of the

1. GP. I. 6. 72-73
   एतत्सर्वं हरे रूपं राजानो दानवा: सुरा: ।
   सूर्यादिपरिचारेण मन्वाद्या ईजिरे हरिम्
2. Ibid. III. 12. 59:
   निन्दां कुर्वन्ति ये विष्णोर्जिह्वाछेदं करोम्यहम् ।
   तदर्थमेव वायोश्च अवतार: सदा भुवि ॥

   Ibid. III.12.79
   अवैष्णवान् दूषयिष्ये सदाहं
   सद्वैष्णवान् पालयिष्ये मुरारे ॥
   विष्णुद्रुहां छेदयिष्ये च जिह्वां
   तच्छृण्वतां पूरयिष्ये त्रपूल्का: ॥

   Ibid. I. 41
   न चास्ति विष्णो: सदृशं च दैवं
   न चास्ति वायो: सदृशं गुरुश्च ।
   न चास्ति तीर्थं सदृशं विष्णुपद्या
   न विष्णुभक्तेन समोऽस्ति भक्त: ॥
3. GP. I. 228. 3
   कर्मणा वध्यते जन्तुर्ज्ञानान्मुक्तो भवाद्भवेत् ।
   आत्मज्ञानमाश्रयेद्वै अज्ञानं यदतोऽन्यथा ॥

Individual Self with the Supreme Self and describes the realization of this identity as liberation.[1]

Considering the Purāṇa as a whole we find that though the worship of Viṣṇu predominates and though for different objects and desires the aspirant is advised to worship different deities[2] Indra, Sūrya, Agni, Vināyaka, Candra, Vāyu and the rest in the prescribed way, liberation could be achieved by focusing thought on Viṣṇu alone.[3] In this process no distinction was made among the deities—Brahmā, Viṣṇu and Śiva.[4] The Purāṇa refers to the composite nature of the supreme deity in the concept of Amṛteśa who is the embodiment of Bhairava, Sūrya, Kṛṣṇa, Śiva and Brahmā.[5] The Supreme lord is conceived in his impersonal form, devoid of attributes, pure, changeless, eternal, unborn, devoid of acts, beyond the states of waking, dream and deep sleep, nameless, without beginning and without end.[6] It is known only by the formulas—'tat tvam asi', 'ahaṁ Brahmāsmi', 'prajñānaṁ Brahma', 'ayam ātmā Brahma." Such concepts indicate the metaphysical trend and the cosmopolitan character of the Garuḍa Purāṇa.

1. GP. I. 226, 227
   अद्वैतयोगसम्पन्नास्ते मुच्यन्तेऽतिबन्धनात् ।
   सोऽहमस्मीति मोक्षाय नान्यः पन्था विमुक्तये
   Ibid. I. 226, 227
   वेदान्तसाङ्ख्यसिद्धान्तं ब्रह्मज्ञानं ददाम्यहम् ।
   अहं ब्रह्म परं ज्योति र्विष्णुरित्येव चिन्तयन् ॥
2. Ibid. I. 51. 16-20
3. Ibid. I. 51. 21
   मुमुक्षुः सर्वसंसारात्प्रयत्नेनार्चयेद् हरिम् ।
   अकामः सर्वकामो वा पूजयेत्तु गदाधरम् ॥
4. Ibid. I. 51
   ब्रह्मविष्णुशिवान् देवान् न पृथग् भावयेत्सुधीः ।
5. Ibid. I. 18
6. Ibid. I. 91 2ff
   देहेन्द्रियमनोबुद्धिप्राणाहङ्कारवर्जितम् ।
   आकाशेन विहीनं वै तेजसा परिवर्जितम् ॥
   उदकेन विहीनं वै तद्धर्म परिवर्जितम् ।
   पृथिवीरहितं चैव सर्वभूतविवर्जितम् ॥
   भूताध्यक्षं तथा बद्धनियन्तारं प्रभुं विभुम् ।
   चैतन्यरूपतारूपं सर्वाध्यक्षं निरञ्जनम् ॥
   रूपेण रहितञ्चव गन्धेन परिवर्जितम् ।
   अनादि ब्रह्मरन्ध्रान्तमहं ब्रह्मास्मि केवलम् ॥

CHAPTER ONE

Incarnations of Viṣṇu

1. I bow to Lord Hari, the un-born, un-ageing, endless, identical with Knowledge, Supreme, auspicious, pure, beginningless, devoid of physical body and sense-organs, the inner presiding deity of all living beings, the unsullied and the only omnipresent force that transcends all illusions.

2. With mind, speech and actions, ever and anon, I offer my obeisance unto Hari, Rudra, Brahmā, Gaṇeśa and the Goddess Sarasvatī.

3-5. The learned Sūta,[1] well-versed in all paurāṇika lore, ever-calm, a master of all sacred scriptures and a great devotee of Lord Viṣṇu happened to visit the holy forest Naimiṣa[2] in the course of his pilgrimage. As he was sitting on a holy seat contemplating on the sinless Lord Viṣṇu the learned Sūta was adored by Śaunaka[3] and other holy sages of the Naimiṣa forest—the sages who were effulgent like the sun, yet ever calm and ever engaged in the celebration of sacrifices.

The Sages said :

6. O Sūta, we ask you, since you know everything. Who, among the gods, is the most godly, almighty, worthy of our worship ?

7. Whom are we to contemplate upon ? Who creates the universe ? Who protects it ? Who destroys it ? Who is the source of religion ? Who is known to be the suppressor of the wicked ?

8. What is the form of that God ? How is the process of creation explained ? What are the religious rites to propitiate him ? By which Yoga can he be attained ?

1. The *sūtas* in the Paurāṇika age were regarded as venerable persons who preserved the genealogies of deities, sages and kings in the form of songs and ballads. [Vide details in *ŚP* (*AITM*) p.l. fn. 2.]

2. A forest near the Gomatī-river. Here Sauti related the Mahābhārata to the sages. (Also refer *ŚP* (*AITM*) p. 2107; *Liṅga* (*AITM*) p. 800).

3. A great sage, the author of the Ṛgveda Prātiśākhya and other Vedic compositions. (Also see *ŚP* (*AITM*) p.l. fn. 1).

9-10. What are his incarnations ? What is the origin of different lineages ? Who assigns the various duties to persons of different castes[1] and āśramas[2] of life ? Who controls him ? O wise sage, narrate to us all this and everything else. Tell us the most excellent stories of Nārāyaṇa.

Sūta said :

11. I shall recount to you the *Garuḍa* Purāṇa, the essence of the anecdotes of Viṣṇu. Formerly, this was narrated to Kaśyapa[3] by Garuḍa. I heard it from Vyāsa[4] in the past.

12. The Lord Nārāyaṇa alone is the most powerful almighty of all gods. He is the supreme soul. He is the supreme Brahman.[5] All this world originates from him.

13. For the preservation of the universe the unborn, unageing, deathless Vāsudeva assumes various incarnations[6] in the form of Kumāra etc.

14. At first, that god, Hari, assumed the form of Kumāra[7]

1. There are four main castes prevalent among the Hindus : (i) *Brāhmaṇa*, (ii) *Kṣatriya*, (iii) *Vaiśya* and (iv) *Śūdra*. (Vide *ŚP AITM*) p. 2098).

2. According to Hindu scriptures, man's life-span is divided into four periods (*āśramas*) viz., (i) *Brahmacarya*, (ii) *Gṛhastha*, (iii) *Vānaprastha*, (iv) *Sannyāsa*. That is to say, (i) a period of studentship totally devoted to study and preparation for life, (ii) a period of householdership enjoying the worldly life, (iii) a period of retired life in the forest and (iv) a period of complete renunciation.

3. A great sage, the legendary father of deities and demons. (Also refer *ŚP* (*AITM*) p. 2104, *Liṅga* (*AITM*) p. 798).

4. The renowned sage, author of the Mahābhārata. (vide *Liṅga* (*AITM*) p. 808.)

5. *Brahman*—an indefinable supreme power.

6. Viṣṇu's preserving and restoring power is manifested in a variety of forms called *avatāras* literally 'discents' but more intelligibly 'incarnations' in which a portion of his divine essence is embodied in a human or supernatural form possessed of super-human powers. All these *avatāras* became manifest for correcting some evil or effecting some good in the world. (*CDHM* p. 361). Ten incarnations of Viṣṇu are accepted universally—Fish, Tortoise, Boar, Man-lion, Dwarf, Paraśurāma, Rāma, Kṛṣṇa, Buddha and Kalki. Bhāgavata-Purāṇa enumerates twenty-two incarnations and asserts that in reality they are innumerable. Garuḍa-Purāṇa follows the suit. (Vide details in *CDHM* pp. 33-8.)

7. A son of Śiva : generally known as Kārttikeya. (*ŚP* (*AITM*) p. 2104; *Liṅga* (*AITM*) p. 798).

and O Brahman, performed the unbroken vow of Brahmacarya (celibacy), very difficult for every one.

15. Secondly, the lord of sacrifices took up the form of a boar lifting up the earth that had sunk deep into the nether region.

16. The third incarnation was in the form of a sage. Assuming the form of the divine sage (Nārada[1]) he expounded the Sātvata Tantra[2]—the philosophy of inactivity of actions.

17. In the fourth incarnation Lord Hari, assuming the form of Nara-Nārāyaṇa[3] practised penance for the preservation of religion. He was honoured by gods as well as demons.

18. The fifth was in the form of Kapila,[4] the foremost among the *Siddhas*[5] who instructed Āsuri in the philosophy of *Sāṅkhya*[6] which had been ravaged by the lapse of time and categorised the (twenty five) *tattvas* (elements).

1. The famous legendary sage, a great devotee of Viṣṇu. (*ŚP* (*AITM*) p. 2108; *Liṅga* (*AITM*) p. 801.)

2. Obviously refers to Nārada-Saṁhitā of *Pañcarātra*—a ritualistic work on *Vaiṣṇavism.*

3. They are said to have been practising austere penance on the Himālayas, which excited the fear of Indra who sent down several damsels to disturb their austerities. But Nārāyaṇa put all of them to shame by creating a nymph Urvaśī from a flower on his thigh who excelled them in beauty. (*SSED* p. 281; *ŚP* (*AITM*) p. 2108; *Liṅga* (*AITM*) p. 801.)

4. A renowned sage who reduced to ashes the sixty-thousand sons of Sagara. (*ŚP* (*AITM*) p. 2104, *Liṅga* (*AITM*) p. 798).

5. *Siddhas*—A class of semi-divine beings. (refer *ŚP* (*AITM*) p. 2114; *Liṅga* (*AITM*) p. 804).

6. One of the six systems of Hindu Philosophy attributed to sage Kapila. This philosophy derives its name from the fact that it describes twenty-five *tattvas* (true principles) with the object to achieve the final emancipation of the twenty-fifth *tattva*, viz., the *Puruṣa* or Soul, from the bonds of his worldly existence—the fetters of phenomenal creation. It conveys a correct knowledge of the twenty-four *tattvas* and effects the disentanglement of the Soul from their vicious influence. It regards the whole universe to be a development of an inanimate principle—*Prakṛti*, while *Puruṣa* is altogether passive and simply a looker-on. It agrees with the *Vedānta* in being synthetical, and differs from the analytical *Nyāya* or *Vaiśeṣika*; but its great point of divergence from the *Vedānta* is that it maintains certain principles which the *Vedānta* denies, chief among them being that it does not admit God as the creator and controller of the Universe, which *Vedānta* affirms. (*SSED*. p. 596.)

19. The sixth incarnation was in the form of Datta,[1] the son of Atri[2] and Anasūyā[3]. When Lord expounded the philosophy of Ānvīkṣikī (Metaphysics) to Alarka, Prahlāda[4] and others,

20. Then in the seventh incarnation he was born as Yajña,[5] the son of Ruci[6] and Ākūti,[7] as a result of propitiation by Indra and other gods in the Svāyambhuva era.[8]

21. In the eighth incarnation he was born as Urukrama the son of Nābhi and Merudevī. He indicated to women the path of duty deserving respect of people of all stages of life.

22. In the ninth incarnation, as requested by the sages, he took up the form of Pṛthu.[9] With the milk of potential herbs he resuscitated the *brāhmaṇas* and other creatures.

23. He took the form of a fish in the great Deluge at the end of Cākṣuṣa Manvantara[10] and saved Vaivasvata Manu[11] by putting him in a terrestrial boat.

1. Popularly known as Dattātreya, he is regarded as an incarnation of Brahmā, Viṣṇu and Śiva.

2. The name Atri occurs in the Ṛgveda as well as in the Epic and Purāṇic literature. (*CDHM* p. 32. Also refer *ŚP* (*AITM*) p. 2096; *Liṅga* (*AITM*) p. 624).

3. Wife of Sage Atri. She is taken as a model for chastity. Brahmā, Viṣṇu and Śiva incarnated as her son Dattātreya. (*ŚP* (*AITM*) p. 2095; *Liṅga* (*AITM*) p. 642.)

4. Son of Hiraṇyakaśipu.

5. He had the head of a deer and was killed by Vīrabhadra at Dakṣa's sacrifice. According to the Harivaṁśa, he was raised to the planetary sphere by Brahmā, and made into the constellation Mṛga-Śiras. (*CDHM* p. 371.)

6. Father of Yajña and Dakṣiṇā.

7. A daughter of Manu Svāyambhuva and Śatarūpā.

8. Svāyambhuva was the first Manu and his period of reign is called Svāyambhuva.

9. Son of Vena. He milked the earth in the form of a cow and gave a new life to the creatures who were suffering on account of a famine. (For details, *CDHM* pp. 242-3.)

10. The period of the reign of the sixth Manu (*ŚP* (*AITM*) p. 2106; *Liṅga* (*AITM*) p. 800; *SSED*. p. 423; *SED*. p. 784; *CDHM* pp. 199-201 for *Manu* and *Manvantara*).

11. The seventh Manu, father of Ikṣvāku etc. (*ŚP* (*AITM*) p 2106; *Liṅga* (*AITM*) p. 800; *SSED*. p. 423; *SED* p. 784; *CDHM* pp. 199-201).

24. In the eleventh incarnation the all-pervasive Lord took the form of a tortoise and bore the Mount Mandara[1] on his back while the gods and demons churned the ocean.

25. In his twelfth and thirteenth incarnations as Dhanvantari[2] and a woman Mohinī respectively,[3] the Lord gratified the gods and charmed others.

26. In the fourteenth incarnation as Man-Lion[4] he tore the powerful demon with his fierce claws just as the mat-maker tears the willow-barks.

27. In his fifteenth incarnation, assuming the form of Vāmana[5] he went to the sacrificial altar of Bali.[6] Wishing to regain heaven, he begged of him three steps of space.

28. In his sixteenth incarnation as Paraśurāma[7] seeing the princes inimical to the *brāhmaṇas* he became infuriated and made the earth devoid of *kṣatriyas* twenty-one times.

29. In his seventeenth incarnation he was born of Satyavatī[8] and Parāśara.[9] Seeing men deficient in intellect, he created branches of the tree of Veda.

30. After that in his eighteenth incarnation he became a Prince Rāma[10] and, in his desire to do work of the gods, performed many deeds such as bridging the ocean.

31. In his nineteenth and twentieth incarnations

1. Mandara—a famous mount in Indian legends. (*ŚP AITM*) p. 2106; *Liṅga* (*AITM*) p. 799).

2. Dhanvantari—The deity of medicines, (*ŚP* (*AITM*) p. 101 fn. 82)

3. Mohinī—a celestial nymph; according to the legend of *Samudra manthana*, Viṣṇu assumed the form of Mohinī to cheat the demons of the distribution of nectar.

4. Viṣṇu assumed this form of half-man and half-lion to kill Hiraṇyakaśipu who was empowered with a boon that neither men nor animals could kill him.

5. Vāmana—the dwarf. *Liṅga* (*AITM*) p. 514).

6. Bali—the celebrated king of the nether world (*ŚP* (*AITM*) p. 750; fn. 147, 955; *Liṅga AITM*) p. 514).

7. He vowed to destroy the *Kṣatriyas* altogether from the earth (*ŚP* (*AITM*) p. 751 fns. 151-2 p. 1453; fn. 211).

8-9. The parents of sage Vyāsa.

10. A son of Daśaratha, the king of Ayodhyā; (*ŚP* (*AITM*), p. 751 fn', p. 1236 fn. p. 94, 1613; *Liṅga* (*AITM*) p. 118.)

obtaining birth as Balarāma[1] and Śrīkṛṣṇa,[2] in the family of the Vṛṣṇis[3] the Lord lessened the burden of the earth.

32. At the juncture of Kali[4] era, in order to delude demons, he will be born in the Kīkaṭa[5] country as the son of Jina[6] and named as Buddha.[7]

33. Again in the eighth juncture (change of cycles) when all kings will be on the verge of extinction, the Lord of the universe will be born of Viṣṇuyaśas[8] and named as Kalki.[9]

34. Thus O *Brāhmaṇas* ! innumerable are the incarnations of Hari, the Omnipotent Lord.

35. From them originate creations etc. They have to be worshipped and propitiated by *Vrata*[10] and other religious rites. Long ago, Vyāsa narrated to me this *Garuḍa* Purāṇa.

CHAPTER TWO

Tradition of Garuḍa Purāṇa

The sages said :

1. How did Vyāsa narrate this *Garuḍa* Purāṇa to you ? Please elucidate this in full, for it is essentially based on the anecdotes of Viṣṇu.

1-2. Well-known brothers celebrated in Indian Literature. Kṛṣṇa killed Kaṁsa, the demonic ruler of Mathura. (*ŚP* (*AITM*) p. 2104)

3. Vṛṣṇi was a descendant of Yadu. His descendants were called Vṛṣṇis.

4. The last incarnation in the cycle of four eras (*yugas*), supposed to have begun after the Mahābhārata war. (*ŚP* (*AITM*) p. 2103, *Liṅga* (*AITM*) p. 798).

5. *Kīkaṭa*—famous for Gayā, a holy place of the Hindus. It is identified with Magadha (modern South Bihar).

6. Jina—there seems to be some confusion here about the name of Buddha's father.

7. Son of Śuddhodana. (*ŚP* (*ATIM*) 2098).

8-9. The last incarnation is yet to take place (*ŚP* (*AITM*) p. 2103).

10. *Vratas* means religious austerities. (*Liṅga* (*AITM*) p. 808).

Sūta said :

2. In the company of the sages I had been to Badarikā Āśrama.[1] There I saw Vyāsa in deep contemplation on the Supreme Lord.

3. With due salutation to the great sage, I sat down there and asked him.

Sūta said :

O sage Vyāsa, please explain the form of Hari and narrate the full process of creation of the universe.

4. Since you ponder over the all-pervasive Lord, I think you know him. Thus asked, what he said, the same O *brāhmaṇas* ! you learn from me.

Vyāsa said :

5. O Sūta, hear. I shall narrate *Garuḍa* Purāṇa as it has been narrated to me by Brahmā, in the presence of Nārada, Dakṣa[2] and others.

Sūta said :

6. How did Brahmā narrate the holy *Garuḍa* Purāṇa—expounding all essential things—to you accompanied by Nārada, Dakṣa and others ?

Vyāsa said :

7. Nārada, Dakṣa, I, Bhṛgu[3] and others saluted Brahmā in his *Brahmaloka* and requested him to tell us what was essentially important.

1. A place sacred to Viṣṇu, on the Ganges in the Himālayas, particularly to Viṣṇu's dual form of Nara-Nārāyaṇa. Thus in the Mahābhārata, Śiva, addressing Arjuna, says, "you were Nara in the former body and, with Nārāyaṇa for your companion, you performed dreadful austerity at Badarī for myriads of years". It is now known as Badarīnātha though this is properly a title of Viṣṇu, as Lord of Badarī. (Vide *ŚP* (*AITM*) p. 927 fn. 142; *CDHM* p. 39).

2. A son of Brahmā. (for details *ŚP* (*AITM*) p. 2099, *Liṅga* (*AITM*) p. 795).

3. A Vedic sage, one of the Prajāpatis and founder of the race of the Bhṛgus or Bhārgavas. (*ŚP* (*AITM*) p. 2097; *Liṅga* (*AITM*) p. 794; *CDHM* pp. 54-55).

Brahmā said :

8. O Vyāsa, I shall narrate to you the story of *Garuḍa* Purāṇa just as narrated by Viṣṇu to me and Rudra in the company of the gods.

Vyāsa said :

9. O Brahman, How did Lord Hari narrate in the past the essence of *Garuḍa* Purāṇa, pregnant with meaning to Rudra accompanied by the gods ?

Brahmā said :

10. I had been to the mount Kailāsa[1] accompanied by Indra and other gods. There I saw Rudra contemplating upon the highest state.

11-12. After due salutation, I asked him, O Lord Śaṅkara, whom do you ponder over ? Since I do not know of a greater god than you, please tell me the essential of all essentials. I am desirous of hearing along with the gods.

Rudra said :

It is Lord Viṣṇu whom I contemplate upon. He is the Supreme Soul, the Almighty.

13. He is the giver of everything, the omnipresent, the cosmic form, and present in the form of every living being. I have smeared the sacred ash all over my body. I have decorated my head with matted hair.

14. O Pitāmaha, this is the sacred rite I follow for the worship of Lord Viṣṇu. We shall go to him and ask him about the essence I have been contemplating upon.

15. Lord Viṣṇu known as Padmanābha and Hari is devoid of physical body and is ever victorious. He is pure, the source of purity, he is Supreme Soul, the Almighty, connected by the word *Tad* (in the Upaniṣads).[2]

1. Name of a mountain in the Himālaya-range. (*Mbh* iii 503; *ŚP* (*AITM*) p. 2103; *Liṅga* (*AITM*), p. 798, *SED*. p. 301).

2. The mystical and philosophical writings of the ancient Indian sages. These discuss the nature of *Brahman* the supreme soul, *jīvātman*, the personal soul, worldly existence, human action (*karma*) etc. These are also called *Vedānta*. They generally form the last stage of the Vedic texts. Their number is plenty but Śaṅkara has commented only upon ten *Upaniṣads*. (Vide details in *CDHM* pp. 325-6; *CSL* pp. 354-55).

16-17. Uniting myself with that universal Soul, I am meditating on that very God—The Lord of creatures, the uniting string, in whom the entire universe consisting of all living beings lies preserved and later on, becomes merged, like closely clustering beads in thread.

He who has thousand eyes, thousand feet, thousand thighs and a handsome face;

18. Who is the subtlest among the subtle, the stablest among the stable, the biggest among the big and the sublimest among the sublime.

19. Who is preserved in the sacred literature and the Upaniṣads, in sentences and phrases and the true Sāmans,[1] as true and of true activities.

20. He is called *purāṇa puruṣa* (the Primordial being), among the twice-born. He is spoken of as Brahman[2] and in the process of annihilation he is termed as Saṁkarṣaṇa.[3] We adore that adorable one.

21. All the worlds quicken in him like the Śakula-fish in water. He who is *Ṛta*[4] (the cosmic order) and the one-syllabled god, the syllable Om[5], is beyond the existent and the non-existent.

1. The mantras of the Sāmaveda are called *sāmans* since they are meant for singing. Majority of them occur in the Ṛgveda.

2. Vide P. 2. fn. 5.

3. Name of Balarāma. This conforms to the system of *Pañcarātra* which enjoins the worship of Viṣṇu in five forms viz., Vāsudeva, Saṅkarṣaṇa, Pradyumna, Aniruddha and Nārāyaṇa.

4. *Ṛta* is a significant term in the Vedic literature. It generally means 'cosmic order' 'divine law or truth', 'settled rule or sacred custom.'

5. *Om* is a word of solemn affirmation and respectful assent. It is generally placed at the beginning of a treatise, as a mark of auspiciousness. It appears in the *Upaniṣads* as a mystic monosyllable set forth as the object of profound religious meditation, the highest spiritual efficacy being attributed not only to the whole word but also to the three sounds *a u m*, of which it consists. In later times *Om* is the mystic name for the Hindu triad, and represents the union of the three gods; viz., *a* (Viṣṇu) *u* (Śiva), *m* (Brahmā); it may also be typical of the three Vedas. It is also called *akṣara* or *ekākṣara*, (Also refer *ŚP* (*AITM*), p. 2108; *Liṅga* (*AITM*) p. 801; *SED* p. 235).

22. Who is worshipped by the deities, Yakṣas,[1] Rākṣasas[2] and serpents, whose mouth is fire, crest the firmament, navel the horizon, feet the earth;

23. Eyes the sun and the moon. I am contemplating upon that lord, in whose belly are the three worlds and whose arms are the different directions.

24. I am contemplating upon that Lord whose breath is the wind, in whose hair are the clouds and in whose joints are the rivers.

25. I am contemplating upon that Lord whose belly are the oceans, who is beyond sacrifices and beyond the Existent and the Non-existent.

26. He is beginningless but the beginning of the universe can be traced to him. I am contemplating upon him. The moon has come out of his mind and the sun out of his eyes.

27. The fire has come out of his mouth. I am contemplating upon him. The earth has come out of his feet, the quarters out of his ears.

28-29. The heaven has come out of his head. I am contemplating upon him. The creation, the subsidiary creation, the lineage, the Manvantaras and the records of kings and great personages can all be traced to him. I am contemplating upon him. We shall go to him to see the True Essence on whom I contemplate.

Brahmā said :

30. Thus I was spoken to by Rudra who, having worshipped and bowed to Viṣṇu, the dweller of *Śvetadvipa*[3], stood by, along with the gods desirous of hearing the narrative.

31. From amongst us Rudra addressed Viṣṇu the almighty, the essence of essences and after due salutations asked him.

1. A class of demi-gods. Attendants of Kubera, the deity of wealth. *ŚP* (*AITM*), p. 2120; (*Liṅga* (*AITM*) p. 808).

2. The demons (for details, *ŚP* (*AITM*), p. 2111; *Liṅga* (*AITM*) p. 802; *CDHM*, pp. 252-5).

3. Refer (*ŚP* (*AITM*) p. 2118; *Liṅga* (*AITM*) p. 806).

Brahmā said :

32. As Vyāsa asked me, so Lord Rudra asked Viṣṇu while the gods, along with other immortals stood listening.

Rudra said :

33. O Lord Viṣṇu, the foremost among gods, please tell us, who is the most powerful among gods ? Who has to be contemplated upon ? Who is the most worthy of our worship ? By what sacred rites, is that great Lord propitiated ?

34. With what sacred rituals, observations, pious worships and conduct of life can he be pleased ? What is his divine form like ?

35. Of what god is the universe born ? Who protects it and by what sort of incarnations ? In whom does the universe merge ultimately ?

36. The creation, the subsidiary creation, the lineage, the Manvantaras—from what god do they proceed ? In whom are these well-established ?

37. O Hari ! please narrate all this, and also if there is anything else. Then Lord Hari narrated to Rudra the glory of the almighty, the yogic means etc. and also the eighteen varieties of lores (vidyās).[1]

Hari said :

38. O Rudra, listen along with Brahmā and other gods. I shall tell you I am the God of gods, the master of all the worlds.

39. I am the most worthy of contemplation and worship. I am to be praised with prayers by the gods.

40. O Rudra, I award the loftiest of positions on being worshipped and gratified by sacred rites, observances and good conduct by men.

41. O Śiva, I am the seed of the existence of the world. I am the creator of the world. I punish the wicked. I protect religion.

1. Eighteen *Vidyās* constitute 4 Vedas, 4 Upa-Vedas, 6 Vedāṅgas, Purāṇas, Mīmāṁsā, Nyāya and Dharma.

42. I sustain the entire universe by my incarnations as fish etc. I am the sacred *mantras*[1] and their purport. I am engaged in worship and contemplation.

43. I am the creator of Heaven and other worlds. Verily I am myself the heaven and other worlds. I am the first *yogi* and also the *yoga*.[2] I am the Purāṇas.

44. I am the knower, the hearer, the thinker, the speaker and the object of speech. I am all. I am the soul of all. I am the highest god who bestow enjoyment and find beatitude.

45. O Rudra, verily I am the activity of contemplation, worship and offering. I am the mystical orbs[3] and mythological epics.[4] O Śiva, I know everything.

46. O Śambhu, I am all knowledge. I am the universal soul. O Śiva, I am Brahmā. I am the entire universe. I am the inner soul of all gods.

47. Verily, I am the good conduct. I am the Vaiṣṇava[5] cult. I am the castes and the āśramas, and their ancient religion I am.

48. I am the various religions and moral curbs and observances. I am the different kinds of rites. O Rudra, I am the Sun, the Moon and the Mars etc.

49. In days of yore, Garuḍa propitiated me with penance which he undertook on the earth. Feeling gratified I said : "ask me a boon", and he chose a boon.

Garuḍa said :

50-52. O Hari, my mother Vinatā[6] has been made a

1. Generally used to denote Vedic prayers, specially the *ṛks*. Also used for a prayer or formula sacred to any deity.

2. Deep meditation on the Supreme Soul with an aim to unite one's own soul with It. A system of philosophy, propounded by Patañjali, elaborating the aforesaid idea.

3. The mystical drawings, generally known as *maṇḍalas* for worship, particularly in Tāntric treatises.

4. The Rāmāyaṇa and the Mahābhārata.

5. One of the three main cults of Modern Hinduism. Its followers believe in the supremacy of Viṣṇu. The other two sects *śaiva* and *śākta* believe in the supremacy of Śiva and Śakti respectively.

6. A daughter of Dakṣa, a wife of Kaśyapa.

slave by serpents. Act thus, O god, that conquering them I may bring the nectar; that I, your carrier, may secure her release from bondage; that I may become strong, mighty, omniscient, destroyer of serpents and expounder of Purāṇa Saṁhitā.

Viṣṇu said :

O Garuḍa, everything shall happen as you have requested for.

53. You will secure the release of your mother, Vinatā from her slavery to the serpents. Conquering the gods, you will bring the divine nectar.

54-55. You will be strong. You will be my carrier. You will be the devourer of poison. With my blessings you will know the Purāṇa glorifying me and expounding my divine form. By your name, it will be celebrated in the world as Garuḍa Purāṇa.

56. O son of Vinatā, just as I am known as the essential glory of all gods, so also Garuḍa Purāṇa will attain the greatest fame among the Purāṇas.

57. You too shall be glorified like me, O Garuḍa. O chief of birds, contemplating upon me propound this *Garuḍa* Purāṇa.

58-59. Thus initiated by me, Garuḍa expounded this Purāṇa to Kaśyapa who sought it from him. By the power he received on hearing *Garuḍa* Purāṇa, he resuscitated a burnt tree. With his mind fixed on another, he revived others by means of this learning. *Yakṣi om uṃ svāhā.* This is the sacred *vidyā Gāruḍī.* O Rudra, please hear the *Garuḍa* Purāṇa dealing with my personality and narrated by Garuḍa.

CHAPTER THREE

Statement of Contents

Sūta said :

1. Thus Rudra and Brahmā heard this from Viṣṇu, sage Vyāsa from Brahmā and I heard this from Vyāsa. I shall now narrate this to you, O Śaunaka, in the sacred forest Naimiṣa.

2. In this august audience consisting of sages, will be narrated the details of creation, the mode of worship of the gods, places of pilgrimage, the treasures of the world and the *Manvantaras*.

3-4. The rights and duties of the various classes of society and stages of life, the mode of gifts, the ways of administration by the King, conduct of life, sacred rites, the families, the medical science along with Pathology, the various ancillary subjects, pralaya[1] (dissolution), the perfect knowledge of virtue, wealth and love, how Lord Viṣṇu had elaborated and annihilated the universe—all this is being told here.

5-7. In the *Garuḍa* Purāṇa, Garuḍa is bhagavān, who acquiring inordinate ability by the favour of Lord Vāsudeva, becoming the vehicle of Hari, the cause of creation, conquering the gods, brought the divine nectar, whose hunger was appeased, whose *brahmāṇḍa*[2] is in the belly of Hari, seeing whom or even remembering whom, the serpents etc perish.

8. Garuḍa is Lord Hari himself. Hence Kaśyapa could resuscitate the burnt tree by the *Garuḍa* (*-vidyā*) mentioned by Garuḍa to Kaśyapa.

9. That holy glorious *Garuḍa* Purāṇa, when read, bestows everything. Bowing to Vyāsa, I shall narrate it to you. O Śaunaka ! listen now how it is so.

1. The destruction of the whole world at the end of a *Kalpa*. (*SED* p. 311.)

2. Brahmāṇḍa, lit. the egg of *Brahman* is generally used to denote Cosmos.

CHAPTER FOUR

Beginning of Creation

Rudra said :

1. O Janārdana, please narrate to us the details of creation, subsidiary creation, lineage, manvantaras and records of kings and great personages.

Hari said:

2. O Rudra, listen. I shall narrate the details of creation etc. which wipe off all sins. I shall describe the old sport of Lord Viṣṇu in creating, preserving and annihilating the universe.

3. Un-sullied Lord Vāsudeva, Nara-Nārāyaṇa is the Supreme Soul, the infinite Brahman, the creator and destroyer of the universe.

4. All this visible universe, with its manifest and unmanifest phases exists in the form of the great *Puruṣa*[1] and the primordial Time.[2]

5. Lord Viṣṇu is both manifest and un-manifest, the great Puruṣa as well as primordial Time. Listen to his divine sport like that of a sportive child.

6-7. The creator, the limitless great Puruṣa, is devoid of beginning and death. He created the un-manifest and from that the soul. From the soul evolved intellect and from it the mind. From mind was evolved firmament. From firmament air. From air the fire. From fire water. The earth evolved out of it.

8. O Rudra, there is a cosmic golden egg and within it the Lord takes for himself a physical body for the sake of creation.

1. In *Sāṅkhya* Philosophy *Puruṣa* means soul, as opposed to *Prakṛti*, (primordial matter) (*ŚP* (*AITM*), p. 2111; *Liṅga* (*AITM*), p. 802).

2. According to Indian thinkers, it is Time (*kāla*) alone that controls the universe. Its destructive powers are unsurpassed. According to the *Vaiśeṣikas*, it is one of the nine *dravyas*. (*ŚP* (*AITM*), p. 2118; *Liṅga* (*AITM*), p. 806),

9. With rajas[1] element in profusion, the four-faced Brahmā takes a physical body and creates the movable and the immovable.

10. The creator creates himself along with the deities and human beings within the cosmic egg. He protects what is to be protected.

11. In the end, he destroys everything. The annihilator too is Lord himself, O Hara. Taking the form of Brahmā, Viṣṇu creates the universe. Hari himself maintains it.

12-13. At the end of the Kalpa,[2] in the form of Rudra, he destroys the universe. At the time of creation Brahmā takes up the physical form of a boar and by means of curved teeth lifts up the earth, learning that it is submerged in water. O Śaṅkara, listen : I *shall* briefly describe the process of creation of Gods and others.

14. The creation of *mahat*[3] (the cosmically great) is the first one. It is a metamorphosis of Brahman. The second creation is called *bhūta sarga*, i.e. the creation of the intrinsic essences (tanmātras) of elements.

15. The third one is called *vaikārika sarga* (modificatory creation) or *aindriyaka sarga* (the creation of sense-organs). All these three together constitute the *prākṛta sarga* (natural creation) beginning with the cosmic intellect (the cosmic great).

16. The fourth creation is called *mukhya sarga* (the principal creation). The stationary things are called principal creatures. The fifth creation is that of the sub-human beings *tiryak-yonayaḥ*) known as *tiryaksrotas*.

1. *Rajas* : the second of the three constituent qualities *guṇas* of all material substances (the other two being *sattva* and *tamas*). *Rajas* is the cause of all activities pertaining to the creatures; it predominates in men, as *sattva* predominates in deities and *tamas* predominates in demons. *SSED* p. 462.

2. A fabulous period of time, a day of Brahmā (*ŚP* (*AITM*), p. 1070 fn., p. 1364 fn. 160; *Liṅga* (*AITM*) p. 15 fn. 22, pp. 86 ff; *SED* p. 262).

3. The great principle, the intellect (distinguished from *manas*) *Liṅga* (*AITM*) p. 799, SSED p. 429.

17. The creation of super-human gods is the sixth one known as *ūrdhvasrotas*. The creation of human beings is the seventh one known as *arvāksrotas*.

18. The eighth creation is what is known as *anugraha sarga*. It is both *sāttvika* and *tāmasika*. These five constitute the *vaikṛta sarga*. I have already told you about the three that constitute the *prākṛta sarga*.

19. The ninth creation known as *kaumāra* is both *prākṛta* and *vaikṛta*.[1] O Rudra, thus there are four types of creation beginning with gods and ending with stationary things.

20-21-22. While engaged in this creation, the *mānasa* (mentally created) sons were born of Brahmā. Desirous of creating the fourfold beings—deities, demons, manes[2] and human beings—and also these waters, he engaged himself in the task. When his self became evident then from the loins of Prajāpati who desired to create, came out the demons who increased through tamas. He then cast off that body preponderant with *tamas*[3].

23-24. O Śaunaka, this discarded body preponderant with *tamas* became the night. The yakṣas and the demons found

1. In this connection, the following chart will be helpful

Prākṛta-Sarga

Mahat | Bhūta-sarga (Tanmātras) | Vaikārika-Sarga (aindriyika-Sarga)

Vaikṛta-Sarga

Mukhyasarga | Tiryaksrotas | Ūdhvasrotas | Arvāksrotas | Anugraha-Sarga

Prākṛta and Vaikṛta

Kaumāra.

2. The *Pitṛs* or deceased ancestors. They are of two classes, viz., the deceased father, grandfather and great grandfather of any particular person, and the progenitors of mankind generally;. in honour of both these classes rites called *śrāddhas* are performed and oblations called *piṇḍas* presented; they inhabit a peculiar region, which according to some, is the *bhuvas* or region of the air. *Śp* (*AITM*) *p*. 286, pp. 1615-19; *liṅga* (*AITM*), p. 407; *SED* p. 626.

3. Vide p. 16. fn 1.

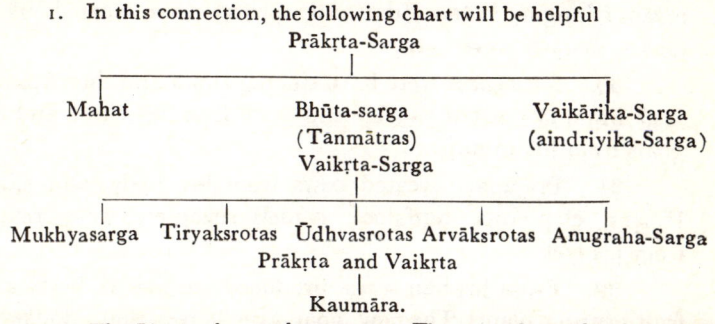

pleasure in that body. Then from the mouth of Brahmā were born the deities who increased in sattva, O Hara. This body with the preponderant *sāttvika* element was cast off evolving the day.

25. Hence, the demons are more powerful in the night and the gods during the day. The manes further evolved themselves by taking up the interspaces of *Sāttvika* element.

26. When that body was cast off, the twilight in between day and night was evolved, the human beings evolved themselves by taking up the inter-spaces of *rajas*-element.

27. That body being cast off became the moonlight or the twilight of the dawn (prāk-sandhyā). Thus his bodies are four, namely, the moonlight, the night, the day and the twilight.

28. By taking up *rajas*-element, hunger, darkness and anger were evolved. Then were created the giants (*rākṣasas*) emaciated with hunger and thirst, consumers of blood, called so on account of *rakṣaṇa* (protection).

29. *Yakṣas* were created and known so on account of *yakṣaṇa* (eating). The serpents were created and they were known so on account of movement of hair (*keṣasarpaṇa*). By means of anger, *bhūtas* (the evil spirits) were created. Then the *Gandharvas*[1] were born.

30. *Gandharvas* were born singing aloud and then Apsarasas.[2] Brahmā created heaven and earth from his chest and the goats from his mouth.

31. Prajāpati created cows from his belly and sides. Horses, elephants, buffaloes, camels, sheep etc. were created from his feet.

32. From his hair were produced medicinal herbs and fruit-bearing plants. The cow, goat, ram, horses, mule, donkey—

33. These are the domestic animals already told; now I describe the wild ones. They are the beasts of prey, the cloven-

1. A class of demi-gods, adept in singing and music. (Also vide *Liṅga* (AITM) p. 796, CDHM pp. 105-6).

2. The celestial nymphs. (Also refer *ŚP* (*AITM*), p. 2095; *Liṅga* (*AITM*), p. 798; *CDHM*, pp. 19-20).

hoofed, elephants and monkeys. The birds constitute the fifth creation (among lower animals).

34. The sixth is the creation of aquatic animals and the seventh that of reptiles. The Ṛgveda and other texts came out of his eastern and other mouths.

35. The *brāhmaṇas* were born of his mouth. The *kṣatriyas* originated from his arms. The *vaiśyas* came out of his thighs and the *śūdras* out of his feet.

36. The world of Brahmā can be attained by the *brāhmaṇas*, that of Śakra (Indra) by *Kṣatriyas*. The goal of *vaiśyas* is the world of the Maruts and that of *śūdra* is the world of *Gandharvas*.

37. Again those who are steady in the *brahmacarya-vrata* (celibacy) attain *brahmaloka*[1] and the householders steadfast in the performance of their ordained duties attain the *Prājāpatya*[2] world.

38. The forest-dwellers (vānaprasthas) attain the world of the seven *ṛṣis*. The *sannyāsins* go at will to the imperishable region.

CHAPTER FIVE

Creation of Progenitors

Hari said :

1. After mentally creating the order of things here and there at the time of *Prajā-sarga*, the Lord created the mental sons who were the progenitors of *prajā*.

1. The world of Brahman, the best of all the worlds. Having attained it one becomes free from re-birth. (Vide *ŚP* (*AITM*) p. 2098; *GDHM* pp. 179-80.)

2. The world of Prajāpatis.

2-3-4-5. The mind-created sons are Dharma, Rudra, Manu, Sanaka, Sanātana, Bhṛgu, Sanatkumāra, Ruci, Śraddhā Marīci, Atri, Aṅgiras, pulastya, Pulaha, Kratu, Vasiṣṭha, Nārada and the seven types of manes, namely, *Barhiṣads, Agniṣvāttas, Kravyādas, Ājyapas, Sukālins, Upahūtas* and *Dīpyas* of whom three are formless and four having forms. The Lotus-born Lord created Dakṣa from his right thumb; from his left thumb he created Dakṣa's wife.

6. Dakṣa begot meritorious daughters on her and gave them in marriage to the sons of Brahmā. Satī[1] was given to Rudra in marriage.

7. Rudra's sons were innumerable and very powerful. He gave his daughter Khyāti of un-rivalled grace to Bhṛgu[2].

8. She gave birth to Dhātṛ and Vidhātṛ from Bhṛgu. She also gave birth to Śrī,[3] the wife of Nārāyaṇa.

9. From her Hari himself begot Bala and Unmāda. Āyati and Niyati were the daughters of the high-souled Manu.[4]

10. They became the wives of Dhāṭṛ and Vidhāṭṛ of whom two sons were born—Prāṇa and Mṛkaṇḍu. Mārkaṇḍeya[5] was the son of Mṛkaṇḍu.

11. Sambhūti, the wife of Marīci, gave birth to Paurṇamāsa. Virajas and Sarvaga were his sons.

12. Aṅgiras begot on Smṛti many sons and daughters—Sinīvālī, Kuhū, Rākā and Anumati.

13. Anasūyā, the wife of Atri, gave birth to the sinless sons—Soma, Durvāsas[6] and Dattātreya the *yogin*.

14-15. Pulastya begot on his wife Prīti a son Dattoli, Karmaṣa, Arthavīra and Sahiṣṇu—these three sons were born of Kṣamā, the wife of Prajāpati Pulaha. Sumati, the wife of Kratu, gave birth to Bālakhilyas[7].

1. The first wife of Śiva. His second wife was Pārvatī, the daughter of Himālaya.

2. The progenitor of the Bhārgava race to which Paraśurāma belonged.

3. Lakṣmī, goddess of wealth.

4. The progenitor of mankind.

5. The author of the Mārkaṇḍeya-Purāṇa.

6. A well-known sage with a fiery temperament.

7. The authors of the Bālakhilya-hymns.

16. Sixty-thousand in number, resplendent like the blazing sun, though they were of the size of a thumb—They became sages of sublimated vitality.

17-18. Vasiṣṭha[1] begot on Ūrjā seven sons—Rajas, Gātra, Ūrdhvabāhu, Śaraṇa, Anagha, Sutapas and Śukra. They are known as the sinless Sapta-ṛṣis[2]. Dakṣa gave his daughter Svāhā in marriage to God fire who had assumed body.

19. From him, O Hara, she got three sons, known as Pāvaka, pavamāna and Śuci, who were of exalted virility and habitually consuming water.

20-21-22-23. Svadhā who married the manes gave birth to Menā and Vaitaraṇī both of whom became *brahma-Vādinīs*[3] (experts in the discussion of Brahman. From Menā, Himācala got a son Maināka[4] and a daughter[5] Gaurī who was Satī formerly. O Hara, Lord Brahmā appointed his son Svāyambhuva Manu, who was really Brahmā himself, in the task of preserving the subjects. Then the all-pervasive lord Svāyambhuva Manu married lady Śatarūpā who had destroyed her sins by ascetic austerities. Śatarūpā gave birth to two sons:

24. Priyavrata and Uttānapāda, and three daughters—Prasūti, Ākūti and Devahūti. Manu gave Ākūti in marriage to Ruci.

25. Prasūti to Dakṣa and Devahūti to Kardama, Ruci's children were Dakṣiṇā and Yajña.

26. They had twelve sons, the powerful yāmas[6]. Dakṣa had twenty-four daughters excellent in all respects.

1. The family of the Vasiṣṭhas was very illustrious one. The seventh Maṇḍala of the Ṛgveda is ascribed to them. Vasiṣṭha was also the priest of Daśaratha and Rāmacandra of Ayodhyā.

2. This list of the seven sages varies from the well-known list.

3. It proves that the women were not debarred from the Vedic studies.

4. A famous mountain. Opinions defer regarding its location. (Refer *CDHM*, p. 94)

5. Well known as Pārvatī, the second wife of Śiva.

6. The reference is to the great moral or religious duties of observances. (*SSED*, p. 455).

27. They were Śraddhā (faith), Lakṣmī (wealth), Dhṛti, (fortitude), Tuṣṭi (satisfaction), Puṣṭi, (Nouishment), Medhā, (Retentiveness), Kriyā (Action), Buddhi (Intelligence), Lajjā (bashfulness), Vapuḥ (Beauty), Śānti (Peace) Ṛddhi (prosperity) and Kīrti (fame) the thirteenth.

28. Dharma married Dākṣāyaṇī the daughter of Dakṣa. The eleven other daughters were Khyāti (praise), Sati (chastity) Sambhūti (production), Smṛti (Memory), Prīti (Affection), Kṣamā (Forgiveness).

29. Sannati (Obeisance), Anasūyā (absence of malice) Ūrjā, (Energy) Svāhā[1] and Svadhā.[2] The great sages Bhṛgu, Bhava, Marīci, Aṅgiras.

30-31. Pulastya, Pulaha, Kratu, Atri, Vasiṣṭha, Vahni and the manes married respectively Khyāti and others. Śraddhā gave birth to Kāma (Desire), calā (Lakṣmī) to Darpa (Pride), Dhṛti to Niyama (Restraint).

32. Tuṣṭi to Santoṣa (Contentment) and (Puṣṭi gave birth to Lobha (Greatness). Medhā gave birth to Śruta (knowledge) and Kriyā to three sons : Daṇḍa, (Punishment) Laya (Adherence) and Vinaya (humanity).

33. Buddhi to Bodha (enlightenment) and Lajjā to Vinaya (Humility). Vapus gave birth to the son Vyavasāya (Effort) and Śānti to Kṣema (Welfare).

34. Ṛddhi gave birth to Sukha (Happiness) and Kīrti to Yaśas (Renown). These are the sons of Dharma. Kāma's wife was Rati (Love) and their son Harṣa (Joy).

35. Once Dakṣa performed a horse-sacrifice to which all his sons-in-law were invited.

36. They were accompanied by their wives. Satī, though not invited, went there, without Rudra, and was disrespected by Dakṣa.

37. Satī cast off her body and was born again as the daughter of Menā and Himavān. She was then known as

1. Generally an exclamation used in offering oblations to the gods. It also means an oblation or offering made to all gods indiscriminately [Refer *STED* p. 633).

2. Generally an exclamation uttered when offering an oblation to the manes. It also means the food offered to the manes. (*SSED*, p. 631].

Gaurī and she married Śambhu. She gave birth to Vināyaka (Gaṇeśa).

38. And Kumāra, Rudra, the Lord of *Bhṛṅgins*, (the attendants of Śiva) and most powerful bearer of *Pināka*, (the famous bow of Śiva) being infuriated destroyed the sacrifice and cursed Dakṣa: "You will be born as a man in the line of Dhruva".[1] (son of Uttānapāda).

CHAPTER SIX

Description of families

Hari said :

1. Uttānapāda's son born of Suruci was Uttama. Another son of his born of Sunīti was Dhruva who attained a lofty position.

2. Due to the favour of the sage (Nārada) and through the propitiation of Lord Janārdana, Dhruva's son was Śliṣṭi who was very powerful.

3. His son was Prācīnabarhis whose son was Udāradhīḥ. His son was Divañjaya whose son was Ripu.

4. Ripu's son was well-known as the glorious Cākṣuṣa Manu. Glorious Ruru was his son whose son was Aṅga.

5. Aṅga's son was Vena who was a non-righteous atheist. The tyrant Vena was killed by the sages by means of the *kuśa* grass.

6. They churned his thigh for the sake of a son whereupon a purely dark-skinned boy was born. They asked him to sit down.

7. He was then known as Niṣāda and he took up his abode in the Vindhya mountains. The *Brāhmaṇas* again churned Vena's right hand.

1. A son of Uttānapāda. A great devotee of Viṣṇu. The pole-star is known as *Dhruva star* after him. (Also *CDHM*, p. 91).

8. Therefrom a son bearing the mental image of Lord Viṣṇu was born. He became famous as Pṛthu. He (Vena) attained heaven.

9. In order to resuscitate the subjects, the king (Pṛthu) milked the Earth. Pṛthu's son was Antardhāna whose son was Havirdhāna.

10. His son Prācīnabarhis shone as the sole emperor of the world. He married Sāmudrī, the daughter of Lavaṇa (the salt-ocean).

11. Sāmudrī gave birth to ten sons, Prācīnabarhiṣas, who were known as Prācetasas. They were well-acquainted with the science of archery.

12. Performing sacred rites collectively, they practised great penance. They also submerged in water of the ocean for ten thousand years.

13. They attained the status of Prajāpati. They married Māriṣā. Dakṣa,[1] who had been cursed by Bhava, became her son.

14. He then mentally created four kinds of progeny. They did not flourish, because they were cursed by Lord Hara.

15. Thereupon Dakṣa Prajāpati desired creation by means of physical intercourse. He married Asiknī, the daughter of Vīraṇa Prajāpati.

16. Vairaṇī (the daughter of Vīraṇa) gave birth to thousand sons. At the instigation of Nārada, they set out in search of the extremities of the world but never returned.

17. When the first set of thousand sons was thus lost, Dakṣa begot another set of a thousand sons. Riding briddled horses, they too followed the footsteps of their elder brothers, O Hara.

18. This infuriated Dakṣa who cursed Nārada, "You will be born in the world". Nārada was born as the son of Sage Kaśyapa.

19. When formerly his sacrifice was destroyed by Śiva, Dakṣa cursed Śiva furiously, "O Śaṅkara, (those who, will praise and worship you with religious Performances,

1. The first father-in-law of Śiva.

20. Will perish even in another birth due to your enmity." Hence, never should one have the feeling of enmity. From Queen Asiknī, Dakṣa got daughters.

21. Sixty beautiful daughters, two of whom were given in marriage to Aṅgiras, two to Kṛśāśva, ten to Dharma.

22. Fourteen to Kaśyapa and twenty-eight to Indu. Suprabhā and Bhāminī were given to Bahuputra.

23. O Mahādeva, Dakṣa gave four of his daughters, Manoramā, Bhānumatī, Viśālā, and Bahudā to Ariṣṭanemi.

24-25. He gave Suprajā and Jayā to Kriśāśva. Dharma's ten wives are Arundhatī, Vasu, Yāmī, Lambā, Marudvatī, Saṅkalpā, Muhūrtā, Sādhyā and Viśvā. Now I shall tell those of Kaśyapa.

26. Aditi, Diti, Danu, Kālā, Anāyu, Siṁhikā, Muni, Kadrū, Sādhyā, Irā, Krodhā, Vinatā, Surabhi and Khagā.

27. Viśvā (wife of Dharma) gave birth to Viśvedevas[1], Sādhyā to Sādhyas[2]. Marutvatī to Marutvans[3] and Vasu to Vasus[4].

28. O Rudra , Bhānu's sons were known as Bhānus[5] Muhūrtā's Muhūrtas[6]. Lambā's son was Ghoṣa and Yāmī's son Nāgavīthi.

29. Arundhatī gave birth to all earthly objects and Saṅkalpā gave birth to Saṅkalpa present in everyone.

30. The Vasus are eight in number, namely, Āpa, Dhruva, Soma, Dhava, Anila, Anala, Pratyūṣa and Prabhāsa.

31. Āpa's sons are Vaituṇḍi, Śrama, Śrānta and Dhvani. Dhruvā's son was Lord Kāla who organised the time-factor in the world.

32-33-34-35. Soma's son was Varcas instilling vigour in the world. Dhara begot of Manoharā the sons Druhiṇa, Hutahavyavāha, Śiśira, Prāṇa and Ramaṇa. Anila begot of

1. Literally "all the deities". (Vide details in *DHM*, p. 363).
2. A class of inferior deities. (Vide details in *CDHM* p. 271).
3. The clouds.
4. Eight minor deities, attendants upon Indra. (Vide details in *DHM* p. 342).
5. The rays of light or the suns.
6. Moments.

his wife Śiva two sons—Pulomajā and Avijñātagati. Agni's son, Kumāra, born in the *śara* (willow)-grove, was otherwise called Kārttikeya, since he was nurtured by the *Kṛttikās*. Śākha, Viśākha and Naigameya were born after him.

36. Pratyūṣa's son was the sage Devala. Prabhāsa's son became famous as Viśvakarman, the architect of the gods.

37. Ajaikapāt, Ahirbudhnya, Tvaṣṭṛ and Rudra the powerful were his other sons. Tvaṣṭṛ's son was Viśvarūpa of great penance.

38-39. The eleven Rudras who became Lords of the three world's are, Hara, Bahurūpa, Tryambaka, Aparājita, Vṛṣākapi, Śambhu, Kapardin, Raivata, Mṛgavyādha, Śarva and Kapālin, O sage.

40. The twelve suns (*dvādaśa* Ādityas) born to Aditi and Kaśyapa are—Viṣṇu, Śakra, Aryaman, Dhātṛ, Tvaṣṭṛ, Pūṣan.

41. Vivasvat, Savitṛ, Mitra, Varuṇa, Aṁśumat and Bhaga—These are the twelve sons known.

42. The twenty-seven wives of Soma (moon) are the twenty-seven constellations. Hiraṇyakaśipu and Hiraṇyākṣa were the sons of Diti.

43. A daughter was also born by name Siṃhikā who became the wife of Vipracitti. Hiraṇyakaśipu had four sons of great valour.

44. Anuhrāda, Hrāda, Prahrāda (Prahlāda) and Saṁhrāda (who was the last one). Among them Prahlāda was a great devotee of Viṣṇu.

45. Saṁhrāda's sons were Āyuṣmat, Śivi and Bāṣkala. Virocana was the son of Prahrāda. Bali[1] was the son of Virocana.

46. O Śiva ! Bali had a hundred sons of whom the eldest was Bāṇa[2]. All the sons of Hiraṇyākṣa were very strong.

47. They are Utkura, Śakuni, Bhūtasantāpana, Mahānāga, Mahābāhu and Kālanābha.

48. The following were the sons of Danu—Dvimūrdhan, Śaṅkara, Ayomukha, Śaṁkuśiras, Kapila, Śambara.

49. Ekacakra of long arms, Tāraka the powerful, Svarbhānu, Vṛṣaparvan, the great demon Puloman.

1. See p. 5. fn. 6
2. Father of Uṣā.

50. And the powerful Vipracitti. These are the known sons of Danu. Svarbhānu's daughter was Suprabhā. Vṛṣaparvan[1] begot Śarmiṣṭhā[2].

51. Upadānavī and Hayaśiras who became famous. The two daughters of Vaiśvānara were Pulomā and Kālakā.

52. Both of them were the wives of Mārīci[3]. Sixty-thousand sons were born of them.

53. These sons of Mārīci were known as Paulomas and Kālakañjas. The Sons of Siṁhikā and Vipracitti were—

54. Vyaṁśa, Śalya the strong, Nabha the powerful, Vātāpi, Namuci, Ilvala, Khasṛmat,

55. Añjaka, Naraka, and Kālanābha. The Nivātakavaca demons were born in Prahrāda's line.

56. Tāmrā gave birth to six daughters of great vigour, namely, Śukī, Śyenī, Bhāsī, Sugrīvī, Śuci and Gṛdhrikā.

57. Śukī gave birth to Śukas (parrots), Ulūkī to owls, Śyenī to hawks, Bhāsī to kites and Gṛdhrī to vultures.

58. Śukī gave birth to water-birds, Sugrīvī to horses, camels and donkeys. Thus I have explained the lineage of Tāmrā.

59. Vinatā had two sons celebrated as Garuḍa and Aruṇa[4]. Surasā gave birth to a thousand serpents of un-limited strength.

60. Kadrū's sons consisting of a thousand *phaṇins* (serpents) of unlimited strength, O Śaṅkara, have the following[5] as their leaders—Śeṣa[6], Vāsuki,[7] Takṣaka,

1. A demon King who struggled hard with the gods for a long time aided by Śukra, the preceptor of the demons.

2. The beloved of Yayāti. Yayāti married Devayānī, daughter of Śukra, and Śarmiṣṭhā, daughter of the king of *asuras* was told by her father to be her servant as a sort of recompense, for her insulting conduct towards her on a previous occasion. But Yayāti fell in love with this servant and privately married her. (Refer *SSED* p. 455).

3. One of the ten Prajāpatis.

4. The lame charioteer of Sun-god.

5. A serpent with one thousand hoods, who is the Cauch and canopy of Viṣṇu. [*CDHM* 291-2].

6. A serpent who was used as a rope around the mountain Mandara for churning the ocean.

7. A serpent who bit King Parikṣit. [Vide details *Pk* p. 192; *Mbh* p. 193].

61. Śaṅkha[1], Śveta, Mahāpadma, Kambala, Aśvatara, Elāpatra, Nāga, Karkoṭaka[2] and Dhanañjaya.

62. All these are easily irritable and all of them have curved fangs. Krodhā gave birth to highly powerful Piśācas (evil-spirits).

63. Surabhi gave birth to cows and buffaloes. Irā gave birth to trees, creepers, turning plants and all kinds of grass-species.

64. Khagā gave birth to Yakṣas and Rākṣasas. Muni gave birth to Apsarasas. Ariṣṭā gave birth to Gandharvas of inordinate strength.

65. There are forty-nine Maruts Ekajyoti, Dvijyoti, Trijyoti, Caturjyoti,

66. Ekaśukra, Dviśukra, Triśukra the powerful, Īdṛk, Sadṛk, Anyādṛk, Pratisadṛk,

67. Mita, Samita, Sumita the powerful, Ṛtajit, Satyajit, Senajit having good army,

68. Atimitra, Amitra, Dūramitra, Ajita, Ṛta, Ṛtadharmā, Vihartṛ, Varuṇa, Dhruva,

69. Vidhāraṇa; this is one group called Durmedhas; Īdṛśa, Sadṛkṣa, Etādṛkṣa eating little,

70. Etena, Prasadṛkṣa, Surata engaged in penances, Hetumat, Prasava, glorious Surabha,

71. Valorous Nādi, Dhvani, Bhāsa, Vimukta, Vikṣipa, Saha, Dyuti, Vasu, Anādhṛṣya, Lābha, Kāma, Jayī, Virāṭ,

72. This is the second group named Udveṣaṇa in the seventh layer of atmospheric minds. All these kings, demons and gods are forms of Lord Hari, surrounded by the sun etc.

73. Manu and others worshipped Lord Hari.

1. A serpent who stole the Vedas. (Vide details in *PK*, p 483-4].

2. A serpent who was saved by King Nala, yet bit him. (Vide details in *PK*, p. 89].

CHAPTER SEVEN

Worship of the sun etc.

Rudra said :

1. Please narrate the details of the worship of Sūrya (the sun) and others as practised by Svāyambhuva Manu and the rest.

Brahmā said :

O Vyāsa, this yields both enjoyment and salvation. Listen to it in brief.[1]

Hari said :

2. I shall explain the worship of the sun etc. that brings about virtue (*dharma*), love (*kāma*) and other (aims in life).

3. *Oṁ* obeisance to Sūrya's seat. *Om* obeisance to the solar form, *Om Hrām Hrim Saḥ* obeisance to Sūrya. *Om* obeisance to Soma (the moon). *Om* obeisance to Maṅgala (Mars). *Om* obeisance to Budha (Mercury). *Om* obeisance to Bṛhaspati (Jupiter). *Om* obeisance to Śukra (Venus). *Om* obeisance to Śanaiścara (Saturn). *Om* obeisance to Rāhu. *Om* obeisance to Ketu. *Om* obeisance to *Tejaścaṇḍa* of fierce refulgence.

4-5. O Śiva, the various rites to the sun and others, namely *āsana* (seat), *āvāhana* (invocation) *pādya*, (water for washing feet), *arghya* (offering), *ācamana* (water for sipping), *snāna* (bathing), *vastropavīta* (cloth and sacred thread), *gandha*, (scent) *puṣpa* (flowers), *dhūpa* (incense), *dīpu* (lamp), *namaskāra* (obeisance), *pradakṣiṇā* (circumambulation) and *visarjana* departure (of deity) are to be performed by means of these *mantras*.

6. *Om Hrām* obeisance to Śiva. *Om Hrām* obeisance to the auspicious form of Śiva. *Om Hrām* obeisance to the heart. *Om Hrām* Svāhā to the head. *Om Hrūm* vaṣaṭ to the tuft. *Om Hrai Hum* to the armour. *Om Hraum* vauṣaṭ to the three eyes. *Om Hraum* vauṣat to the three eyes. *Om* Hraḥ obeisance to the weapon. *Om Hrām* obeisance to Sadyojāta. *Om Hrim* obeisance to Vāmadeva. *Om Hrām* obeisance to Aghora. *Om Hrim* obeisance to Tatpurusa. *Om Hrim* obeisance to Īśāna. *Om Hraum* obeisance

1. Missing in Veṅkaṭeśvara edition.

to Gaurī. *Om Hraum* obeisance to the preceptors. *Om Hraum* obeisance to Indra. *Om Hraum* obeisance to Caṇḍa. *Om Hrām* obeisance to Aghora. *Om* obeisance to Vāsudeva's seat. *Om* obeisance to Vāsudeva's form. *Om Ām Om* obeisance to Lord Aniruddha. *Om* obeisance to Nārāyaṇa. *Om* to *Tat Sad* Brahman. *Om* Hrām obeisance to Viṣṇu. *Om kṣauṃ* obeisance to Lord Narasiṁha. *Om* Bhūḥ. *Om* obeisance to Lord Varāha (the boar-incarnation. *Om Kam Ṭam Pam Śam* obeisance to Vainateya (Garuḍa). *Om Jam Kham Ram* obeisance to Sudarśana (the divine discus). *Om Kham* Ṭhaṁ Phaṁ Ṣaṁ obeisance to the Gadā (the divine club). *Om Vam Lam mam Kṣam* (obeisance to Pāñcajanya (the divine conch) Oṁ *Gham* Ḍhaṁ *Bham Ham* obeisance to goddess Śrī. *Om Gam Dam Vam Sam* obeisance to *Puṣṭi* (nourishment). *Om Dham Ṣam Vam Sam* obeisance to the Vanamālā (the divine garland). *Om Sam Dam* Lam obeisance to Śrīvatsa (the divine mark on the breast). *Om Ṭham Caṁ Bham* Yam obeisance to Kaustubha[1] (the divine jewel). *Om* obeisance to the preceptors. *Om* obeisance to Indra and other dikpālas[2] (guardians of the directions). *Om* obeisance to Viṣvaksena.

7. Offerings of the seat and other things to Lord Hari should be made, O Śiva, by means of these mantras. Now hear the procedure of worship to Sarasvatī[3] a power of Lord Viṣṇu. It is very auspicious.

8. *Om Hrīm* obeisance to Sarasvatī. *Om Hrām* obeisance to heart. *Om Hrīm* obeisance to the head. *Om Hrūm* obeisance

1. Name of a celebrated jewel obtained with thirteen other precious things at the churning of the ocean and suspended on the breast of Kṛṣṇa or Viṣṇu (*SED* p. 318.)

2. Each of the ten directions, beginning with the east, has one guardian deity—namely, Indra, Agni, Yama, Nirṛti, Varuṇa, Vāyu, Kubera Īśa, Brahmā and Ananta. The last two are for upward and downward directions respectively.

3. The goddess of eloquence and learning who is opposed to Śrī or Lakṣmī, and sometimes considered to be the daughter and also the wife of Brahmā, the proper wife of that god being rather Sāvitrī or Gāyatrī. She is also identified with Durgā, or even with the wife of Viṣṇu and of Manu and held to be the daughter of Dakṣa. [vide *ŚP* (*AITM*], p. 350, *SED* p. 1182).

to the tuft. *Om Hraim* obeisance to the armour. *Om Hraum* obeisance to three eyes. *Om Hraḥ* obeisance to weapon.

9. Goddess Sarasvatī's powers are : Śraddhā (faith), Ṛddhi (prosperity), Kalā (arts), Medhā (intellect), Tuṣṭi (satiation) Puṣṭi(nourishment), Prabhā (light), Mati (intelligence), those beginning with *Om Hrīm* and ending with namaḥ (obeisance).

10. *Om* obeisance to *Kṣetrapāla* (the guardian of the field (the body). *Om* obeisance to the preceptors. *Om* obeisance to the grand-preceptors.

11. Offering of seat etc. to Sarasvatī seated on the divine lotus, and investiture with the sacred thread (*yajñopavīta*) of Sūrya etc., should be performed by their own *mantras*.

CHAPTER EIGHT

Worship of Viṣṇu and Vajranābha maṇḍala

Hari said :

1-2. O Rudra ! after the due bath Viṣṇu should be worshipped in the *Maṇḍala* (mystic diagram) prepared in a *Maṇḍapa* (consecrated temple or hall) on the ground. This mystic diagram should be drawn with powders of five colours and should consist of sixteen apartments. It is known as *Vajranābha*. The string should be first placed on the fourth and the fifth corners.

3. The well-versed devotee should then extend the strings into those corners too, which are on either side of the original corners.

4. On the alternative corners too this should be done. In the interval juncture of the lines the first centre is to be taken.

5. In all the interstices, there are such eight centres. The thread should be whirled round from the earlier and the middle centres.

6. O Śiva, ! in the interstics the learned *brāhmaṇa* should whirl (the thread) about three fourth (in length). By this the hypotenuse of the central thread should be whirled.

7. The well-versed devotee should draw the filaments of the lotus in two parts on either side of the hypotenuse. The petals should be drawn on the top of it.

8. O you of firm vows, the instructor who knows reality should make the figure of lotuses in all the regions around the centres.

9. Openings should be made (drawn) in proportion to the first thread—length. The opening should be embellished about half-way.

10. In the mystic diagram the colours chosen (for the powders) should be as follows—The hypotenuse in yellow, the filaments in white and red, the interstices in blue, the petals in black.

11-12. The four borders in black, the openings in white and the five lines in the mystic diagram too likewise. White, red, yellow and black lines should be in this order. Having prepared the mystic diagram and after performing the *nyāsa*[1] one should begin the worship of Hari.

13-14. The *nyāsa* (assignment) of Viṣṇu is in the middle of the heart, of Saṅkarṣaṇa in the throat, of Pradyumna in the head of Aniruddha in the tuft, of Brahmā in all the limbs and that of Śrīdhara in both the hands. After cotemplating "I am Viṣṇu" one should fix Hari in the pericarp of the lotus.

15. One should fix Saṅkarṣana in the east, Pradyumna in the south, Aniruddha in the west and Brahmā in the north.

16. Śrīdhara is to be fixed in Rudra's Corner (North-east), Indra and others should be fixed in the four quarters. Thereafter due worship by means of fragrant incense and other articles one attains the greatest status.

1. Assignment of the various parts of the body to different deities, which is usually accompanied with prayers and corresponding gesticulations. (*SSED*, p. 306.)

CHAPTER NINE

Viṣṇu-dīkṣā

Hari said :

1. The disciple, duly consecrated in proper time, should be blindfolded with a cloth. He should be made to offer oblations with the original *mantra* hundred and eight times.

2. If the consecration is for the acquisition of a son, the oblations offered are twice in number, if it is for a *sādhaka* (aspirant after spiritualism) it is thrice. O Rudra, if it is the case of a preceptor who had to attain salvation, it is four times.

3. If the consecration were to be omitted, it amounts to killing a preceptor, Vaiṣṇva *brāhmaṇa* and woman. The details of the consecration will now be narrated by me. The consecration destroys *adharma.*

4. After making the disciples sit outside, they should be made to contemplate. O Rudra, they should be considered as being dried up by a portion of wind.

5. They should be considered as being scorched by a portion of fire, and being inundated by a portion of water. *Tejas* will make that being one with it and then leave it out.

6. He should think upon *Praṇava*[1] (the mystic syllable *Om*) as the cause in the heaven, the cause in the body being the other one. There he should unite one soul with another, that being the cause of the body.

7. Then having aroused, he should attach each one, O Śaṅkara. If one is incompetent to worship Hari in the mystic diagram, one should adore him in contemplation.

8. This (adoration) should have four openings (doors) beginning with Brahmatīrtha in order. The hand is the lotus and the fingers are the petals.

9. The palm is the pericarp and the nails are the filaments. He should adore, having contemplated Hari there in the midst of the sun, the moon and fire.

10. He, with due contemplation, should place the palm on the head of the disciple. Since there is Viṣṇu in the palm,

1. Vide fn. 5 on p. 9.

this palm is that of Viṣṇu; and all sins perish on coming in contact with it.

11. The teacher should honour the disciple, whose eyes are covered with a piece of cloth, and then keeping him face to face with the Lord should offer a flower so that it falls there where the head of Lord Viṣṇu is.

12.. He should give him a name. The names of ladies should be self-chosen. The learned preceptor shall fix the names of the *Śūdras*, ending with *dāsa*.

CHAPTER TEN

Worship of Lakṣmī

Hari said :

1. I shall narrate the worship of Śrī and others in the altar for the sake of prosperity. *Srīṁ Hrīm* obeisance to Mahālakṣmī. *Śrāṁ Śrīṁ Śrūm Śraim Śrauṁ Śraḥ* in order, the heart, the head, the tuft, the armour, the eyes, the weapon, the seat and the idol should be worshipped.

2-4. In the mystic diagram with the lotus drawn within, having four passages abounding in dust, (everything pervades the firmament, the eyes, the moon and the sun, in view of the subsistence on the sky, the Vedas and the moon) having sixty-four extremities and eight beginnings, he who wishes to fulfil his desires, should offer oblations in the sacrificial fire to Lakṣmī and her limbs in one corner and Durgā, *Gaṇa* the preceptor and the *Kṣetrapāla*[1] in another. *Oṁ Ghaṁ Ṭaṁ Ḍaṁ Ham* obeisance to Mahālakṣmī.

5. With this (*mantra*) one should worship Lakṣmī with all the members of the family as narrated before. *Oṁ Saum* obeisance to Sarasvatī. *Oṁ Hrīṁ Saum.* Obeisance to Sarasvatī.

6. *Oṁ Hrim* say, say Vāgvādini *Svāhā*. *Oṁ Hrim* obeisance to Sarasvatī.

1. A tutelary deity; their number is given as 49. *SED* p. 332.

CHAPTER ELEVEN

Nava-vyūha[1] *worship of Viṣṇu*

Hari said :

1. I shall now narrate the procedure of *Nava-vyūhārcana* which had been mentioned to Kaśyapa. Extricating the vital breath through the cerebral passage one should fix it in navel, in the sky.

2. Then with the mystic *bija*[2] *ram* the physical body shall be burnt. With the *bīja yam* he should destroy all.

3. With the *bija lam* all movable and immovable beings should be deluged. With the *bīja bam* he should ponder over the *amṛta* (the imperishable).

4. Then, in the middle of the bubbles with the thought 'I am yellow-clad, four-armed Viṣṇu' he should contemplate mentally.

5-6. He should then perform the three-fold *mantra-nyāsa* in the hands and the body with the *bija* consisting of twelve mystic syllables. Then with the help of aforesaid *bijas* and through six *aṅgas*[3] (limbs of the body) he should so perform that Hari is realised. Starting with the right thumb, he should place the centre of the thumb on the petal.

7. After fixing two mystic *bijas* in the centre, he should place them again on the *aṅga*. He should place them in heart, head, tuft, vital limbs, mouth, eyes, stomach, back,

8. Arms, hands, knees and feet. Keeping the hands shaped like lotus, he should place the thumb in the middle.

9. And contemplate on Viṣṇu, the lord of all, the supreme entity. He should place these mystic *bijas* in the forefinger and other fingers.

10. Then on head, eyes, mouth, neck, heart, navel private part, knees and feet respectively.

1. *Vyūha*—a form, manifestation, especially of Viṣṇu.

2. *Bīja*—a mystical letter or syllable which forms the essential part of the *mantra* of any deity.

3. Six parts of the body: two thighs, two arms, head and the middle part. *SSED*. p. 569.

11. After placing the *ṣaḍaṅga bījas*[1] in the hands he should place them over the body. Then the five *bījas* should be placed beginning with thumb and ending with the little finger.

12. The *netra-bīja* should be placed in the middle of the hand, the same order is to be followed in *aṅga-nyāsa.* After placing the heart in the heart, the head should be placed on the head.

13. After placing the tuft on the tuft, the armour should be placed all over the body; the eyes should be placed over the eyes and the weapon in both the hands.

14. Binding all the quarters with that alone, he should begin the process of worship. At first with concentration, he should think of the *yoga-pīṭha,* (the sacred seat) in the heart.

15. He should place virtue, knowledge, renunciation and prosperity in the quarters beginning with the south-east respectively and un-righteousness etc. in the quarters beginning with the east.

16. Therefore he should place the infinite that had been well-covered by these, that identifies itself with them, that acts as the supporting seat and that is raised in the fore-part.

17-18. Then contemplating on the white lotus born of the pond of *vidyā,* having eight similar petals in the form of the quarters, having a hundred leaves, and with the upper pericarp scattered about; he should think about the upper and upper zones of the sun, the moon, fire and soul by means of the Vedas and others.

19. Then he should place the eight-fold powers of Keśava, i.e. *Vimalā* and others, resting in the quarters beginning with the east; and also the ninth power vested in the pericarp.

20. Contemplating thus and worshipping the *yoga-pīṭha,* he should thereafter place Lord Viṣṇu, the holder of the bow, invoking him mentally.

21. Then he should place the eye in the middle, the

1. The six *bījas* for the six parts of the body.

astra-mantra in the corners, uniting the heart etc. with the four-petals of the four-quarters beginning with the east.

22. Uniting the *bījas* of Saṅkarṣaṇa and others with the east etc. in order, he should place Vainateya (garuḍa) in the eastern and western doors.

23. He should assign Śrī to the south and Lakṣmī to the north, and Śudarśana with a thousand spokes to the southern door.

24. He should then place the conch in the corners after placing the club in the northern door. The intelligent devotee should place Śārṅga-bow either on the right or on the left of the lord.

25. Similarly, he should place the sword and the discus (*cakra*) on either side and thereafter the guardians of the quarters (Indra and others) in accordance with their respecttive quarters (east etc.)

26. In the same manner, he should place the weapons *Vajra* etc. Then he should contemplate *Brahman* above and *Ananta*[1] below.

27. After contemplating and worshipping them, all *mudrās*[2] (mystic signs) should be shown. The first *mudrā* is *Añjali* which propitiates the lord quickly.

28-29. *Vandanī* is the next when placed on the heart with the right hand raised up. When the left fist is kept with the thumb lifted up and then locked up with the right thumb it is *Ūrdhvāṅguṣṭha.* These three are common. There are others according to the different forms of the idols.

30. With the use of the little finger (and other fingers) eight *mudrās* are formed in order (five plus three). It should be borne in mind that the order is those of the eight *bījas* mentioned before.

31. Bending the three fingers ending with the little finger, with the thumb and keeping both the hands bent down, *Narasiṁha-mudrā* is formed.

1. Names of Viṣṇu, also of serpent Śeṣa, *SED*, p. 16.

2. Name of particular positions or intertwinings of the fingers (24 in number). Commonly practised in religious worship and supposed to possess an occult meaning and magical efficacy. Ibid., p. 822.

32. Keeping the left hand raised up, whirl it slowly. This is the ninth one known as *Varāha-mudrā*.

33. Keeping both the fists raised up and straight, release them one by one and then again contract all. This is called *Aṅga-mudrā*.

34. Keeping both the fists tight one after another the *mudrās* of the ten guardians of the quarters are formed in order.

35. The first vowel, the second, the penultimate and the final signify Vāsudeva, Bala, Kāma, and Aniruddha in due order.

36. *Oṁ*, *Tat Sat*, *Huṁ*, *Kṣaum*, *Bhūḥ*, these are the *mantras* for Nārāyaṇa, Brahmā, Viṣṇu, (Nara-) siṁha and the lordly Boar.

37. In view of the different hues, the names are nine-fold—white, red, yellow, blue, black, purple, cloud-coloured, fire-coloured and honey-coloured.

38. *Kaṁ*, *Ṭaṁ*, *Paṁ*, *Saṁ* Garuḍa; *Jaṁ*, *Khaṁ*, *Vaṁ*—Sudarśana; *Ṣaṁ*, *Caṁ*, *Phaṁ*, *Ṣaṁ—Gadā* (the divine club); *Vaṁ*, *Laṁ*, *Maṁ*, *Kṣam*—Conch;

39. *Ghaṁ*, *Ḍhaṁ*, *Bhaṁ*, *Ham*— Śrī; *Gaṁ*, *Jaṁ*, *Vaṁ*, *Śaṁ—Puṣṭikā*; *Ghaṁ*, *Vam—Vanamālā*; *Daṁ—Sam—Śrīvatsa*;

40 *Chaṁ*, *Ḍaṁ*, *Paṁ*, *Yam*—Kaustubha and *Ananta* is I myself. Thus the limbs of the lord of lords are ten duly.

41. Garuḍa resembles the lotus in colour, the club has a black form, the halo (*Puṣṭi*) has the colour of *Śirīṣa*-flower; Lakṣmī has a golden complexion.

42. The conch resembles the full-moon, Kaustubha has red hue, the discus has the brilliance of a thousand suns and *Śrīvatsa* resembles white *Kunda*-flower.

43. The garland is of five colours, *Ananta* is like the cloud, the weapons have the forms of lightning which may not have been mentioned.

44. One should offer *arghya* and *pādya* in accordance with *Puṇḍa īkākṣa-vidyā*.

CHAPTER TWELVE

Order of worship

Hari said :

1. I shall describe the order in the procedure of worship for achieving its success. At first the remembrance of the Supreme Soul with *Oṁ Namaḥ* (obeisance)'.

2. *Yaṁ*, *Raṁ*, *Vaṁ*, *Lam*—thus the purification of the body. *Om* obeisance, thus the formation of *caturbhuja*- (four armed) soul.

3. Then threefold placement of *Ākāra*. Then the worship of the *yoga*-seat embedded in the heart. *Om* obeisance to *Ananta*. *Om* obeisance to *dharma*. *Om* obeisance to knowledge. *Om* obeisance to renunciation. *Om* obeisance to prosperity. *Om* obeisance to evil. *Om* obeisance to ignorance. *Om* obeisance to non-detachment. *Om* obeisance to non-prosperity. *Om* obeisance to the lotus. *Om* obeisance to the solar-sphere. *Om* obeisance to the lower sphere. *Om* obeisance to the fiery sphere. *Om* obeisance to Vimalā. *Om* obeisance to Utkarṣiṇī. *Oṃ* obeisance to Jñānā. *Om* obeisance to Kriyā. *Om* obeisance to Yogā. *Om* obeisance to Prahvī. *Om* obeisance to Satyā. *Om* obeisance to Īśānā. *Om* obeisance to Sarvatomukhī. *Om* obeisance to Hari's seat with all *aṅgas* and *upāṅgas*. Then in the pericarp—*Am* obeisance to Vāsudeva. *Ām* obeisance to the heart. *Īm* obeisance to the head. *Ūm* obeisance to the tuft. *Aim* obeisance to the armour. *Aum* obeisance to the trio of eyes. *Āḥ Phaṭ* obeisance to the weapon. *Ām* obeisance to Saṅkarṣaṇa. *Am* obeisance to Pradyumna, *Aḥ* obeisance to Aniruddha. *Om Aḥ* obeisance to Nārāyaṇa. *Oṁ Tat Sat* obeisance to Brahman. *Om Hum* obeisance to Viṣṇu. *Kṣaum* to Narasiṁha. *Bhūḥ* to Varāha. *Kam* to Vainateya. *Jaṁ Khaṁ Vaṁ* to Sudarśana. *Khaṁ Cam*, *Pham*, *Sam* to *Gadā*. *Vum*, *Lam*, *Mam*, *Kṣaṁ* to Pāñcajanya. *Ghaṁ Dhaṁ Bhaṁ Ham* to Śrī. *Gam*, *Ḍam*, *Vam*, *Śaṁ* to *Puṣṭi*, *Dham*, *Vam* to *Vanamālā*. *Daṁ Saṁ* to *Srīvatsa*, *Chaṁ Daṁ*, *Yam* to Kaustubha. *Saṁ* to Śārṅga. *Īm* to the two quivers. *Cam* to the hide. *Kham* to the sword; to Indra, the lord of gods; to Agni, the lord of lustre; to Yama, the lord of *dharma*, *Kṣam* to Nairta, the lord of demons; to Varuṇa, the lord of water. *Yam*

to Vāyu, the lord of breath. *Dham* to Dhanada, the lord of wealth. *Hām* to Īśāna, the lord of learning. *Om* to Vajra, to Power. *Om* to *Daṇḍa* (punishment), to the sword. *Om* to the noose, to the banner, to the club, to the trident. *Lam* to *Ananta*, the lord of nether-worlds. *Kham* to Brahman, the lord of all worlds. *Om* obeisance to Lord Vāsudeva. *Om Om* obeisance. *Oṁ Nam* obeisance. *Oṁ Mam* obeisance. *Oṁ Bham* obeisance. *Oṁ Gam* obeisance. *Oṁ Vam* obeisance. *Oṁ Tem* obeisance. *Oṁ Vām* obeisance. *Om Sum* obeisance. *Om Dem* obeisance *Om Vām* obeisance. *Om Yam* obeisance. *Om Om* obeisance. *Om Nam* obeisance *Om Mom* obeisance. *Om Nām* obeisance. *Om Rām* obeisance. *Om Yam* obeisance *Om Nām* obeisance. *Om Yām* obeisance *Om Naṁ moṁ Bhaṁ Gaṁ Vaṁ Teṁ Vāṁsuṁdeṁvām Yam Om* obeisance to Nārāyaṇa. *Om* obeisance to Puruṣottama.

4. Obeisance to you, O Puṇḍarīkākṣa. Obeisance to you O Viśvabhāvana (well-wisher of the universe). Obeisance to you, O Subrahmaṇya (well-embedded in the Brahman), O Great-being, O Elder.

5-6-7. In the *havana*-rites[1] of these the word *svāhā* should be added at the end of these *mantras*. Thus repeating this hundred and eight times and giving *arghya*, obeisance should be made repeated with the *mantra jitaṁ teno*, (he has won). Then the devotee well-versed in *mantras* should worship duly that god of gods, Acyuta, with, first having mentioned *praṇava*, his own *bīja*, *aṅgas* and the rest.

8. After kindling fire, he should keep it well in the sacred pit with the auspicious results thereof. After contemplating everything, he should meditate upon the *maṇḍala*.

9. Having performed *havana*, hundred and eight times with the principle called Vāsudeva, he should offer six oblations with Saṅkarṣaṇa—*bīja*.

10. Three each time to the *aṅgas* and one each to the guardians of the quarters. The *pūrṇāhuti*[2] should be made in the end.

1. Offering oblation into fire.
2. The final offering into fire.

11. The soul should be merged with the greatest principle beyond the pale of speech. After sitting and showing the *mudrās*, he should bow down again.

12. This *homa* is called *nitya*; and *naimittika* requires twice this ritual. Go, I go to the greatest destination where there is Lord Nirañjana (the unsullied one).

13. May the gods go back to their respective places. Sudarśana, Śrī, Hari, Acyuta, Trivikrama.

14. Caturbhuja, Vāsudeva, Pradyumna, Saṅkarṣaṇa, Puruṣa—these constitute the ten with the nine *vyūhas*.

15. Aniruddha, Dvādaśātmā, beyond that Anantaka—these *devas* should be known as signified by the wheels beginning with one.

16. They should be worshipped by me in a house marked with the wheels. *Om Svāhā* to *Cakra*. *Oṁ* Svāhā to *Vicakra*. *Oṁ Svāhā* to *Sucakra*. *Oṁ Svāhā* to *Mahācakra*. *Oṁ Mahācakra* the destroyer of demons, *Huṁ Phaṭ*. *Oṁ Hum* to the thousand-spoked, *Huṁ Phaṭ*.

17. This Dvārakā-cakra-pūjā in the house is auspicious and well-protecting.

CHAPTER THIRTEEN

Viṣṇupañjarastotra

Hari Said:

1-2. I shall now expound Viṣṇu's auspicious *Pañjara* (protective cage) Obeisance, obeisance to Thee, O, Govinda. Taking up the discus Sudarśana protect me in the east. O Viṣṇu, I seek refuge in Thee. O Padmanābha, take up the club Kaumodakī, obeisance to Thee.

3-10. O Viṣṇu, protect me in the South. I seek refuge in Thee. Taking up the plough-share Saunanda protect me in the west, O Puruṣottama, obeisance to Thee. I seek refuge in Thee. Taking up the destructive Mortar O Puṇḍarīkākṣa (lotus-eyed one) protect me in the north. O Jagannātha (lord of the universe) I seek refuge in Thee. Taking up the Sword the shield and the other weapons protect me, O Hari, killer of *Rākṣasas*, in the north east, Obeisance to Thee. I have sought refuge in Thee. O Viṣṇu, taking up the great Conch Pāñcajanya[1] and the lotus Anudbodha protect me in the South-east, O Boar, protect me. O Nṛkesarin (Man-lion) of divine form, Taking up the sun and the moon and the *Cāndramas* a (Lunar Sword,) protect me in the South west. Taking up Vaijayantī and the necklace *Srīvatsa*[2] protect me in the north-west. O Lord Hayagrīva[3], obeisance to Thee. Riding on Vainateya high over in the sky O Janārdana, the unconquered, protect me always. O un-vanquished, obeisance to Thee. Riding on Viśālākṣa protect me in the nether worlds, obeisance to Thee O shoreless Ocean, Obeisance to Thee O Great Fish ! O Truth ! making the *Bāhupañjara* (Protective Cage of Arms) protect me in the hands, fingers, head and other parts. O Viṣṇu, foremost among men, obeisance to Thee. Thus was expounded to Śaṅkara the Great *Vaiṣṇava Pañjara* formerly for the protection of Kātyāyanī,[4] the wife of Īśāna. O Śaṅkara, by this she destroyed Cāmara, Mahiṣāsura the demon Rakta-bīja and other enemies of gods. By reciting this with devotion a man always conquers his enemies.

CHAPTER FOURTEEN

Meditation

Hari Said:

1. I shall now expound *Yoga* conducive to enjoyment and final beatitude. Hari, the lord, is to be contemplated, so say the devotees who regularly contemplate.

1. It is Kṛṣṇa's conch. It derives its name from the sea-demon Pañcajana.
2. A particular mark (a curl of hair) on the breast of Viṣṇu (and also Kṛṣṇa).
3. According to some, Viṣṇu took this form to save the Vedas. Refer *CDHM* p. 120.
4. A name of the goddess Durgā.

2. O Īśa listen, Viṣṇu, the lord of all, is infinite, remover of all sins, devoid of ground of rest for the feet.[1]

3. I am Vāsudeva, the lord of the universe, the soul of Brahman, the immanent soul, the eternal, free from all kinds of physical bodies.

4. Devoid of the attributes of the body, free from *kṣara* (perishable) and *Akṣara* (imperishable) presiding over the six types (of living beings), the seer, the hearer, the smeller and beyond the pale of the senses.

5. Free from its attributes, the creator, devoid of name and race, the thinker residing in the mind, the lord free from mind.

6. Devoid of the attributes of the mind, he is the worldly knowledge, the spiritual knowledge, the knower the presiding being in the intellect, the omniscient witness devoid of (the attributes of) the intellect.

7. Free from the attributes of the intellect, all in-all, the omnipresent mind, free from all living beings, and devoid of the attributes of the vital breath.

8. The Vital breath of living beings, the quiet, devoid of fear, free from egotistic feelings and devoid of the attributes (of the ego).

9. The witness (of ego), the controller; (of ego), Bliss personified, the presiding being of (the three states of) wakefulness, dream and sleep, devoid of their attributes.

10. The fourth, the great Creator *Dṛgrūpa* (Having the form of the Vision), free from qualities, the independent, the enlightened, the unageing, the all-pervading, the Truth. I am the soul, the auspicious one.

11. Those men of knowledge who contemplate upon (me) and the lord thus, attain the great status and also that form; no doubt need be entertained.

12. O Śaṅkara of good vows, thus I have narrated to you the procedure of contemplation. He who reads this constantly attains to Viṣṇu's world.

1. The reading पद्भिर्भूपरिवर्जित: is suggested.

CHAPTER FIFTEEN

Viṣṇu-sahasra-nāma-stotra

Rudra said :

1. O Lord, what is to be muttered by a man so that he is released from the terrible ocean of worldly existence. O Janārdana, you narrate to me that great *stotra*.[1]

Hari Said :

2. Praising Lord Viṣṇu (the great Brahman, the Supreme Soul, the immutable) by thousand names a man becomes free.

3-160. I shall tell you O Śaṅkara, the holy and great object of recitation[2] which removes all sins. Listen with full attention. *Om*

Vāsudeva—son of Vasudeva.
Mahāviṣṇu—the great Viṣṇu the omnipresent.
Vāmana—the dwarf (who put down the demon Bali).
Vāsava—Indra.
Vasu—the eight semi-divine beings.
Bālacandranibha—resembling the crescent moon.
Bāla—the child.
Balabhadra—Balarāma.
Balādhipa—highly powerful.
Balibandhanakṛt—who fettered the demon Bali.
Vedhas—the creator.
Vareṇya—the excellent.
Vedavit—knower of Vedas.
Kavi—poet.
Vedakartṛ—producer of Vedas.
Vedarūpa—Vedas personified.
Vedya—worthy of being known.
Vedaparipluta—filled with Vedas.

1. A hymn to recite one thousand names of Viṣṇu. It is rather different form the one found in the Mahābhārata.

2. Japya—a hymn of adoration; that which is to be recited and muttered.

Vedāṅgavettṛ—knower of the Vedāṅgas.[1]
Vedeśa—lord of the Vedas.
Balādhāra—store of strength.
Balārdana—suppressor of the strong.
Avikāra—unchanging.
Vareśa—lord of Boons.
Varada—(or Varuṇa) he who grants boons (or Varuṇa).
Varuṇādhipa—overlord of Varuṇa.
Vīrahā—slayer of heroes.
Bṛhadvīra—greater hero.
Vandita—the adored.
Parameśvara—the great Īśvara.
Ātman—the soul.
Paramātman—the Supreme Soul.
Pratyagātman—the inner Self.
Viyatpara—beyond the sky.
Padmanābha—lotus-navelled.
Padmanidhi—the treasure trove Padma.
Padmahasta—the holder of a lotus in the hand.
Gadādhara—the holder of club.
Parama—the greatest.
Parabhūta—beyond the elements.
Puruṣottama—most excellent of puruṣas.
Īśvara—the powerful.
Padmajaṅgha—lotus-wristed.
Puṇḍarīka—white in colour.
Padmamālādhara—wearing garland of lotuses.
Priya—beloved of all.
Padmākṣa—lotus-eyed.
Padmagarbha—lotus-wombed.
Parjanya—rainbearing cloud.
Padmasaṁsthita—seated in a lotus.
Apāra—beyond the range.
Paramārtha—the greatest entity.
Parāṇāṁpara—greatest of the great.
Prabhu—lord.

1. Six subsidiary treatises related to the Vedas. They are शिक्षा, कल्प, व्याकरण, निरुक्त, छन्दस्, ज्योतिष्

Paṇḍitebhyaḥ Paṇḍita—scholarly of Scholars.
Pavitra—holy.
Pāpamardaka—suppressor of sins.
Śuddha—Pure.
Prakāśarūpa—of refulgent form.
Pavitra—purifier.
Parirakṣaka—protector.
Pipāsā-Varjita—free from thirst.
Pādya—holy wāter (offered at the feet of the lord).
Puruṣa—the divine being.
Prakṛti the divine Nature.
Pradhāna the divine intellect.
Pṛthivīpadma—the lotus of the earth.
Padmanābha—lotus-navelled.
Priyaprada—giver of desire.
Sarveśa—lord of all.
Sarvaga—going everywhere.
Sarva—the all-in-all.
Sarvavid—omniscient.
Sarvada—bestower of all.
Para—he who is beyond everything.
Sarva—identical with all.
Jagato dhāma—the abode of the universe.
Sarvadarśin—the witness of all.
Sarvabhṛt—upholder of all.
Sarvānugrahakṛd—Deva the deity benevolent to all.
Sarvabhūtahṛdisthita—residing in the hearts of all living beings.
Sarvapa—protector of all.
Sarvapūjya—worthy of every one's worship.
Sarvadevanamaskṛta—saluted by all devas.
Sarvasya jagato mūlam—root-cause of all universe.
Sakala—the entire, the whole.
Niṣkala—the undivided.
Anala—the fire.
Sarvagoptṛ—the protector of all.

Sarvaniṣṭha—all-pervasive.
Sarvakāraṇakāraṇam—cause of all causes.
Sarvadhyeya—worthy of meditation by all.
Sarvamitra—friend of all.
Sarvadevasvarūpadhṛk—holding the forms of all gods.
Sarvādhyāya—object of study by all.
Surādhyakṣa—presiding deity of gods.
Surāsuranamaskṛta—adored by gods and demons.
Duṣṭānām asurāṇāṁ ca sarvadā ghātaka—the perpetual slayer of the wicked and the *asuras*.
Antaka—the destroyer.
Satyapāla the protector of truth.
Sannābha—central cynosure of the good.
Siddheśa—lord of *Siddhas*.
Siddhavandita—respected by *Siddhas*.
Siddhasādhya—one who has achieved everything achievable.
Siddhasidha—obtained by the *Siddhas*.
Sādhyasiddha—obtained by *Sādhyas*.
Hṛdīśvara—lord of the heart.
Jagataḥ śaraṇam—refuge of the universe.
Jagataḥ śreyaḥ—glory of the Universe.
Jagataḥ kṣema—affluence of the Universe.
Śubhakṛt—doer of good.
Śobhana—beautiful.
Saumya—gentle.
Satya—reality.
Satyaparākrama—of true valour.
Satyastha—stationed in truth.
Satyasaṅkalpa—of true volition.
Satyavid—knower of truth.
Satyada—giver of truth.
Dharma—virtue.
Dharmin—virtuous.
Karmin—observer of sacred rites.
Sarvakarmavivarjita—free from all activities.
Karmakartṛ—ordainer of actions.
Karman—the action.

Kriyā—sacred rite.
Kāryam—the result.
Śrīpati—lord of splendour.
Nṛpati—lord of men.
Śrīmat—glorious.
Sarvasya pati—lord of all.
Ūrjita—the powerful.
Devānāṁ pati—lord of *devas*.
Vṛṣṇīnāṁ pati—lord of *Vṛṣṇis*.
Hiraṇyagarbhasya pati—lord of Hiraṇyagarbha.
Tripurāntaḥpati—lord of slayer of *Tripuras*.
Paśūnāṁ pati—lord of beasts.
Prāya—abundance.
Vasūnām pati—lord of *Vasus*.
Ākhaṇḍalasya pati—lord of India.
Varuṇasya pati—lord of Varuṇa.
Vanaspatīnāṁ pati—lord of plants.
Anilasya pati—lord of wind.
Analasya pati—lord of fire.
Yamasya pati—lord of Yama.
Kuberasya pati,—lord of Kubera.
Nakṣatrāṇāṁ pati—lord of Stars.
Oṣadhīnāṁ pati—lord of medicinal herbs.
Vṛkṣāṇāṁ pati—lord of trees.
Nāgānāṁ pati—lord of the Nagars.
Arkasya pati—lord of the Sun.
Dakṣasya pati—lord of Dakṣa.
Suhṛdāṁ pati—lord of friends.
Nṛpāṇāṁ pati—lord of Kings.
Gandharvāṇāṁ pati—lord of the *Gandharvas*.
Asūnām uttamaḥ pati—most excellent lord of vital breaths.
Parvatānāṁ pati—lord of mountains.
Nimnagānaṁ pati—lord of rivers.
Surāṇāṁ pati—lord of *devas*.
Śreṣṭha—the most excellent.
Kapilasya pati—lord of Kapila.
Latānāṁ pati—lord of creepers.

Vīrudhāṁ pati—lord of spreading creepers.
Munīnāṁ pati—lord of Sages.
Sūryasya uttama pati—most excellent lord of the sun.
Candramasaḥ śreṣṭha pati—most excellent lord of the moon.
Śukrasya pati—lord of Śukra.
Grahāṇāṁ pati—lord of the *planets*.
Rākṣasānāṁ pati—lord the Rākṣasas.
Kinnarāṇāṁ pati—lord of the *Kinnaras*.
Dvijānām uttama pati—most excellent lord of the twice born.
Saritāṁ pati—lord of rivers.
Samudrāṇāṁ pati—lord of the oceans
Sarasāṁ pati—lord of the lakes.
Bhutānāṁ pati—lord of the goblins.
Vetālānāṁ pati—lord of the *Vetālas*.
Kūṣmāṇḍānāṁ pati—lord of the pumpkins.
Pakṣiṇām pati—lord of birds.
Paśūnām pati—lord of beasts.
Mahātman—noble soul.
Maṅgala—the auspicious.
Meya—that can be measured.
Mandara—the mountain Mandara.
Mandareśvara—lord of Mandara.
Meru—mountain Meru.
Mātṛ—the measurer.
Pramāṇa—means of valid knowledge.
Mādhava—lord of Lakṣmī.
Manuvarjita[1]—Devoid of mantras.
Mālādhara—wearing garlands.
Mahādeva—great Lord.
Mahādevena pūjita—adored by Śiva.
Mahāśānta—very quiet.
Mahābhāga—the fortunate.
Madhusūdana—slayer of Madhu.
Mahāvīrya—of great heroism.
Mahāprāṇa—of great vital breath
Mārkaṇḍeya pravandita[2]—saluted by Mārkaṇḍeya

1. *v.l. malavarjita.*
2. *v.l. mārkaṇḍeyarṣivandita.*

Māyātman—identified with illusion.
Māyayā baddha—fettered by illusion.
Māyayā Vivarjita—free from illusion.
Munistuta—lauded by the sages.
Muni—identified with sages.
Maitra—great friend.
Mahānāsa—having long nose.
Mahāhanu—having large cheeks.
Mahābāhu—having long arms.
Mahādanta[1]—having big teeth.
Maraṇena vivarjita—devoid of death.
Mahāvaktra—having a large mouth.
Mahātmā—having a huge body.
Mahākāra[2]—having a big size.
Mahodara—having a great belly.
Mahāpāda—having large feet.
Mahāgrīva—having a long neck.
Mahāmānin—highly respected.
Mahāmanas—high-minded.
Mahāmati[3]—of great intellect.
Mahākīrti—of great fame.
Mahārūpa—of great form.
Mahāsura—identified with great Asura.
Madhu—honey.
Mādhava—spring season.
Mahādeva—great Deva.
Maheśvara—the great Īśvara.
Makheṣṭa[4]—pleased with sacrifices.
Makharūpin—of the form of a sacrifice.
Mānanīya—the laudable.
Makheśvara—lord of sacrifices.
Mahāvāta—the violent wind.
Mahābhāga—having great share.
Maheśa—great lord.
Atītamānuṣa—the Superman.

1. *v.l. mahādānta.*
2. *v.l. mahākāya.*
3. *v.l. mahāgati.*
4. *v.l. makhejya.*

Mānava—the mankind.
Manu—Manu (himself).
Mānavānāṁ Priyaṅkara—doing good to men
Mṛga—the deer.
Mṛgapūjya—adored by the deer.
Mṛgāṇāṁ pati—lord of the deer.
Budhasya pati—lord of Mercury.
Bṛhaspateḥ pati—lord of Jupiter.
Śanaiścarasya pati—lord of Saturn.
Rāhoḥ pati—lord of Rāhu.
Ketoḥ pati—lord of Ketu.
Lakṣmaṇaḥ—having good mark.
Lakṣaṇa—good sign.
Lamboṣṭha—having hanging lips.
Lalita—handsome to look at.
Nānālaṅkārasaṁyukta—bedecked with many ornaments of variety.
Nānācandanacarcita—anointed with sandal pastes of various sorts.
Nānārasojjvaladvaktra—with mouth shining with different kinds of juices.
Nānāpuṣpopaśobhita—adorned with flowers of various sorts.
Rāma—(identified with prince) Rāma.
Ramāpati—Lord of Lakṣmī.
Sabhārya Parameśvara—ardhanārīśvara.
Ratnada—giver of jewels.
Ratnahartṛ—confiscator of jewels.
Rūpin—possessed of forms.
Rūpavivarjita—devoid of forms.
Mahārūpa—having immense form.
Ugrarūpa—having terrific form.
Saumyarūpa—having gentle form.
Nīlameghanibha—resembling blue cloud.
Śuddha—the pure.
Kālameghanibha—resembling dark cloud.
Dhūmavarṇa—of smoke-colour.
Pītavarṇa—of yellow colour.
Nānārūpa—of various forms.
Avarṇaka—having no colour.

Virūpa—of hideous form.
Rūpada—bestower of comely appearance.
Śuklavarṇa—of white colour.
Sarvavarṇa—of all colours.
Mahāyogin—the great yogin.
Yajña[1]—the sacrifice.
Yajñakṛt—the sacrificer.
Suvarṇa—having good colour.
Varṇavat—having colour.
Suvarṇākhya—named gold.
Suvarṇāvayava—having golden parts.
Suvarṇasvarṇamekhala—having a golden girdle of good colour.
Suvarṇasya pradātṛ—giver of gold.
Suvarṇāṁśa[2]—having parts of gold.
Suvarṇasya priya—fond of gold.
Suvarṇāḍhya—possessing gold.
Suparṇin—of beautiful wings.
Mahāparṇa—of huge wings.
Suparṇasya kāraṇam—cause of Suparṇa.
Vainateya—Vinatā's son.
Āditya—Aditi's son.
Ādi—the beginning.
Ādikara—creator of beginning.
Śiva—Śiva.
Mahataḥ kāraṇam—cause of the intellectual principle.
Purāṇasya[3] kāraṇam—cause of purāṇas.
Buddhīnāṁ kāraṇam—cause of intellects.
Manasaḥ kāraṇam—cause of mind.
Ceṭasaḥ kāraṇam—cause of thought.
Ahaṅkārasya kāraṇam—cause of the ego.
Bhūtānāṁ kāraṇam—cause of the elements.
Vibhāvasoḥ kāraṇam—cause of fire.
Ākāśakāraṇam—cause of the ether.
Pṛthivyāḥ paraṁ kāraṇam—the great cause of the earth.
Aṇḍasya kāraṇam—cause of the cosmic egg.
Prakṛteḥ kāraṇam—cause of the Prakṛti.

1. *v.l. yājya.*
2. *v.l. suvarṇeśa.*
3. *v.l. pradhānasya kāraṇam.*

Dehasya kāraṇam—cause of body.
Cakṣuṣaḥ kāraṇam—cause of the eye.
Śrotrasya kāraṇam—cause of the ear.
Tvacaḥ kāraṇam—cause of the skin.
Jihvāyāḥ kāraṇam—cause of the tongue.
Prāṇasya kāraṇam—cause of the vital breath.
Hastayoḥ kāraṇam—cause of hands.
Pādayoḥ kāraṇam—cause of feet.
Vācaḥ kāraṇam—cause of speech.
Pāyoḥ kāraṇam—cause of the organ of evacuation.
Indrasya kāraṇam—cause of Indra.
Kuberasya kāraṇam—cause of the Kubera.
Yamasya kāraṇam—cause of Yama.
Īśānasya kāraṇam—cause of Īśāna.
Yakṣāṇāṁ kāraṇam—cause of Yakṣas.
Rakṣasāṁ paraṁ kāraṇam—great cause of demons.
Bhūṣaṇānāṁ śreṣṭhaṁ kāraṇam[1]—excellent cause of ornaments.
Dharmasya kāraṇam—cause of the virtue.
Jantūnāṁ kāraṇam—cause of the creatures.
Vasūnāṁ paraṁ kāraṇam—great cause of Vasus.
Manūnāṁ kāraṇam—cause of Manus.
Pakṣiṇāṁ paraṁ kāraṇam—great cause of birds.
Munīnāṁ śreṣṭhaṁ kāraṇam—excellent cause of sages.
Yogināṁ paraṁ kāraṇam—great cause of ascetics.
Siddhānāṁ kāraṇam—cause of Siddhas.
Yakṣāṇāṁ paraṁ kāraṇam—great cause of Yakṣas.
Kinnarāṇāṁ kāraṇam—cause of Kinnaras.
Gandharvāṇāṁ kāraṇam—cause of Gandharvas.
Nadānāṁ kāraṇam—cause of west flowing rivers.
Nadīnāṁ paraṁ kāraṇam—great cause of east-flowing rivers.
Samudrāṇāṁ kāraṇam—cause of seas.
Vṛkṣāṇāṁ kāraṇam—cause of trees.
Vīrudhāṁ kāraṇam—cause of creepers.
Lokānāṁ kāraṇam—cause of worlds.
Pātāla-kāraṇam—cause of Pātāla.
Devānāṁ kāraṇam—cause of Devas.
Sarpāṇāṁ kāraṇam—cause of serpents.

1. *v.l. nṛpāṇām.*

Śreyasāṁ kāraṇam—cause of glory.
Paśūnāṁ kāraṇam—cause of animals.
Sarveṣāṁ kāraṇam—cause of all.
Dehātman—soul of the body.
Indriyātman—soul of sense-organs.
Buddheḥ ātman[1]—soul of intellect.
Manasaḥ ātman—soul of mind.
Ahaṅkāracetasaḥ ātman—soul of egoistic mind.
Jāgrataḥ ātman—soul of the wakeful.
Svapataḥ ātman—soul of the slumbering.
Paramahadātman—soul of the cosmic intellect.
Pradhānasya parātman—great soul of *Pradhāna*.
Ākāśātman—soul of ether.
Apām ātman—soul of waters.
Prithivyāḥ paramātman—great soul of Earth.
Vayasyātman[2]—soul of friends.
Gandhasya paramātman—great soul of smell.
Rūpasya Para ātman—great soul of colour.
Śabdātman—soul of sound.
Vāgātman—soul of speech.
Sparśātman—soul of touch.
Puruṣa—the Being.
Śrotrātman—soul of ears.
Tvagātman—soul of skin.
Jihvāyāḥ paramātman—great soul of tongue.
Ghrāṇātman—soul of smell.
Hastātman—soul of hands.
Paramapādātman—great soul of feet.
Upasthasya ātman—soul of the organ of generation.
Parama pāyvātman—great soul of organ of evacuation.
Indrātman—soul of Indra.
Brahmātman—soul of Brahmā.
Rudrātman—soul of Rudra.
Manoḥ ātman—soul of Manu.
Dakṣasya prajāpateḥ ātman—soul of Dakṣa the patriarch.
Paramasatyātman—great soul of truth.

1. *v.l. ātmā buddhiḥ.*
2. *v.l. rasātman.*

Īśātman—soul of Īśa.
Paramātman—great soul.
Rudrātman—soul of Rudra.
Mokṣavid—knower of salvation.
Yati—ascetic.
Yatnavān—striving.
Yatna—efforts.
Carmin—having leather.
Khaḍgin—having sword.
Asurāntaka[1]—slayer of *Asuras*.
Hrīpravartanaśīla—habitually practising modesty.
Yatīnāṁ hite rata—engaged in the welfare of ascetics.
Yatirūpin—having the form of an ascetic.
Yogin—*yogi*.
Yogidhyeya—worthy of meditation by *yogīns*.
Hari—remover (of sins).
Śiti—the dark
Saṁvit—perfect knowledge.
Medhā—genius.
Kāla—time.
Ūṣmā—heat (summer).
Varṣā—rain (rainy season).
Mati—determination.
Saṁvatsara—year.
Mokṣakara—bringing about salvation.
Mohapradhvaṁsaka—remover of delusion.
Duṣṭānāmmohakartṛ—stupefying the wicked.
Māṇḍavya—sage Māṇḍavya.
Baḍavāmukha—having submarine fire in the mouth.
Saṁvartaka—the whirling fire at the time of final dissolution.
Kālakartṛ—creator of time.
Gautama—sage Gautama.
Bhṛgu—sage Bhṛgu.
Aṅgiras—sage Aṅgiras.
Atri—sage Atri.
Vasiṣṭha—sage Vasiṣṭha.
Pulaha—sage Pulaha.

1. *v.l. murāntaka*.

Pulastya—sage Pulastya.
Kutsa—sage Kutsa.
Yājñavalkya—sage Yājñavalkya.
Devala—sage Devala.
Vyāsa—sage Vyāsa.
Parāśara—sage Parāśara.
Śarmada—giver of Welfare.
Gāṅgeya—Gaṅgā's son (Bhīṣma).
Hṛṣīkeśa—Master of sense organs.
Bṛhacchravas—having large ears.
Keśava—having luxuriant hair.
Kleśahantṛ—remover of pain.
Sukarṇa—having good ears.
Karṇavarjita—devoid of ears.
Nārāyaṇa—having waters for abode.
Mahābhāga—immensely lucky.
Prāṇasya pati—Lord of vital breath.
Apānasya pati—Lord of Apāna.
Vyānasya pati—Lord of Vyāna.
Udānasya śreṣṭha pati—Lord of Udāna.
Samānasya pati—Lord of samāna.
Sabdasya śreṣṭha pati—excellent lord of speech.
Sparśasya pati—Lord of touch.
Rūpāṇāmādyanṛpati—first lord of colour.
Khaḍgapāṇi—having sword in hand.
Halāyudha—using ploughshare as weapon.
Cakrapāṇi—having discus in hand.
Kuṇḍalin—having earrings.
Śrīvatsāṅka—having Śrīvatsa mark on the chest.
Prakṛti—the prakṛti (Nature).
Kaustubhagrīva—having Kaustubha gem in the neck.
Pitāmbaradhara—having yellow garment.
Sumukha—having nice face.
Durmukha—having wry face.
Mukhena vivarjita—without face.
Ananta—endless.
Anantarūpa—of endless form.
Sunakha—having nice nails.

Surasundara[1]—most beautiful of all *devas.*
Sukalāpa[2]—having good collection.
Vibhu—present everywhere
Jiṣṇu—victorious.
Bhrājiṣṇu—resplendent.
Iṣudhi—the quiver.
Hiraṇyakaśipuhantṛ—slayer of Hirayakaśipu.
Hiraṇyākṣavimardaka—suppressor of Hiraṇyākṣa.
Pūtanānihantṛ—slayer of Pūtanā.
Bhāskarāntavināśana—slayer of demon Bhāskarānta.
Keśidalana—splitter of Keśin.
Muṣṭikavimardaka—suppressor of Muṣṭika.
Kaṁsadānavabhettṛ—slayer of demon Kaṁsa.
Cāṇūrapramardaka—suppressor of Cāṇūra.
Ariṣṭanihantṛ—slayer of Ariṣṭa.
Akrūrapriya—fond of Akrūra.
Akrūra—not cruel.
Krūrarūpa—of cruel features.
Akrūrapriyavandita—adored by Akrūra's friends.
Bhagahā—destroyer of glory.
Bhagavān—having lordly powers.
Bhānu—the sun.
Bhāgavata—devotee of Lord.
Uddhava—Uddhava, uncle of Kṛṣṇa.
Uddhavasya Īśa—Lord of sacrificial fire.
Uddhavena vicintita—thought of by Uddhava.
Cakradhṛk—holder of wheel.
Cañcala—ever moving.
Calācalavivarjita—devoid of movable and irmmovable.
Ahaṁkāra—the ego.
Mati[3]—decision.
Cittam—wavering mind.
Gaganam—the firmament.
Prithivī—the earth.
Jalam—water.

1. *v.l. suramandara.*
2. *v.l. sukolapa.*
3. *v.l. upama.*

Vāyu—wind.
Cakṣus—the eye.
Śrotram—the ear.
Jihvā—the tongue.
Ghrāṇam—the nose.
Vākpāṇipāda—speech, hand, foot.
Javana—the quick.
Pāyu—the organ of evacuation.
Upastha—the organ of generation.
Śaṅkara—giver of auspiciousness.
Kharva[1]—thousand crores.
Kṣāntida—giver of forgiveness.
Kṣāntikṛt—forgiver.
Nara—man.
Bhaktapriya—fond of devotees.
Bhartṛ—Lord.
Bhaktimān—endowed with devotion.
Bhaktivardhana—Increasing devotion.
Bhaktastuta—lauded by votaries.
Bhaktapara—attached to votaries.
Kīrtida—bestower of fame.
Kīrtivardhana—enhancer of fame.
Kīrtidīpti—resplendence of fame.
Kṣamā—forgiveness.
Kānti—splendour.
Bhakti—devotion.
Parā Dayā—greatest compassion.
Dāna—the gift
Dātṛ—the giver.
Kartṛ—the agent.
Devadevapriya—fond of god of gods.
Śuci—the pure.
Śucimān—possessing the pure.
Sukhada—giver of happiness.
Mokṣa—emancipation.
Kāma—Love.
Artha—wealth.

1. *v.l. śarva.*

Sahasrapāt—having 1000 feet.
Sahasraśīrṣā—thousand-headed.
Vaidya—the physician.
Mokṣadvāra—entrance to salvation.
Prajādvāram—passage of subjects.
Sahasrānta[1]—having thousand ends.
Sahasrakara—having thousand hands.
Śukra—the essence.
Sukirīṭin—having good coronet.
Sugrīva—having good neck.
Kaustubha—the Kaustubha gem.
Pradyumna—Pradyumna.
Aniruddha—Aniruddha.
Hayagrīva—Hayagrīva.
Śūkara—the Boar.
Matsya—the Fish.
Paraśurāma—Paraśurāma.
Prahlāda—Prahlāda.
Bali—Bali.
Śaraṇya—worthy of being refuge.
Nitya—the permanent.
Buddha—the enlightened.
Mukta—the emancipated.
Śarīrabhṛt—the embodied.
Kharadūṣaṇahantṛ,—slayer of Khara & Dūṣaṇa.
Rāvaṇasya Pramardana—slayer of Rāvaṇa.
Sītāpatī—husband of Sītā.
Bharata—Bharata.
Vardhiṣṇu—the flourishing.
Kumbhendrajit-nihantṛ—slayer of kumbhendrajit.
Kumbhakarṇapramardana—grinder of Kumbhakarṇa.
Narāntakāntaka—slayer of Narāntaka.
Devāntakavināśana—slayer of Devāntaka.
Duṣṭāsuranihantṛ—slayer of wicked demons.
Śambarāri—enemy of Śambara,
Narakasya nihantṛ—slayer of Naraka.
Triśīrṣasya vināśana—slayer of Triśīrṣa.

1. *v.l. sahasrākṣa,*

Yamalārjunabhettṛ—splitter of twin Arjunas.
Tapohitakara—ençourager of penance.
Vāditra—the player on instruments.
Vādyam—the musical instrument.
Buddha—the enlightened.
Varaprada—the giver of boons.
Sāra—the essence.
Sārapriya—fond of essence.
Saura—belonging to the Sun.
Kālahantṛ—slayer of Kāla.
Nikṛntana—the splitter.
Agastya—sage Agastya.
Devala—sage Devala.
Nārada—sage Nārada.
Nāradapriya—fond of Nārada.
Prāṇa—vital air Prāṇa.
Apāna—vital air Apāna.
Vyāna—vital air Vyāna.
Rajas—the quality of baseness.
Sattva—the quality of goodness.
Tamas—the quality of ignorance.
Śarat—the Autumn.
Udāna—the vital air Udāna.
Samāna—the vital air Samāna
Bheṣaja—the medicine.
Bhiṣak—the physician.
Kūṭastha—the unchanging.
Svaccharūpa—having clean form.
Sarvadehavivarjita—devoid of all kinds of bodies.
Cakṣurindriyahīna—devoid of sense of vision.
Vāgindriyavivarjita—devoid of sense of speech.
Hastendriyavihīna—devoid of hands.
Pādābhyāṁ vivarjita—devoid of feet.
Pāyūpasthavihīna—devoid of organs of generation and evacuation.
Mahātapavisarjita[1]—discarded from great penance.
Prabodhena vihīna—devoid of good perception.

1. *v.l marutāpavivarjita.*

Buddhyā vivarjita—devoid of intellect.
Cetasā vigata—devoid of consciousness.
Prāṇena vivarjita—devoid of Prāṇa.
Apānena vihīna—devoid of Apāna.
Vyānena vivarjita—devoid of Vyāna.
Udānena vihīna—devoid of Udāna.
Samānena vivarjita—devoid of Samāna.
Ākāśena vihīna—devoid of ether.
Vāyunāparivarjita—devoid of wind.
Agninā vihīna—devoid of fire.
Udakena vivarjita—devoid of water.
Prithivyāvihīna—devoid of earth.
Śabdena vivarjita—devoid of sound.
Sparśena vihīna—devoid of touch.
Sarvarūpavivarjita—devoid of all forms.
Rāgeṇa vigata—devoid of passion.
Aghena parivarjita—devoid of sins.
Śokena rahita—devoid of grief.
Vacasā parivarjita—devoid of speech.
Rajovivarjita—devoid of quality of rajas.
Ṣadvikāravivarjita—devoid of six deviations.
Kāmavarjita—devoid of lust.
Krodhena parivarjita—devoid of anger.
Lobhena vigata—devoid of covetousness.
Dambhena vivarjita—devoid of pride.
Sūkṣma—the subtle.
Suṣūkṣma—the very subtle.
Sthūlāt sthūlatara—grosset of the gross.
Viśārada—the clever.
Balādhyakṣa—leader of armies.
Sarvasya kṣobhaka—agitator of all.
Prakṛteḥ kṣobhaka—agitator of Prakṛti.
Mahataḥ kṣobhaka—agitator of intellectual principle.
Bhūtānāṁ kṣobhaka—agitator of elements.
Buddheḥ kṣobhaka—agitator of the intellect.
Indriyāṇām kṣobhaka—agitator of the senses.
Viṣayakṣobhaka—agitator of objects.
Brahmaṇaḥkṣobhaka—agitator of Brahmā.
Rudrasya kṣobhaka—agitator of Rudra.

Cakṣurādeḥ agamya—beyond the range of eyes.
Śrotrāgamya—beyond the range of ears.
Tvacā na gamya—unknown by the skin.
Kūrma—the tortoise.
Jihvāgrāhya—beyond the perception of tongue.
Ghrāṇendriyāgamya—beyond the perception of smell,
Vācāgrāhya—unknown by speech.
Pāṇibhyām agamya—Incomprehensible by hands.
Pādāgamya—beyond the reach of feet.
Manasaḥ agrāhya—beyond the reach of mind.
Buddhyā agrāhya—beyond the reach of intellects.
Hari—remover of evil.
Ahambudbhyā grāhya—realizable by the perception of *aham.*
Cetasā Grāhya—realizable by the mind.
Śaṅkhapāṇi—having conch in the hand.
Avyaya—undecaying.
Gadāpāṇi—having the club in the hand.
Śārṅgapāṇi—having the bow Śārṅga in the hand.
Kṛṣṇa—(dark in colour).
Jñānamūrti—of the form of knowledge.
Parantapa—slayer of enemies.
Tapasvin—ascetic.
Jñānagamya—realisable by knowledge.
Jñānin—endowed with knowledge.
Jñānavid—knower of knowledge.
Jñeya—the object of knowledge.
Jñeyahīna—devoid of objects of knowledge.
Jñapti—knowledge.
Caitanya rūpaka—having the form of consciousness.
Bhāva—the purport.
Bhāvya—to be conceived.
Bhavakāra—cause of origin.
Bhāvana—the conceiver.
Bhavanāśana—the destroyer of birth.
Govinda—lord of cows.
Gopati—master of kine.
Gopa—cowherd.
Sarvagopīsukhaprada—giver of happiness to all cowherdesses.
Gopāla—protector of cows.

Gopati—lord of speech.
Gomati—with the mind directed to cows.
Godhara—lifter of kine.
Upendra—Indra's younger brother.
Nṛsiṁha—the Man-lion.
Śauri Kṛṣṇa—grandson of Śūra.
Janārdana—tormentor of the wicked.
Āraṇeya—produced from *Araṇi*.
Bṛhadbhānu—of long rays.
Bṛhaddīpta—Immensely shining.
Dāmodara—tied with a rope.
Trikāla—threefold time.
Kālañjara—cognizer of time
Kālavarjita—devoid of time.
Trisandhya—of threefold junctions.
Dvāparam—the Dvāpara Age.
Tretā—the Tretā Age.
Prajādvāra—the gateway of subjects.
Trivikrama—having three steps.
Vikrama—the valorous.
Daṇḍahasta—having the staff in the hand.
Ekadaṇḍin—having a single staff.
Tridaṇḍadhṛk—holding three staffs.
Sāmabheda—variety of Sāma.
Sāmopāya—having sāmopāya (peaceful means).
Sāmarūpin—having Sāma as form.
Sāmaga[1]—reached by Sāmans.
Sāmaveda—the Sāma Veda.
Atharva—the Atharva Veda.
Sukṛta—well-framed.
Sukharūpaka[2]—happily formed.
Atharvavedavid—knower of Atharva veda.
Atharvācārya—preceptor of Atharva veda.
Ṛgrūpin—having the form of Ṛks.
Ṛgveda—the Ṛgveda.
Ṛgvedeṣu pratiṣṭhita—well-stationed in the Ṛgveda.

1. *v.l. tathyopāya.*
2. *v.l. sutarūpaṇaḥ.*

Yajurvettṛ—knower of Yajur mantras.
Yajurveda—the Yajur Veda.
Yajurvedavid—knower of Yajur Veda.
Ekapāt—single-footed.
Bahupāt—many-footed.
Supāt—nice-footed.
Sahasrapāt—thousand footed.
Catuṣpāt—four-footed.
Dvipāt—two-footed.
Smṛti—the Smrit text.
Nyāyopama[1]—comparable to Nyāya.
Balin—the powerful.
Sannyāsin—the renouncer of the world.
Sannyāsa—renunciation.
Caturāśrama—having the four stages of life.
Brahmacārin—the student.
Gṛhastha—the householder.
Vānaprastha—the retired.
Bhikṣuka—the mendicant.
Brāhmaṇa—the Brahmin.
Kṣatriya—the Kṣatriya.
Vaiśya—the Vaiśya.
Śūdra—the Śūdra.
Varṇa—the class of society.
Śīlada—provider of good character.
Śīlasampanna—endowed with good character.
Duḥśīlaparivarjita—devoid of bad character.
Gokṣa[2]—having eyes fixed on the world.
Adhyātmasamāviṣṭa—engaged in Spiritual acts.
Stuti—the praising verse.
Stotṛ—the praiser.
Pūjaka—worshipper.
Pūjya—worthy of worship.
Vākkaraṇam—the organ of Speech.
Vācya—object of statement.
Vācaka—the reciter.

1. *v.l. nyāyo yamo.*
2. *v.l. mokṣa.*

Vettṛ—the knower.
Vyākaraṇam—grammar.
Vākyam—the sentence.
Vākyavit—conversant with sentences.
Vākyagamya—within the reach of words.
Tīrthavāsin—living in sacred places.
Tīrtha—the sacred shrine.
Tīrthin—of the shrines.
Tīrthavid—knower of holy places.
Tīrthādibhūta—abiding in all tīrthas.
Sāṁkhya—the Sāṁkhya system.
Niruktam—the science of etymology.
Abhidaivata—face to face with the deity.
Praṇava—the sacred syllable *om*.
Praṇaveśa—lord of *Praṇava*.
Praṇavena pravandita—adored by *Praṇava*.
Praṇavena lakṣya—indicated by Praṇava.
Gāyatrī—the mystic verse Gāyatrī.
Gadādhara—holder of the club.
Śālagrāmanivāsin—living in Śālagrāma.
Śālagrāma—the Śālagrāma itself.
Jalaśāyin—lying in waters.
Yogaśāyin—lying in Yoga.
Śeṣaśāyin—lying on serpent Śeṣa.
Kuśeśaya—the mystic lotus.
Mahābhartṛ—the great lord.
Kāryam—the result.
Kāraṇam—the reason.
Pṛthivīdhara—the holder of earth.
Prajāpati—the patriarch.
Śāśvata—the eternal.
Kāmya—worthy of being desired.
Kāmayitṛ—the creator of desire.
Virāṭ—the lord Paramount.
Samrāṭ—the emperor.
Pūṣan—the sun.
Svarga—the heaven.
Rathastha—stationed in a car.
Sārathi—the charioteer.

Balaṁ—the strength.
Dhanin—the rich.
Dhanaprada—the giver of riches.
Dhanya—the blessed.
Yādavānāṁ hite rata—engaged in the wellbeing of Yādavas.
Arjunasya priya—fond of Arjuna.
Arjuna—Arjuna himself.
Bhīma—Bhima himself.
Parākrama—valour (personified).
Durviṣaha—the unbearable.
Sarvaśāstraviśārada—efficient in all Śāstras.
Sārasvata—devotee of Sarasvati.
Mahābhīṣma—the great terrifier.
Pārijātahara—remover of pārijāta.
Amṛtasya pradātṛ—giver of nectar.
Kṣīroda—the ocean of milk.
Kṣīra—the milk itself.
Indrātmaja,—son of Indra (Jayanta).
Indragoptṛ—protector of Indra.
Govardhanadhara—upholder of Govardhana mountain.
Kaṁsasya nāśana—slayer of Kaṁsa.
Hastipa—keeper of elephant.
Hastināśana—slayer of elephant.
Śipiviṣṭa—pervaded by rays.
Prasanna—the cheerful.
Sarvalokārtināśana—remover of vexations of the whole world.
Mudra—the mysterious.
Mudrākara—showing the mystic sign with the hand.
Sarvamudrāvivarjita—devoid of all *Mudras*.
Dehin—the embodied.
Dehasthita—Immanent in the body.
Dehasya niyāmaka—Organizer of the body.
Śrotṛ—the hearer.
Śrotraniyantṛ—the controller of the ears.
Śrotavya—worthy of being heard.
Śravaṇa—power of hearing.
Tvaksthita—present in the skin.
Sparśayitṛ—the toucher.
Sparśya—object of touching.

Sparśanam—power of touching.
Cakṣustha—present in the eye.
Rūpadraṣṭṛ—seer of forms.
Cakṣuṣaḥ niyantṛ—the controller of eyes.
Dṛśyam—the object of vision.
Jihvāstha—present in the tongue.
Rasajña—knower of the taste.
Jihvāniyāmaka—controller of the tongue.
Ghrāṇastha—seated in the nose.
Ghrāṇakṛt—creator of smell.
Ghrātṛ—the smeller.
Ghrāṇendriyaniyāmaka—the controller of the organ of smell.
Vākstha—seated in speech.
Vaktṛ—the speaker.
Vaktavya—the object of speech.
Vacana—the action of speech.
Vāṅniyāmaka—controller of speech.
Prāṇistha—seated in living beings.
Śilpakṛt—creator of fine arts.
Śilpa—the fine arts.
Hastayoḥ niyāmaka—controller of hands.
Padavyaḥ—the roads.
Gantṛ—the goer.
Gantavya—the place going to.
Gamana—the act of going.
Pādayoḥ niyantṛ—the controller of feet.
Pādyabhāk—receiver of pādya.
Visargakṛt—the excretor.
Visargasya niyantṛ—controller of excretion.
Upasthastha—seated in the organ of generation.
Sukha—pleasure.
Upasthasya niyantṛ—controller of the organ of generation.
Upasthānandakara—creator of pleasure through the organ of generation.
Śatrughna—slayer of enemies.
Kārtavīrya,—the king Kārtavīrya.
Dattātreya—the sage Dattātreya.
Alarkasya hite ratah—engaged in the welfare of Alarka.
Kārtavīryanikṛntana—slayer of Kārttavīrya.

Kālanemi—rim round the wheel of time.
Mahānemi—the great rim.
Megha—the cloud.
Meghapati—Lord of clouds.
Annaprada—purveyor of food.
Annarūpin—of the form of food.
Annāda—the eater of food.
Annapravartaka—producer of food.
Dhūmakṛt—producer of smoke.
Dhūmarūpa—of the form of smoke.
Devakīputra—son of Devakī.
Uttama—the most excellent.
Devakyānandana—delighter of Devakī.
Nanda—foster father.
Rohiṇyāḥ priya—beloved of Rohiṇī.
Vasudeva priya—beloved of Vasudeva.
Vasudevasuta—son of Vasudeva.
Dundubhi—the trumpet Dundubhi.
Hāsarūpa—of the form of laughter.
Puṣpahāsa—smiling like flowers.
Aṭṭahāsapriya—loving boisterous laugh.
Sarvādhyakṣa—presiding deity over all.
Kṣara—the decaying.
Akṣara—the undecaying.
Acyuta—the undefaulting.
Satyeśa—lord of truth.
Satyāyāḥ priya—lover of Satyā.
Vara—the excellent.
Rukmiṇyāḥ pati—lord of Rukmiṇī.
Rukmiṇyāḥ vallabha—lover of Rukmiṇī.
Gopīnāṁ vallabha—lover of cowherdesses.
Puṇyaśloka—of meritorious fame.
Viśruta—famous.
Vṛṣākapi—Vṛṣākapi.
Yama—the god of death.
Guhya—seated in caves.
Maṅgala[1]—the auspicious.

1. *v.l. mukula.*

Budha—the planet Mercury.
Rāhu—the planet Rāhu.
Ketugraha—the planet Ketu.
Grāha—the crocodile.
Gajendramukhamelaka—associate of the lord of elephants.
Grāhasya vinihantṛ—slayer of crocodile.
Grāmaṇi—the leader of the village.
Rakṣaka—the protector.
Kinnara—the semidivine Kinnara.
Siddha—the semidivine Siddha.
Chandas—the prosody.
Svachandas—the free.
Viśvarūpa—having the Cosmic form.
Viśālākṣa—having wide eyes.
Daityasūdana—slayer of demons.
Anantarūpa—having endless forms.
Bhūtastha—seated in elements.
Devadānavasaṁsthita—standing between *devas* and *dānavas*.
Suṣuptistha—stationed in sleep.
Suṣupti—deep slumber.
Sthānam—the permanent abode.
Sthānānta—end of abode.
Jagatstha—standing in the Universe.
Jāgartṛ—the wakeful.
Jāgaritaṁ sthānam—the seat of the wakeful.
Svapnastha—standing in dream.
Svapnavid[1]—knower of dream.
Svapna—the dream.
Sthānastha—remaining in his own place.
Sustha—well stationed.
Jāgradvihīna—devoid of wakefulness.
Svapnavihīna—devoid of dream.
Suṣuptivihīna—devoid of slumber.
Caturthaka—the fourth.
Vijñānam—the precise knowledge.
Caitrarūpa[2]—of the form of the month Caitra.

1. *v.l.* Veṅkaṭeśvara edition adds *svapnasthānam* after this.
2. *v.l. vedyarūpam.*

Jīva—the life.
Jīvayitṛ—the life giver.
Bhuvanādhipati—lord of the universe.
Bhuvanānāṁ niyāmaka—controller of worlds.
Pātālavāsin—residing in Pātāla.
Pātāla—the nether world.
Sarvajvaravināśana—destroyer of all fevers.
Paramānandarūpin—of the form of great bliss.
Dharmāṇāṁ pravartaka—organizer of *dharmas*.
Sulabha—easily acessible.
Durlabha—difficult of access.
Prāṇāyāmapara—engaged in holding breath.
Pratyāhāra—the redeemer.
Dhāraka—the supporter.
Pratyāhārakara—organizer of redemption.
Prabhā—splendour.
Kānti—brilliance.
Arcis—lustre.
Śuddha—the pure.
Sphaṭikasannibha—like glass.
Agrāhya—incomprehensible.
Gaura—the white-coloured.
Sarva—the all.
Śuci—the clean.
Abhiṣṭuta—the adored.
Vaṣaṭkāra—the mantra Vaṣaṭ.
Vaṣaṭ—Vaṣaṭ.
Vauṣaṭ—the mantra Vauṣaṭ.
Svadhā—the offering Svadhā.
Svāhā—the offering Svāhā.
Rati—the pleasurable love.
Paktṛ—the cook.
Nandayitṛ—the delighter.
Bhoktṛ—the enjoyer.
Boddhṛ—the knower.
Bhāvayitṛ—the conceiver.
Jñānātman—the soul of knowledge.
Ūhātman[1]—the soul of inference.

1. *v.l. dehātman.*

Bhūmā—the prolific.
Sarveśvareśvara—supreme Lord of all.
Nadī—the river.
Nandin—the delighted.
Nandīśa—lord of Nandin.
Bhārata—engaged in lustre
Tarunāśana—destroyer of trees.
Cakrapa—protector of the wheel.
Śrīpati—Lord of Lakṣmī
Nṛpa—the king.
Cakravartināmīśa[1]—lord of emperors.
Sarvadevānāmīśa—lord of all *devas*.
Svāvakāśasthita[2]—abiding by his space.
Puṣkara—the lotus.
Puskarādhyakṣa—presiding over lotus.
Puṣkaradvīpa—the continent Puṣkara.
Bharata—the nourisher.
Janaka—the king Janaka.
Janya—the resultant.
Sarvākāravivarjita—devoid of all forms.
Nirākāra—having no form.
Nirnimitta—having no cause.
Nirātaṅka—having no calamity.
Nirāśraya—having no support.
Deva[3]—the lord.
Viṣṇu[4]—the omnipresent.
Īśa[5]—the master.

O Vṛṣabhadhvaja (Śaṅkara) thus I have mentioned to you the thousand names of Lord Viṣṇu that wipe off all sins. The Brahmin who recites this attains Viṣṇuhood, the Kṣatriya becomes victorious, the Vaiśya realises wealth and Śūdra attains happiness full of Viṣṇu's devotion.

1. *v.l. nṛpāṇāṁ cakravartinām*
2. *v.l. Dvārakā-saṁsthita.*
3. Not found in Veṅkaṭeśvara edition.
4. —do—
5. —do—

CHAPTER SIXTEEN

Contemplation of Hari and Sun-worship

Rudra said :

1. O Lord, the holder of conch, discus and club, please narrate to me further the process of contemplation on Lord Viṣṇu, the pure and the Supreme soul.

Hari said :

2-3. O Rudra, listen to the procedure in the contemplation of Lord Hari which destroys the tree of worldly existence. There is the great Brahman whose form is invisible, whose end cannot be seen, who is omnipresent, unborn, immutable, imperishable, all-pervasive, eternal the root-cause of the whole universe and the supreme lord of all.

4. He is seated in the heart of all living beings. He is the great lord of all creatures. He is the support of all. He is not supported by any thing else. He is the cause of all causes.

5-6. He is stainless, free from bondage, contemplated by sages who are emancipated. He has no gross body, he is devoid of eyes, vital airs and sense-organs, all qualities of living beings, organs of excretion and generation and all senses.

7. He is without mind as well as all its qualities. He is devoid of intellect and thought yet (functions as lord of all gods.

8-9. He is devoid of ego and functions of the intellect. He is free from *Prāṇa*[1] *and Apāna*[2]; he is without the vital air called Prāṇa[3] and all its qualities. (Such a Brahman must be contemplated).

Hari said :

I shall expound again the process of worship of the Sun that had already been explained to Bhṛgu before.

1. The first of the five vital airs enumerated as *prāṇa*, *apāna*, *samāna*, *vyāna* and *udāna*. *Prāṇa* has its seat in the beings, hence it means the breath.
2. One of the five vital airs which comes out of the arms.
   v.l. vyāna.

10. *Oṁ khakholkāya namaḥ* (*Om* salutation to the Sun, the meteoric planet of the sky). This is the *Mūlamantra* (the basic mystic verse) that gives worldly enjoyment and final beatitude (*Mukti*).

11. [Special Sūrya mantra] *Om* obeisance to lord Khakholka[1]. *Om* in the rays that spread (*vici*) ṭha ṭha obeisance to the head.

Oṁ ṭha ṭha unto the knowledge. Obeisance to the tuft of hair. *Oṁ ṭha ṭha* to the thousand-rayed, obeisance to the armour (amulet and mystic syllable).

12. *Oṁ ṭha ṭha* to the lord of all brilliance, obeisance to the weapon. *Oṁ* burn, burn, blaze, blaze *ṭha ṭha* obeisance.

13. This is the Sun's *mantra* of fiery species that destroys all sins.

[*Sakalīkaraṇa mantra*]

Oṁ Ādityāya Vidmahe Viśvabhāvāya dhīmahi Tannaḥ Sūryaḥ pracodayāt.

14. With this Gāyatrī (a particular metre) of the sun the worshipper should perform the *Sakali-karaṇa* (summing up). Then the salutation (special gesture with joined palms) to Dharma in the east, to Yama in the south.

15. To Daṇḍanāyaka and then to Vaivarṇa in the north. The dark-tawny (form) in the north-east and the Dīkṣita in the south-east to be worshipped.

16. To Indra, the holder of thunderbolt in the hand, is to be worshipped in the South-west and the mystic syllables *Bhūrbhuvaḥ svaḥ* in the north-west.

To Bull-bannered Śaṅkara, the following should be worshipped in the eight directions beginning with east and ending with north-east. *Oṁ* obeisance to the moon, the lord of stars. *Oṁ* obeisance to Aṅgāraka (Mars) the son of the Earth. *Oṁ* obesance to Budha (Mercury) the son of the moon. *Oṁ* obeisance to the lord of speech (Bṛhaspati), the lord of all learning. *Oṁ* obeisance to sage Śukra the son of Bhṛgu. *Oṁ* obeisance to Śanaiścara (Saturn) the son of the Sun. *Oṁ* obeisance to Rāhu. *Oṁ* obeisance to Ketu.

1. Veṅkaṭeśvara edition adds *tridaśāya*.

17. *Oṁ* obeisance to Anūruka[1]. *Oṁ* obeisance to the Lord of *Pramatha* (goblins attending on Śiva). Om obeisance to the enlightened.

18. O Lord ! having rays measured all round, O Lord of the entire universe, having seven horses for vehicles, the four-armed one, giver of the great *siddhis*[2] tawny in colour due to the flames, the gentle one ! Come on, Come on. This is water-offering. Salutation unto the head. Take back the terrific form. O the un-naked, burn, burn *ṭha ṭha* obeisance.

19. With this mantra he should invoke the sun. He should discharge him with the mantra. *Om* salutation to the lord Āditya (sun) of thousand rays, go as you please, to come again.

CHAPTER SEVENTEEN

Worship

Hari Said :

1. Next I shall expound the process of worship of the sun which had been explained to Dhanada (the lord of wealth—Kubera).

In a clean place the figure of a lotus with eight petals should be drawn with the pericarp.

2. Showing the mystical sign *Āvāhinī* (the invoking) with the fingers, the worshipper should invoke Hari. The Sun-god Khakholka should be placed in the middle in the form of a *Yantra* (mechanical device) and sprinkled with holy water.

1. *v.l. anūru.*

2. Superhuman faculty or power which is achieved by a *sādhaka* when he reaches the highest stage of *sādhanā*. The following are the names of the eight *siddhis—aṇimā, laghimā, mahimā, prāpti, prākāmya, īśitva, vaśitva* and, *karmāvasāyitā*. (*ŚP* (*AITM*) p. 2114; *CSL* p. 458).

3. O Śiva, let him place the heart of the god in the south-eastern direction. The head should be placed in the north-eastern direction. Let him place the tuft in the South-west.

4. With the mind solely concentrated let him fix Dharma to the east, the eye to the north-west and the *Astra* (missile) to the west.

5. Let him place soma (Moon) in the north-east and Lohita (Mars) in the east. Moon's sun (Budha—Mercury) is to be placed in the south-east and Bṛhaspati (Jupiter) in the south.

6. The preceptor of demons (Śukra-Venus) is to be placed in the south-west and Śanaiścara (saturn) in the west. Let him place Ketu in the north-west and Rāhu in the north.

7-8. In a second square the twelve suns should be worshipped. The twelve suns are Bhaga, Sūrya, Aryaman, Mitra, Varuṇa, Savitṛ, Dhātṛ, vivasvat the powerful, Tvaṣṭṛ, Pūṣan, Indra and the twelfth is Viṣṇu.

9. Indra and other deities should be worshipped with reverence by the worshipper. (The four forms of the goddess Durgā, Jayā, Jayantī and Aparājitā should be worshipped. So also Śeṣa, Vāsuki and other serpents.

CHAPTER EIGHTEEN

Worship of Amṛteśa Mṛtyuñjaya

Sūta said :

1. I shall now expound the process of worship of Mṛtyuñjaya (the conqueror of death) narrated to Kaśyapa by Garuḍa. It is holy, has redeeming features and covers all the deities.

2. *Oṅkāra* (The mystic syllable *Om*) should be placed first. *Juṅkāra*[1] (the syllable *Jum*) next. The third one is *sa* with a *visarga* (*saḥ*). This mantra (*Oṁ juṁ saḥ*) suppresses death and poverty.

1. *v.l. huṅkāra.*

3. This *mahāmantra* is the lord of Nectar. It consists of three syllables. The recital and worship of this mantra are equally efficacious. By its recital people can become free from death and all kinds of sins.

4. By its recital a hundred times a man attains the fruits of the recital of Vedic passages or pilgrimage to holy places. By reciting it a hundred and eight times, three times during the day (dawn, midday and dusk) he can conquer death and enemies.

5. He should contemplate on the god Varada (giver of boons) as seated on a white lotus indicating fearlessness through gestures. The lord of Nectar should be thought of as holding the jar of nectar with both the hands.

6. He should think of the goddess of nectar, true of speech, as seated on his limb holding the jar in the right hand and the lotus in the left.

7. Reciting this *mantra* eight thousand times, three times a day, for a month he conquers old age, death, pestilence and enemies and accords peace and benevolence to all living beings.

8-11. A real worshipper must know all these things in detail—the site of a place of worship, the consecration (of an idol), the checking (of breath), the proximity, the placing, the water (for washing the feet), the water for ritualistic drink with the palm, the water for bathing, the materials of worship, the application of unguents, the holy lamp, the cloth, ornament, food offering and the water for drinking (offered to the deity), the *mātrās* or quantities, mystical signs and gesticulations, the gift for the priests, the ghee offerings in the fire, the prayer, playing on musical instruments, vocal music, dancing in attendance, assignment of fingers etc, the proper assemblage, going round in reverence, kneeling down, chanting of mystic syllables, sacrifices, offering obeisance, and Visarjana (the final summing up and conclusion)—this process of worship involving the use of six limbs (*ṣaḍaṅgas*, viz., two thighs, two arms, head and heart (or navel) as mentioned in order and emanated from the mouth of the great Lord.

12. First of all, *arghya* should be offered and *pāśārcana*[1]

1. *v.l. arghyapātrārcanaṁ dadyādastreṇaiva tutāḍanam.*

performed, then fanning is done with a piece of cloth. It is then purified with the *kavaca mantras* followed by the rite of *Amṛtīkaraṇa.*

13-14. Then follows the worship of *Ādhāraśaktis* (the presiding goddesses of the materials of worship), *Prāṇāyāma*[1] (holding the breath), yogic postures, purification of the *Piṇḍa*[2] (ball of food) for the manes by drying it up. Then remember the soul as in the form of god, assign the various gestures with fingers of the hand, pray to the soul in the form of refulgence in the middle of the lotus of the heart.

15. Then he should scatter brilliant flowers on the idol or on the ground all round. For the worship of its *Dvāra* (entrance-passage), the soul and the *Ādhāra-śaktis* are worshipped.

16. Then follows *sānnidhyakaraṇa* of the *devas* (invoking them to be near one) and the worship of the followers. For the *pūjā*[3] of the six limbs the quarters are divided.

17. Dharma and others, Indra and others are duly worshipped along with their weapons and followers. Worship of the cycles, the Vedas and the *muhūrtas* yields enjoyment and salvation.[4]

18. The groups of Mothers Nandī and Gaṅgā, Mahākāla and Yamunā are to be worshipped at the threshold.

19. *Om* obeisance to Bhairava the lord of Nectar. Similarly, *Om juṁ saḥ*[5] obeisance to sun.

20. In the same manner he should perform the worship of Śiva-Kṛṣṇa, Brahman, the *Guṇas*, Caṇḍikā[6] Sarasvatī, Mahālakṣmī and others.

1. Exercising the breath. It is of three types—*pūraka, kumbhaka* and *recaka.*
2. *v.l. pīṭhaśuddhi.*
3. *v.l. kartavyā ca vipaścitaiḥ.*
4. An association of, specially, attendants of Śiva.
5. *v.l. haṁsaḥ.*
6. Durgā.

CHAPTER NINETEEN

Prāṇeśvarī Vidyā

Sūta said :

1. I shall now narrate the *prāṇeśvarī* rite of Garuḍa as explained by Śiva. I shall at first mention the places where a person bitten by a cobra does not remain alive.

2. If he is bitten in the funeral pyre, anthill, well, and the cavities of trees or if the marks of the bite are indistinct and there are three lines, he does not survive.

3-4. A person cannot survive the serpent bite if he is bitten on the sixth day of the fortnight or when the sun is in the Zodiac, Cancer or Aries, or the moon in the constellations Mūlā, Āśleṣā and Maghā; If he is bitten in the armpit, loins, throat, joints, temples, ears, belly, mouth, arms, neck or the back; If the messenger going to the physician is a man with a stick or a weapon, a mendicant or a naked person the patient is sure to die.

5-7. There are six *vivartanas* (or units of session) during the day and five *vivartanas* during the night. During the day the sun has the first session for a yāma[1], the other ten planets (adding Rāhu and Ketu also) have half yāma each. ($10 \times \frac{1}{2} = 5$ sessions). During the night the serpents have their sessions (Śeṣa one and eight other serpents together four, five sessions). Among serpents Seṣa is Sun, Phaṇipa is moon, Takṣaka is Mars, Karkoṭa is Jupiter, Padma and Mahāpadma (jointly) Venus and Śaṅkha is saturn. Rāhu and Kulika are themselves serpents and planets.[2]

8. When Jupiter presides during the day or in the night he is the slayer of even gods. Saturn is death by day. When Rāhu presides along with kulika at the hours of confluence of two half-yāmas, the period is destructive

1. *Yāma* generally means one eighth part of a day, a period of three hours, (*SSED* p. 457)

2. This list of eight main serpents is somewhat different from that found elsewhere.

9-11. The fifteen parts of the human body, viz—toes, feet, calves, knees, genital, navel, heart, breast tips, neck, nose-tip, eyes, ears, brows temples and the head are allotted a day each from *pratipad* (the first day of the fortnight). These parts are assigned, in order, to so many *muhūrtas* (one sixtieth of a day) as follows :—five to the toe, twelve to the feet, five to the calf, two to the knee, one to the genital, six to the navel, four to the breast tip, eight to the throat, fifteen to the nosetip and one each to the eyes, ears eye-brow, temple and the head.

12-13. If the moon presides over the right part of the man's body he may survive. In regard to a woman it is the left part of the body. Consciousness is restored by rubbing with the hand and setting the wind in motion. The great *Bīja* (mystic seed) of the soul is called *haṁsa*, it is as pure as crystal.

14. It is known as the queller of poison and sin. Its *Bīja* is fourfold. The first *Bīja* is *Bindu* (the point in *Om*). The second consists of five vowels; the third stands on the sixth and the fourth is with *visarga*.

15. *Oṁ kuru Kunde*[1] *Svāhā.*

This Vidyā (mystical knowledge) was kept by Garuḍa formerly for the protection of the three worlds.

16. A man desirous of killing the serpents shall place *Praṇava* (*Om*) in the mouth. The wise man shall place *Kuru* in the neck, *Kunde*[2] in the calves, Svāha in the feet. This *nyāsa* (placing) is called *yugahā.*

17. The house in which this *mantra* is written and placed is abandoned by serpents. After reciting this *mantra* a thousand times the sacred thread shall be placed on the ear.

18. Serpents leave off the house where sand particles are scattered after reciting this *mantra*. By reciting it seven lakhs of time[3] *siddhi* has been obtained by *Devas* and *Asuras*.

19. *Oṁ svāhā* unto the fowl-formed of golden lines (*Oṁ Suvarṇarekhe kukkuṭavigraharūpiṇi svāhā*), he should write, on a lotus of eight petals, two letters in each petal.

1. *v.l. kule.*
2. *Ibid.*
3. Reading altered to saptalakṣa from Japtalakṣa.

20. The patient bitten by a serpent should be sprinkled with water of that lotus. He then leaves off the poison.

21. *Oṁ Pakṣi Svāhā*

Reciting this mantra the fingers beginning with the thumb and ending with the little finger should be placed, (Nyāsa) in order, on the head, mouth, heart, genital and the feet.

22. Even in dreams the poisonous serpents do not step on his shadow. The person who recites this a hundred thousand times is competent to quell poison by a mere glance.

23. *Oṁ Hriṁ Hrauṁ Hrīṁ Bhīruṇḍāyai Svāhā*

This *mantra* recited into the ear of the patient removes poison.

24-25. *Nyāsa*

a	ā	to be placed at the tip of the	feet
i	ī	,,	calf
u	ū	,,	knee
e	ai	,,	waist
o		,,	navel
āu		,,	heart
am		,,	mouth
aḥ		,,	head

This *Haṁsa-mantra-nyāsa* when recited, contemplated or worshipped removes poison.

26. 'I am Garuḍa'—meditating like this the process of destroying poison should be done. The *Ham* mantra with the *nyāsas* on the body is said to be quelling poison.

27. Placing *Haṁsa* on the left hand, the operator shall close nostrils and mouth. This mantra shall destroy poison in the skin as well as flesh.

28. He should draw out the poison of the patient by blowing the wind and place it over his body. He then shall remember the blue-throated God Śiva and others.

29. The root of *Pratyaṅgirāḥ*[1] drunk with rice water removes poison. The roots of *Punarnavā*[2] *Phalinī*[3] and *Cakrajā*[4] are also like this.

1. Identity not clear.
2. Spreading Hogmeed, *VN* p. 233.
3. Also called *priyangu—Callicarpa macrophylla, VN*, p. 236.
4. *v.l. vakrajā.* Suśruta describes a shrub called *cakrakā.* There is also a herb named *vakra* (valleriana wallichii). *GUDB*, pp. 150 and 173.

30. The roots of white *Bṛhatī*[1] and *Karkoṭi*[2] are also destructive of poison. *Gairikarṇikā*[3] (a clod of earth) kneaded with water and mixed with ghee should be applied over the part bitten. The appliance of paste will remove poison.

31-32. If the patient drinks hot ghee, the poison does not spread. Five parts of the root of *Śirīṣa*[4] with one part of *Gṛñjana*[5] (red garlic) either drunk or applied over the body removes poison. The mantra *Oṁ Hrīm* removes the poison of *Gonasa* (a kind of snake).

33. When this mantra (*Oṁ Hrīm*) ending with *visarga* is contemplated in the heart and forehead it gives the power to influence every one. If this mantra is placed in the vaginal passage the girl comes under his influence, putting forth secretions of intoxication profusely.

34. Having recited this mantra 7×8 (fifty-six) thousand times, one becomes competent to go everywhere like Garuda, and a poet, well-read in Vedas and obtains a wife who will be under his control.

Indeed, the central theme of Sage Vyāsa story is destructive of poison.

CHAPTER TWENTY

Mantras for removing poison

Sūta said :

1-2. I shall now expound the highly secret collection of mantras described by Śiva. The usual weapons of a king are noose, bow, discus, heavy club (pestle), trident and spear.

1. Solanum indicum. *GVDB*, p. 277.
2. Name of a kind of *Karkoṭaka* (momordica divica). *GVDB*, p. 81.
3. *Gairika* generally means red chalk. *SSED*, p. 192
4. Albizzia lebback. *GVDB*, p. 399.
5. Allium ascalonicum. *GVDB*, p. 143.

With mantras, as with these weapons the king shall conquer his enemies.

3. In the lotus beginning with the petal towards the east and ending with the petal to the north-east (the eighth) a, ā etc. should be written as *Mantroddhāra*. They are *Aṣṭavargas*.

4. *Oṁkāra* shall be the *Bīja* of Brahmā. *Hrīṁkāra* is Viṣṇu himself. *Hrīṁkāra* should be written three times on the head of Śiva and placed in order.

5. *Oṁ Hrīm Hrīm*

Taking up the trident by the hand, he should whirl it facing the sky. On seeing it, the evil planets and the serpents are destroyed.

6. Holding the smoke-coloured bow in the middle of the hand he should contemplate over it in the sky. Evil planets, serpents, clouds and *Rākṣasas* are destroyed.

7. This mantra can protect the three worlds, not to speak of the land of mortals.

8. *Oṁ Jūṁ Sūṁ Hūṁ Phaṭ*

Eight pegs of *Khadira*[1] wood after the invocation with *mantras* shall be fixed up in the field. There can be no harm from thunderbolts or explosions in that place.

9. Invoke the great *mantra* mentioned by Garuḍa over the eight pegs and dig the earth in the field twenty one times at night.

10. This wards off troubles from lightning, vats and thunderbolt.

11. *Hara Kṣara Mala Vaṣat* with the bindu (Oṁ) is always auspicious. *Oṁ Hrām* obeisance to Sadāśiva. He should then place the *piṇḍa* (rice-ball) shining like the pomegranate flowers with the forefinger.

12. By only seeing it the evil clouds, lightnings, poisons, *Rākṣasas* and goblins flee unto the ten quarters.

13. *Oṁ Hrīm* obeisance to Gaṇeśa. *Oṁ Hrīm* obeisance to *Stambhanādicakra*. *Om Aiṁ Yāum* obeisance to Trailokyaḍāmara.

14. This *piṇḍa* is called Bhairava. It removes poisons and evil planets. It protects the field. It suppresses goblins (*Rākṣasas*) as well as others.

1. Acacia catechu. *GVDB*, p. 129.

15. *Oṁ* obeisance. Contemplating Indra's thunderbolt in the hand he can destroy evil clouds etc. By *Vajramudrā* poison, enemies and goblins are destroyed.

16. *Oṁ Kṣum* obeisance. One shall remember the noose on the left hand. Poisons, goblins etc are destroyed.

Oṁ Hrām obeisance. By mere repetition the *mantra* shall remove poison, evil clouds and evil planets.

17. By contemplation it can burn even death as the whole world by means of splitting missiles.

Oṁ Kṣṇam obeisance. By contemplating on Bhairava the *mantra* can be made to quell planets, goblins and poisons.

18. *Oṁ lasad dvijihvākṣa Svāhā.* This *mantra* prevents evil planets, goblins poison and birds affecting the field.

19. *Oṁ kṣām* obeisance. After writing this *mantra* on a kettle drum with blood the names of planets should be inserted.

Oṁ Mara Mara Māraya Māraya Svāhā

Oṁ Huṁ Phaṭ Svāhā

20. The trident should be invoked eight hundred times mentally with the mantras. It destroys hosts of enemies.

The lower energies should be blunted and bent by the pouncing of higher energies.

21. The mantras should be practised in *Pūraka* (in-take of breath), well-invoked at the time of *Kumbhaka* (retention of breath) and well-developed with *Praṇava.* Thus developed mantras yield fruits even as servants.

CHAPTER TWENTYONE

Worship of Pañca-vaktra Śiva

Sūta said :

1. I shall now severally relate the worship of *Pañcavaktra*[1] (Śiva) which gives enjoyment and salvation.

1. The five forms of Śiva who has five faces are — *Sadyojāta, Vāmadeva, Aghora, Tatpuruṣa,* and *Īśāna.*

Oṁ Bhūḥ obeisance to Viṣṇu, the primordial principle, the form that supports everything, *Svāhā*.

2. The invocation of *Sadyojāta* (Śiva) should be made with this *mantra* at first.

Oṁ obeisance to *Sadyojāta*. Of him the eight *Kalās* are well praised.

3. They are *Siddhi* (achievement), *Ṛddhi* (prosperity) *Dhṛti* (courage), *Lakṣmī* (wealth), *Medhā* (intellect), *Kānti* (splendour) *Svadhā* (oblation) and *Sthiti* (sustenance).

Oṁ Hām obeisance to Vāmadeva.

His Kalās are thirteen.

4. *Rājā* (the king), *Rakṣā* (protection), *Rati* (love), *Pālyā* (that which should be preserved), *Kānti* (splendour), *Tṛṣṇā* (thirst), *Mati* (reflection), *Kriyā* (action), *Kāmā* (lust), *Buddhi* (Intellect), *Rātri* (Night), *Trāsanī*, (that which terrifies) and *Mohinī* (that which enchants).

5. There are eight terrific *Kalās*[1] viz *Manonmanī* (suppressing the mind), *Aghorā* (not awful), *Mohā* (delusion), *Kṣudhā* (hunger), *Kalā* (digit), *Nidrā* (sleep), *Mṛtyu* (death) and *Māyā* (illusion).

6. *Oṁ Hraīm* obeisance to *Tatpuruṣa* alone. (His *Kalās* are) *Nivṛtti* (return), *Pratiṣṭhā* (Stabilization), *Vidyā* (learning) *Śāntī* (Peace).

7. *Oṁ Hraum* obeisance to *Īśāna*. (His *Kalās* are) *Niścalā* (unmoving), *Nirañjanā* (unsullied), *Śaśinī*, (bright) *Aṅganā* (woman), *Marīci* (ray) and *Jvālinī* (having flames),

CHAPTER TWENTYTWO

Worship of Śiva

Sūta said:

1. I shall now explain the process of worship of Śiva which brings enjoyment and salvation. He is quiet, omnipresent, void and stationed in a diagram of twelve parts.

1. These obviously belong to *Aghora*.

2. The five faces are short vowels. His limbs are long vowels with *bindu*.

His missile is represented by *visarga*. Above that the word Śiva should be written.

3-4. In the sixth apartment the great mantra *Haum* should be written below. It bestows all wealth.

The great *Mudrā* is as follows. With both the hands grasp the feet. The head then shall be placed over the tips of the feet. Then perform *Karāṅganyāsa* (the placing of the fingers as a mystic ritual)

With the palm of the hand using the *Astra mantra* purify the back.

5. Then perform *Aṅgavinyāsa* beginning with the little finger and ending with the forefinger.

I shall now explain the worship in the pericarp of the lotus of the heart.

6. Perform *arcanā*[1] of virtue, knowledge, unattachment, prosperity etc. with the heart.

With the heart offer the invocation, installation of the deity, the *pādya* and *arghya*.

7-8. The *Ācamana* (mystical drinking of water), the bathing, and the worship of similar base should be performed.

I shall now narrate the rites in five *Ullekhana-s* (prodding with the tip) performed with the *Śastra*. With the coat of mail sprinkling should be made. *Śaktinyāsa* should be made with the heart.

Throw fire either in the pit of Śakti or in the heart.

9. After performing *Garbhādhāna* and other rites (mystical conception), performing all activities with the heart he should perform *Homa* of Śiva with all the *Aṅgas* (parts).

10. Śambhu should be worshipped in the altar and in the *Padma Garbha*; let there be a mark of a cow.

The *maṇḍala* (altar) of *Svākṣi*, *Svādhya* and other things has eight in the beginning and sixty-four in the end.

11. *Svākṣi* (one's own eye) goes up to Indra and Sun by means of fortyone *vartanas* (revolutions) in the whole sky,

1. Adoration.

The auspicious pit should be made in the south-east in the form of a crescent moon.

12. The groups of *Śastra hṛdaya* are devoted to the *Śastra* of five. Astra should be placed in the border of the quarters and Śadāśiva in the pericarp.

13. I shall now mention *Dikṣā* (preparation for sacred rite) and the ground, etc. settled in the five *tattvas*. *Nivṛtti* (returning) is the ground, then *Pratiṣṭhā* (establishing); learning is five; *Śānti* is the ray.

14. In the *homa*[1] *Śānti* goes beyond. After that the immutable is quiescent. For each there shall be a hundred *homa*. Thus *homa* shall be performed five times.

15-16. After giving the *Pūrṇāhuti* (the final ghee-offering) he should meditate upon Śiva for his favour.

In order to purify the atonement each *Āhuti* should be gradually made with the *Astrabīja*. Thus Dīkṣā is concluded.

Except the actual performance of the sacrifice all other rituals should be kept confidential.

17. If the devotee thus becomes purified ritualistically he attains to Śivahood, indeed.

CHAPTER TWENTYTHREE

Worship of Śiva

Sūta said :

1-2. I shall now explain the worship of Śiva conducive to the achievement of virtue and love etc. With the following three mantras, beginning with *Om* and ending with *Svāhā*, *Ācamana* shall be performed.

Oṁ Hām Ātmatattvāya[2] Svāhā
Oṁ Hiṁ Vidyātattvāya[3] Svāhā
Oṁ Hūṁ Śivatattvāya[4] Svāhā

The salutation to the ears should be made with the heart.

1. *v. l. vyoma.*
2. To soul-element.
3. To knowledge-element.
4. To Śiva-element.

3. For the bath of ashes and *Tarpaṇa*[1] the mantras are *Oṁ Hāṁ Yāṁ Svāhā*. For all *devas*, all sages the adoration is with the *Mantra* ending with *Namaḥ* and *Vauṣaṭ*[2].

4. For all the *Pitṛs* and *Pitāmahas* (fathers and grandfathers) the *mantra* should end with *Svadhā*.

Oṁ Hām to the great-grand-fathers and maternal grand fathers as well.

5. *Hāṁ Namaḥ* to all mothers. Then *Prāṇāyāma* should be performed. *Ācamana* and *Mārjana*[3] should be made. *Gāyatri*[4] be recited next.

6. *Oṁ Hāṁ Tan Maheśāya Vidmahe / Vāgviśuddhāya Dhīmahi/Tanno Rudraḥ Pracodayāt//*[5]

7. After *Sūryopasthāpana* (special recital of prayers with mystic gesticulations with the hand) he should begin worship with solar *mantras*.

Oṁ Hāṁ Hīṁ Hūṁ Haiṁ Hauṁ Haḥ. Salutation to Śiva-Sūrya. *Oṁ Ham* obeisance to *Khakolka*, the form of Sun.

1. Presenting libations of water to the manes.

2. An exclamation uttered while offering oblations to the deities.

3. Cleansing, sprinkling water by means of hand or a blade of *kuśa* grass.

4. Gāyatrī generally means a verse composed in the Vedic metre called Gāyatrī which is of 24 syllables, usually a triplet of eight syllables each.

But in the Indian culture it has assumed a specific meaning and the following Ṛgvedic Verse is popularly known as Gāyatrī (because it is also composed in the Gāyatrī metre).

Tat savitur vareṇyaṁ
bhargo devasya dhīmahi/
dhiyo yo naḥ pracodayāt//
(ṚV 3.62.10)

Every caste Hindu is expected to repeat this verse during morning and evening devotions (sandhyā). As it is addressed to Savitṛ, the sun, it is also called Sāvitrī.

Gāyatrī is also personified as a goddess and is said to be the wife of Brahmā and the mother of the four Vedas and the first three castes.

It is held very sacred and attributed with many mystical and philosophical potentialities. The Tāntrikas have a number of mystical verses, each one attributed to a particular deity, and these are also known by the name of Gāyatrī. (Also *Liṅga* (*AITM*), p. 796, *SED*, p. 352;*CDHM*, pp. 111-2).

Nonetheless the verse given here beginning with *Oṁ hām* is quite different to that one generally accepted as Gāyatrī and quoted above.

5. This verse, also composed in Gāyatrī metre, is addressed to Śiva and seems to be composed on the model of the ṚV 3.62.10.

8. *Oṁ Hṛām Hrim Saḥ* obeisance to the sun. *Daṇḍin* and *Piṅgala* and other *Bhūtas* should be systematically remembered. After propitiating the pure Īśāna in fire great pleasure shall be obtained.

9-10. He should worship *Padmā* with *Rām*; *Diptā* with *Rīm*; *Sūkṣmā* with *Rūm*; *Jayā* with *Rem*; *Bhadrā* with *Raim*, *Vibhūti* with *Rom*; *Vimalā* and *Amoghikā* with *Raim*; *Vidyutā* with *Ram* in the eastern and other quarters; *Rom* in the middle, *Sarvatomukhī* with Ram; the sun's seat and the form of sun with *Hrām* and *Hrūm*; and the sun with *Saḥ*.

11. *Om* and *Ām* for the sun in the heart; head and tuft of hair and *Bhūḥ*, *Bhuvaḥ*, *Svaḥ*, *Om*. *Jvālinī* should be worshipped with *Hrām*. Coat of mail and weapon should be assigned duly.

12. The queen properly initiated should be worshipped with *Sūrya-Hṛdaya Mantra*. The planet *Soma* (Moon) should be worshipped with *Som*; *Maṅgala* (Mars) with *Mam*; *Budha* (Mercury) with Bam; Bṛhaspati (Jupiter) with *Bṛ*; *Bhārgava* (*Śukra-venus*) with *Bham*; the planet *Śanaiścara* (Saturn) with *Śam*.

13. *Rāhu* with *Ram*; *Ketu* with *Kam* and the fierce lustre should be worshipped with *Om*. After worshipping the sun and performing *Ācamana* the *Aṅganyāsa* should be made beginning with the little finger.

14. *Hāṁ Him* for the head; *Hūm* for the tuft, *Haim* for the coat of mail and *Haum* for the eyes. *Haḥ* for the weapon. Having fixed *Śakti*, *Nyāsa* should be made for the purification of elements.

15. Then making a vessel for *Arghya* it shall be sprinkled with holy water.

16. The *Ātman* should be worshipped as seated on the lotus. With *Hauṁ Śivāya* the exterior should be worshipped. *Nandin*[1] and *Mahākāla*[2] at the gate; Gaṅgā, Yamunā, Sarasvatī,[3].

1. The bull of Śiva. His image of white colour is always put before the idol of Śiva in every temple of Śiva. He is supposed to be the guardian of all four-footed animals. He is one of Śiva's *gaṇas* and accompanies him during his *tāṇḍava* dance.

2. The chief of Śiva's *gaṇas* (personal attendants).

3. *v.l. gauḥ.*

17. *Śrivatsa*, *Vāstvadhipati* (presiding deity of the plot); Brahmā, *Gaṇa*, preceptor, *Śakti* and *Ananta*—all these in the middle, *Dharma*[1] and others in the east;

18. *Adharma*[2] in the south-east; *Vāmā* and *Jyeṣṭhā* in the middle and in the pericarp of the lotus; *Raudrī*, *Kālī*, Śiva and Sītā in the east.

19-20. *Oṁ Haum* obeisance to *Kalavikariṇī*. The following should be worshipped in the middle of the seat in front of Śiva. *Balavikāriṇī*, *Balapramathinī* *Sarvabhūtānāṁ damanī* & Manonmanī, the great form of Śiva's seat and in its middle Śiva.

21-23. All these rites should be performed duly—*Āvāhana*, *Sthāpana*, *Sannidhāna*,[3] *Nirodhana*,[4] *Sakalīkaraṇa*, *Mudrādarśana*, *Arghya*, *Pādya*, *Ācamana*, *Abhyaṅga*,[5] *Udvarta*,[6] *Snāna*, *Nirmañcana*.[7] Next he should offer garments, unguents, flowers, incense, lamp, food offerings, *Ācamana*, fragrant spices, betel leaves, water for washing hands, umbrella, chowries and sacred thread and perform *Paramīkaraṇa*.

24. After imagining the deity in its solitary form recital of prayers and the dedication thereof should be performed. This is called *Nāmāṅga* worship—i.e. prayer, kneeling etc. by means of the heart.

25. In the south-east, north-east, north-west and south-west, the worship mentioned for the east should be made in the middle. He should worship Indra and others and *Nirmālya* should be applied to *Caṇḍa*.

26-29. The prayer shall be:—O Lord Śiva, thou art the protector of the secret of secrets. Please accept this chanting of prayer performed by us. Let there be successful achievement for me by thy grace in thy presence. Whatever sin I may

1. A personification of Religion or Righteousness or virtue. *Dharma* is also a name of *Yama*, the god of death. (*SSED*, p. 268).

2. A personification of Vice. It is very peculiar that *adharma* is also to be worshipped with *dharma*.

3. Receiving or putting down together.

4. Endorsing, covering up.

5. Smearing with oily substances.

6. Smearing with perfumes.

7. *v.l. nirmohana*.

have committed do thou destroy that since I am in Śiva's region. Thou art the giver of Renown. Śiva is the giver, Śiva is the enjoyer, Śiva is this entire world, Śiva is victorious everywhere. I am he who is Śiva. Whatever I have done, whatever I will do let everything be sacred unto thee. O Śiva thou art the saviour, the leader of the universe. I do not have any other lord."

30-35. I shall explain another method of worship of Śiva. Beginning from the east these should be placed in the gates:—*Gaṇa*, *Sarasvatī*, *Nandī*, *Mahākāla*, *Gaṅgā*, *Yamunā*, & *Vāstvadhipa*. Indra and others should be worshipped. The *Tattvas* (principles) should be worshipped viz:—Earth, Water, Fire, Wind, Ether, smell, taste, form, Sound, touch, speech, hands, feet, anus, penis, ears, skin, eyes, tongue, nose, mind, intellect, ego, *Prakṛti*,[1] *Puruṣa*, *Rāga*,[2] *Dveṣa*,[3] *Vidyā*, *Kāla*, *Akāla*,[4] *Niyati*,[5] *Māyā*,[6] pure learning, Īśvara, Sadāśiva, Śakti and Śiva. Having known all these he should become wise and liberated. He who is Śiva is Hari and Brahmā and I am Brahman due to liberation.

36-37. I shall explain the purification of elements, through which a man being purified becomes Śiva. The mantra is in the lotus of the heart. The return is immediate. These two are the *Nāḍis*, (nerves) *Iḍā*[7] and *Piṅgalā*.[8] The two

1. Nature.
2. Passion.
3. Jealousy.
4. Obviously opposite of *Kāla* (time).
5. Destiny.
6. Illusion, Deception. Illusion is personified as a female form of celestial origin, created for the purpose of beguiling some individual. In Vedānta philosophy, it means illusion by virtue of which one considers the unreal universe as really existent and as distinct from the supreme spirit. It is regarded as a power of God. *Māyā* is considered by some to be synonymous with *Ajñāna* or *Avidyā* which is the cause of false knowledge. In *sāṅkhya* philosophy it means the *Pradhāna* or *Prakṛti*. (Vide *CDHM*, p. 207; *CSL*, p. 437).
7. According to the *Tantras*, it is the principal nerve in the human nervous system, being on the left side of the body. (*CSL*, p. 446).
8. The principal nerve on the right side of the body. (*CSL*, p. 446).

Prāṇa and *Apāna* in the square *Maṇḍala* (diagram) shall be the bodies of Indra and Brahmā.

38-40. The *maṇḍala* is marked by *Vajra*[1] and illuminated. The arrows are of the quality of single stroke. The quiver in the place of heart is spacious and contains hundred chambers. *Oṁ Hrīm Pratiṣṭhāyai Huṁ Haḥ Phaṭ*; *Oṁ Hrām Vidyāyai Hrām Haḥ Phaṭ*. The Bhūmi Tantra is eightyfour crores in height. In its centre he should contemplate the *Bhavavṛkṣa* (the tree of worldly existence) and the soul.

The Earth should then be thought of as with a face downwards. Then everything should be made pure.

41. *Vāmā Devī* is the *Pratiṣṭhā* (base). *Suṣumṇā*,[2] is *dhārikā* (the supporting prop). The deities are *Samāna, Udāna* and *Varuṇa*. Viṣṇu is the cause.

42. *Udghātas* (beginnings) are four times. The *dhyāna* is *Śveta* (white). The lotus of the neck should be made thus. The *maṇḍala* (diagram) shall be called *Ardhacandra* (Crescent moon).

43. Marked by a lotus it shall extend to two hundred crores. The *Ātman* ninetyfour (times) in height shall be thought of as with face downwards.

44. There are places and lotuses. The *Aghora* (non-terrific)shall be accompanied by learning.

Nāga (Serpent) and the deity of fire are to be contemplated as the tongue of an elephant with the lips in the centre.

45. Rudra is the cause. The *Udghāta* is for three times. Its colour is that of blood. It is in the form of a blaze, triangular in shape. Its altitude and width are four hundred crores.

46-48. Rudra *Tattva* should be contemplated thus.

It is in the forehead that the *Puruṣa* has his *Śakti*. A grassy place with tortoise and partridge, O scholars. Vāyu is the deity. Īśvara is the cause.

The *Vāyu Tattva* should be contempiated as extending to fourteen crores. *Udghāta* is for two times. The *maṇḍala* is

1. *v.l.vakra.*

2. The most important nerve in the human nervous system, being in the middle of the body. (*CSL*, p. 461.)

haxagonal in shape called *Vṛṣa*. It is marked by a dot. The width and the altitude are eight crores.

49. In a lotus of twelve ends the *Īśvaras* are beyond. *Śānti* (peace) *Kuhū*, *Śaṅkhinī*, *Devadatta* and *Dhanañjaya* are the *Nāḍis*.

50. The cause is *Śikheśāna* and *Sadāśiva*. The *Udghāta* is for once only. It should be remembered as resembling bright glass.

51. The width is sixteen crores. The altitude is twenty five crores. Thus the abode should be contemplated as circular in shape. *Bhūta Śuddhi* has been explained thus.

52. *Gaṇaguru*, *Bījaguru*, *Śakti*, *Ananta*, *Dharmaka*, *jñāna*, *Vairāgya*, *Aiśvarya*—all these are in the petals beginning with that in the east.

53. Both of them are prone-faced and supine-faced. The pericarp and filaments of the lotus are contemplated. One should always contemplate the *Ātmavidyā* (study of soul) and those others beginning with *Vāmā*.

54. The *Tattva* named *Śiva* should be thought of in the seat of Śiva. The *Mūrti* is *Ho Haum*. Obeisance to *Vidyādeha*.

Lord Śiva is seated in the pose *Padmāsana*[1], white in colour and sixteen years old.

55. He has five faces. Of his ten hands, the five on the right carry *Abhaya*,[2] *Prasāda*, *Śakti*,[3] *Śūla* (trident) and *Khaṭvāṅga*.[4]

56. And the left ones carry Serpent, *Akṣasūtra*[5] drums, blue lotus and the pomegranate.

57. Sadāśiva is three-eyed. He has *Icchā śakti* (will-power), *Jñanaśakti* (knowledge-power), and *Kriyāśakti* (Action-

1. A particular posture in religious meditation.
ūrūmūle vāmapādaṁ punastu dakṣiṇaṁ padam /
Vāmorau sthāpayitvā tu padmāsanamiti smṛtam // (SSED, p. 314).

2. A particular *mudrā* of hand promising protection.

3. A kind of missile, spear, dart, pipe or lance.

4. A club or staff with a skull at the top considered to be a weapon of Śiva and carried by ascetics and yogins. (SSED, p. 174).

5. A rosary.

power). A person who worships Śiva like this and contemplates thus will be devoid of Kāla (become deathless).

58. If one circle of worship is completed in a day and night, the worshipper shall live for three years, if in two days, he shall live for two years.

59. If in three days he shall live for one year. He will never have premature death or death due to cold or heat.

CHAPTER TWENTYFOUR

Worship of Tripurā

Sūta said :

1. I shall now describe the most excellent worship of *Gaṇas*. Inferior deities attending on Śiva under the supervision of Gaṇeśa[1] which will yield everything, even heavenly bliss. The seats of the *Gaṇas* should be adored. He should worship the idols of the *gaṇas* and the lord of *gaṇas*

2. Heart and other limbs should be assigned to *Durgā*[2] with *Gāṁ* and other *mantras*. The sandals of the preceptor, the seat of *Durgā* and her idol should be adored with the mantra—*Hrīṁ Durge Rakṣiṇi*.

3. With the heart etc. assignment should be made to the eight *Śaktis*[3]:— *Rudracaṇḍā, Pracaṇḍā, Caṇḍogrā, Caṇḍa-Nāyikā, Caṇḍā, Caṇḍavatī.*

1. He is the son of Śiva and Pārvatī, or of Pārvatī only, for, according to one legend, he sprang from the scurf of her body. He is the god of wisdom and remover of obstacles; hence he is invoked and worshipped at the commencement of every important undertaking. He is usually represented in a sitting posture—short and fat—with a protuberant belly, and four hands riding a mouse; and with the head of an elephant. This head has only one tusk. (*SSED*, p. 178; *CDHM*, pp. 106-8).

2. A name of Pārvatī, the second wife of Śiva (the first was Satī). (Vide note on *Devī CDHM*, pp. 86-8).

3. The active power of a deity is called *Śakti*, regarded as his wife. *Śaktis* may be eight or nine or even fifty.

4. *Caṇḍarūpā*, and *Caṇḍikā* with the mantra—*Durge Durge'tha rakṣiṇi*. The *Mudrās* (mystic signs) *Vajra*, *Khaḍga* etc. shall be assigned to Śiva and others in the south-east.

5. Then *Sadāśiva*, the lord of the big goblins and the lotus-seat also shall be worshipped.

Aiṁ Klīm Svaḥ. Obeisance to *Tripurā Oṁ Hrāṁ Hrīṁ Kṣeṁ Kṣaiṁ Strīṁ Skoṁ roṁ Spheṁ Sphoṁ Śāṁ* ! the lotus-seat and the heart etc. of *Tripurā*.

6. Then in the lotus-*Pīṭha* (altar) should be adored *Brahmāṇī, Maheśvarī, Kaumārī Vaiṣṇavī, Vārāhī, Indradevatā.*

7. *Cāmuṇḍā, and Caṇḍikā.* Then the devotees shall worship the *Bhairavas*[1]. There are eight *Bhairavas*: *Asitāṅga, Rura, Caṇḍa, Krodha, Unmattabhairava.*

8-9. *Kapālin, Bhīṣaṇa* and *Saṁhāra*. The devotee should meditate in his heart, in a *maṇḍala* (diagram) with a lotus inside and triangular in shape, on these :— *Rati*,[2] *Prīti, Kāmadeva*[3], the five arrows, *Yoginī, Vaṭuka, Durgā, Vighnarāja, Guru* and *Kṣetrapa.*

10. By reciting for a hundred thousand times the names of *Śuklā, Varākṣa sūtra pustakābhaya samanvitā* (having the excellent *Akṣasūtra*, book, and offer of fearlessness in her hands) and *havana* (sacrificial offering) *Tripura* gives *Siddhi* (full achievement).

CHAPTER TWENTYFIVE

Adoration of āsana

Sūta said :

1. *Aim Krīṁ Śrīm Spheṁ Kṣaum.* I worship the sandal of *Ananta-Śakti* (Endless power). Obeisance (unto it).

2. *Aiṁ Hrīṁ Śrīṁ Phrauṁ Kṣāum.* I worship the sandal of *Ādhāra-Śakti* (Supporting power). Obeisance (unto it).

1. These are eight inferior forms or manifestations of Śiva, all terrific. (See *CDHM*, p. 45).
2. Wife of Kāmadeva, the deity of love, literally means love.
3. The deity of love. cupid. Literally means passion.

3. *Oṁ hrīṁ Hūṁ* I worship the *Pādukā* (sandal) of *Kālāgni Rudra*. Obeisance (unto it).

4. *Oṁ Hrīṁ Śrīm*. I worship the *Pādukā* of lord *Hāṭakeśvara*. Obeisance (unto it).

Oṁ Hrīṁ Śrīm. I worship the seat called *Ananta* of the earth, its syllables, the universe, islands, oceans and the quarters.

5. *Oṁ Hrīm*. I worship the *Pādukā* of *Śeṣa Bhaṭṭāraka*. Obeisance unto it.

6. *Hrīm Śrīṁ Nivṛtti* and other *Kalās*; the earth, the *Tattvas*, *Ananta* and other worlds, *Oṁkāra* and other syllables. The nine-syllabled word beginning with Hakāra is the *mantra* of *Sadyojāta* (Quick-born) etc. *Hām* the heart and other limbs. This is the *Māheśvara* mantra. It is the ocean of the great nectar. It is identical with *Siddhavidyā* (the accomplished learning).

In all the quarters around the six *aṅgas* (parts) the water of the ocean of Śadāśiva, the side of the full ocean is identical with the base of *Śrī* and *Māna*. *Vidyā*, *Umā*, *Jyeṣṭhā* with the characteristics of complete knowledge and the state of being the doer, *Rūpacakra*[1], *Rudra*, *Śaktyātmaka*, *Karṇikā*, *Nava-Śakti* with the three *maṇḍalas* (zones) of the Tridents of Śiva and others. I worship the *Pādukā* of *Nyastapadmāsana* in the form of a lotus. Obeisance unto it.

CHAPTER TWENTYSIX

Assignment of limbs over the body

Sūta said :

1. After that, *Karanyāsa* and the purification conducive to *Vidyā* are to be performed. After making the mystic sign of *Padma*, *Mantra-Nyāsa* shall be performed.

2. Then the assignments over the body (*Deha Nyāsa*) shall be performed. *Kam* obeisance to *Maṇibandha* (the west),

1. *v.l. Jyeṣṭhā-cakra*.

Aiṁ Hrīṁ Śrīṁ obeisance to *Kāraskara* (a tree with a bitter fruit). *Mahātejorūpam* (the great effulgent form) shall be contemplated upon and with *Huṁ Huṁkāra* hands shall be washed.

3. *Aiṁ Hrīṁ Śrīṁ Hraiṁ Sphaiṁ* obeisance to Bhagavān (the great lord). *Sphaiṁ* obeisance to *Kubjikā* (an unmarried girl of eight years). *Hrūṁ Hrīṁ Krauṁ* Ṅa Ña *Ṇa Na* and *Ma* to *Aghoramukhī. Hāṁ Hiṁ Kili Kili* dependent on *Vidyā* and the *Vyaṅga* (the crippled). *Hrīṁ Hrīṁ Śrīṁ Aiṁ* obeisance to Lord *Urdhvavaktra* (to the North). *Sphauṁ* to the *Kubjikā*. Obeisance to Pūrvavaktra (face turned east). *Hrīṁ Śrīṁ Hrīṁ* Ṅa Ña *Ṇa Na Ma* obeisance to *Dakṣiṇa Vaktra* (face turned to the South). *Oṁ Hrīṁ Śrīṁ Kili Kili* obeisance to *Paścimavaktra* (face turned to the west). *Oṁ Aghoramukhi* obeisance to *Uttaravaktra* (face turned to the north). OṀ obeisance to the lord *Hṛdaya* (Heart) obeisance. *Kṣem Aim* to the *Kubjikā*. *Svāhā* to the head. *Hrīṁ Krīṁ Hrīṁ Prāṁ* Ṅa Ña *Ṇa Na Ma* to the tuft. *Aghoramukhi, Hum* to the *Kavaca* (coat of mail). *Haiṁ Haim īṁ Vauṣaṭ* to the three eyes. *Kili Kili Vivve Phaṭ* to the *Astra* (*weapon*).

4. *Aiṁ Hrīṁ Śrīṁ* obeisance to the *Mahāśūlamaṇḍala* (surrounded by great tridents) having the form of an unsplit zone. *Aiṁ Hrīṁ Śrīṁ* obeisance to the *Vāyumaṇḍala* (the zone of wind). *Aiṁ Hrīṁ Śrīm* obeisance to *Somamaṇḍala* (the zone of the moon). *Aiṁ Hrīṁ Śrīṁ* obeisance to *Mahākula Bodhāvali Maṇḍala* (surrounded by the cluster of conceptions of the great family). *Aiṁ Hrīṁ Śrīm* obeisance to *Kaulamaṇḍala. Aiṁ Hrīṁ Śrīm* obeisance to *Gurumaṇḍala* (the zone of Jupiter). *Aiṁ Hrīṁ Śrīm* obeisance to *Sāmamaṇḍala. Aiṁ Hrīṁ Śrīṁ* obeisance to *Samagramaṇḍala, Siddhamaṇḍala, Yogimaṇḍala, Pīṭhamaṇḍala, Apapīṭha Maṇḍala, Kṣetramaṇḍala, Apakṣetramaṇḍala* and *Santāna-maṇḍala*. Thus all the twelve *maṇḍalas* are to be worshipped in order.

CHAPTER TWENTYSEVEN

Mantra to cure snake-bite

Sūta said :

1. O ! the skeletal form of *Kāla* and *Vikāla* ! O *Carviṇi !* (the chewing); *Bhūtahāriṇi* (destroying creatures); *Phaṇiviṣiṇi* (Venom of serpents); *Virathanārāyaṇi* (Nārāyaṇi devoid of a chariot) : Ume; burn, burn in the hand *Caṇḍe* (O ! fierce), *Raudri*, *Māheśvari*, *Mahāmukhi* (large-faced), *Jvālāmukhi* (flame-mouthed), *Śaṅkukarṇi* (dart-eared), *Śukamuṇḍe* (parrot-headed), destroy the enemy *Sarvanāśini* ! (destroyer of all). *Khakha* thou seest the blood in every limb. O Goddess *Manasā*, enchant, enchant. Thou born of the heart of Rudra ! Thou art stationed in the heart of Rudra. Thou hast the form of Rudra O ! *Devi* Protect me, Protect me. *Hūṁ Mām Phapha Ṭhaṭha*. Thou hast the girdle of *Skanda*. Thou removest the poison of planets and enemies.

Oṁ Śāle Māle, remove, remove. O Viśoka (free from sorrow).

Hāṁ Hāṁ Śavari
Hūṁ Śavari Prakoṇaviśare Sarve ! *Viñca Meghamile* !

These mantras (recited properly) are conducive to the removal of poison of all serpents.

CHAPTER TWENTYEIGHT

Worship of Gopāla

Sūta said :

1-3. I shall now describe the worship of Gopāla (Lord Kṛṣṇa) that yields worldly enjoyment and salvation. In the door-ways *Dhātṛ*[1], *Vidhātṛ*[2], *Gaṅgā*, *Yamunā*, *Saṅkhanidhi*, *Padma-*

1. Brahmā.
2. Dispenser of Destiny.

nidhi, *Sāraṅga*,[1] *Śarabha*[2] and *Śrī* are to be worshipped. In the east *Bhadra* and *Subhadra* are worshipped, in the South *Caṇḍa* and *Pracaṇḍaka* are worshipped, in the west *Bala* and *Prabala* and in the north *Jaya*[3] and *Vijaya* are to be worshipped. In the four main doors, *Śrī*, *Gaṇa*, *Durgā* and *Sarasvatī*[4] are to be worshipped.

4. In the corners of south-east of the field, Nārada, Siddha, Guru and Nalakūbara[5], are to be worshipped. In the corner one should worship *Bhāgavata*.[6]

5. In the east, the devotee should worship Viṣṇu, Viṣṇu's *Tapas* (penance) and Viṣṇu's *Śakti* (power). Then in the middle he shall worship the family of Viṣṇu, *Śakti* and *Kūrma* (the tortoise).

6. He shall worship *Ananta*, *Earth*, *Virtue*, *Knowledge* and *Vairāgya* (non-attachment) in the South-east. Prosperity shall be worshipped in the north-west and in the north the *Prakāśātman* (*brilliant*-souled).

7. Worship shall be offered to *Sattva* of the nature of *Prakṛti*; to *Rajas* of the nature of delusion and to *Tamas* the lotus of *Ahaṅkāra Tattva* (the principle of ego).[7]

8. The principle of learning, the great principle. The zones of Sun, Moon and fire—all these shall be worshipped. The seat of *Vimalā* and others shall be worshipped in the east with *Hrīṁ Śrīṁ*.

9-10. To the lover of cowherd lasses the mantra ending with *Svāhā* is mentioned. In the east of the corners of the heart the weapons—*Ācakra*, *Sucakra*, *Vicakra*, *Trailokya-*

1. Chātaka, peacock, deer or elephant.
2. A fabulous animal or a young elephant.
3. Jaya and Vijaya are the well-known attendants of Viṣṇu.
4. The goddess of speech. The wife of Brahmā. An ancient river (which is now lost). In the Ṛgveda, she is lauded both as a river and as a deity. But she became the goddess of learning only in the post- Ṛgvedic literature. (Also refer *CDHM*, pp. 284, *ŚP* (*AITM*), p. 350 fn. 268; *Liṅga* (*AITM*), p. 804).
5. Name of a son of Kubera.
6. Bhāgavata-Purāṇa or a follower of Viṣṇu.
7. In the Veṅkaṭeśvara edition, the second half of this verse is *tamase kandapadmāya yajet kaṁ kākatattvakam*.

rakṣaṇa (protecting the three worlds) *Asurāricakra*, *Sudarśana*,[1] *Astra* and *Śakti* shall be worshipped.

11. *Rukmiṇi*[2] *Satyabhāmā*,[3] *Sunandā*[4] *Nāgnajiti*[5] *Lakṣmaṇā*[6] *Mitravṛndā*[7] *Jāmbavati*[8] and *Suśīlā*[9] (shall be first worshipped).

12. Then *Śaṅkha*,[10] *Cakra*[11], *Gadā*[12], *Padma*[13], *Musala*[14] and *Śārṅga*[15] shall be worshipped.

Then the sword, the noose, the goad shall be worshipped in the east. *Śrīvatsa Kaustubha*, coronet, garland of wild flowers, Indra and others, the principal leaders of the banner shall be worshipped. *Kumuda*[16] and others, *Viṣvaksena*,[17] Kṛṣṇa along with Śrī shall be worshipped.

By the recital of the name, contemplation and worship the devotee shall obtain all desires.

1. It is the well-known discus of Lord Kṛṣṇa. According to legends Agni gave it to him.
2. Daughter of Bhīṣmaka, king of Vidarbha. The chief wife of Kṛṣṇa.
3. Another wife of Kṛṣṇa. Daughter of Satrājit.
4. A wife of Kṛṣṇa.
5. A wife of Kṛṣṇa.
6. A wife of Kṛṣṇa.
7. A wife of Kṛṣṇa.
8. A wife of Kṛṣṇa. Daughter of Jāmbavat.
9. A wife of Kṛṣṇa.
10. Conch.
11. Discus.
12. Club.
13. Lotus. Kṛṣṇa holds a conch, a discus, a club and a lotus in each of his four hands.
14. Pestle. It is held by Balarāma, as his weapon.
15. The bow is generally associated with Viṣṇu.
16. An obvious reference to Kaumodakī, the mace of Viṣṇu.
17. Viṣṇu.

CHAPTER TWENTYNINE

Trailokya-mohinī

Hari said :

1. I shall now describe the worship of *Trailokya Mohini*[1] (the enchantress of the three worlds) a chief form of *Puruṣottama* (Lord Viṣṇu) and also the *mantras* for the worship of *Śrī Rādhā*[2] that yields virtue, desire etc.

2. *Oṁ Hrīṁ Śrīṁ Klīṁ Hūm Om* obeisance. O ! foremost among men ! O thou the unrivalled in features ! the abode of goddess of Fortune ! the exciter of the entire universe ! the breaker of the hearts of all woman ! O thou who heightenst the elation of the three worlds ! Distress the minds of the beautiful women among the gods and demons; dry, dry (them) ; beat, beat (them) ; win, win (them) ; melt, melt (them); attract attract (them). O thou the fine-featured ! O thou the giver of fine features that grant good fortune. O thou the giver of all desires !

Kill kill so-and-so with the discus, club and sword. Pierce, pierce with all the arrows; pound and beat with the goad and noose. Why dost thou tarry ? Save, save, till my desired object is achieved. *Hrūṁ Phaṭ* obeisance.

3. *Śrīm* obeisance to *Śrīdhara* the enchanter of the three worlds. *Klīṁ* obeisance to Puruṣottama the enchanter of three worlds !

4. *Hūm* obeisance to Viṣṇu the enchanter of the three worlds.

Oṁ Śrīṁ Hrīṁ Klīm obeisance to the enchanter of the three worlds, Viṣṇu.

5. All the *mantras* of the enchanter of the three worlds are conducive to the achievement of all objects. All can be meditated upon collectively, separately analytically or succinctly.

1. An obvious reference to the form of a most beautiful woman assumed by Viṣṇu, at the time of distributing of nectar, to cheat the demons.

2. *v.l. Śrīdhara.*

6-7. After the worship of the seat, idol, weapon, the six ancillary objects of the sacrifice viz ;—*Cakra*, *Gadā*, *Sword*, *Pestle*, *Conch* and the *Śārṅga*, arrow, noose, goad and *Viṣvaksena* (Viṣṇu) accompanied by Lakṣmī and Garuḍa, in detail or otherwise, the devotee shall obtain everything.

CHAPTER THIRTY

Worship of Śrīdhara

Sūta said :

1. I shall now describe the auspicious worship of Śrīdhara The *Parivāra* (attendants, followers) is the same (as in *Gopāla Pūjā*). Scholars shall note it.

2. *Oṁ Śrāṁ* obeisance to the heart. *Oṁ Śrīṁ Svāhā* to the head. *Oṁ Śruṁ Vaṣaṭ* to the tuft. *Oṁ Śraiṁ Huṁ* to the *Kavaca* (coat of mail). *Oṁ Śrauṁ Vauṣaṭ* to the three eyes. *Oṁ Śraḥ Phaṭ* to the *Astra* (weapon).

3. Having meditated upon the *Ātman* known as Śrīdhara, bearing conch, discus, and the club, the *Mudrās* (mystical signs) of conch, discus, and the club shall be shown.

4. Then the devotee shall worship the deity in the *Svastika*[1] *maṇḍala* (mystical diagram). With these *mantras*, O Śaṅkara, the great god, the devotee shall worship the seat of Śārṅgin (Viṣṇu) the god of Gods. Please hear those *mantras*.

5. *Om* O ye deities of the seat of Śrīdhara, come. *Om* obeisance to the seat of *Acyuta* attended by all followers.

6. *Om* obeisance to *Dhātṛ*. *Om* obeisance to *Vidhātṛ*. *Om* obeisance to *Gaṅgā*. *Om* obeisance to *Yamunā*. *Om* obeisance to *Ādhāra-Śakti*. *Om* obeisance to *Kūrma* (the tortoise). *Om* obeisance to *Ananta* (the endless). *Om* obeisance to *Pṛthivī* (Earth). *Om* obeisance to *Dharma* (virtue). *Om* obeisance to *Jñāna* (knowledge). *Om* obeisance to *Vairāgya* (non-attachment). *Om*

1. It is in fact a mystical mark put on persons or things, to bless them with good luck.

obeisance to *Aiśvarya* (prosperity). *Om* obeisance to *Adharma* (evil). *Om* obeisance to *Ajñāna* (ignorance). *Om* obeisance to special attachment to world. *Om* obeisance to *Anaiśvarya* (impoverished state). *Om* obeisance to *Skanda*. *Om* obeisance to *Nīla*. *Om* obeisance to *Padma* (lotus). *Om* obeisance to *Vimalā* (the untarnished). *Om* obeisance to *Utkarṣiṇī* (the prosperous). *Om* obeisance to *Jñāna* (the power to know). *Om* obeisance to *Kriyā* (the action). *Om* obeisance to *Yoga* (the power of fixing the mind). *Om* obeisance to *Putrī*. *Om* obeisance to *Pṛthvī* (the humble). *Om* obeisance to *Satyā* (the truthful). *Om* obeisance to *Īśānā* (the lordly). *Om* obeisance to *Anugrahā* (the blessed).

7. Having worshipped all, O Rudra, Hari shall be invoked. The wise devotee then shall invoke and worship Hari with these *mantras* destroying all sins.

8. *Oṁ Hrīm* obeisance to Śrīdhara, the enchanter of the three worlds, Viṣṇu (Himself).

9. *Om* obeisance to *Śrī*. *Oṁ Śrām* obeisance to the heart. *Oṁ Śrīm* obeisance to the head. *Oṁ Śrūm* obeisance to the tuft. *Oṁ Śraim* obeisance to the *Kavaca* (coat of mail). *Oṁ Śraum* obeisance to the three eyes. *Oṁ Śraḥ* obeisance to the *Astra* (weapon). *Om* obeisance to the couch. *Om* obeisance to the lotus. *Om* obeisance to the discus. *Om* obeisance to the club. *Om* obeisance to *Śrīvatsa*. *Om* obeisance to the *Kaustubha*. *Om* obeisance to the *Vanamālā* (the garland of wild flowers). *Om* obeisance to the yellow-robed. *Om* obeisance to *Brahman*. *Om* obeisance to *Nārada*. *Om* obeisance to the preceptor. *Om* obeisance to *Indra*. *Om* obeisance to the Fire-god. *Om* obeisance to *Yama*. *Om* obeisance to *Nirṛti*. *Om* obeisance to *Varuṇa*. *Om* obeisance to *Vāyu* (wind god). *Om* obeisance to *Soma* (Moon). *Om* obeisance to *Īśāna*. *Om* obeisance to *Ananta*. *Om* obeisance to *Brahman*. *Om* obeisance to *Sattva*. *Om* obeisance to *Rajas*. *Om* obeisance to *Tamas*. *Om* obeisance to *Viṣvaksena*.

10-11. With the following *mantras* shall be offered the *Abhiṣeka* (bathing of the idol), garments, sacred thread, sandal paste, flower, incense, lamp, food oblation, and circular peregination. After completing the same, let him recite the *mantra* one hundred and eight times. Then dedicate this to the deity.

12-13. Then for a *muhūrta* (24 minutes) he should meditate in his heart the deity seated in the heart, as bright as the pure crystal, brilliant like a crore of Suns, pleasant in face, gentle, wearing the two earrings shaped like the *Makara*[1] and coronets, beautiful of limbs, bedecked by a garland of wild flowers, identical with the Supreme Soul.

14. The scholarly devotee shall thus worship and contemplate upon Śrīdhara. Let him eulogise the great lord with this prayer hymn.

15. Obeisance to Lord Śrīnivāsa[2], obeisance to Śrīpati[3] obeisance to Śrīdhara with the *Śārṅga* (the bow), obeisance to the donor of prosperity.

16. Obeisance to Śrīvallabha[4] (Lover of Śrī), obeisance to the calm deity endowed with splendour. Obeisance to the deity whose abode is in Śrīparvata[5] mountain. Obeisance to the giver of renown.

17. Obeisance to the lord of all benefits; obeisance to the refuge (of all); obeisance to the renown-featured; obeisance to Śrīkara[6].

18. Obeisance to *Śaraṇya* (worthy of Refuge). Obeisance to *Vareṇya* (the foremost); obeisance again and again unto him. After reciting the hymn let him prostrate and mystically discharge the deity (*Visarjana*).

19. Rudra, I have thus explained the worship of *Viṣṇu*, the great soul. He who does this with great devotion attains the supreme region.

20. He who reads this chapter which sheds light on the worship of Viṣṇu shakes off all sins and attains Viṣṇu's supreme region.

1. A crocodile or a shark.
2. A name of Viṣṇu.
3. A name of Viṣṇu.
4. A name of Viṣṇu.
5. A hill situated in Karnul district to the south of the river Kṛṣṇā. At present there are numerous *Śiva-liṅgas* here, including the famous Mallikārjuna, one of the nine *Jyotirliṅgas*. It is also known as *Śrīśaila* (*CSL*, p. 500; *ŚP* (*AITM*) p. 2117; *Liṅga* (*AITM*) p. 806).
6. A name of Viṣṇu.

CHAPTER THIRTYONE

Worship of Viṣṇu

Rudra Said:

1. O ! Lord of the Universe ! Please explain further the worship of the deity whereby I shall cross the ocean of worldly existence which is very difficult to cross.

Hari said:

2. O Vṛṣabhadhvaja (Śiva) ! I shall explain to you the adoration of Lord Viṣṇu. O Fortunate Śiva ! Hear it *which* is auspicious and which yields worldly pleasure and salvation.

3-4. The devotee shall take bath, perform Sandhyā (prayers) and enter the room for sacrifice. After washing the hands and feet and performing *Ācamana* particularly he shall assign the *Mūlamantra* (the root *mantra*) to his hand. O Rudra ! I shall tell you the *Mūla Mantra.*

5-6. *Oṁ Śrīṁ Hrīm* obeisance to Śrīdhara, Viṣṇu (Himself). This *mantra* is of Viṣṇu expressing him as the lord of deities, dispelling all sickness, all defects in planets, all sins and giving enjoyment and salvation.

7. O skilful Śiva, the devotee shall then perform the *Aṅganyāsa* with these *mantras. Oṁ Hām* obeisance to the heart; *Oṁ Hīm Svāhā* to the head; *Oṁ Hūm Vaṣaṭ* to the tuft; *Oṁ Haiṁ Hum* to the *Kavaca, Oṁ Hauṁ Vauṣat* to the eyes; *Oṁ Haḥ Phaṭ* to the *Astra.*

8. Powerful that I am I have explained the *mantra* to you. The devotee having conquered his *soul* shall show the *Mudrā* of the *Ātman* after performing the *Nyāsa.*

9. Then the devotee shall meditate on the supreme lord Viṣṇu residing in the hollow of the heart, holding conch and discus and white as the *Kunda*[1] flower and the moon.

10. After performing the purificatory rite the devotee shall meditate 'I am Viṣṇu'—Viṣṇu with Śrīvatsa and Kaustubha, bedecked with garlands of wild flowers, wearing coronet and diamond necklace and the great Lord.

1. Jasminum multiflorum (*GVDB*, p. 105).

11. With the *Bijas* (mystic seeds) *Yaṁ Kṣaṁ* Ram and the names he shall (in imagination) prepare an egg and harden it and then pierce it with *Praṇava* itself.

12-14. Then, O Vṛṣabhadhvaja, thinking of the form as mentioned before, the devotee shall perform the *Ātmapūjā* with auspicious fragrant flowers. All the deities of the seat shall be invoked with these *mantras*. O Śaṅkara ! Hear those mantras. O ye deities of the seat of Viṣṇu ! Come.

15. *Oṁ* obeisance to Acyuta with all attendents; *Oṁ* obeisance to *Dhātṛ*; *Oṁ* obeisance to *Vidhātṛ*; *Oṁ* obeisance to *Gaṅgā*; *Oṁ* obeisance to *Yamunā*. *Oṁ* obeisance to the treasure *Śaṅkha*; *Oṁ* obeisance to the treasure *Padma*; *Oṁ* obeisance to *Caṇḍa*; *Oṁ* obeisance to *Pracaṇḍa*; *Oṁ* obeisance to the splendour of gate; *Oṁ* obeisance to the *Ādhāra Śakti*; *Oṁ* obeisance to *Kūrma*; *Oṁ* obeisance to *Ananta*; *Om* obeisance to *Śrī*; *Oṁ* obeisance to *Dharma*; *Oṁ* obeisance to *Jñāna*; *Oṁ* obeisance to *Vairāgya* (non-attachment); *Oṁ* obeisance to *Aiśvarya* (*prosperity*);*Oṁ* obeisance to *Adharma* (evil); *Oṁ* obeisance to *Ajñāna* (ignorance); *Oṁ* obeisance to *Avairāgya* (attachment); *Oṁ* obeisance to *Anaiśvarya* (impoverished state); *Oṁ Sam* obeisance to *Sattva*; *Oṁ Ram* obeisance to *Rajas*; *Oṁ Tam* obeisance to *Tamas*; *Oṁ Kam* obeisance to *Skanda*; *Oṁ Nam* obeisance to *Nīla*; *Oṁ Lam* obeisance to *Padma*; *Oṁ Am* obeisance to the solar zone; *Oṁ Sam* obeisance to the lunar zone; *Oṁ Vam* obeisance to the fiery zone; *Oṁ* obeisance to *Vimalā*; *Oṁ* obeisance to *Vikarṣiṇī*. *Oṁ* obeisance to the Power of knowledge; *Oṁ* obeisance to *Kriyā* (Action); *Oṁ* obeisance to *Rogā* (deity of diseases); *Oṁ* obeisance to *Prahvī* (the humble); *Oṁ* obeisance to *Satī*; *Oṁ* obeisance to *Īśānā*; *Oṁ* obeisance to *Anugrahā* (the blessed one).

16-17. With these *mantras* and fragrant flowers, the devotee shall worship these deities. After that he shall invoke into the *Maṇḍala* and worship Viṣṇu the great lord, the creator and destroyer, Hari the remover of all sins.

18. Just as in the *Ātman*, so in the lord too, the *Nyāsa* shall be performed from the beginning and afterwards show of *Mudrā* and then *Arghya* etc. shall be given.

19-20. Then in order shall be performed bathing, offering of garment, *Ācamana*, fragrant flowers, incense, light, food offering and circular peregrination. The *Japas* shall be recited and dedicated to the deity. With their own respective *mantras* the worship of the *Aṅgas* (parts) shall be performed by the *Sādhaka* (devotee).

21. O Vṛṣadhvaja know this to be with the root-*mantra* alone. Please listen, O Three-eyed Śiva, to the *mantras* being recited by me.

22. *Oṁ Hāṁ* obeisance to the heart. *Oṁ Hīm* obeisance to the head. *Oṁ Hūm* obeisance to the tuft. *Oṁ Haim* obeisance to the *Kavaca*; *Oṁ Haum* obeisance to the three eyes: *Oṁ Haḥ* obeisance to the *Astra*; *Oṁ* obeisance to *Śrī*; *Oṁ* obeisance to the *Śaṅkha*; *Oṁ* obeisance to *Padma*, *Oṁ* obeisance to *Cakra*; *Oṁ* obeisance to *Gadā*; *Oṁ* obeisance to *Śrīvatsa*. *Oṁ* obeisance to *Kaustubha*; *Oṁ* obeisance to *Vanamālā* (garland of wild flowers); *Oṁ* obeisance to *Pītāmbara* (the yellow-robed); *Oṁ* obeisance to *Khaḍga* (sword). *Oṁ* obeisance to *Musala* (Pestle); *Oṁ* obeisance to the noose; *Oṁ* obeisance to the goad. *Oṁ* obeisance to *Śārṅga* (the bow) *Oṁ* obeisance to *Śara* (arrow); *Oṁ* obeisance to *Brahman*; *Oṁ* obeisance to *Nārada*; *Oṁ* obeisance to all *Siddhas* (*yogins*). *Oṁ* obeisance to all *Bhāgavatas* (devotees); *Oṁ* obeisance to all preceptors: *Oṁ* obeisance to all great preceptors; *Oṁ* obeisance to Indra, the lord of gods seated in his vehicle and attended by followers; *Oṁ* obeisance to *Agni* (Fire-god) lord of lustres seated in his vehicle and attended by his followers; *Oṁ* obeisance to Yama, the lord of the dead, seated in his vehicle and attended by his followers. *Oṁ* obeisance to *Nirṛti* lord of demons seated in his vehicle and attended by followers; *Oṁ* obeisance to *Varuṇa* lord of waters seated in his vehicle, attended by his followers; *Oṁ* obeisance to *Vāyu* lord of vital airs seated in his vehicle and attended by his followers; *Oṁ* obeisance to *Soma*[1] lord of the stars, seated in his vehicle and attended by followers; *Oṁ* obeisance to *Īśāna*[2] lord of learning seated in his vehicle and attended by his followers; *Oṁ* obeisance to *Ananta*[3] the lord of serpents seated in his vehicle attended by his followers;

1. The moon.
2. A name of Śiva or Rudra, or of one of his manifestations. (Vide *CDHM* p. 128).
3. Popularly known as *Śeṣanāga*.

Oṁ obeisance to *Brahman* the lord of worlds seated in his vehicle, attended by his followers; *Oṁ Huṁ Phaṭ* obeisance to *Vajra*; *Oṁ Huṁ Phaṭ* obeisance *to Śakti*; *Oṁ Huṁ Phaṭ* obeisance to *Daṇḍa* (baton); *Oṁ Huṁ Phaṭ* obeisance to sword; *Oṁ Huṁ Phaṭ* obeisance to the noose; *Oṁ Huṁ Phaṭ* obeisance to the banner; *Oṁ Huṁ Phaṭ* obeisance to *Gadā*; *Oṁ Huṁ Phaṭ* obeisance to the trident; *Oṁ Huṁ Phaṭ* obeisance to the *Cakra*; *Oṁ Huṁ Phaṭ* obeisance to *Padma*; *Oṁ Vaum* obeisance to *Viṣvaksena.*

23. O Mahādeva ! *Aṅga* etc. shall be worshipped with these *mantras*. After worshipping *Viṣṇu* the great soul of the form of *Brahman*.

24. The supreme Soul shall be sung in praise by this hymn. Obeisance to *Viṣṇu* the god of gods; obeisance to *Prabha-Viṣṇu* (the powerful).

25. Obeisance to *Vāsudeva* the sustainer; obeisance to the *grasping*; obeisance to the *Pralayaśāyin* (lying in the waters of deluge).

26. Obeisance to the lord of gods; obeisance to the lord of sacrifices. Obeisance to the lord of sages. Obeisance to the lord of *Yakṣas*.

27. Obeisance to the conqueror of all gods; obeisance to the omnipresent of great soul. Obeisance to the lord of all, honoured by Brahmā, Indra and Rudra.

28. Obeisance to the beneficiary of all worlds; obeisance to the presiding deity of the Universe; Obeisance to the protector of all; doer of all, destroyer of all.

29. Obeisance to the giver of boons; the quiet; the foremost. Obeisance, obeisance, to the refuge, to the self-formed and the giver of Virtue, love and wealth.

30. After singing the hymn, the devotee shall meditate in his heart on the imperishable in the form of Brahman, let him worship Viṣṇu with the root mantra, O Śaṅkara.

31. Or, Let him recite the Mūla mantra. He shall attain Hari. O Rudra, thus I have narrated the excellent worship of Viṣṇu.

32. This is to be kept as a great secret. It gives enjoyment and salvation. The scholar who reads this becomes a great devotee of Viṣṇu. He who hears or recites to others attains the world of Viṣṇu.

CHAPTER THIRTYTWO

Worship of Pañca-Tattvas[1]

Maheśvara said:

1. O ! Lord ! bearing *śaṅkha*, *cakra*, and *gadā* ! Please expound the *Pañca-Tattvārcana* (the worship of five principles) of worship by knowing which entirely a man attains the supreme region.

Hari said:

2. O Śaṅkara of splendid vows ! I shall expound the worship of *Pañca-Tattvas* that is auspicious, divine, esoteric and yields all wishes.

3-4. It is holy and destructive of the bad effects of Kali age. Listen. Vāsudeva is the only eternal supreme soul, imperishable, tranquil, permanent, pure, omnipresent and unsullied. Hari himself by means of his *Māyā* stands five-fold.

5-6. To bless the Universe and destroy the wicked entirely. The five-fold forms are: — Vāsudeva[2], Saṅkarṣaṇa,[3] Pradyumna[4], Aniruddha,[5] and Nārāyaṇa[6]. Viṣṇu alone stands in all these forms.

7. O Vṛṣadhvaja ! Listen to the *mantras* expressing these. *Oṁ Am* obeisance to Vāsudeva; *Oṁ Ām* obeisance to Saṅkarṣaṇa; *Oṁ Am* obeisance to Pradyumna; *Oṁ* obeisance to Aniruddha, *Oṁ* obeisance to Nārāyaṇa.

8. Thus I have expounded the *mantras* expressing the five deities. They remove all sins, destroy all sicknesses. They are holy.

1. Here pañca-*tattvas* obviously mean the five-fold forms of Viṣṇu, namely, (i) Vāsudeva, (ii) Saṅkarṣaṇa, (iii) Pradyumna, (iv) Aniruddha and (v) Nārāyaṇa. The worship of the five-fold forms of Viṣṇu is the basis of the *Pāñcarātra* sect of *Vaiṣṇavism*.

2. Kṛṣṇa, a son of Vasudeva.

3. Balarāma, another son of Vasudeva.

4. Son of Kṛṣṇa by Rukmiṇī, father of Aniruddha.

5. Son of Pradyumna. Grandson of Kṛṣṇa.

6. A common name for Viṣṇu. Literally it means the son of *Nara*, the primordial man.

9. Now I shall explain the auspicious worship of *Pañcatattvas*, by what all means it shall be performed and with what all mantras, O Śaṅkara.

10-11. The devotee shall first take his bath and then perform *Sandhyā*. Then going to the chamber of worship let him wash his hands and feet and perform Ācamana. He shall then sit in a comfortable position as he wishes; then let him perform the rite of *Śoṣaṇa* etc. (wiping dry) with the mantras *Aṁ Kṣrauṁ Ram*.

12. By unhardening the *Sāmans* let him prepare an egg and breaking it meditate on the supreme god in the egg.

13-14. In the heart lotus of oneself he shall first meditate on Vāsudeva the lord of the universe, wearing the silken yellow robes, resplendent like a thousand suns, and with glittering earring shaped like Makara fish. Afterwards Saṅkarṣaṇa the lord of self shall be meditated upon.

15. Thereafter Pradyumna, Aniruddha and *Śrimān*[1] (prosperous)Nārāyaṇa shall be meditated upon. Then he should think of the gods Indra and others springing from that Lord of lords.

16. Then *Nyāsa* shall be performed on both the hands. The pervading *Aṅganyāsa* shall be with the root *mantra* and *Aṅgamantras*.

17. Mahādeva of good vows! listen to those *mantras*. *Oṁ Ām* obeisance to the heart. *Oṁ Īm* obeisance to the head. *Oṁ Ūm* obeisance to the tuft. *Oṁ Aim* obeisance to the *Kavaca*. *Oṁ Aum* obeisance to the three eyes. *Om Aḥ* phaṭ to the *Astra*.

18. *Oṁ* obeisance to *Acyuta*[2] with all his followers; *Oṁ* obeisance to *Dhātṛ*; *Oṁ* obeisance to *Vidhātṛ*; *Oṁ* obeisance to *Ādhāra Śakti*; *Oṁ* obeisance to *Kūrma*[3]; *Oṁ* obeisance to *Adanta*; *Oṁ* obeisance to the earth; *Oṁ* obeisance to *Dharma*; *Oṁ* obeisance to *Jñāna* (knowledge); *Oṁ* obeisance to *Vairāgya* (non-attachment); *Oṁ* obeisance to *Aiśvarya* (prosperity); *Oṁ* obeisance to *Adharma* (evil); *Oṁ* obeisance to *Ajñāna* (Ignorance); *Oṁ* obeisance to *Anaiśvarya* (impoverished State); *Oṁ* obeisance

1. Literally it means 'with Lakṣmī'.
2. Viṣṇu or Kṛṣṇa.
3. The tortoise incarnation of Viṣṇu.

to the solar zone; *Oṁ* obeisance to Lunar zone; *Oṁ Mam* obeisance to the fiery[1] zone; *Oṁ Vam* obeisance to Vāsudeva the supreme *Brahman*, the auspicious, the lustre-featured, the pervading and the imperial lord of all deities. *Oṁ* obeisance to *Pāñcajanya*. *Om* obeisance to *Sudarśana*. *Oṁ* obeisance to *Gadā*. *Om* obeisance to *Padma*. *Oṁ* obeisance to *Śrī* (prosperity); *Om* obeisance to *Kriyā* (action, rite); *Oṁ* obeisance to *Puṣṭi* (Nourishment); *Oṁ* obeisance to *Gīti*; *Oṁ* obeisance to *Śakti*; *Oṁ* obeisance to *Prīti* (satisfaction); *Oṁ* obeisance to *Indra*, *Oṁ* obeisance to *Agni* (Fire-god). *Oṁ* obeisance to *Yama* (God of Death); *Oṁ* obeisance to *Nirṛti*; *Oṁ* obeisance to *Varuṇa*; *Om* obeisance to *Vāyu* (Wind-god); *Oṁ* obeisance to *Soma* (Moon); *Oṁ* obeisance to *Īśāna*; *Oṁ* obeisance to *Ananta*; *Oṁ* obeisance to *Brahman*; *Oṁ* obeisance to *Viṣvaksena*; *Oṁ* obeisance to *Padma*.

19. O Rudra, I have succinctly expounded the *Mantras*. The worship has to be performed in such zones (mystic diagrams) as *Svastika* etc.

20. After performing *Aṅganyāsa* all *Mudrās* shall be shown. The *Ātman* and *Vāsudeva* the great lord shall be meditated upon.

21. The devotee shall then worship the seat after duly invoking it. O *Vṛṣadhvaja*, the worship of *Dhātṛ* and *Vidhātṛ* shall be performed at the doorway.

22. O Śaṅkara, in front of *Vāsudeva* the devotee shall worship Garuḍa and in the middle (all his paraphernalia) from *Śaṅkha* to *Padma* shall be worshipped.

23. From east onwards (in the four quarters) *Dharma*, *Jñāna*, *Vairāgya* and *Aiśvarya* shall be worshipped and in the four corner quarters beginning with south-east *Adharma* and the three others shall be worshipped.

24. The seat is fixed in the middle of the two *Maṇḍalas*. *Saṅkarṣaṇa* and others are to be worshipped in the eastern and other petals.

25. In the pericarp Vāsudeva the great Lord shall be worshipped. *Pāñcajanya* and others are to be worshipped as fixed in the north-east, etc.

1. The solar zone.

26. O Śaṅkara ! the *Śaktis* of the god of gods are to be worshipped in the east. Indra and other guardians of quarters are to be worshipped fixed in their respective stations.

27. The *Nāga* (Serpent) shall be worshipped below and the *Brahmā* high above by the scholarly devotee. O Śaṅkara ! The order of fixation shall be understood thus by you.

28. After invoking the Lord in the Maṇḍala and performing his *Nyāsa* and showing the *mudrā*, O Śaṅkara, *Pādya* (water for washing feet) shall be given at the foot.

29. Bathing garment offering, *Ācamana*, *Namaskāra* (bowing down), circular peregrination—all these shall be offered at the foot. Then the *Japa* shall be dedicated.

30. Afterwards remembering Vāsudeva let this hymn be recited : *Oṁ* obeisance unto Vāsudeva, obeisance unto Saṅkarṣaṇa.

31. Obeisance unto Pradyumna the first deity; obeisance to Aniruddha; obeisance to Nārāyaṇa the lord of men.

32. Obeisance, obeisance, unto the primordial Being, worthy of respect of men, of being glorified, of being honoured; the giver of boons and devoid of beginning and death.

33. Obeisance unto Him the creator and destroyer, the lord of Brahmā; obeisance unto Him who can be known through Vedas and who holds *Śaṅkha* and *Cakra*.

34. Obeisance unto the Lord of gods who destroys the sin of *Kali*-age, who cuts down the tree of worldly existence and who pierces *Māyā* (the ignorance, Illusion). Obeisance, obeisance.

35. Obeisance unto Him of diverse forms, the holy of holies, having the three *Guṇas*, obeisance, obeisance. Obeisance to Him who awards salvation and who manifests Himself as Brahmā, Viṣṇu and Īsvara[1]. Obeisance, obeisance.

36. Obeisance unto him who is the path to salvation, who is virtue, who is the extinction (of bondage), who gives all desires, who has the form of *Parabrahman*[2].

37. O Lord of the Universe, save me deeply immersed in the ocean of worldly existence of terrific nature. Other than you there is no better saviour.

1. Śiva.
2. The Supreme Being, God.

38. I have sought refuge under you the omnipresent: release me from darkness by giving me the lamp of knowledge.

39. O Nīlalohita (Śiva) ! for the destruction of all pain, the lord of gods shall be praised by means of this hymn and similar hymns from the Vedas.

40. The devotee shall meditate within his heart on Viṣṇu accompanied by the Five *Tattvas.* Then the *Visarjana* shall be performed. Thus I have ex-pounded the worship.

41. By reciting this, O Śaṅkara, the hymn shall award him all desires. He shall be having the satisfaction of having done his duty.

42. He who reads this worship entitled *Pañcatattvārcana,* he who hears this and he who repeats this shall attain the region of Viṣṇu.

CHAPTER THIRTYTHREE

Worship of Sudarśana

Rudra said :

1. O Lord holding *Śaṅkha, Cakra* and *Gadā*, please expound to me the worship of *Sudarśana,* by performing which the evil effects of planets, and illness are destroyed.

Hari said :

2. O Vṛṣadhvaja, listen to the worship of *Cakra Sudarśana.* The devotee shall first take his bath and then worship Hari.

3. The *Nyāsa* is done by means of the *Mūla mantra.* Listen to it. It is *Oṁ Sahasrāraṁ* (having thousand spokes) *Huṁ Phaṭ* obeisance (with the *Praṇava* in the beginning).

4. This piercing *Mantra* is said to be the destroyer of all wicked persons.

The devotee shall meditate in the lotus of his heart Sudarśana the hinings.

5-6. Then after invoking the gentle deity wearing *Śaṅkha*, *Cakra*, *Gadā* and *Padma* and coronet in the mystic diagram by means already mentioned, O Hara, let him worship Him with the offerings of fragrant flowers, etc. After worship the *mantra* is to be recited one hundred and eight times.

7. He who performs the excellent worship of the *Cakra* thus, shall be free from all sickness and shall attain the world of Viṣṇu.

8. Thereafter let him recite the following hymn destructive of all diseases. Obeisance unto *Sudarśana* lustrous like a thousand suns.

9. Lighted by a series of flames and having a thousand spokes and eyes (obeisance unto Him) who destroys all the wicked, and suppresses all sins.

10. Obeisance unto *Sucakra*, *Vicakra* and piercer of all *mantras*. Obeisance unto the originator of the world, the sustainer of the world and the destroyer of the world.

11. Obeisance unto the destroyer of all wicked demons for the protection of the world.

Obeisance, obeisance unto Him who is fierce and gentle and terrific in form.

12. Obeisance unto Him who is in the form of the eye of the world and who dispels the fear of worldly existence.

Obeisance unto Him who breaks asunder the cage of *Māyā*, obeisance, obeisance unto the benefactor.

13 Obeisance unto Him who is in the form of a planet and surpasses all the other planets. Obeisance to the lord of planets.

Obeisance, obeisance unto Him who is Time (Supreme) and Death and the terrific.

14. Obeisance to the blesser of devotees. Obeisance, obeisance to the protector of devotees. Obeisance unto Him who is in the form of Viṣṇu, who is tranquil, and who bears all weapons.

15. Again and again obeisance unto the weapon of Viṣṇu; unto the *Cakra* obeisance. This hymn, highly meritorious of the *Cakra* that I explained to you shall be read with great devotion.

16. He who does so attains the world of Viṣṇu.

17. O Rudra ! he who reads the scheme of the worship of the *Cakra*, with all the sense-organs under his control shall burn all sins to ashes and become competent to ascend to the world of Viṣṇu.

CHAPTER THIRTYFOUR

Worship of Hayagrīva[1]

Rudra said :

1. O Hṛṣīkeśa[2] (Viṣṇu) bearing the club ! Please expound again the worship of the lord. The more you speak in detail about the worship the more I delight in hearing it. I am never satiated.

Hari said :

2. I shall narrate the worship of Lord Hayagrīva whereby the lord of the universe Viṣṇu, is propitiated. Listen to it.

3. O Mahādeva, I shall explain the holy *Mūla mantra* expressing *Hayagrīva*. O Śaṅkara listen to that first.

4. *Oṁ haum Kṣrauṁ Śirase Namo haum.* This mantra of nine syllables gives all learning.

5. O Mahādeva, Vṛṣadhvaja, listen to its limbs. *Oṁ Kṣrām* obeisance to the heart. *Oṁ Hrīṁ Svāhā* to the head (*Śiraḥ* is said to be attached with *Svāhā*). *Kṣrūm Vaṣat* is also likewise.

6. O Vṛṣadhvaja, the lord's tuft is to be known as accompanied by *Oṅkāra*. *Oṁ Kṣraim* to the *Kavaca*. *Hum* is described as *Kavaca*.

7. *Oṁ Kṣauṁ Vauṣat* to the three eyes. This is described as the lord's eye. *Oṁ Haḥ Phaṭ* to the *Astra*. This is described as the lord's weapon.

8. I shall explain the procedure of worship. Please listen to me as I narrate. First the devotee shall take his bath.

1. Viṣṇu (*CDHM*, p. 120).
2. Literally, the lord or conqueror of the five sense-organs.

Then after performing *Ācamana* he shall go to the chamber of Sacrifice.

9-10. After entering let him perform the mystical rite of Śoṣaṇa (wiping dry). After creating the egg with the *Bīja mantras—Yaṁ Kṣauṁ Raṁ Lam*—and hardening it, let him split it with *Oṅkāra* itself. Let him meditate on *Hayagrīva* within his self in the middle of the egg.

11-13. (*Hayagrīva* who is) as white as conch, moon and the flower *Kunda*, shining like the lotus stalk and silver, bearing *Śaṅkha*, *Cakra*, *Gadā* and *Padma* in his four hands ; Hayagrīva wearing a crown, earrings and garland of wild flowers ; he is crimson-coloured in his cheeks and wears yellow robes; after meditating on the all-pervasive noble soul accompanied by all deities let him perform the *Nyāsa* with the *Aṅga mantras* and the *Mūla mantra*.

14. Then O Śaṅkara, let him show the *Mudrās* of *Śaṅkha*, *Padma*, etc. Thereafter let him meditate upon and worship Viṣṇu by means of the *Mūla mantra*.

15. Let him then, O Rudra, invoke those deities who preside over the seats "*Oṁ* O ye deities of the seat *Hayagrīva*, come."

16. After invoking let him worship them in the *Svastika maṇḍala*. O Vṛṣadhvaja, the worship of *Dhātṛ* and *Vidhātṛ* shall be performed in the doorway.

17. "Obeisance to *Acyuta* with the entire attendants," saying so in the middle the worship shall be performed. Then the worship of *Gaṅgā*.

18. *Yamunā*, *Mahādevī* and the two *Nidhis Śaṅkha and Padma* and Garuḍa are to be worshipped in front. In the middle *Śakti* is to be worshipped.

19. The *Śakti* is called *Ādhāra Śakti*. Then let him worship *Kūrma*. Afterwards let him worship *Ananta* and the earth. Then *Dharma* and *Jñāna*.

20. Let him worship *Vairāgya* and *Aiśvarya* in the corners south-east, etc.

Adharma, *Ajñāna*, *Avairāgya* and *Anaiśvarya* are to be worshipped in the east.

21. Let him worship in the middle place *Sattva*, *Rajas* and *Tamas*. Let him worship *Nanda*, *Nala* and *Padma* only in the middle.

22. The worship of the *maṇḍalas* of Sun, Moon and Fire shall be performed in the middle place. O Rudra, it is so narrated.

23. The *Śaktis* and the following *Vimalā*, *Utkarṣiṇī Jñānā*, *Kriyā*, *yogā*, *Prahvī*, *Satyā*, *īśānā* and *Anugrahā*.

24. The first eight *Śaktis* are to be worshipped in the petals beginning with that in the east and Anugrahā in the pericarp by men who wish for lasting good.

25. The devotee shall worship the seat with these *mantras* keeping the names in the dative case, prefixing Praṇava and ending with "Namaḥ."

26. The worship of the seat shall be auspicious by duly offering bath, fragrant pastes, flowers, incense, light and the food offerings.

27. This is the scheme as adumbrated and is to be followed. Then he shall invoke Lord *Hayagrīva*, lord of gods.

28. O Śaṅkara, the deity shall be meditated upon as entering through the left nostril. The *Mūla mantra* is to be employed while he arrives.

29. The invocation of the god of gods *Śaṅkhin* (holding *Śaṅkha*) shall then be performed. After invoking, the devotee shall cautiously perform the *Nyāsa* in the *Maṇḍala*.

30-31. After performing the *Nyāsa* let him think of the god seated there, *Hayagrīva*, the great god, bowed to by gods and demons, accompanied by the guardians of the quarters Indra and others, the imperishable Viṣṇu Himself. After the contemplation he shall show the auspicious *Mudrās*, *Śaṅkha*, *Cakra*, etc.

32-33. *Pādya*, *Arghya*, *Ācamanīya* (water for *Ācamana*) shall be offered to *Viṣṇu*. Then the devotee shall bathe the lord *Padmanābha* free from illness. After fixing the lord duly, O Vṛṣadhvaja, he shall offer the garments, then *Ācamana* and the auspicious sacred thread.

34. Then he shall meditate on the great Lord in the *maṇḍala*, O Rudra. After meditation he shall again give *pādya* and other things to the deity, O Śaṅkara.

35. He shall give it to *Bhairava-deva* with the *Mūla-mantra*. *Oṁ Kṣām* obeisance to the heart. With this he shall worship the heart.

36. *Oṁ Kṣim* obeisance to the head, then the worship of the head. *Oṁ Kṣūm* obeisance to the tuft. With this let him worship the tuft.

37. *Oṁ Kṣaim* obeisance to the *Kavaca*; let him worship the *Kavaca*. *Oṁ Kṣaum* obeisance to the eye. With this let him worship the eye.

38. *Om Kṣaḥ* obeisance to the weapon. With this let him worship the weapon. (Thus let him worship) the heart, head, tuft and *Kavaca*.

39. In the places beginning with the east let him worship these. O Rudra, let him worship the *Astra* in the corners and the eye in the middle.

40. Let him worship the great goddess Lakṣmī, the auspicious giver of prosperity. He shall worship *Śaṅkha, Padma Cakra* and *Gadā* beginning with the east.

41. O Rudra, let him worship the sword, pestle, noose, goad and the bow with the arrow from the east with these *mantras* with their own name.s

42-43. O Rudra, from the east itself let him worship *Śrīvatsa*, *Kaustubha*, garland, and the auspicious yellow garment. Then let him worship the deity bearing *Śaṅkha*, *Cakra* and *Gadā*, Brahmā, Nārada, Siddhaguru (the preceptor with yogic achievements), and Paraguru (the supreme Preceptor). Similarly (let him worship) the sandals of the preceptor and the supreme preceptor.

44-45. O Vṛṣabhadhvaja, let him worship beginning with the east and ending with *Ūrdhva* (above) Indra along with his vehicle and followers Agni, Yama, Nirṛti, Varuṇa, Vāyu, Soma, Īśāna, Nāga and Brahmā.

46. Let him then worship the ten weapons *Vajra* (thunderbolt), *Śakti*, *Daṇḍa*, sword, noose, banner, trident, discus and lotus.

47. Let him worship then in the north-east, *Viṣvaksena* with these mantras, with the *Praṇava* in the beginning and *Namaḥ* in the end, O Vṛṣadhvaja.

48. Then let the worship of *Ananta* be performed O Vṛṣadhvaja. It is with the *mūlamantra* that the worship of the deity shall be done, O Vṛṣadhvaja.

49. Fragrant unguents, flowers, incense, lamp, oblations circular peregrinations, prostrations and *Japyas* (recital of prayers) shall be dedicated to him.

50. Let him sing this hymn with *Praṇava* in the beginning. O Vṛṣadhvaja. *Oṁ* obeisance to *Hayaśiras* the presiding deity of learning.

51. *Oṁ* obeisance to the deity who is of the form of learning and the giver of learning. Obeisance, obeisance.

Obeisance to the quiet lord, obeisance to the *Ātman* of the three *Guṇas*.

52. Obeisance to the destroyer of gods and demons and the slayer of the wicked.

Obeisance unto the deity who is the lord of all worlds, in the form of Brahmā.

53. Obeisance to the deity worthy of respect of *iśvara*. Obeisance to the deity who bears *Śaṅkha* and *Cakra*. Obeisance to the primordial deity, the fully controlled, conducive to the benefit of all living beings.

54. Devoid of three *guṇas* and equipped with *guṇas* in the form of Brahmā, Rudra and Viṣṇu, the doer, the destroyer, the lord of gods, obeisance to the omnipresent.

55-56. O Rudra, after singing the hymn he shall meditate on the god of gods in the pure lotus of the heart, the god bearing *Śaṅkha*, *Cakra* and *Gadā*, refulgent like a crore of suns, beautiful in every limb, the great lord *Hayagrīva*, the noble, *Ātman* the imperishable.

57. O Śaṅkara, thus I have expounded to you the worship of *Hayagrīva*. He who reads this with great devotion shall go to the supreme region.

CHAPTER THIRTYFIVE

Worship of Gāyatrī

Hari Said :

1. I shall expound the *Nyāsa*, etc. and the metre of *Gāyatrī*; Viśvāmitra is the sage; Savitṛ[1] is the deity.

2. It has Brahmā for its head, Rudra for its tuft, it is stationed in Viṣṇu's heart. The application is its eye. It is *Sagotra* (of the same family) with *Kātyāyana*.[2]

3. It must be known as having three worlds for its feet. It has the bowels of the earth for its base. Knowing it thus *Gāyatrī* is to be repeated one million two hundred thousand times.

4. It has three feet of eight syllables each or four feet of six syllables for *Japa* (repetition) ; it is three-footed and for worship it is four-footed.

5. In *Nyāsa Japa*, *Dhyāna* (contemplation), *Agnikārya* (sacred rites in fire) and *Arcana* (worship) the devotee shall employ *Gāyatrī* always. It dispels all sins.

6-7. The devotee shall assign the outline to the toes, insteps, calves, knees, thighs, private parts, scrotum, blood vessel, navel, belly, the nipples, the heart, throat, lips, mouth, palate, the shoulders, eyes, eyebrows, forehead, the four quarters and the head. I shall tell you the colours.

8-10. The sapphire colour, the colour of fire, yellow, deep black, tawny, white, lightning colour, silvery white, dark, crimson, darkblue, white, yellow, grey, ruby colour, conch colour, grey red as wine, sun colour, similar to the colour of the moon and white as the lustre of conch-shell.

11. Whatever the devotee touches with his hand and whatever he sees with his eyes it becomes pure. They know nothing superior to *Gāyatrī*.

1. Literally means the 'generator'. It is a solar deity and many hymns are addressed to him in the Ṛgveda.

2. A great sage. The *Vārttikas* are ascribed to him. (*CDHM* p. 154; *CSL* p. 57).

CHAPTER THIRTYSIX

Method of performing Sandhyā[1]

Hari said :

1. O Rudra, I shall explain the mode of performance of *Sandhyā* prayer. It destroys sins. Listen. After performing *prāṇāyāma* (holding of the breath) thrice, the devotee shall take the *Sandhyā* bath.

2. It is called *prāṇāyāma* when one repeats the *Gāyatrī* along with *praṇava* and the *Vyāhṛtis* (*Oṁ Bhūḥ Bhuvaḥ Svaḥ Oṁ*) three times while holding the breath.

3. A twice-born will be able to burn off all mental, verbal and physical defects by *prāṇāyāma*. Hence, he shall practise the same always.

4. The *Ācamana mantra* during the evening *Sandhyā* is the Vedic *Ṛk*: *Agniśca mā*; during the morning it is *Sūryaśca mā*; in the mid-day it is: *Āpaḥ punantu*. Let him duly perform *Upasparśa*[2] also.

5. He shall perform *Mārjana* (mystical wiping) with the *Ṛk* : *Āpo hi ṣṭhā* and water by means of *Kuśa* grass shall be sprinkled at every step with the recital of *praṇava*.

6. With these nine (three times daily three main rites) the devotee shall burn off the nine sorts of defects arising from *Rajas*, (passion) *Tamas* (ignorance), *Moha* (delusion) waking state, dreaming state and state of sound sleep, from speech, from thought and from actions.

7. Taking water in the joint palms (in the form of a cup) and reciting the mantra, *Aghamarṣaṇa* water shall be offered three, eight or twelve times.

8. The sun shall be worshipped with the two Ṛks *Udu tyam* and *Citram*. The sins committed during the day or night shall be destroyed instantly.

1. Morning. noon and evening prayers.
2. Bathing or rinsing the mouth, sipping and ejecting water as a religious act.

9. The *Sandhyā* prayer shall be recited in the morning standing and in the evening, sitting. The *Gāyatrī* shall be recited with *praṇava* prefixed and accompanied by *Mahāvyāhṛtis*.[1]

10. If it is recited ten times *Gāyatrī* removes the sin of this birth; if it is recited hundred times it destroys the sins of all previous births and if it is recited a thousand times it removes the sins of three *yugas*[2] (Ages i.e. *Kṛta*, *Tretā* and *Dvāpara*).

11. *Gāyatrī* is crimson-coloured. *Sāvitrī*[3] is white-hued and *Sarasvatī*[4] shall be known to be dark in colour. These are the three *Sandhyās* as explained.

12-13. After fixing *Oṁ Bhūḥ* in the heart, *Oṁ Bhuvaḥ* shall be fixed on the head; *Oṁ Svaḥ* shall be in the tuft. The scholarly devotee shall fix the first *pāda* (group of six syllables, here) of *Gāyatrī* in the *Kavaca*; the second in the eyes. The *Aṅga-vinyāsa* is to be done with the third (*pāda*) and he shall fix the fourth (*pāda*) all over (the body).

14. During the *Sandhyās* (morning, mid-day and evening) *Gāyatrī* the mother of Vedas shall be recited after due *Nyāsas*. He shall be blessed with welfare in all limbs if the *Nyāsa* is accompanied by *prāṇāyāma* too.

15. *Gāyatrī* of three *pādas* (3×8 syllables) is identical with Brahmā, Viṣṇu and Maheśvara. The *Japa* shall be begun only after knowing the *Viniyoga* (application), *Ṛṣi* (sage) and the *Chandas* (metre).

16. Then he shall be free from all sins and shall attain *Brahmā's* world. The fourth *pāda* (last group of six syllables) is mentioned to be the essence beyond all *Rajas* (passion).

17. The sun destroys the person who does not perform the *Sandhyā* prayer. The sage of the fourth *pāda* is "Nirmala".

18. The *Chandas* is *Gāyatrī* the divine; and the deity is *paramātmā* (the supreme soul).

1. *Bhūr*, *bhuvaḥ* and *svaḥ* are called the *Mahāvyāhṛtis*.

2. According to the Post-Ṛgvedic Hindu traditions Time is divided into the cycle of four ages or *yugas*. They are *Kṛta-yuga* (also called *Satyayuga*), *Tretāyuga*, *Dvāparayuga* and *Kaliyuga*. (Vide details in *Liṅga* (*AITM*) p. 809; *CDHM*, pp. 381-3).

3. Name of Gāyatrī, for the morning-worship.

4. It is note-worthy here that Sarasvatī is a name of Gāyatrī and it is dark-coloured for the evening-worship.

CHAPTER THIRTYSEVEN

Gāyatrī Kalpa

Hari said :

1. *Gāyatrī* is the great goddess. All the great sins of the person who recites *Gāyatrī* are destroyed.

2. I shall now describe the *Gāyatrī Kalpa* (eulogy of *Gāyatrī*). It is conducive to enjoyment here and salvation hereafter. The devotee shall repeat it one thousand and eight times, or one hundred and eight times.

3. Thrice daily during the period of conjunctions he shall attain *Brahmaloka*. After repeating a hundred times he is allowed to take water. In the *Sandhyā* the divine deity destroying all sins shall be invoked and worshipped.

4. Along with twelve names with her own *mantra* : *Bhūḥ Bhuvaḥ Svaḥ*. Obeisance to *Gāyatrī*; obeisance to *Sāvitrī*; obeisance to Sarasvatī.

5. Obeisance to the mother of *Vedas* to *Sāṅkṛti*, to *Brahmāṇī* to *Kauśikī*, to *Sādhvī*, to *Sarvārthasādhinī* (who can accomplish all desired objects), to Sahasrākṣī (having thousand eyes).

6-7. In the fire let the devotee offer the *Ājya* (melted ghee) and *Haviṣyaka* (food offering with *Bhūḥ Bhuvaḥ Svaḥ*). In order to get all virtues and desired objects he shall pour *ghee* (in the fire) one thousand and eight times or one hundred and eight times.

After worshipping the idol made of sandal wood or gold,

8. The devotee shall repeat it one hundred thousand times, taking only milk, bulbous roots and fruits. Pouring twenty thousand Āhutis he shall obtain all desires.

9. (The *Visarjana mantra*) is: "O Goddess, born in the land of northern Summit and permitted to stay on the Mountain by Brahmā, please repair as please you".

CHAPTER THIRTYEIGHT

Worship of Durgā

Hari said :

1. On *Navamī*[1], the devotee shall worship *Durgā* with the mantra *Hrīṁ Durge Rakṣiṇi*. O Mother, O excellent mother Goddess *Durgā*, the giver of all implements of love and wealth ! Grant unto me all desires accepting this offering.

2-3. In the *mārgaśīrṣa*[2] month(Oct-Nov.) beginning with the third day of the lunar fortnight the devotee shall worship in order these goddesses :—*Gaurī*, *Kālī*, *Umā*, *Durgā*, *Bhadrā*, *Kānti*, *Sarasvatī*, *Maṅgalā*, *Vijayā*, *Lakṣmī*, *Śivā* and *Nārāyaṇī*. He will never have the sorrow of separation.

4-5. The devotee shall meditate on the goddess with eighteen hands bearing *Kheṭaka* (club), bell, mirror, *Tarjanī* (censuring symbol), bow, banner, *Ḍamaruka* (small drum), axe, noose, *Śakti* (Javelin), pestle, *Śūla* (trident), *Kapāla* (skull), *Vajraka* (thunderbolt) goad, arrow, *Cakra* and a probe.

6. I shall now explain the process of *Japa* of *Śrī* Bhagavatī[3] along with the requisite *mantras*.

7. Om obeisance to Thee Goddess *Cāmuṇḍā*,[4] living in the cremation ground, having a skull in the hand, riding on a great spirit having a cluster of *mahāvimānas* (aerial chariots) around *Kālarātri* (terrific like a nightmare), surrounded by a number of attendants, having a huge mouth and many arms, bearing bell, drum and *kiṅkiṇī*, loudly laughing with the sound *kili-kili*. *Hum* unto thee. O deity producing all sorts of sounds, body covered with the hide of an elephant, smeared with blood and flesh, having a terrific dangling tongue, O great *Rākṣasī*, terrific with hideous crooked teeth, laughing boisterously, effulgent like the glittering lightning, O *Karālanetrā* (having awful eyes) move on, move on. *Hili-Hili*. *Hum* unto Thee.

1. The ninth day in the lunar fortnight.

2. The ninth month of the Hindu calendar which now-a-days begins with *chaitra*.

3. Durgā.

4. A form of Durgā who killed the demons Caṇḍa and Muṇḍa (*CDHM*, pp. 65-6).

Put both thy tongues into the mouth. O *Bhṛkuṭimukhi* (with face having knit eyebrows), having *Oṅkāra* for thy auspicious seat, wearing a garland of skulls, having matted hair crown and moon on the head, boisterously laughing *Kili-Kili Huṁ Huṁ* unto Thee. With thy hideous crooked teeth thou dost bring about a terrific darkness. O thou who dispellest all obstacles achieve this (such and such as specified) work. Do it quickly. *Kaha Kaha* allow me to enter along with the goad. *Vaṅga* ! *Vaṅga* make him tremble, make him tremble, move on, move on, lead, lead. O deity fond of blood, flesh and wine ! kill, kill, pound, pound; cut, cut; strike, strike; let us speak requesting you to make the body adamantine; destroy all wicked persons in the three worlds, whether taken or not taken; make him enter, make him enter (thy presence); make him go ahead, make him go ahead; dance ! dance ! bind ! bind ! trot ! trot. O deity with sunken eyes ! with hair tied up; O owl-faced ! having *kiṅkiṇis* in the hand. O deity having a garland of skeletons, burn ! burn ! cook ! cook ! grasp ! grasp ! make him enter the middle of the *maṇḍala*, why dost thou delay ? On oath unto Brahmā ! on oath unto Viṣṇu, on oath unto sages, on oath unto Rudra. Inspire him ! Inspire him *Kili-Kili-Khili-Khili-mili-mili cili-cili*; O thou deformed deity ! with body encircled by a black serpent! O Thou who takest in all planets, of lips drooping down, of nose sunken between eyebrows; of grim face, of grey matted hair ! *O Brāhmi* ! break ! break ! blaze ! blaze, O *Kālamukhi* (having dark face) *Khala* ! *Khala* ! strike, strike down. O ! thou red-eyed ! roll them, make others roll them, fell them to the ground; hold, hold the head; opene open thy eyes; break, break; take, take, thy feet; show the *mudrās*, *Huṁ Hūṁ phaṭ* unto thee. Pierce, pierce, tear, tear with the trident; kill, kill with the thunderbolt; strike, strike, with the baton, chop off, chop off with the *cakra*, pierce, pierce with the *Śakti*, chew, chew with the curved tooth; nail, nail with the pin; mince, mince with the scissors; catch hold of, catch hold of with the goad; release me from the fever recurring daily with headache; from the fever recurring every two days, three days, four days; release me from *Ḍākiniskandagraha* (the haunting of the spirit *Ḍākinī*) catch *Lala*, *Lala*, lift up lift up? strike down, strike down to the ground; catch. O *Brahmāṇi*, come,

come. O *Māheśvari* come, come; O *Kaumāri* come, come; O *Vārāhi* come, come; O *Aindri* come, come; O *Cāmuṇḍā* come, come; O *Vaiṣṇavi* come, come; O *Nārasiṁhi* come, come; O *Śvadūti* come, come; O *Kapālini* come, come; O *Mahākāli* come, come; O *Revati* come come; O *Śuṣka Revati* come, come; O *Ākāśa Revati* come, come; O *Himavantacāriṇi*[1] come, come; O *Kailāsacāriṇi*[2] come, come; cut, cut the enemies; *mantra*: *Kili Kili Bimbe!* O *Aghorā*; O *Cāmuṇḍā* of terrific form originating from the fury of *Rudra!* O thou deity who makest *Asuras* dwindle in numbers and goest along the firmament; bind, bind with the noose the time! stop, stop, make it enter, make it enter the *maṇḍala*; cause it to fall; cause it to fall; grasp it, grasp it; bind, bind its face (mouth); bind bind the eves, bind, bind the heart; bind, bind hands and feet; bind, bind all evil planets, bind, bind the quarters; bind, bind the corners; bind, bind above; bind, bind below; Inspire them with ashes, water, earth or with mustard seeds; strike them down, strike them down. O! *Cāmuṇḍā Kili Kili Vicce, Huṁ phaṭ Svāhā.*

8. This is the garland of one thousand eight letters in the form of *mantras* for repeated *Japa*. Each word (letter) is to be repeated eight thousand times. Then homa is to be performed eight thousand times with gingelly seeds coated with *Trimadhura* (three sweet things sugar, honey and clarified butter).

9. With the great flesh (human flesh) coated with the three sweet things *homa* shall be performed one thousand and eight times repeating each letter one thousand eight times. Or merely gingelly seeds coated with *trimadhura* can be used for *homa.*

10. In the case of war, by throwing water, mustard seed or ashes one's victory is assured.

11. The deity can be meditated upon as having twenty-eight, eighteen, twelve, eight or four arms.

12. One pair of hands has sword and club, the other mace and baton, the third bow and arrows and the fourth sword and pestle.

1. Moving in the Himālayas.
2. Moving in the Kailāsa mountain.

13. Another pair of hands has *Śaṅkha* and bell; another banner and pole; another pair axe and discus; and another pair small drum and mirror.

14. In one pair a hand holds *Śakti* and the other gesticulates; another pair has *Musalas* (pestles); another pair has noose and a long javelin; still another has *Ḍhakkā* and *Paṇava* (two kinds of drums).

15. With one hand the goddess is threatening (the demons), with another she produces a tinkling sound; with one hand she shows the *Abhaya Mudrā*[1] and with the other the *Svastika Mudrā.*[2] Such is *Mahiṣaghnī* (the slayer of the demon *Mahiṣa*) riding on a lion.

16. Victory unto thee, O goddess of goblins, surrounded by all spirits. Protect me from your spirits. Accept this oblation. Obeisance unto thee.

CHAPTER THIRTYNINE

Worship of the Sun

Rudra said :

1. O *Janārdana,* please expound again succinctly the worship of the Sun-god who is identical with *Viṣṇu.* The worship that affords enjoyment in this world and salvation hereafter.

Vāsudeva said :

2. O Rudra, listen, I shall again expound the mode of worship of sun. *Om* obeisance unto *Uccaiśravas.*[3] *Om* obeisance unto *Aruṇa. Om* obeisance unto *Daṇḍin. Om* obeisance unto *Piṅgala.* O *Vṛṣadhvaja* with these *mantras* they are to be worshipped at the door.

1. Promising protection.
2. Promising good luck.
3. The horse obtained at the churning of the ocean.

3. *Om Am* obeisance unto *Bhūta*, the devotee shall worship him in the middle, him whose name is *Prabhūtāmala*.

Om Am obeisance unto *Vimala*. *Om Am* obeisance unto *Sāra*. *Om Am* obeisance unto *Ādhāra*. *Om Am* obeisance unto *Paramamukha Vimala* and others are to be worshipped in the south-east and other corners.

4. *Om* obeisance to *Padma*. *Om* obeisance to the *Karṇikā* the pericarp. A devotee shall worship these inside the mystical diagram. *Dīptā* and others are to be worshipped in the east and other directions and *Sarvatomukhī* is to be worshipped in the middle. *Oṁ Vām* obeisance unto *Dīptā*. *Oṁ Vin* obeisance unto *Sūkṣmā*. *Oṁ Vūm* obeisance unto *Bhadrā*. *Oṁ Vaim* obeisance unto *Jayā*. *Oṁ Vīm* obeisance unto *Vibhūti*. *Oṁ Vam* obeisance unto *Aghorā*. *Oṁ Vam* obeisance unto *Vidyutā*. *Oṁ Vaḥ* obeisance unto *Vijayā*. *Oṁ* obeisance unto *Sarvatomukhī*.

5. *Oṁ* obeisance unto the seat of Sun. *Oṁ Hrām* obeisance to the idol of the Sun. These are to be worshipped in the middle. O *Śaṅkara*, listen to the *Hṛnmantras*. *Oṁ Haṁ Saṁ Khaṁ Khakholkāya Krāṁ Krīṁ Saḥ Svāhā*. Obeisance unto the idol of the Sun. With this the *Āvāhana* (invocation), *Sthāpana* (installation) and *Sannidhānaka* (bringing near) are to be performed. *Sakalīkaraṇa* (summing up) is to be with the *mantra* for *Sannirodhana* (warding off).

6. *Mudrās* are to be shown likewise. O Rudra, let him worship with the *Mūlamantra*, the sun brilliant in form, crimson in colour, seated in a white lotus, in a chariot with a single wheel, having two arms, holding a lotus.

7. The sun shall be meditated upon this. Listen to the *Mūlamantra* :—*Oṁ Hrāṁ Hrīṁ Saḥ* obeisance unto the sun.

8. The devotee shall show *Padmamudrā* and *Bimba-Mudrā* three times. *Oṁ Ām* obeisance to the heart. *Oṁ Svāhā* to the sun, to the head. *Oṁ Aḥ Bhūrbhuvaḥ Svaḥ Vaṣaṭ* to *Jvālinī* to tuft. *Oṁ Huṁ Huṁ* to *Kavaca*. *Oṁ Bhām Vauṣat* to the two eyes. *Oṁ Vaḥ Phaṭ* to the weapon.

9. The devotee shall worship the heart, etc. in the south-east, north-east, south-west or north-west and the eye in the middle.

10. In the directions he shall worship the weapon and

the white-hued *Moon*. In the eastern petal, O Rudra, he shall worship the gold-coloured *Budha* (mercury).

11. O Rudra, in the south he shall worship yellow-coloured Jupiter. He shall worship *Bhūteśa* (the lord of spirits) in the north and the white-hued *Venus*.

12. In the south-east, O *Hara*, he shall worship the red-hued *Aṅgāraka*(Mars). He shall worship black-hued *Saturn* in the south-west.

13. In the north-west, O *Hara*, he shall worship *Rāhu* of the colour of the flower *Nandyāvarta* and in the north-east he shall worship *Ketu* the smoke-coloured.

14. These are the *mantras* O *Śaṅkara*, listen:

15. *Oṁ Som* obeisance to the moon. *Oṁ Bum* obeisance to *Budha* (Mercury). *Oṁ Bṛm* obeisance to *Bṛhaspati* (Jupiter). *Oṁ Bham* obeisance to *Bhārgava* (Venus). *Oṁ Am* obeisance to *Aṅgāraka* (Mars). *Oṁ Śam* obeisance to *Śanaiścara* (Saturn). *Oṁ Ram* obeisance to *Rāhu*. *Oṁ Kam* obeisance to *Ketu*.

16. O *Śaṅkara*, after giving *Pādya*, etc. with the *Mūla-mantra*, the best of devotees (the aspirant) shall show the *Dhenumudrā* at the end of offering food.

17. After repeating the *mantra* eight thousand times, he must dedicate the same to the deity; O *Bhūteśa* (Śiva), he shall worship the *Tejaścaṇḍa* (the fierce splendour) in the north-east, etc.

18-19. *Oṁ Huṁ Phaṭ Svadhā Svāhā Vauṣat* to *Tejaścaṇḍa*. He shall dedicate unto him the *Nirmālya* and *Arghya* consisting of gingelly seeds and rice grains, mixed with red sandal ground into a paste with unguent water accompanied by flowers and incense.

20. He shall place that vessel above the head and kneeling on the earth, O *Vṛṣadhvaja*, he shall give *Arghya* to the Sun with the *Hṛnmantra*.

21. After worshipping the *Gaṇa* and the preceptors, he shall worship all deities. *Oṁ Gam* obeisance to *Gaṇapati*. *Oṁ Am* obeisance to the preceptors.

22. Thus the worship of Sun has been described. Performing this, the devotee shall attain the world of *Viṣṇu*.

CHAPTER FORTY

Worship of Maheśvara

Śaṅkara said :

1. O Lord, bearing *Śaṅkha* and *Gadā*, please narrate to me the *Māheśvarī Pūjā* (worship) after knowing which men attain *Siddhi* (achievement).

Hari said :

2. O *Vṛṣadhvaja*, listen to the mode of worship of *Maheśvara* even as I describe the same. After taking bath, and performing *Ācamana* let the devotee sit on a seat and perform Nyāsa.

3. He shall then worship *Maheśvara* in the *maṇḍala* (mystic diagram). With these *mantras* (he shall worship) *Maheśvara* accompanied by all followers.

4. *Oṁ Hām*, O ye deities of the seat of *Śiva*, come. He shall invoke the deities of the seat with this.

5. *Oṁ Hām* obeisance to *Gaṇapati*. *Oṁ Hām* obeisance to *Sarasvatī*. *Oṁ Hām* obeisance to *Nandin*. *Oṁ Hām* obeisance to *Gaṅgā*. *Oṁ Hām* obeisance to *Lakṣmī*. *Oṁ Hām* obeisance to *Mahākāla*. *Oṁ Hām* obeisance to the *Astra*.

6. O *Hara*, these are to be worshipped at the door with bathing, unguent, etc. *Oṁ Hām* obeisance to *Brahman* the lord of *Vāstu* (plot). *Oṁ Hām* obeisance to the preceptors. *Oṁ Hām* obeisance to the *Ādhāraśakti*. *Oṁ Hām* obeisance to *Ananta*. *Oṁ Hām* obeisance to *Dharma*. *Oṁ Hām* obeisance to *Jñāna* (knowledge). *Oṁ Hām* obeisance to *Vairāgya* (non-attachment). *Oṁ Hām* obeisance to *Aiśvarya* (prosperity). *Oṁ Hām* obeisance to *Adharma* (Evil). *Oṁ Hām* obeisance to *Ajñāna* (ignorance). *Oṁ Hām* obeisance to *Avairāgya* (attachment). *Oṁ Hām* obeisance to *Anaiśvarya* (Poverty). *Oṁ Hām* obeisance to *Ūrdhvacchandas* (the metre lifted up). *Oṁ Hām* obeisance to *Adhaścchandas* (the metre shelved down). *Oṁ Hām* obeisance to *Padma*. *Oṁ Hām* obeisance to the *Karṇikā* (pericarp). *Oṁ Hām* obeisance to *Vāmā*. *Oṁ Hām* obeisance to *Jyeṣṭhā*. *Oṁ Hām* obeisance to *Raudrā*. *Oṁ Hām* obeisance to *Kālī*. *Oṁ Hām* obeisance to *Kalavikariṇī*. *Oṁ Hām* obeisance to *Balapramathinī*. *Oṁ Hām* obeisance to *Sarvabhūta*-

damanī (suppressor of all living beings). *Oṁ Hām* obeisance to *Manonmanī*. *Oṁ Hām* obeisance to the three *maṇḍalas*. *Oṁ Hām Hauṁ Ham* obeisance to the idol of Śiva. *Oṁ Hām* obeisance to the presiding deity of learning. *Oṁ Hām Hīṁ Hauṁ* obeisance to Śivā. *Oṁ Hām* obeisance to the heart. *Oṁ Hīm* obeisance to the head. *Oṁ Hūm* obeisance to the tuft. *Oṁ Haim* obeisance to the *Kavaca*. *Oṁ Haum* obeisance to the three eyes. *Oṁ Haḥ* obeisance to the *Astra*. *Oṁ* obeisance to the *Sadyojāta*.

7. *Oṁ Hām* obeisance to *Siddhi*. *Oṁ Hām* obeisance to the *Ṛddhi* (prosperity). *Oṁ Hām* obeisance to *Vidyutā*.[1] *Oṁ Hām* obeisance to *Lakṣmī*. *Oṁ Hām* obeisance to *Bodhā*.[2] *Oṁ Hām* obeisance to *Kālī*.[3] *Oṁ Hām* obeisance to *Svadhā*. *Oṁ Hām* obeisance to *Prabhā*.[4]

8. These are the eight *Kalās* (digits) of *Satya* situated in the east, etc.

9. *Oṁ Hām* obeisance to *Vāmadeva*. *Oṁ Hām* obeisance to *Rajas*. *Oṁ Hām* obeisance to *Rakṣā*.[5] *Oṁ Hām* obeisance to *Rati*. *Oṁ Hām* obeisance to *Kanyā*.[6] *Oṁ Hām* obeisance to *Kāmā*.[7] *Oṁ Hām* obeisance to *Jñānī*.[8] *Oṁ Hām* obeisance to *Kriyā*. *Oṁ Hām* obeisance to *Vṛddhi*.[9] *Oṁ Hām* obeisance to *Kāryā*.[10] *Oṁ Hām* obeisance to *Rātri*.[11] *Oṁ Hām* obeisance to *Bhrāmī*.[12] *Oṁ Hām* obeisance to *Mohinī*.[13] *Oṁ Hām* obeisance to *Tvarā* (Hurry).

O *Vṛṣadhvaja*, the *Kalās* of *Vāmadeva* are to be known as thirteen.

10. *Oṁ Hām* obeisance to *Tatpuruṣa*. *Oṁ Hām* obeisance to *Vṛtti*.[14] *Oṁ Hām* obeisance to *Pratiṣṭhā*.[15] *Oṁ Hām* obeisance to

1. of lightning-colour.
2. Having knowledge.
3. The black one.
4. Lustre.
5. Security.
6. Virgin.
7. The loving one
8. The knowing one.
9. Prosperity.
10. That which is to be done.
11. Night.
12. Roaming.
13. Enchanting.
14. Existence.
15. Position.

Vidyā.[1] *Oṁ Hām* obeisance to *Śānti.*[2] O ! *Vṛṣabhadhvaja*, the *Kalās* of *Tatpuruṣa* are to be known as four.

11. *Oṁ Hām* obeisance to *Aghora*[3]. *Oṁ Hām* obeisance to *Umā.*[4] *Oṁ Hām* obeisance to *Kṣamā.*[5] *Oṁ Hām* obeisance to *Nidrā* (sleep). *Oṁ Hām* obeisance to *Vyādhi* (sickness). *Oṁ Hām* obeisance to *Kṣudhā* (hunger). *Oṁ Hām* obeisance to *Tṛṣṇā* (thirst). These six are the terrific *Kalās* of *Aghora*, O Hara.

12. *Oṁ Hām* obeisance to *Īśāna. Oṁ Hām* obeisance to *Samiti* (Association). *Oṁ Hām* obeisance to *Aṅgadā.*[6] *Oṁ Hām* obeisance to *Kṛṣṇā.*[7] *Oṁ Hām* obeisance to *Marīcī.*[8] *Oṁ Hām* obeisance to *Jvālā* (flame). O *Vṛṣabhadhvaja*, know these five are *Kalās* of *Īśāna.*

13. *Oṁ Hām* obeisance to *Śiva's* followers. *Oṁ Hām* obeisance to Indra the lord of deities. *Oṁ Hām* obeisance to *Agni* the lord of brilliance. *Oṁ Hām* obeisance to *Yama* the lord of departed spirits. *Oṁ Hām* obeisance to *Nirṛti* the lord of demons. *Oṁ Hām* obeisance to *Varuṇa*[9] the lord of waters. *Oṁ Hām* obeisance to *Vāyu*[10] the Lord of vital airs. *Oṁ Hām* obeisance to *Soma*[11] the lord of eyes. *Oṁ Hām* obeisance to *Īśāna* the lord of all learning. *Oṁ Hām* obeisance to *Ananta* the lord of *Nāgas. Oṁ Hām* obeisance to *Brahman* the lord of all the worlds. *Oṁ Hām* obeisance to *Dhūlicaṇḍeśvara.*

1. Knowledge.
2. Peace.
3. Beautiful.
4. Tranquillity.
5. Forgiveness.
6. Having an armlet.
7. Black.
8. Ray of light.
9. A very important deity in the Ṛgveda where he is treated as the king of the universe. He is, in fact, a solar deity, or a personification of the sky. In later times, he became a minor deity, the Lord of water. (*ŚP* (*AITM*) p. 1598; *Liṅga* (*AITM*) p. 494 note 865; *CDHM* pp. 336-8).
10. A minor deity in the Ṛgveda. However, in the later days, he came to be regarded as the Lord of air and also bore the name Marut : whereas in the Ṛgveda, the Maruts enjoy a separate identity. (*ŚP* (*AITM*), p. 2119; *CDHM* pp. 343-4).
11. In the Ṛgveda, he is identical with Soma-juice and is praised in one whole *maṇḍala* (IX). However, in the same Ṛgveda he is sometime identified with the moon : whereas in later mythology he is completely identified with the moon. (*CDHM*, pp. 301-3).

14-19. The devotee shall duly perform *Āvāhana*, *Sthāpana*, *Sannidhāna*, *Sannirodha*, *Sakalīkaraṇa*, *Tattvanyāsa* (fixation of principles), showing of *Mudrās*, meditation, *Pādya*, *Ācamana*, *Arghya*, offerings of flowers and scented oils, *Udvartana*, *Snāna*, application of scented unguents offering of garments, ornaments etc. *Aṅganyāsa*, Incense, Lamp, food offerings, washing of hands, *Pādya*, *Arghya*, *Ācamana*, *Gandha*, betel leaves, musical play, dance offering of umbrella, *Mudrās*, *Rūpa*, *Dhyāna*, *Japa*, *Ekavadbhāva* (identification), etc. He shall dedicate *Japa* with the *Mūla-mantra*. O Rudra, I have, described the worship of *Maheśa*, that destroys all sins.

CHAPTER FORTYONE

Mantras to obtain Woman

Vāsudeva said :

1. *Oṁ* there is a *Gandharva Viśvāvasu*[1] the lord of girls. I am getting him for thy sake. After begetting a girl *Svāhā* unto *Viśvāvasu*. Acquisition of girls by the recitation of this *mantra*. Now I shall describe the Night-mare (*Kālarātri*).

2. *Oṁ* obeisance unto thee, Goddess *Ṛkṣakarṇi* (Bear-eared), having four arms, hair tied up, three-eyed one. *Kālarātri* feeding on fat and blood of men, giver of death to so-and so whom god of death has approached. *Huṁ Phaṭ*. Kill, kill; burn, burn; digest, digest flesh and blood. *Svāhā* unto thee, O *Ṛkṣapatni* (wife of the constellation 'Great Bear'). Neither the day of the lunar fortnight nor star nor fasting is being stipulated.

3. The devotee in all fury shall smear blood over his hands, lift the phallic emblem and strike the unbaked clay pot. *Oṁ* obeisance ! all round are these *Yantras* (mechanical devices) such as *Jambhanī* (the yawning), *Mohanī* (the

1. The legendary chief of the Gandharvas.

charming) and *Sarvaśatruvidāriṇī* (tearer of all enemies); protect me—so and so protect me—from all fear and harassments, *Svāhā* unto thee. When *Śukra* is destroyed after the *japa* has been performed twice, I shall explain further.

CHAPTER FORTYTWO

Pavitrāropaṇa of Śiva

Hari said :

1. I shall now describe the sacred rite of *Śiva*, named *Pavitrāropaṇa* (the rite of putting the sacred thread consisting of three yarns around the image). O *Hara*, only the preceptor, the aspirant or his son observing the vow shall perform the worship.

2. Otherwise *Vighneśa* removes the effects of a worship performed over a year. This worship has to be performed in the month of *Āṣāḍha*,[1] *Śrāvaṇa*,[2] *Māgha*[3] or *Bhādrapada*.[4]

3. In the *Kṛtayuga* the sacred thread is made of gold thread; In the *Tretāyuga* it is of silver; in *Dvāpara* it is of copper and in the *Kali* age it is of cotton thread. A virgin shall spin it and cut the ends.

4. Three yarns are to be twisted into one and such three new yarns constitute the *Pavitraka*. The knots shall be made with *Vāmadeva-mantra* and washed with *Satya mantra*.

5. The knots shall be purified with *Aghora-mantra* and tied with *Tatpuruṣa-mantra*. It shall be incensed with *Īśa-mantra*. The deities of the yarn are these.

6. *Oṅkāra*, *Candramas* (moon), *Vahni* (fire); *Brahmā*, *Nāga*, *Śikhidhvaja* (Lord *Subrahmaṇya*), *Ravi* (sun), *Viṣṇu* and *Śiva* are the deities of the yarn.

1. The fourth month in the Hindu lunar calendar. It generally heralds the beginning of rainy season. June-July.

2. The fifth month in the Hindu lunar calendar: July-August.

3. The eleventh month in the Hindu lunar calendar: January-February.

4. The sixth month in the Hindu lunar calendar: August-September.

7. O Rudra, each yarn shall be of length one hundred and eight, fifty or twentyfive *hastas*. There are ten knots.

8-9. Between two knots the intervals shall be of four *aṅgulas*.[1] The names of the knots are :—*Prakṛti*[2] *Pauruṣī*[3] *Virā*,[4] *Aparājitā*,[5] *Jayā*,[6] *Vijayā*,[7] *Rudrā*,[8] *Ajitā*,[9] *Manonmanī*,[10] and *Sarvamukhī*,[11] O *Sadāśivā*,[12] the inter-spaces of the knots can be two *aṅgulas* or one *aṅgula* too.

10. Either in the bright half or the other, the *Pavitraka* can be made on the seventh or thirteenth day. It shall be coloured with fragrant *Kuṅkuma* and other substances (saffron).

11. After bathing the *liṅga* (phallic emblem) with milk etc., it shall be worshipped with fragrant unguents, etc. The fragrant *Pavitraka* shall be offered to *Brahman* the *Ātman*.

12. In the north-east, fragrant flower shall be offered; in the east the pole-shaft and in the north the fruit of myrobalan shall be offered.

13. The devotee conversant with the use of *mantras* shall place clod of earth in the west, ashes in the south, *Aguru*[13] in the south-west with the *Śikhā mantra*.

14. In the north-west he shall place mustard with the *Kavaca-mantra*, O Vṛṣadhvaja. The house shall be encircled with the thread and *Gandhapavitraka* shall be offered.

15. The *Homa* shall be performed in the sacred fire and *Bhūtabali* (Oblation) shall be offered. O *Maheśvara*, lord of gods, thou art invited along with thy followers.

1. In ancient Indian metrics, one *aṅgula* is equal to a finger's breadth. (12 *aṅgulas* make a *vitasti* and 24, a *hasta*).
2. Nature.
3. Valorous.
4. Heroic.
5. That which cannot be conquered.
6. Victorious.
7. Ever-victorious
8. Fierce.
9. Unconquered.
10. Exciting.
11. All-faced.
12. Who is always benevolent.
13. Fragrant aloe.

16. "I shall worship thee in the morning. Be present here." With these words the devotee shall invite the deity in the night and send it by singing hymns.

17. The *mantra*-inspired *Pavitras* shall be placed near the deity. On the fourteenth day of the dark fortnight let him bathe the image of the Sun and worship *Rudra*.

18. Meditating on the self (*Ātman*) as *Viśvarūpa* (omniformed) stationed on the forehead let him worship it.

He shall dedicate incense to the deity, after sprinkling the same with *Astra mantra*, worshipping it with the *Hṛdaya-mantra*.

19. and inspiring it with the *Saṁhitā mantra*. He shall worship the *Śiva tattva* first, *Vidyātattva* next,

20. and then *Ātmatattva* and *Devaka*. *Oṁ Haum* obeisance to *Śivatattva*. *Oṁ Him* obeisance to *Vidyātattva*.

21. *Oṁ Hām*, obeisance to *Ātmatattva*; *Oṁ Hāṁ, Hiṁ, Hūṁ Kṣauṁ* obeisance to *Sarvatattva*.[1] *Oṁ* thou art identical with time (*Kālātmaka*). Whatever has been seen by thee in my rites performed wrongly, omitted, secretly offered,

22. O *Śambhu*, by thy will let it be holy.

23. *Oṁ* fulfil, fulfil the sacrificial rite. Obeisance unto thee who art the lord of its control, who art identical (*Sarvatattvātmaka*), with all principles and *Sarvakāraṇapālita* (protected by all reasons). *Oṁ Hām Hiṁ Hūṁ Haiṁ Hauṁ* obeisance to *Śiva*.

24. He who gives four *Pavitrakas* shall do so with this and the previous ones. After giving the *Pavitra* to the sacred fire, *Dakṣiṇā* shall be given to the preceptor.

25. The oblation shall then be given and the Brahmins fed. Finally *Caṇḍa* shall be discharged after worship.

1. The universal element.

CHAPTER FORTYTHREE

Pavitrāropaṇa of Viṣṇu

Hari said :

1. I shall expound the rite of *Pavitrāropaṇa* that yields worldly enjoyment and salvation. Formerly at the time of their war with the demons, Brahmā and others sought refuge in *Hari*.

2. *Viṣṇu* gave them a banner and a necklace. Hari told them that they can overcome the demons by seeing them (the banner and necklace).

3. When Viṣṇu said thus, the serpent, brother of *Vāsuki* said :

"O *Vṛṣadhvaja*, I plead thee for the *Pavitra*; grant me this boon.

4. Let this necklace given by Hari be famous under his name." When he said thus, he granted that boon.

5. During the rainy season if they do not worship by means of *Pavitrakas*, the full year's worship of those men shall be fruitless.

6. Hence, *Pavitrāropaṇa* is essential for all deities.

Beginning with the first day and ending with *Paurṇamāsī* (full moon), the *deities* shall be worshipped on their respective days.

7. O *Hara*, the worship of *Viṣṇu* shall be performed on the twelfth day, either during the bright half or during the dark half. During calamities, in *Dakṣiṇāyana*[1], during Solar or Lunar eclipses.

8 When any rite for prosperity is performed, at the advent of the preceptor, this *Pavitra* rite for Viṣṇu has to be performed. During the rainy season it is essential.

9. The sacred thread can be made of silk, cotton or linen. For Brahmins it can be made of *Kuśa* grass. For kings it can be of red silk.

1. It means a period of six months during which the sun moves from the north to the south, as seen in India. Roughly 15th July to 15th January.

10. For *Vaiśyas* it shall be woollen or silken; for *Śūdras* it shall be of fresh barks of trees.[1] O Īśvara, a sacred thread made of cotton or fibres of lotus stalk is praiseworthy in regard to all castes.

11. The thread spun by a brahmin lady and twisted three times three shall be used. The deities for the yarn are *Oṅkāra*,[2] *Śiva*, *Soma*, *Agni*, *Brahmā*, *Phaṇin*,[3] *Ravi*.[4]

12. *Vighneśa*[5] and *Viṣṇu*. The deities of the *Trisūtra* are *Brahmā*, *Viṣṇu* and *Rudra*.

13. The thread shall be placed in a vessel of gold, silver, copper, bamboo or earth (clay). The best vessel is sixtyfour *aṅgulas* large; the middling — half of it.

14. And the smallest still half of it. The best thread is one hundred and eight *aṅgulas* long; *Madhyama* — half of it and the smallest — still half as explained before.

15. The best knot shall be of the size of the thumb, the middling — of the size of the middle finger and the smallest — of the size of the little finger.

16. In length and in the size of the vessel this is the principle to be followed.

O Śiva, the devotee shall place the thread on the idol.

17. Such that it passes through the chest, navel and thigh and resets on the knee.

18. The length of the thread may be one thousand and eight *aṅgulas*. With four, thirtysix, twentyfour, or twelve knots.

19. The *Pavitraka* shall be dyed with Saffron turmeric or sandal paste.

The devotee who has observed fast shall consecrate the *Pavitra*.

20. He shall dedicate to *Saṅkarṣaṇa* in the east the twig and *Kuśa* grass placed in a vessel made of banyan tree leaves in all the eight quarters.

1. Variant: *Śaṇa-valkajam*.
2. Here we find deification of *Om*.
3. Ananta or Śeṣa-nāga.
4. The sun.
5. Gaṇeśa.

21-22. The same dyed with yellow pigment and saffron shall be dedicated to *Pradyumna* in the south. The devotee who is about to wage war shall for the sake of good results dedicate the *Pavitra* dyed with sandal, blue ashes, gingelly seeds and rice grains in a mixture, to *Aniruddha* in the west. He shall assign in the south-east and other directions the deities *Śri*, etc.

23. The devotee shall inspire the *Pavitra* with *Vāsudeva-mantra* once, look at it and worship again. He shall then cover it with a cloth carefully.

24. And place it in front of the deity or in front of the mystic diagram of the idol. As before, let him place it in the west-south and north.

25. In order of *Brāhmaṇa*, etc., and worship the pitcher. After making a *Maṇḍala* with the *Astra-mantra*, let him offer the oblation (*Naivedya*).

26-27. After finishing the rite of *Adhivāsa*[1] to the *Pavitra*, he shall encircle the altar, the soul with *Kalaśa* (pitcher), sacrificial pit, *Vimāna* (the resting place of idols), *maṇḍapa* (the raised platform) and the house with three or nine (threads). He shall take one thread and place it on the head of the deity.

28. After that let him perform the worship of *Maheśvara* and recite this *mantra*—"O lord of gods *Parameśvara* ! Thou hast been invoked for the worship.

29. I shall worship thee in the morning. Please be present near the materials got ready." The *Adhivāsa* rite shall thus be performed for one night or three nights.

30. He shall be awake throughout the night and in the morning after worshipping *Keśava*[2] he shall put the three *Pavitrakas*—the best, the middling and the smallest in order.

31. He shall show incense and inspire with *mantras*.

Reciting the names of the knots he shall worship with flowers and other things.

32. It shall again be worshipped with *Gāyatri* and then dedicated to the deity. Let the end of this sacred thread be held by his sons, wife, etc.

1. Application of scents. *Adhivāsa* or *Adhivāsana* also means preliminary consecration of *om* image, making a divinity assume its abode in an image.

2. Viṣṇu.

33. "I am holding in front of you this beautiful *Pavitraka* with pure knots, destructive of the greatest iniquity, dispelling all sins."

34. (Having said so) the devotee shall place the three threads (best, middling and the smallest) in order. "This is the pure refulgence of *Viṣṇu* that destroys all sins.

35. In order to acquire virtue, love and wealth I wear this round my neck."

After worshipping the garland of wild flowers he shall dedicate it with its own *mantra*.

36. After making various kinds of food-offerings, let him make oblations and offerings of flowers.

37. In a sacrificial pit twelve *aṅgulas* in length let him worship fire and offer a *Pavitra* one hundred and eight *aṅgulas* long. Let him first offer *Arghya* to the Sun and then a *Pavitra*.

38. Then O *Hara*, let him worship *Viṣvaksena* and the preceptor with *Arghya*, etc. Then let him recite this *mantra* in front of the deity, standing with the joined palms.

39. O Sureśvara,[1] whether I know it completely or I am ignorant, I have completed the worship. Due to thy grace let it be fulfilled.

40. (As if it was) with jewels, corals and garlands of *Mandāra*[2] flowers, O *Garuḍadhvaja*,[3] let this *Sāṁvatsarī* (Annual) worship be dedicated unto thee.

41. Just as thou wearest the *Vanamālā* and *Kaustubha* always on thy chest, so also be pleased to wear this *Pavitra* — the garland of threads too.

42. After worshipping and reciting the prayer thus, let him feed the brahmins and give them *Dakṣiṇās*[4] and send them off in the evening.

43. The next day he shall say thus :— "O *Pavitraka*, after finishing the *Sāṁvatsarī Pūjā* thou art discharged. Be pleased to go now to the world of Viṣṇu."

1. Lord of the deities.
2. Perhaps calotropis gigantea or C. procera *VN*, p. 32.
3. (Viṣṇu) in whose banner is the image of Garuḍa.
4. An offering, as a fee or remuneration, to the preceptor or to the brāhmaṇas.

CHAPTER FORTYFOUR

(*Contemplation of Brahman or Viṣṇu's form*)

Hari said :

1. After worshipping with *Pavitra*, etc. if the devotee meditates deeply on *Brahman* he shall become identical with *Hari*. I shall now describe the meditation on *Brahman* destructive of the machine of *Māyā* (Illusion).

2. The intelligent shall restrict speech with the mind and the mind in the soul which is of the form of pure knowledge. The intellect shall be confined to the *Mahat* (the great principle) if one wishes for pure knowledge in the soul.

3-5. *Samādhi*[1] or *Spiritual Trance* is the realisation I am *Brahman*—the *Brahman* that is shorn of body, sense organs, mind, intellect, the vital airs, the ego, the subtle particles of the five elements, the three *Guṇas*, birth and feeding; the *Brahman* that is self-luminous, devoid of forms, beginningless and of the nature of perpetual Bliss; the *Brahman* that is eternal, pure, conscious, flourishing, true, blissful, without a second (real entity). It is the fourth imperishable *Brahman* the supreme position. (Fourth—beyond the trinity and the three *Guṇas*).

6. Know the Soul to be like a charioteer, the body is the chariot; know the intellect to be the driver and mind the rein; the sense-organs are the horses; the objects are subsidiary to senses.

7-9. The learned speak of the soul in conjunction with sense-organs and the mind as the *Bhoktṛ* (Enjoyer of worldly experience). He who is endowed with the vehicle of *Vijñāna* (Real perception) and a full concentrated mind attains that supreme position. He is not born again. With real knowledge as the charioteer and mind as the rein the soul crosses the Divine *Gaṅgā*. That is the supreme position of Viṣṇu. Non-violence etc. is called *Yama* (Restraint). Purity, etc. is called *Niyama* (religious ritual).

1. *Samādhi* means perfect absorption of thought into one subject of meditation, e.g. the supreme spirit.

10. The *Yogic* pastures of *Padma* (squatting posture) etc. are called *Āsanas*. Full control over the breath is called *Prāṇāyāma.*

The withdrawal (of the senses from the objects) is called *Jaya*; *Dhyāna* is the meditation on the Lord.

11. The stabilisation of the mind is *Dhāraṇā* and *Samādhi* is the existence in *Brahman.* (i.e. Realisation that I am Brahman). If at first, it is not possible to concentrate the mind, then the devotee shall meditate on an idol.

12. In the middle of the pericarp of the lotus of the heart the form of Viṣṇu bearing *Śaṅkha*, *Cakra* and *Gadā* shall be meditated upon endowed with *Śrīvatsa* (the indelible congenital mark) and the gem *Kaustubha*, refulgent with the glow of the garland of forest flowers.

13. He is the supreme Lord the eternal, the pure, the intelligent and known as Truth and Bliss. The devotee shall always be conscious—"I am the *Ātman*, the supreme *Brahman*, the great Light."

14. Viṣṇu of twenty-four different forms[1] (incarnations) is seated on the *Śālagrāma* stone. Hari can also be meditated upon or worshipped as staying in Dvārakā,[2] etc.

15. The devotee shall acquire all desires and become *Deva* moving about in *Vimāna* (aerial chariot). Contemplating on the idol, singing prayers and reciting the names, the devotee, free from desires, shall attain salvation.

1. A stone held sacred and worshipped by the Vaiṣṇavas, because its spirals are supposed to contain or to be typical of Viṣṇu. It is an ammonite found in the river Gaṇḍaka, and is valued more or less highly according to the number of its spirals and perforations. (*CDHM* p. 275.)

2. Kṛṣṇa's capital in Gujrat sea-coast after the Yādavas migrated there from North India. There is a modern city of this name in Gujrat.

CHAPTER FORTYFIVE

Characteristics of Śālagrāma

Hari said :

1. Relevent to the context I shall explain the characteristics of *Śālagrāma* stone a touch of which destroys the sins of a crore of births.

2. *Gadādhara* (Viṣṇu) bearing *Śaṅkha, Cakra, Gadā* and *Padma* is called *Keśava*. (In this and those that follow, the order of the weapons shall be preserved for the success of meditation]. The supreme lord holding *Abja* (Padma), *Kaumodakī* (gadā) *Cakra* and *Śaṅkha* is *Nārāyaṇa*.

3. *Śrīgadādhara* (Viṣṇu) bearing *Cakra, Śaṅkha, Abja and Gadā* is *Mādhava Gadādhara* (Viṣṇu). He can be worshiped as *Govinda* wearing *Gadā, Abja, Śaṅkha* and *Cakra*.

4. Obeisance unto thee of the form of Viṣṇu bearing *Padma, Śaṅkha, Cakra* and *Gadā*. Obeisance to *Madhusūdana mūrti* (form bearing *Śaṅkha, Abja, Gadā* and *Cakra*.

5. Obeisance unto *Traivikrama* (the incarnation *Vāmana* who took three steps) bearing *Gadā, Cakra, Śaṅkha* and *Abja*. Obeisance unto *Vāmana mūrti*, bearing *Cakra, Kaumodakī, Padma* and *Śaṅkha*.

6. Obeisance unto *Śrīdhara-mūrti* bearing *Cakra, Abja, Śaṅkha* and *Gadā*. Obeisance unto *Hṛṣikeśa* bearing *Abja, Gadā* and *Śaṅkha* and *Cakra*.

7. Obeisance unto thee in the form of *Padmanābha*[1] bearing *Abja, Cakra, Gadā* and *Śaṅkha*. O *Dāmodara*,[2] obeisance, obeisance unto thee bearing *Śaṅkha, Cakra, Gadā* and *Padma*.

8. Obeisance unto *Vāsudeva* bearing *Cakra, Śaṅkha, Gadā* and *Abja*. Obeisance unto *Saṅkarṣaṇa* bearing *Śaṅkha, Abja, Cakra* and *Gadā*.

1. Name of Viṣṇu, literally meaning 'from whose navel comes out a lotus'.

2. Name of Viṣṇu. more properly of Kṛṣṇa because his foster mother tried to tie him up with a rope (*dāman*) round his belly (*udara*). (*CDHM* p. 80.)

9. Obeisance to *Pradyumna-mūrti* bearing *Śaṅkha, Gadā, Abja* and *Cakra*. Obeisance unto *Aniruddha* bearing *Gadā, Śaṅkha, Abja* and *Cakra*.

10. Obeisance to *Puruṣottama-mūrti* bearing *Abja, Śaṅkha, Gadā* and *Cakra*. Obeisance unto thee in the form of *Adhokṣaja*[1] bearing *Gadā, Śaṅkha, Cakra* and *Padma*.

11. Obeisance unto *Nṛsiṁha-mūrti* bearing *Padma, Gadā, Śaṅkha* and *Cakra*. Obeisance to *Acyuta-mūrti*[2] bearing *Padma, Cakra, Śaṅkha* and *Gadā*.

12. I invoke *Janārdana*[3] here bearing *Śaṅkha, Cakra, Abja* and *Gadā*. Obeisance, obeisance unto thee, O *Upendra*[4] having *Gadā, Cakra, Padma* and *Śaṅkha*.

13. Obeisance unto *Hari-mūrti*[5] bearing *Cakra, Abja, Gadā* and *Śaṅkha*. Obeisance unto *Śrikṛṣṇa-mūrti* bearing *Gadā, Abja, Cakra* and *Śaṅkha*.

14. The *Śālagrāma* stone white in colour that has two ring-like marks at the entrance is called *Vāsudeva*. Let Lord Viṣṇu presiding over it protect you all.

15. The stone red in colour, having the mark of a lotus in front, with two clearly defined ring-like marks, is called *Saṅkarṣaṇa*. If it is yellow in colour with ringlike marks not clearly defined it is called *Pradyumna*.

16-17. *Aniruddha* stone is blue in colour; it has a long aperture at the top, it has three lines at the lateral aperture. It is circular in shape. The *Nārāyaṇa* stone is black in colour with the form of *Gadā* in the middle, with the *Cakra* lines at the

1. Name of Viṣṇu.

2. Unfallen; a name of Viṣṇu or Kṛṣṇa. It has been variously interpreted as signifying "he who does not perish with created things", in the Mahābhārata as "he who is not distinct from final emancipation", and in the Skanda Purāṇa as "he who never declines (or varies) from his proper nature". It can also mean 'one who is firm, one who does not yield to passions. (*CDHM* p. 2; *SSED* p. 7).

3. The adored of mankind; A name of Kṛṣṇa or Viṣṇu; but other derivations are offered, as 'extirpator of the wicked, by Śaṅkarācārya. (*CDHM* p. 133).

4. Name of Viṣṇu as the younger brother of Indra in his fifth or dwarf incarnation. (*SSED* p. 116.)

5. A name of Viṣṇu.

centre that is lifted up. The stone called *Nṛsiṁha* has a stout chest and three dots. It is tawny in colour. May it protect us.

18. Or it may have five dots. Only *Brahmacārins* (students) shall worship it. The *Śālagrāma* with two uneven ring-like marks is called *Varāhaśaktiliṅga.*[1] May it protect us.

19. The *Kūrma mūrti*[2] is blue in colour. It has three lines. It is stout and has dots. May the stone called *Kṛṣṇa* depressed at the back and having circular curb protect you.

20. Let the *Śrīdhara* stone marked with five lines, a garland of forest flowers and club protect us. *Vāmana* stone is circular and short. *Sureśvara* stone has a ringlike mark on the leftside.

21. The *Anantaka* stone is of various colours and forms with serpentine marks. The *Dāmodara* stone is stout and of blue colour. In its middle there is a ring-like mark of deep blue colour.

22. The *Brahmā* stone is of crimson colour. It has a small aperture. May it protect you. It has a long line and a ringlike mark and a large lotus in the aperture.

23. *Hayagrīva* stone has a big aperture, a stout ring-like mark and dark spots. That which has five lines in the form of a goad is *Kaustubha* stone.

24. *Vaikuṇṭha*[3] stone is lustrous like a precious gem. It has a single ringlike mark and a lotus. It is dark in colour. The Matsya[4] stone is of great length in the form of a lotus with lines at the aperture. May it protect you.

25. May the *Trivikrama*[5] stone with ringlike mark on the left and lines on the right and dark in colour protect you. Obeisance unto the lord with *Gadā* staying in *Śālagrāma* in *Dvārakā*.

26-27. May the *Lakṣmīnārāyaṇa*[6] stone protect us — the stone that has one aperture with four ringlike marks, which

1. The indicator of the power of the Boar (incarnation of Viṇṣu).
2. Refers to the Tortoise-incarnation of Viṣṇu.
3. This is supposed to be a paradise where Viṣṇu resides. Sometimes Viṣṇu is also called *vaikuṇṭha*.
4. Refers to the Fish-incarnation of Viṣṇu.
5. Viṣṇu is called *Trivkrama* because he took three steps at the time of Ṭāmasa-incarnation.
6. Name of Viṣṇu. Literally Lakṣmī and Nārāyaṇa.

is bedecked with garland of forest flowers. It has golden lines in the form of cow's hoofs. It is of the shape of a *Kadamba*[1] flower. The *Sudarśana* class of stones is marked with a single characteristic.

28. May Viṣṇu presiding over it protect us. The *Lakṣmī nārāyaṇa* class is marked with two features, the *Trivikrama* class with three features. The *Caturvyūha*[2] class is marked with four features: the *Vāsudeva* class with five.

29. The *Pradyumna* class with six and the *Saṅkarṣaṇa* class with seven. The *Puruṣottama* class is marked with eight features, the *Navavyūha*[3] class with nine.

30. The *Daśāvatāra*[4] class is marked with ten features and *Aniruddha* with eleven. May it protect us. The *Dvādaśātmā*[5] class is marked with twelve features and the Ananta class with more features.

31. He who reads this prayer consisting of Viṣṇu's forms shall go to Heaven. *Brahmā* is four-headed. It (the image) has a staff and two waterpots.

32. That of *Maheśvara*[6] has five faces, ten hands and the emblem of a bull. It has suitable weapons and the attendants *Gaurī*, *Caṇḍikā*, *sarasvatī*,

33. And *Mahālakṣmī*. The idol of the Sun has a lotus in the hand. The *Gaṇādhipa*[7] has the face of an elephant. *Skanda* has six faces.

34. These images of the different characteristic features shall be duly worshipped and installed in mansions after duly consecrating the plot of land. Then the owner of that building shall obtain Virtue, Wealth, fulfilment of desires, emancipation and other benefits.

1. Anthocephalus indicus. (*GVDB* p. 70.)
2. It refers to the worship of Viṣṇu in four-fold forms of Vāsudeva, Saṅkarṣaṇa, Pradyumna and Aniruddha.
3. The worship of Viṣṇu in nine forms. They are, according to Garuḍa Purāṇa—Vāsudeva. Balarāma, Kāma (Pradyumna), Aniruddha, Nārāyaṇa, Brahmā, Viṣṇu, Siṁha (Nṛsiṁha) and Varāha (*GPEA* pp. 332-3).
4. For ten incarnations of Viṣṇu see p. 2, fn. 6.
5. Twelve forms of Viṣṇu, to be worshippd in each month of the year, viz., Keśava, Nārāyaṇa, Mādhava, Vāsudeva, Trivikrama, Vāmana, Śrīdhara, Pradyumna, Hṛṣikeśa, Padmanābha, Dāmodara and Aniruddha. (*GPEA*, p. 333).
6. Śiva.
7. Gaṇeśa.

CHAPTER FORTYSIX

Vāstu-pūjā[1]

Hari said :

1. I shall now briefly describe the *Vāstu Pūjā* (worship of the site) which destroys obstacles in the building of houses. Beginning from the north-east corner the worship shall extend to eighty-one feet.

2-3. The *Vāstu Puruṣa's*[2] head is worshipped in the north-east; the feet in the south-west and the hands in the south-east and north-west. In building temporary sheds, houses, cities, villages, bazaars, palaces, parks, forts, temples and monasteries the twentytwo deities shall be worshipped outside the plot and thirteen within.

4-7. The deities are :—*Īśa*, *Parjanya*,[3] *Jayanta*[4], *Kuliśāyudha* (Indra), *Sūrya*, *Satya*[5], *Bhṛgu*[6], *Ākāśa* (sky), *Vāyu*, *Pūṣan*, *Vitatha*[7], *Graha*[8], *Kṣetra*,[9] the two *Yamas*, *Gandharva*, *Bhṛgurāja*,

1. *Vāstu* means the site for building and also the house. Hence *Vāstu-pūjā* means the worship of the site chosen for building a temple or a house. It is treated as a must for the safe and sound construction.

2. *Vāstu-puruṣa* is the presiding deity of the site. According to a legend in the Matsya-purāṇa, Lord Śiva assumed a ferocious form to kill the demon, Andhaka. Drops of perspiration fell from Śiva's forehead and therefrom a fierce ghost came out. He was given a boon by Śiva. Thereafter he fell down covering the entire earth. Then he came to be worshipped. In Vedic literature, we come across Vāstoṣpati, the Protector of Houses. (*GPEA*, p. 395; *CDHM*, p. 342).

3. A Ṛgvedic deity. He is the deity of the rains or the rains personified.

4. Son of Indra.

5. Truth (personified).

6. A famous sage, progenitor of the Bhārgavas. The planet Venus is also called Bhṛgu.

7. Falsehood (personified).

8. The planet. It also means a class of demons supposed to seize upon children and produce convulsions. (*SSED* p. 195.)

9. Field or ground.

Mṛga,[1] *Pitṛgaṇa*, *Dauvārika*,[2] *Sugrīva*[3], *Puṣpadanta*,[4] *Gaṇādhipa*. *Asura*,[5] the two *Seṣapādas*, *Roga*,[6] *Ahimukhya*[7], *Bhallāṭa*, *Soma*, *Sarpa*[8], *Aditi*, *Diti*—these thirty two are to be worshipped outside. Listen to the four to be worshipped within.

8. In the four corners beginning with the north-east, the four *devas* stationed therein shall be worshipped by the scholarly devotee. They are *Āpa*, *Sāvitra*[9], *Jaya* and *Rudra*.

9. In the middle, *Brahmā* and his eight attendants all round shall be worshipped *from* the east. Their names are as follows :—

10. *Aryaman*[10], *Savitṛ*, *Vivasvān*[11], *Vibudhādhipa*[12], *Mitra*, *Rājayaṣkmā*[13], *Pṛthvīdhara*.

11. And the eighth *Āpavatsa*. These are to be placed all round *Brahmā*. The group of deities beginning with north-east is called *Durga*.

12. And that beginning with south-east is called *Durdhara*. These *Vāstudevas*—*Aditi*, *Himavanta*[14], *Jayanta*,

13. *Nāyikā*, *Kālikā*, *Śakra*[15], and *Gandharvaga* shall first be worshipped and then only the work of building houses and palaces should be commenced.

14. The image of *Bṛhaspati*[16] shall be installed in front. The kitchen shall be made in the south-east with a ventilator

1. The constellation Mṛgaśiras.
2. A door-keeper.
3. The monkey-chief mentioned in the Rāmāyaṇa. He helped Rāma in his war against Rāvaṇa. (*CDHM*, p. 306).
4. One of the attendants of Śiva: Puṣpadanta is also the name of one of the guardian elephants.
5. *Asura* generally means a demon. However, it is also the name of Rāhu.
6. Disease (personified).
7. Reference may be to Vāsuki.
8. Generally means a serpent.
9. The sun.
10. One of the Ādityas.
11. The sun.
12. Indra.
13. The disease called consumption.
14. Himālaya.
15. Indra.
16. Bṛhaspati is a Ṛgvedic deity. He is also called Brahmaṇaspati. He is invoked as the deity of the prayers. He is as well called *Purohita*. In

just enough to let a monkey pass through. In the east, the sacrificial altar shall be erected.

15. The room for storing scents and flowers shall be made in the north-east paved with slabs. The store-room shall be made in the north and the cowshed in the north-west.

16. The water-shed (Bath room ?) having windows is to be made in the west. The room for storing sacrificial twigs, *Kuśa*-grass, fuel, weapons, etc. shall be constructed in the south-west.

17. The guest-room shall be in the south. It shall be furnished with beds, seats, sandals, water pots, fire, lamps, etc. It shall be beautifully laid out and servants shall be employed to look to their comfort.

18. Other houses shall be made fully bedecked with flowers of five colours, plantain trees, water sheds, etc.

19. An outer wall shall be erected five *hastas* (cubits) high. Thus *Viṣṇu-Āśrama* shall be made with gardens and parks.

20. In the case of palaces, etc., the *Vāstu* of sixty-four feet is to be worshipped. In the middle, *Brahmā* occupies four feet and *Aryaman*, etc., are to have two feet each.

21. In the hypoteunse *Śikhī*[1] etc, are the Deities. Along with them the other deities shall have two feet each.

22. Thus it has been explained how the deities come to occupy sixty-four feet. *Carakī*, *Vidārī*, *Pūtanā*[2] and *Pāparākṣasī*,

23. Shall be worshipped in the north-east and other corners. *Hetuka* and others are to be adored outside—*Hetuka*, *Tripurānta*, *Agni Vetālaka*, *Yama*,

24. *Agnijihva*, *Kālaka*, *Karāla*, and *Ekapādaka*. In the north-east *Bhīmarūpa* (Terrific in appearances) is to be worshipped; in *Pātāla Pretanāyaka*.

later mythology he is referred to more as the preceptor of the deities than as a deity. It is also the name of the planet Jupiter. (*CDHM*, pp. 63-4).

1. Fire.

2. A demoness who was killed by Kṛṣṇa when he was still a child.

25. And in the sky *Gandhamālin*. Then Kṣetrapālas are to be worshipped. The length divided by the width—that number is considered to be the *Rāśi*[1] of the *Vāstu*.

26. Divided by eight, the remainder is called *Āya*. Multiply it by eight and divide by seven. (*Ṛkṣabhāga*).

27-28. Consider what remains as *Ṛkṣa*. Multiply this by four. Then divide by nine. What remains is *Vyaya* according to Devala[2]. If it is multiplied by eight it shall be *Piṇḍa*.[3] Divide it by sixty.

29. What remains is *Jīva*. The quotient is *Maraṇa* (death). No one shall build houses behind the *Vāstu*. They are to be built inside the *Vāstu*.

30. He shall sleep on his left side. No hesitation in this matter. For persons born in the zodiacal sign of *Siṁha*,[4] *Kanyā*,[5] and *Tulā*[6] the main door is good if made in the north.

31. For the persons born of Vṛścika,[7] etc. the door is advised in the east, south and west in order. The door shall have two units of length and one unit of width. There must be eight doors at least in a house.

32. If the bed is slanting to the south, death due to a serpent, issuelessness and impotency may result.

33. If it is slanting to the south-east, imprisonment is the result, if towards north-west, birth of a son and satisfaction; if it is to the north, harassment by the king, if towards west, sickness.

34-35. If the door is in the north then there is fear from king, death of infants, issuelessness, enmity, wealth, loss of wealth, faults, death of son. I shall now say about the eastern doors. Fear from fire, plenty of daughters, wealth and honour,

36. Death of king, sickness, these are the results if the door is in the east. In the north-east, etc., let it be in the east; in the south-east, etc., let it be in the south.

1. The numbers or figures put down for any arithmetical operation such as adding, multiplying, etc. (*SSED*, p. 469).
2. There are several men of this name. One was an astronomer. (*CDHM* p. 85).
3. Sum, total amount in arithmetic. (*SSED* p. 336.)
4. Leo.
5. Virgo.
6. Libra.
7. Scorpio.

37. In the south-west, etc. let it be in the west; in the north-west, etc. let it be in the north. When divided by eight, these are the results of doors.

38. If *Aśvattha,*[1] *Plakṣa,*[2] *Nyagrodha*[3] and *Udumbara*[4] are planted in the east and *Śālmali*[5] (Silk cotton tree) in the north-east and they are worshipped, it shall be beneficent to the house and palace.

CHAPTER FORTYSEVEN

Characteristics of Palaces

Sūta said :

1-2. I shall now describe the characteristic features of palaces. O Śaunaka, listen to it. The plot shall be divided into sixty-four squares with the quarters distinctly marked. The doors are twelve in all. Fortyeight divisions are to be set apart for walls.

3. The *Jaṅghā* (calf), i.e. the height of the plinth, shall be equal to the length of the platform above the ground and beyond that it shall be twice that. The *Śukāṅghri,* the height of the inner vault, shall be as large as its base.

4. The depressions on either side shall measure a third or a fifth of the chord of the inner vault, rising upto the half of the entire height of the pinnacle.

5. The whole height of the pinnacle shall be divided into four parts. The super-structure is over the third part and the ornamental figure edging the entire height shall be on the fourth part.

1. Ficus religiosa. (*GVDB*, p. 29.)
2. Ficus Lacor. (*GVDB*, p. 264.)
3. Ficus bengalensis. (*GVDB*, p. 356.)
4. Ficus racemosa. (*GVDB*, p. 51.)
5. Salmalia malabarica. Bombax ceiba. (*GVDB*, p. 397.)

6-7. Or let the *Vāstu* be divided into sixteen equal parts and in the middle the inner vault be constructed over four parts. Over the remaining twelve parts, the wall shall be raised with the height well-proportioned.

8. The height of the pinnacle is twice the height of the wall. The circular verandah shall be one-fourth of the height of the pinnacle in width.

9-10. The outlets on the four sides shall be equal to a fifth of the vault in breadth. The *Mukhamaṇḍapa* or frontal edifice (protruding promontory) shall be equal to the inner vault from above.

11. This is the general feature of a palace (or a temple). I shall now mention the dimensions based on the size of the idol. The pedestal shall be as large as the idol.

12. O Śaunaka, the sanctum sanctorum shall be twice that all round. The wall shall be of the same size and the calf (the height of the plinth) shall be half of it.

13-14. The pinnacle is twice the calf, O Śaunaka; the vault covers the entire space occupied by the pedestal; the depressions and outlets as before. This is called *Liṅga-Māna* (dimensions in accordance with the size of the idol). I shall now mention *Dvāra-Māna* (where the dimensions are in accordance with the size of door-frames).

15. Multiply the total length upto the tip of the hand (of the idol) by four; and one-eighth of the same shall be the width of the door. If one wishes, it shall be twice that also.

16. Upto the half, the door is as usual and above that it contains holes. A part of the door is taken by the wall.

17. The plinth is equal to its width (width of the door); the pinnacle is twice that; the vault shall be made, as before, as high as the outlet.

18-19. I have described the *maṇḍapa-māna* (measurement is accordance with the platform). I shall mention another type. The space occupied by the idols shall be multiplied by twelve which gives the exterior dimensions. The inner rim shall be one fourth in area, all round the temple on the inner side.

20. The sanctum sanctorum shall be twice the area of

the rim. The same is the height of the wall and the pinnacle is twice.

21-22. I shall mention the origin and dimensions of temples. There are five types of temples: 1) *Vairāja*, 2) *Puṣpaka*, 3) *Kailāsa*, 4) *Mālikā*, 5) *Triviṣṭapa*. They are the sources (models) for all other temples. The first one is square in shape; the second is rectangular.

23. The third is circular; the fourth is oval and the fifth is octagonal in shape. All beautiful temples are built on the model of these). They are forty-five in all.

24-27. Temples built on the model of *Vairāja* are square in shape and consist of nine sorts, *viz.*, *Meru*, *Mandara*, *Vimāna*, *Bhadraka*, *Sarvatobhadra*, *Rucaka*, *Nandana*, *Nandivardhana* and *Śrīvatsa*. Temples built on the model of *Puṣpaka* and rectangular in shape are nine :—*Valabhi*, *Gṛharāja*, *Śālāgṛha*, *Mandira*, *Vimāna*, *Brahmamandira*, *Bhavana*, *Uttambha* and *Śibikāveśma*.

28-30. Temples built on the model of *Kailāśa*, circular in shape, are nine: viz. *Valaya*, *Dundubhi*, *Padma*, *Mahāpadma*, *Mukulī*, *Uṣṇīṣi*, *Śaṅkha*, *Kalaśa* and *Guvāvṛkṣa*. Temples built on the model of *Maṇikā Mālikā*, oval or globular in shape, are nine :—*Gaja*, *Vṛṣabha*, *Haṁsa*, *Garuḍa*, *Siṁha*, *Bhūmukha*, *Bhūdhara*, *Srījaya* and *Pṛthivīdhara*.

31-33. Temples built on the model of *Triviṣṭapa*, octagonal in shape, are nine:—viz. *Vajra*, *Cakra*, *Muṣṭika*, *Babhru*, *Vakra*, *Svastikabhaṅga*, *Gadā*, *Śrīvṛkṣa* and *Vijaya*. *Maṇḍapas*[1] are made in the forms of Triangles, Lotus, Crescent, Quadrilateral and Bi-octagonal. If the *maṇḍapa* is triangular, the owner shall win a kingdom; if lotus-shaped, wealth; if crescent, longevity;

34. Quadrilateral, birth of a son and the bi-octagonal, women and prosperity. The banner shall be fixed, *Garbha-gṛha* or sanctum sanctorum shall be made at the entrance.

35. *Maṇḍapas* equal in number and befitting the quality shall be made. *Bhadra* shall be made one-fourth of the *maṇḍapa*.

36-37. It can have windows or not. In some places the *maṇḍapas* are made equal to one and a half times or twice the

1. The halls.

length of the wall. Ornamental cornices shall be made on temples,

38-39. With spaces of unequal length of various shapes in between and lines of different lengths. The temple *Meru* is the best, a base of four doors bedecked with four *maṇḍapas* and a hundred pinnacles or turrets. Cupolas can be constructed over them with three *Bhadras* (arches).

40. In structure, dimensions and shapes they differ variously. There are many with bases and some with no bases.

41-42. Due to the difference in images too, the temples differ. Due to the difference in consecration, structure, special characteristics of the deities, etc., there are varieties of temples. With regard to deities (images) of self-origin (not man-made) there is no rule governing the construction of temples.

43-44. They shall be made according to the dimensions set forth above. They can be square, rectangular, or quadrilateral with long terraces, turrets, etc. In front, small *maṇḍapas* shall be made for the vehicles of the deities.

45-46. Dance-halls (for religious dances) shall be constructed in the proximity of the main door of the temple. In the temples *Dvārapālas* (watch and ward) shall be installed collectively or separately. The rest-houses of those who serve in the temple are to be made a little away from the temple.

47. Covered *hedges* shall be made containing fruits and flowers and profusely watered. The devotee shall worship the deities to be installed in the temples. *Vāsudeva* is the god of all. Persons who *build* his temples enjoy everything.

CHAPTER FORTYEIGHT

Installation of idols

Sūta said :

1. I shall now succinctly explain the mode of installation of the idols of deities. On an auspicious day, the preceptor shall perform the installation rites.

2-3. Along with five or more *Ṛtviks* (sacrificial priests) a brahmin belonging to the central region shall be chosen as the main priest in accordance with the injunctions in his branch of Veda or simply by reciting the *Praṇava*. They must be received with the offerings of *Pādya* and *Arghya*, *mudrikās*, garments, unguents, flowers, sandal pastes, etc.

4. The preceptor shall begin the rite after performing *mantra-nyāsa*. *A maṇḍapa* shall be made ten *hastas* square in front of the temple.

5. Some make *maṇḍapas* twelve cubits square. It must have sixteen pillars. In the middle there shall be the altar four cubits square. There shall be eight flags fitted to the pillars.

6-7. Sand taken from the confluence of two rivers shall be strewn over the altar. The sacrificial pits shall be made of various shapes—square, segment-shaped (bow-like), circular or in the form of a lotus. Or all of them shall be square. They must be five in all.

8. With the preliminary *Śānti rite* (for peaceful completion of the main task) and for the achievement of all desires, the priest shall begin the *homa* (ghee-offering in the fire) at the head of the image.

9-10. Some desire that this be performed in the north-east after scrubbing the floor and applying a coat of cowdung paste. Four main doors shall be made. For festoons, poles of *Nyagrodha*, *Udumbara*, *Aśvattha*, *Bilva*,[1] *Palāśa*[2] and *Khadira* tree branches, five cubits long, shall be fixed and decorated with coloured cloths and flowers.

11. In the four main quarters four pits shall be made each a cubit deep. In the eastern gate the figure of the lion shall be installed; that of *Uccaiśśravas* (the divine horse) in the south.

12. That of a bull in the west and that of divine tiger in the north. The installation of lion shall be with the Vedic *mantra*—*Agnimīle*[3], etc.

1. Aegle marmelos. (*GVDB*, p. 274.)
2. Butea monosperma. (*GVDB*, p. 241.)
3. RV. 1.1.1.

13. The installation of the horse in the south, shall be with the *mantra—Iṣe tvā*,[1] etc., the installation of the bull in the west shall be with the *mantra—Agna Āyāhi*[2], etc.

14. And the installation of the celestial tiger in the north shall be with the *mantra—Śanno Devī*[3], etc. The flag in the east is cloud-coloured, that in the south-east is smoke-coloured.

15. That in the south is dark in colour, that in the south-west is dark-blue a greyish flag is to be hoisted in the west; that in the north-west shall be yellow.

16. The flag in the north is red-coloured and that in the north-east is white. In the middle, a flag of various colours shall be hoisted. The flag in the east is called *Indra-vidyā*.

17. The flag in the south-east shall be consecrated with *Saṁsupti mantra*. The flag in the south is called *Yamo-nāga*. The flag in the west should be worshipped with the mantra—*Rakṣohaṇam*.[4]

18. In the north the consecration is either with the *mantra-Vāta*[5] etc. or *Āpyāyasva*[6] etc. In the north-east too is the same. In the middle—*Viṣṇornu kam*.[7]

19. Near every one of the gates two pots shall be placed. They shall be covered with two cloths; bedecked with sandal-paste,

20. And many varieties of flowers. They shall be inspired with *mantras*. The guardian deities of the quarters shall be worshipped in the manner laid down in the *Śāstras*.

21-22. The efficient devotee shall use these *mantras* for the invocation of the guardian deities :—*Trātāram Indram*,[8] *Agnirmūrdhā*;[9] *Asmin Vṛkṣe, Itaścaiva Pracārī*; *Kiñcedadhāt*; *Ā ca tvā*[10] *Abhi tvā Deva*[11] *and Imā Rudrāya*.[12]

1. VS. 1.1.22.
2. ṚV. 6.16.10.
3. ṚV. 10.9.4. or AV. 2.25.1.
4. ṚV. 10.87.1.
5. ṚV. 10.186.1.
6. ṚV. 1.91.16 or 17.
7. ṚV. 1.154.1.
8. ṚV. 6.47.11 or VS. 8.46.
9. ṚV. 8.44.16.
10. ṚV. 3.43.4 (*ā ca tvām*).
11. ṚV. 1.24.3.
12. *Imā rudrāya* RV. 1.114.1 or 7.46.1.

23. The various articles for *homa* with other ancillary objects shall be placed in the north-west. As laid down in sacred scriptures, the preceptor shall cast glances on and purify the white *Śaṅkhas*.

24. There is no doubt in this that the sacrificial articles become purified by glances. Heart and other limbs shall be assigned by *Praṇava* with the *Vyāhṛtis*.

25. *Astra-mantra* is also used in all assignments as is in vogue for all rites. Raw rice grains and other materials of sacrifice shall be inspired with *Astra mantra*.

26. The preceptor shall touch all the articles together with the *Yāgamaṇḍapa*[1] with the *Kuśa* seat inspired with *Astra mantra*. The rice-grains shall be scattered all around after the purificatory rite.

27-28. Beginning with the east and ending with north-east, the rice grains shall be scattered. Then the *maṇḍapa* shall be smeared with unguents. The preceptor shall assign the *mantras* to the *Arghya*-pot as well. With the water in the *Arghya*-pot he shall sprinkle the *Yāgamaṇḍapa*.

29. The *Kalaśa* (pot) of the deity to be installed shall be known after it and placed in the north-east and in the south the *Vardhanī* (water jar with spout) shall be worshipped with *Astra-mantra*.

30. Just as Kalaśa and water jar so also the planets and *Vāstoṣpati* too shall be worshipped. All these shall be placed in their respective seats and the preceptor shall recite *Praṇava*.

31. And worship the *Kalaśa* with the sacred thread round it and covered with an excellent cloth and smeared with all medicinal herbs and unguents.

32. The deity shall be worshipped in the *Kalaśa* along with the *Vardhanī* and the excellent cloth. Afterwards, let him whirl the *Kalaśa* and *Vardhanī* (water pot with a spout).

33. With water dripping from the *Vardhanī* (water-pot with a spout) he shall sprinkle and place it in front. After worshipping again the *Vardhanī* and the *Kalaśa*, he shall worship the deity on the altarground.

1. The *maṇḍapa* prepared for the sacrifice.

34. Removing the *Kalaśa* to the north-west he shall worship *Gaṇeśa* in the north-east with the *mantra Gaṇānāṁ tvā*[1]. He shall then worship *Vāstupati* with the *mantra Vāstoṣpati*[2] for suppressing the defects in the plot. To the east of the *Kalaśa*, oblations shall be offered to the *Bhūtas* (living beings) and *Gaṇadevas*.

35. Let him read the *Vidyās* and perform *Ālambana* (splitting — evidently the twigs). With the *mantra Yogeyoge*[3], etc. he shall spread the *Kuśa* grass.

36-38. The preceptor in the company of the *Ṛtviks* shall place the deity on the pedestal for bath. Vedic *mantras* shall be sung in chorus (*Brahmaghoṣa*) and the image shall be placed in the *Brahmaratha* (chariot) with the *Puṇyāha*[4] and *Jayamaṅgala mantras*. The pedestal shall be brought to the north-east and placed in the *maṇḍapa* by the preceptor.

39. The image shall be bathed with the *mantra Bhadraṁ karṇebhiḥ*[5] etc. He shall then put the sacred thread on the image and make the entrance, bowing low from far.

40-41. The collyrium for the eye shall be placed in a bell-metal or copper vessel containing honey and ghee. Reciting *Agnirjyoti*[6] *mantra*, the eyes shall be probed with golden probing twig and collyrium shall be applied. At this time the name of the deity shall be mentioned once by the *Sthāpaka* (the installer).

42. With the verse *Imaṁ me Gaṅge*[7] cooling operation of the eyes shall be performed and the dust from the Ant-hill shall be applied with the *mantra—Agnirmūrdhā*[8] etc.

43-45. With the *mantra Yayñāyajñā*[9] the *Kaṣāya* (decoction) of the barks of five trees *Bilva, Udumbara, Aśvattha, Vaṭa*

1. ṚV 2.23.1
2. *Vāstoṣpate* ṚV. 7.54.1.
3. ṚV. 1.30.7.
4. Repeating 'this is an auspicious day' three times at the commencement of most religious ceremonies. (*SSED* p. 340.)
5. ṚV. 1.89.8.
6. SV. 2.1181.
7. ṚV. 10.75.5.
8. ṚV 8.44.16.
9. ṚV. 6.48.1.

and *Palāśa*, along with *Pañcagavya* (the medicinal mixture of five products of cow-milk, butter, curd, cowdung, urine) shall be poured over the image. These medicinal herbs—*Sahadevī*,[1] *Balā*,[2] *Śatamūlī*, *Śatāvarī*,[3] *Kumārī*[4], *Guḍūcī*,[5] *Siṁhī*[6] and *Vyāghrī* shall be soaked in water and the water shall be poured over the image with the *mantra Yā oṣadhī*[7] etc.

46. Thereafter *Phala-snāna* (bathing with the fruit juice) is to be formed with the *mantra—Yāḥ phalinī*[8] etc. *Udvartana* (rubbing off) shall be done with the *Mantra—Drupadādivā*[9], etc.

47. After placing gems, cereals and the herb *Śatapuṣpikā*[10] in the *Kalaśas* beginning with the one in north.

48-49. The waters of the four oceans of pure water. curd, milk and ghee shall be assigned in the four quarters and the *Kalaśas* shall be inspired with the *mantras Āpyāyasva* etc. *Dadhikrāvṇo*[11] etc. *Yā oṣadhīḥ*, etc. and *Tejosi*[12], etc.

50. Then giving the names of the oceans to the *Kalaśas*, the image shall be bathed. After bathing and dressing, incense with *Guggulu* (gumresin) shall be shown.

51-52. For the final *Abhiṣeka* (bathing) different *Tīrthas* (waters from the holy rivers) shall be put in pots separately. Whatever holy river there is in the world or whatever sea, the water from those shall be kept in different pots with the *Mantra Yā oṣadhī*, etc. those pots shall be inspired. Whoever takes his bath with that, water is freed from all sins.

53. After performing the *Abhiṣeka* with *Samudra-mantras*, *Arghya* shall be offered. Sweet scents shall be offered with the

1. Perhaps Abution indicum. (*GVDB*, p. 428, p. 11.)
2. Sida cordifolia. (*GVDB* p. 269.)
3. Asparagus racemosus. (*GVDB*, p. 389.)
4. Aloe barbadensis. (*VN* p. 134.)
5. Tinospora cordifolia. (*GVDB*, p. 141.)
6. Solanum xanthocarpum. (*GVDB*, pp. 68-69.)
7. ṚV. 10.97.1.
8. ṚV. 10.97.15.
9. AV. 6.115.3.
10. Perhaps *Śatapuṣpā*-Peucedanum graveolens or Foeniculum vulgare. (*GVDB*, p. 388.)
11. ṚV. 4.39.6.
12. AV. 7.89.4.

Mantra—Gandhadvārām[1] etc, and *Nyāsa* shall be performed with Vedic *mantras*.

54. Garments shall be offered with the *mantras—Yavaṁ vastra* etc., in accordance with the injunctions of the scripture. Then the idol shall be taken to the *Maṇḍapa* with the *Mantra-Kavihau,* etc.

55. With the *mantra—Śam bhavāya* etc., the idol shall be laid on the bed. The *Sakala-Niṣkalam* rite shall be performed with the *mantra—Viśvataś-cakṣuḥ*.[2]

56. Staying in the Supreme Principle (God) *mantra-nyāsa* shall be done. As laid down in one's own branch of Vedas,

57. The deity is then covered with a sheet of cloth and worshipped. The *Naivedyas* (food offerings) shall be given at the foot.

58. The *Kalaśa* inspired by *Praṇava,* and covered with two cloths, along with the money (gold coin), shall be offered at the head.

59. Then the preceptor shall stand near the sacrificial pit and ignite fire, with the *mantras* laid down in his branch or general Vedic *mantras*.

60. He shall recite the following *Mantras* and hymns in the east:— *Śrīsūkta*[3], *Pavamāna, Vāsa, Dāsya*[4] *Ajina, Vṛṣākapi*[5], *Mitra* and *Bahvṛca.*

61. The *Adhvaryu* (The priest performing the sacrifice) shall recite in the south the following :—*Rudra, Puruṣasūkta*[6], *Ślokādhyāya* (chapter of verses — prayers, *Brahmā* and *Pitṛmaitra.*

62. The *Chandoga* (Vedic School shall recite in the west, *Vedavrata, Vāmadevya,*[7] *Jyeṣṭhasāma*[8], *Rathantara*[9] and *Bheruṇḍa-sāmans.*

1. *Gandhadvārām* (ṚVkh. 5.87.9.)
2. ṚV. 10.81.3.
3. ṚVkh. 5.87.
4. AV. 6.71.3 (dāsyan)
5. ṚV. 10.86.2.
6. Ibid. 10.90.
7. MS. 4.9.11; 132.10.
8. SV. 1. 273.
9. VS. 10.10.

63. *Atharva* (scholar specially well—versed in Atharva Veda) shall recite in the north *Atharvaśiras* (principal portion in that Veda); *Kumbha-sūkta Nīlarudra* and *Maitra.*[1]

64-65. The preceptor shall sprinkle the pit first with *Astra-mantra* and then bring fire in a copper-vessel or mudpot, according to his position, and place it in front. He shall ignite the fire with *Astra-mantra* and envelop it with *Kavaca-mantra.*

66. The preceptor then shall perform the *Amṛtikaraṇa* rite with all *mantras* and holding the vessel with both of his hands whirl it round the pit.

67-68. Put in it *Tejas* with the *Vaiṣṇava-mantra.* With the general *mantra* or that laid down in his own sacred literature he shall place the *Brahma* in the south and *Praṇītā* (sacrificial vessels) in the north. He shall then spread the *Palāśa* twigs along with *Kuśa*[2] grass in different quarters.

69. *Brahmā, Viṣṇu, Hara* and *Īśāna* shall be worshipped with common *mantras.* The fire shall be placed in the *Darbha*[3] grass. Whatever is enveloped in *Darbha* grass,

70-71. Or sprinkled with *Darbha* water becomes pure even without *mantra.* Fire enveloped by uncut *Kuśa* grasses with their tips turned towards east, north and west, comes near of its own accord. Persons well-versed in *mantras* shall do everything for the protection of the fire.

72. Some preceptors maintain that installation of fire shall be after *Jātakarman* (the rite consequent to the birth of a child). Wearing *Pavitra,* the *Ājya* (ghee) shall be consecrated.

73. The preceptor shall see and inspire with *mantras* the *Nīrājana* (waving of lights before the idol). The *Ājya* should be taken just enough to last till the final *Āhuti* is made.

74. For each *Āhuti* five drops are poured into the leaf with which the *Āhuti* is then made. All the rites that one has to perform from the time of *Garbhādhāna* (conception) to *Godāna* (cutting of the forelocks of a child for the first time),

1. VS. 39.5.
2. Desmostachya bipinnata. (*GVDB*, p. 111.)
3. *Kuśa.* (*GVDB*, p. 201.)

75. Are to be performed either in accordance with *Śāstraic* injunction with those *mantras*, or with *Praṇava*. Thereafter *Pūrṇāhuti* (entire ghee poured into the fire) is performed and the devotee gets all his desires fulfilled.

76. A fire thus maintained is conducive to all success in all rites. After performing the worship the fire shall be transferred to the pits.

77. To Indra and other gods one hundred *Āhutis* each shall be given. At the end of hundred *Āhutis* the *Pūrṇāhuti* is performed for all gods.

78-80. The *Hotṛ* shall assign to the *Kalaśa* his own *Āhuti*. Keeping to one's side all the deities, mantras, sacrificial fire and himself the *Pūrṇāhuti* shall be given. After extricating himself the preceptor shall offer oblations to the guardians of the quarters, spirits, gods, and to serpents by means of due rites. Gingelly seeds and sacrificial twigs are the two essential ingreendits.

81. *Ghee* is an auxiliary. The other articles are to be given after smearing them with *ghee*. *Puruṣasūkta* is to be used in the east. *Rudra* in the south.

82. *Jyeṣṭhasāman*[1], *Bhīruṇḍa* and *Tannayāmi* to the west. *Nīlarudra* is a great *mantra*. *Kumbhasūkta* is an important part of the *Atharvaveda*.

83. Each of the *Devas* shall be worshipped with *Havana* a thousand times at the head.

84-85. Similarly in the middle and at the foot. Then with *Pūrṇāhuti*, on all those spots termed 'Head' of the image, the *Āhutis* shall be offered. The brahmin shall offer *Āhutis* in honour of the gods either with the principal *mantras* or the *mantras* of his own scriptural code or with the *Gāyatrī* or with *Gāyatrī*, *Vyāhṛti* and *Praṇava*.

86. Having thus performed the rite of *Homa*, the preceptor shall perform *mantra-nyāsa* :—at the feet with *Agnimīle mantra*, at the ankles with *Iṣe tvā mantra*.

87. At the calves the assignment is with the *mantra*

1. SV. 1.273.

Agna āyāhi, etc. at the knee-joint *Sanno devi mantra*, at the thigh *Bṛhadrathāntara* and in the belly *Ṣvātila mantra*.

88. For longevity the assignment is made in the heart *Śrīś ca te*[1] *galake*, at the chest *Trātāram Indram*, at the eyes *Triyugmaka mantra*.

89. At the top of the head *Mūrdhā bhuvo*[2] *mantra*. Thereafter, he shall raise the deity by saying "O lord of Brahman ! rise".

90. Then reciting the Vedic *Puṇyāha mantras* he shall go round the temple with the *mantra Devasya tvā*[3] he shall split the *Piṇḍikā*.

91. And place the images of gods, gems, minerals, medicinal herbs and *loha-bījas* behind the deity.

92. The image is not to be placed exactly in the centre of the sanctum sanctorum or far removed from it. It shall be placed slightly away from the centre. There is no attendant defect therein.

93. It should be brought a little to the north. "*Oṁ* obeisance, obeisance, be stable, be beneficent to all people."

94. To the six deities he shall make assignments with the *mantra—Devasya tvā savitur vaḥ* and reciting—"All the principles, *Varṇas*, and *Kalās* in the god having the world as his progeny.

95. After assigning all the six he shall inspire them with *mantras* with the *Sampātakalaśa* the installed deity shall be bathed.

96. With lamps, incense and scented sticks he shall worship. After performing *Arghya* and bowing he shall pray for forgiveness.

97. To the *Ṛtviks dakṣiṇā* shall be given according to the capacity and articles, such as a vessel, a pair of cloths, umbrella, good rings, etc.

98. The householder shall then perform the fourth *Homa*, with full concentration. After offering hundred *Āhutis*, the *Pūrṇāhuti* shall be offered.

1. *Śrīś ca te lakṣmīś ca* VS. 31.22.
2. *Mūrdhā bhuvo* ṚV 10. 88.6.
3. VS. 1.21 (Also *DC*. pp. 492-4).

99. The preceptor shall then come out and offer oblations to the guardians of the quarters. With flowers in his hands he shall say "Forgive" and scatter them.

100-101. At the end of the sacrifice, the householder shall give to *ācārya* a grey cow, chowrie, coronet, ear-rings, umbrella, bracelet, girdle, fan, villages, garments, etc., with all subsidiary things. He shall feed lavishly. By the god's grace he shall be liberated.

CHAPTER FORTYNINE

Four Varṇas and āśramas

Brahmā said :

1. O Vyāsa, Hari is the creator of the world, etc. He has to be worshipped by Brahmā the self-created and others. He has to be duly adored by *Brāhmaṇas* and others according to their own *duties*. Please listen to those *duties*.

2. Six duties are assigned to the *Brāhmaṇa*; performing sacrifices for himself, performing them for others, giving gifts, accepting them, studying and teaching others.

3. The common *duty* of *Kṣatriya* and *Vaiśya* is giving gifts, studying and performing *yajñas*. The additional duty of a *Kṣatriya* is maintaining law and order and that of a *Vaiśya* is agriculture.

4. Service of the twice-born is the main duty of *Śūdras*. Maintenance by means of various arts and crafts and *pākayajña*[1] is also their duty.

5. The special duty of a *Brahmacārin* is begging for alms, service to the preceptor, study, sacrificial rites and renunciation.

6. There are two-fold conditions in all *āśramas*. *Brahmacārin* becomes *Upakurvāṇa* or *Naiṣṭhika*. This *Naiṣṭhika* is eager to realise *Brahman*.

1. A simple or domestic sacrifice.

7. After studying the Vedas if he becomes a householder he is called *Upakurvāṇa*. The *Naiṣṭhika* remains a *Brahmacārin* till death.

8. O best brahmin ! the duties of a house-holder are in brief — the preservation of the sacred fire, hospitality to the guests; performance of sacrifices, giving gifts, and worshipping gods.

9. The householder is of two kinds: *Udāsīna* and *Sādhaka*. The householder who endeavours to maintain the house is called *Sādhaka*.

10. After repaying the three debts (to sages, to gods and to the manes) and renouncing wife and wealth, he who seeks salvation alone, is called *Udāsīna*.

11. The duty of a *Vanavāsin* (dealer in a forest) is lying on the ground, sustenance on fruits and roots, study, austerities and sharing of whatever he gets with others.

12. He is the best of ascetics who performs penance in the forest, worships gods, performs sacrifices and is devoted to the study.

13. He is to be considered a sage stationed in *vānaprastha* order who is very much emaciated due to penance and is extremely devoted to meditation.

14. The *Bhikṣu* (mendicant) who is engaged in yogic practices always, aspires to rise up, controls his sense-organs and strives for knowledge is called a *Pārameṣṭhika*.

15. The sage delighting in communion with the soul, ever satiated, who practises yogic exercises and moves about with sandal paste applied all over his body is called *Yogin*.

16. In a *Bhikṣu* these are the essential characteristics :— beggary, Vedic study, vow of silence, austerities, special meditation, perfect knowledge and complete detachment from worldly affairs.

17. The *Pārameṣṭhika* is of three types:— Some renounce *jñāna*. Others renounce *Vedic Rites*. The third renounces all sorts of activities.

18. *Yogin* is of three types *Bhautika*, *Kṣatra* and *Antyāśramin* who relies on the *Yoga-mūrti*.

19. In the first *Yogin* the *Bhāvanā* (Imagination) is primary, in the second there is *Duṣkara* (difficult) *Bhāvanā* in salvation and in the third there is *Pārameśvarī* (Godly) *Bhāvanā*.

20-24. From virtue, salvation is produced; from wealth, *love* issues forth. There are two types of Vedic rites — that which is pursued with knowledge is *Nivṛtti* (withdrawal of sense-organs), and *Pravṛtti* is the performance of fire rites and god-worship. These are the common characteristics of all *Āśramas*:— Forgiveness, self-restraint, compassion, charity, absence of greed, straight-forwardness, want of jealousy, following great religious leaders, truthfulness, contentedness, *theism*, control of sense-organs, worship of deities, respecting Brahmins, non-violence, pleasant speech, absence of backbiting and refraining from harshness. I shall now describe the goal of the four castes. The *Brāhmaṇas* who maintain their sacred rites attain *Prājāpatya* (Brahmā's) region.

25. The *Kṣatriyas* who never quit the battle ground in fear attain Indra's region. The *Vaiśyas* who strictly adhere to their duties attain the region of the *Maruts* (Wind gods),

26-27. The *Śūdras* who serve others attain the region of *Gandharvas*. The region attained by the eightyeight thousand sages who have sublimated their sensual feelings can be attained by pupils who remain continuously with their preceptors. The region of the seven divine sages is obtained by forest-dweller.

28. The region from which the sage never returns, the the region of *Brahman*, the Blissful, is for the ascetics who control their minds, who renounce and who sublimate their base passions.

29. The region of *Yogins* is *Amṛtasthāna* which is imperishable either, the blissful, the divine, from which the liberated soul never returns.

30-31. Salvation is to be attained by the knowledge of the eight constituents [*yama* etc. hereinafter explained]. I shall describe them in brief. *Yama* (restraint) is of five sorts, i.e. 1) *Ahiṁsā* which is not injuring any living being; 2) *Satya* which is the narration of facts beneficent to others, 3) *Asteya* is not taking anything (belonging to others); 4) *Brahmacarya* is refraining from sexual intercourse; 5) *Aparigraha* is the renunciation of all possessions.

32. *Niyama* (control) are of five sorts, *Satya* etc. It is both external and internal. 1) *Śauca* (purity) 2) *Satya* (truthfulness) 3) *Santoṣa* (contentment) 4) *Tapas* (penance) 5) *Indriyanigraha* (controlling sense-organs).

33. *Svādhyāya* is mastery of *mantras*. *Praṇidhāna* is worship of God *Viṣṇu*. *Āsana* is the yogic posture *Padmaka*, etc. *Prāṇāyāma* is the mastery of breath.

34. In *Prāṇāyāma* the *garbha* is attended with meditation and repetition of *mantras*. *Prāṇāyāma* without this is *agarbha*. It is again of three varieties. Inhaling is *Pūraka*.

35. Retention is *Kumbhaka*. Exhaling is *Recaka*. *Laghu* or the simplest is of twelve seconds duration; the higher one is of twentyfour seconds' duration.

36. And the best is of thirty six seconds' duration. *Pratyāhāra* is the withdrawal of sense-organs from the objects. *Dhyāna* is the meditation over the identity of the supreme soul and the individual soul. *Dhāraṇā* is the steadying of the mind.

37. *Samādhi* is that state where one is conscious that I am *Brahman* and retains it. I am the *Ātman*, the supreme *Brahman*, the truth, the knowledge, the endless,

38. *Brahman*, the specific knowledge of the bliss that you are. I am *Brahman*, without the body, sense-organs,

39. And free from mind, intellect, Mahat, ego, etc. I am the Light free from the three states of wakefulness, dream and dreamless sleep.

40. The permanent, the pure, the intelligent, Truth, Bliss, without second. The soul within the Sun is I myself, the unsevered. A brāhmaṇa who meditates over this becomes liberated from the bondage of worldly existence.

CHAPTER FIFTY

Daily routine for the aspirant

Brahmā said :

1. The aspirant who undertakes the following routine daily, without break is sure to achieve enlightenment. He should wake up from bed in the fourth quarter of the night and review his progress in the way of righteousness and prosperity.

2-3. He should meditate upon the joyous and unageing Viṣṇu as seated in his heart on the filament of the lotus. After conducting the necessaries by way of purging himself he should take bath in the pure waters of the river, as this act, viz. bath, absolves him of all his sins.

4. A morning bath should be taken without negligence. The wise proclaim that a morning bath causes fruition of one's acts both perceptible and imperceptible.

5. A person in sound sleep is liable to fall prey to various sorts of pollutions. He should not begin any activity without taking a bath.

6. A morning bath removes sins of poverty, indisposition, bad dream and evil thought. One should not entertain any doubt about it.

7. He should not commence any ceremonious acts without first taking bath. In the performance of the ritual such as sacrifice, or the recitation of mantras a bath is inevitable.

8. When he is indisposed and weak he shall take bath down the neck (without pouring water over the head) or wipe the body with a wet cloth.

9. Purificatory bath is of six types : 1) *Brāhma* 2) *Āgneya*, 3) *Vāyavya*, 4) *Divya*, 5) *Vāruṇa*, 6) *Yaugika*.

10. The *Brāhma* bath means sprinkling the body with drops of water through the holy *Kuśa* grass simultaneously chanting the holy *mantras* and rubbing the body. The *Āgneya* bath means purifying the body by smearing the divine ashes from head to foot.

11. Smearing the body with the dust of dried cow-dung is the excellent form in bath called *Vāyavya*. Taking bath

in the rain when there is simultaneous sunshine is called the *Divya* bath.

12. Plunging into water (of tank rivers, etc.) is called *Vāruṇa* bath. The *Yaugika* bath is the meditation on the Ātman by Yogic means and mental dedication.

13. It is known as the *Ātmatīrtha* (the holy water of the *Ātman*) and is resorted to by philosophers. Twigs for chewing (for cleaning the teeth) are excellent if they are of any of the following trees 1) *Kṣīravṛkṣa* (one of the four trees *Nyagrodha, Udumbara, Aśvattha* or *Madhūka*[1]), 2) *Mālatī*[2],

14. 3) *Apāmārga*[3], 4) *Bilva*[4] 5) *Karavīra*.[5] He shall face the north or the east while cleaning the teeth.

15. After chewing, the cleansing twig shall be washed and thrown carefully in a clean place. After duly finishing the *Ācamana* (the ritualistic drinking of water) and bath, *Tarpaṇa* (offering of water chanting Vedic *Mantras*) shall be performed for the gods, sages and the manes.

16-17. After that he shall silently perform *Ācamana* once again. Let him sprinkle his body with drops of water by means of *Kuśa* grass[6] chanting the Vedic *mantras, Āpo hi ṣṭhā* etc. along with *Sāvitrī mantras*[7] and *Vāruṇa mantras*[8]. Let him then recite the *Gāyatrī mantra* prefixed with the mystic syllable *Om*. This *mantra* is the mother of all Vedic *mantras*.

18-19. He shall then fix his mind on the Sun and make water-offering unto him. The *Śruti* (Veda) has ordained that one should sit on the *Kuśa* grass with mental concentration, do *Prāṇāyāma* (hold the breath chanting the requisite *mantra*) and perform *Sandhyā* (repetition of Vedic *mantras*). This *Sandhyā* gives birth to the universe. It is free from taints. It is beyond *Māyā* (Illusion and ignorance).

1. Madhuca indica *GVDB*, p. 295.
2. Jasminum grandiflorum *GVDB*, p. 166.
3. Achyrandthes aspera *GVDB*, p. 14.
4. Aegle marmelos *GVDB*, p. 274.
5. Nerium indicum *GVDB*, p. 77.
6. ṚV. 10.9.1.
7. ṛcs addressed to Savitṛ.
8. ṛcs addressed to Varuṇa.

20. It is the sole power of *Īśvara* (the Almighty). It has sprung from the three *Tattvas* (Principles). After meditating on (*Sandhyā*) the crimson-coloured, the white and the dark (respectively at dawn, midday and dusk), the learned man shall repeat the *Gāyatrī*.

21. The Brahmin shall always face the east when performing *Sandhyopāsanā*. The person who does not perform *Sandhyā* is impure and unfit for any other (holy) rite.

22-24. Whatever he does he shall not reap the fruit thereof. Brahmins who have mastered the Vedas and performed the *Sandhyā* with single-minded concentration have attained the highest goal. He may be the best of brahmins but if he neglects *Sandhyā* worship and exerts himself in other religious activities he goes to hell and remains there for ten thousand years. Hence, by all means *Sandhyopāsanā* should be performed.

25-27. Verily thereby the Almighty of yogic body, is being propitiated. A scholar, pure and controlling the senses, shall repeat the *Gāyatrī* everyday, facing the east, the maximum number of a thousand times, or a hundred times or at least ten times. Then with various kinds of essential *mantras* from Ṛgveda, Yajurveda and Sāmaveda he shall propitiate the rising sun. After the worship of the sun, the god of gods, the giver of great fortune,

28. He shall prostrate the head touching the ground. He shall then recite this *mantra*. "Om obeisance to *Khakholka*, the quiet, the cause of three-fold causes.

29. I am dedicating myself unto you. Obeisance to thee in the form of knowledge. Thou art the great *Brahman*, the waters, the brilliant lustre, the essential juice, the nectar.

30. Thou art the earth; the upper region; the heaven; the *Oṅkāra*; all the eternal Rudras." Reciting this excellent prayer within the heart,

31. Prostrations shall be made unto the sun both in the morning and at midday. Then the brahmin shall return home and perform *Ācamana* duly.

32. Then let him duly kindle the sacrificial fire and offer oblations to it. The priest, his son, wife, disciple or brother,

33. After being permitted, shall offer special additional offerings of oblations. A religious rite without *mantras* is not conducive to good results either here or hereafter.

34. All deities shall be bowed to and food offerings made unto them. The preceptor shall be revered and what is beneficent to him be performed.

35. Thereafter, the brahmin shall proceed with the study of Vedas to the extent of his ability. Let him recite words of prayer, teach his disciples, ponder over the subjects discussed and retain them in his mind.

36. He shall go through *Dharma-śāstras*[1] and other sacred texts, Vedas and the six *Vedāṅgas*[2] (ancillary subjects) entirely.

37. He shall then approach the king (or a rich man) for the sake of *Yogakṣema* (securing and preserving) and from him he shall receive different articles for the sake of his family.

38. Then at midday for the sake of his ablution he shall take with him a lump of clay, flowers, dry rice grains, gingelly seeds, kuśa grass and pure dry cowdung.

39. He shall take bath only in rivers, or natural lakes or tanks. He shall not bathe in another man's private tank.

40. Without offering the five rice balls (to the manes) the bath becomes imperfect. With one part of the clay lump the head shall be wiped, the portion above the navel with two parts.

41. The nether regions with three parts and the feet shall be wiped with six parts. The clay-lump shall be as big as a ripe *Āmalaka*[3] (Myrobalan).

42. So also the cow-dung. The limbs are to be smeared with it. He then shall wash it and perform *Ācamana*. Let him then take bath with all senses fully controlled.

43. The smearing with clay shall be done sitting on the bank and chanting the *Liṅga-mantras* (of Viṣṇu). The water

1. *Dharma-śāstra* actually means the code-book of conduct. This encompasses the entire Hindu law. Generally the *Smṛtis*, or the sacred books ascribed to Manu, Yājñavalkya, etc. come under *Dharma-śāstra*, (Also *CDHM*, p.89)

2. The ancillary Vedic literature divided under the six headings—*Śikṣā*, *Chandas*, *Vyākaraṇa*, *Nirukta*, *Jyotiṣa* and *Kalpa*.

3. Emblica officinalis *GDVB*, p. 36.

also shall be infused with *Liṅga* and *Vāruṇa mantras* of very auspicious nature.

44. He shall remember God Viṣṇu at the time of bath. Verily the waters are the Lord Nārāyaṇa. Looking at the Sun that is *Oṅkāra* itself let him dip himself in water three times.

45. After performing an *Ācamana* (without *mantra*) let him do another *Ācamana* with this *mantra*, the *mantra*-knower that he is. [*Ācamana mantra*] : thou movest about in the inner cavities in the living beings facing all round.

46. Thou art the sacrifice, the mystic syllable *Vaṣaṭkāra*, thou art the waters, the lustre, the juice, the nectar. Or he shall repeat *Drupadā mantra three times* along with the *Praṇava* and the *Vyāhṛtis* (*Oṁ Bhūḥ Bhuvaḥ Svaḥ*).

47. Or he, the scholar, can repeat the *Sāvitrī* or the *Aghamarṣaṇa mantra*. Then wiping shall be done with the *mantras—Āpo hi ṣṭhā*, etc.

48. Or *Idam āpaḥ pravahata*[1] along with *vyāhṛtis*. Then the water shall be infused with the *mantras—Āpo hi ṣṭhā*.

49. Inside water, he shall silently repeat thrice the *mantra-Aghamarṣaṇa* or *Drupadā* or *Sāvitrī* or *Tad Viṣṇoḥ paramaṁ padam*[2].

50. Or he shall repeat the *Praṇava* frequently. He shall remember *Hari*, the god of gods. If *Mārjana* (wiping) is done with water held in the palm and the *mantra* recited.

51. Or if that water is sprinkled on the head, he becomes free from all sins. After performing *Sandhyā* and *Ācamana* he shall always remember God.

52. Then he shall propitiate the Sun with lifted-up *Puṣpāñjali* (handful of flowers). Scattering (the flowers he shall look at the rising sun with the mantras *Na hanyate*.

53. *Udu tyam*,[3] *Citraṁ devānām*,[4] *Taccakṣuḥ devahitam*[5] etc. Then he shall repeat the *mantras Haṁsaḥ śuciṣad* specially accompanied by the *Sāvitrī*.

1. ṚV. 1.23.22.
2. ṚV. 1.22.20.
3. ṚV. 1.50.1.
4. ṚV. 1.115.1.
5. ṚV. 7.66.16.

54. And other solar *mantras* mentioned in the Vedas and *Gāyatrī* too. Afterwards, sitting on a seat of *kuśa* grass on the eastern bank.

55. He shall repeat various *mantras* with concentrated mind and look at the sun. He shall repeat the *japas* with rosary of beads made of glass, *abjākṣa, Rudrākṣa* or *Putrañjīva*[1] in the interval.

56. If the devotee is wearing wet cloth he shall repeat the beads standing in water.

57. Or if he is wearing dry cloth he shall sit on the ground in a clean place on a mat of *kuśa* grass. The mind shall always be concentrated. After the circular perambulation he shall prostrate on the ground.

58. Then he shall perform *Ācamana* and proceed with the study of Vedas to his capacity. Then *Tarpaṇa* (water offering in propitiation) shall be made to *devas*, sages and the manes.

59. The deities, etc., shall be named with *Oṁkāra* prefixed to them and *Namaḥ* (obeisance) and *Tarpayāmi* (I propitiate) added in the end. In the water-offerings to *devas* and to Brahminical sages there shall be rice grains in the water [and not gingelly seeds as in regard to the manes].

60. The process of offering shall be in accordance with the injunctions in one's own *Sūtra* [the branch of scriptural code one follows].

61. So also offering should be made to *devarṣis*. While offering to deities the sacred thread is worn as usual; while offering to the sages it shall be worn like a garland.

62. While offering to the manes, the sacred thread shall be worn to the left side. After squeezing out the water from the cloth (worn at the time of bath) he shall perform *Ācamana* silently.

63-64. Then the gods shall be worshipped with their respective *mantras*, with flowers, leaves and water. He shall worship all favourite gods Brahmā, Śaṅkara, Sun, slayer of Madhu (Viṣṇu) and other approved deities. Hara (Śiva) is pleased with devotion. Or he shall offer flowers, etc. chanting *Puruṣa sūkta*.

1. Putrañjīva roxburgh *GVDB*, p. 252.

65. The deities of waters may also be worshipped well. With the mind fully concentrated he shall prostrate chanting the *Praṇava*,

66. And offer the flowers separately. Without the *Ārādhanā* (propitiation), no vedic rite becomes meritorious.

67. Hence there, in the beginning, middle and the end, Hari shall be meditated upon. With the *mantra Tad viṣṇoḥ* and the *Puruṣa sūkta*,

68. He shall dedicate himself to *Viṣṇu* of pure effulgence. Repeating the *mantras* he shall remain meditating on God.

69. Then he shall perform the five *yajñas*, (sacrifices) to gods, to the living beings, to the manes, to men and to the *Brahman*.

70. If he has already performed *Brahma yajña*[1] before *Tarpaṇa*, he can proceed with his study of Vedas after performing *manuṣya yajña*[2] (the sacrifice to men

71. *Vaiśva deva* (offering of oblations in the fire before meals, intended for all *deities* collectively) shall be performed—it is called *Devayajña*. The offering to *Bhūtas*—living beings or spirits is to be known as *Bhūtayajña*.

72. Food offerings are made to dogs, *Śvapacas* (degraded people; outcastes), fallen people, on the ground outside (the house) as also to the birds.

73. The *Pitṛyajña* is conducive to the attainment of *salvation*. The best man shall feed a single brahmin *bearing all the manes in mind*. It has to be performed every day faithfully.

74. Or in accordance with one's capacity, he shall take a small quantity of food and offer that with the mind fully concentrated to a brahmin who is a scholar fully conversant with the meanings and principles of Veda.

75. A guest shall be worshipped always. A brahmin who comes to the house and is perfect in mind, speech and actions shall be bowed to and worshipped with words of welcome.

1. One of the five daily *yajñas* or sacrifices to be performed by a householder; teaching and reciting the Vedas. *Adhyāpanam brahmayajñaḥ*, *Manu*. 3.70.

2. In practice, hospitality, reception of guests.

76. If a mouthful of food is given, it is called *Bhikṣā*. A handful is equivalent to four such mouthfuls and is considered sufficient for an *Atithi* (guest).

77. The guest shall wait for as much time as is necessary for milking a cow. The householder shall duly honour according to his ability, visitors and guests.

78. He shall duly give alms to a mendicant who is a *Brahmacārin* (unmarried student). Without *greed*, he shall give food to those who *request* for it, commensurate with his ability.

79. He shall partake of food along with kinsmen while taking food he shall be silent and by no means shall he criticise the food served. If a brahmin takes food without performing the five *yajñas*,

80. He is definitely foolish and shall be reborn as one of the low animals. He shall practise the study of the Vedas every day, even if he is unable to perform great sacrifices.

81. The worship of gods destroys all sins immediately. If he does not perform the worship of god out of delusion or lethargy,

82. And takes food, he goes to hell or is reborn as a boar. I shall now expound the special type of impurity called *Āśauca*. Animpure man is ever a sinner.

83-84. Impurity is due to contact and purity by avoiding it. When people die or a child is born, all brahmins have to observe *Āśauca* for ten days. The duration of *Āśauca* when a child dies before its tonsure ceremony has been celebrated, is only one night.

85. If a child dies before the ceremony of investiture with the sacred thread, the duration of *Āśauca* is for three nights. For deaths thereafter the *Āśauca* is for ten nights. A *Kṣatriya* is freed of this impurity in twelve days; a *vaiśya* in fifteen days,

86. And a *Śūdra* in a month. An ascetic has no such impurity. If abortion or still birth takes place, the freedom from impurity is in as many nights as months. (Abortion in the third month—3 nights of *Āśauca*; Abortion in the fifth month —5 nights of *Āśauca* and so on].

CHAPTER FIFTYONE

Charity

Brahmā said:

1-2. I shall now describe the virtue of making charitable gifts than which there is nothing better. It has been mentioned by those who know it that charitable gift means handing over riches and articles with due faith to those who deserve the same. Charity yields enjoyment in this world and salvation after death. One shall acquire wealth by justifiable means. Its fruit shall be charity as well as enjoyment.

3. A brahmin's usual way of earning is by teaching, presiding over sacrifices and taking *Dakṣiṇās*. [If that is not possible] usury, agriculture and trade (shall be resorted to). Or he can earn by activities of a *kṣatriya* (fighting).

4. The charity given to deserving persons is *Sāttvika* (of pure quality). Charity is of four types 1) *Nitya* (Daily gift), (2) *Naimittika* (casual), (3) *Kāmya* (Desiring a special result) and (4) *Vimala* (free from dirt).

5. The *Nityadāna* is the gift of any article or cash to a Brahmin who does not do anything in return. It shall be given every day without wishing for any result thereof.

6. The *naimittika* charity is performed by all good people. Something is given to scholars for wiping off sins.

7. The charity given, desiring for progeny, success, prosperity or heaven is called *kāmya*[1] by sages who think about *dharma*.

8. The charity given to persons with the knowledge of the *Brahman* with a *Sāttvika* mind, just to please God is called *Vimala*[2]. It is auspicious.

9. The person who gives a land of flourishing sugarcane plants or barley or wheat to a Vedic Scholar has no rebirth in the world.

10. There never was nor ever shall be a charity superior

1. With desire.
2. Pure.

to the gift of lands. By giving the gift of *Vidyā*[1] (by teaching) to a brahmin, the donor is highly revered in the *Brahmaloka.*

11. Everyday this shall be given to a *Brahmacārin* with sincerity. He shall then be freed of all sins and attain *Brahmaloka.*

12. A learned person should observe fast himself on the Full-moon day in the month of *Vaiśākha* and honour twelve brahmins with honey, gingelly seeds and ghee.

13. Having worshipped with fragrant incense, etc., he shall say through someone or himself, "O Dharmarāja, be pleased as you like."

14-16. He can have all sins, *committed throughout* life, wiped off immediately. The person who gives gingelly seeds placed in a deer-skin to a brahmin along with gold, honey and *ghee* to a brahmin crosses all evils. If a person gives cooked rice seasoned with *ghee*, and water to brahmins, after offering the same to *Dharmarāja*, is freed from fear. This is specially done in *Vaiśākha.* If after observing fast (*the previous day*) on the *Dvādaśī* day (12th day in the lunar fortnight) he worships Viṣṇu, the destroyer of all sins,

17. He becomes free from all sins. Whatever deity he may wish to propitiate,

18. It is necessary that he should honour brahmins with great effort and feed women and then worship the gods. A person desiring progeny shall worship Indra always.

19. A person desiring brahminical splendour shall worship brahmins decidedly firm in the *Brahman.* A man desirous of health shall worship the sun; a man wishing for riches shall worship firc.

20. A man cager for the fulfilment of his affairs shall worship *Vināyaka.* A man who yearns for enjoyment shall worship the moon, a man wishing for strength shall worship the wind-god.

21. A man desiring freedom from the entanglement of worldly existence shall worship Lord Hari with sincere effort; a man desiring for all sorts of things or without desire at all shall worship Lord *Gadādhara*[2] (Viṣṇu).

1. Knowledge or instruction.
2. One who holds the club.

22. A man who gives cool water (to the thirsty) attains gratification. A man who gives cooked rice shall enjoy unending happiness. A man who gives gingelly seeds shall obtain wished-for progeny. A man who makes a gift of a lamp shall get keen vision.

23. A man who gifts away lands gets everything worth-having. A man who gives gold obtains longevity. A man who gives house attains excellent worlds. A man who gives silver secures comely features.

24. A man who gives garments attains the world of the moon. A giver of horses gets to the region of Śiva. A man who gifts away oxen obtains full scale prosperity and he who gives cows reaches the solar region.

25. The giver of vehicles and quilts secures a good wife. He who offers protection gets prosperity. The giver of grains gets permanent happiness. The giver of knowledge of the Vedas, attains the eternal *Brahman.*

26. He who imparts knowledge to Vedic scholars is honoured in heaven. He who gives grass to cows becomes free from sins.

27. He who gives fuels becomes brilliant like fire. He who gives medicines to remove the sickness of a patient and furnishes him with food and ghee,

28-29. Becomes happy, free from sickness and lives long. By giving umbrellas and sandals he will be able to cross *Asipatravana*—a forest in the hell where plenty of plants grow with leaves having edges as sharp as sword-edge and where the sunshine is fierce. Whatever is craved for in the world, whatever lovable thing he possesses in his house.

30. Shall be given to a man of good quality by a man who wishes an abundant supply of the same. What is given during any of the equinoxes, in solar or lunar eclipses,

31-32. Or during the migration of planets from one sign of zodiac to the other, becomes never-exhausting. There is no greater virtue to any of the living beings than the virtue of giving away (articles and cash) in holy places like Prayāga[1] etc.

1. The place where the Gaṅgā and the Yamunā meet is known as Prayāga since ancient days.

or particularly at Gayā.[1] Giving of any gift by a person desiring non-severance from heaven is conducive to the destruction of sins.

33. A sinful person, who prevents the offerings made to brahmins, or in fire or at the time of sacrifices, becomes reborn as a lower animal.

34. A person refraining from giving food at the time of famine, when brahmins die, becomes as despicable as a slayer of Brahmins.

CHAPTER FIFTYTWO

Prāyaścitta[2]

Brahmā said :

1-2. O Brahmins, hereafter I shall expound the process of atonement for sin. There are five great sinners:—the slayer of brahmins, the drunkard, the thief, defiler of preceptor's bed, and a person associating with any of these. The deities have mentioned the slaughter of cows, etc. as *Upapāpa* (subsidiary sin).

3. The slayer of a brahmin shall stay in a hut in the forest for twelve years. He shall observe fast, fall from a great precipice,

4. Jump into fire, or drown himself into water. Or he shall cast off his body for the sake of a brahmin or a cow.

5. By giving food to a scholar he can wipe off the evils of the slaughter of a brahmin. A brahmin (slayer of another brahmin) becomes free from the sin by bathing at the ceremonial bath after the horse-sacrifice.

6-7. Or he shall give away everything he possesses to a brahmin knowing Vedas. A brahmin shall fast for three nights

1. A renowned place of pilgrimage in Bihar, sacred to the Hindus and the Bauddhas alike.

2. A religious act to atone for one's sin.

and take bath thrice a day in the famous confluence of River *Sarasvatī*[1]. By taking bath at the *Setubandha*[2] (at *Rāmeśvara*[3] in the south).

8. Or in *Kapālamocana* at Vārāṇasī[4] a man is freed from the sin of slaughtering a brahmin. A brahmin guilty of drinking wine shall be freed from the sin by drinking hot boiling wine,

9. Milk, ghee or cow's urine. A thief stealing gold is freed from that sin if he is struck by the king with a pestle.

10. A brahmin guilty of stealing gold shall wear bark garments and perform the expiatory atonement of a slayer of brahmin. A brahmin who passionately embraces the preceptor's wife,

11. Shall expiate by embracing the redhot iron statue of a woman. All persons guilty of illegitimate intercourse with the preceptor's wife, shall perform the expiatory rites of a slayer of a brahmin.

12. Or he shall perform *Cāndrāyaṇa* vow nine times [Taking fifteen mouthfuls of food on the full moon and decreasing it daily, taking nothing on the new moon day. This is a *Cāndrāyaṇa Vrata*. This, he shall perform nine times]. A brahmin associating with any of the four sinners mentioned above,

13. Shall perform the due expiatory rites for the respective sins to ward off the evil results. Or he shall perform bodily mortification and austerity for a year without fail.

14. He shall offer all he possesses. He shall be freed from all sins. Due performance of *Cāndrāyaṇa* or bodily mortification,

15. Or going to holy places like Gayā is destructive of sin. He shall propitiate Lord *Bhava* (Śiva).

16. After feeding brahmins on the new moon day he shall be freed from all sins.

1. An important river in the Ṛgveda, flowed between Śatadrū and Yamunā but, in later times, it was lost.

2. A bridge mentioned in the Rāmāyaṇa; constructed by Rāma to cross the sea to invade Laṅkā.

3. According to the legends, Rāma worshipped the *Śiva liṅga* here. Now-a-days it is a place of pilgrimage situated on the island of Pāmbau.

4. The modern Vārāṇasī. It was also known as Kāśī.

In the dark-half of the lunar month one shall observe fast on the fourteenth day.

17-18. And on the next day in the morning he shall take bath in a river and offer water libations with gingelly seeds seven times saying *Yamāya* (to Yama , *Dharmarājāya* (to Dharmarāja), *Mṛtyave* (to Mṛtyu) *Antakāya* (to Antaka), *Vaivasvatāya* (to Vaivasvata; *Kālāya* (to Kāla) and *Sarvabhūtakṣayāya* (to Sarvabhūtakṣaya). He shall then be freed from all sins.

19. In all *Vratas* (sacred rites) he shall be quiescent, of controlled mind and shall observe *Brahmacarya* (celibacy), fast and worship of brahmins and shall lie only on the ground (not on a cot).

20. He shall observe fast on the sixth day in the bright half of the lunar month and on the seventh day he shall worship God Sun with mental concentration. He shall be freed from all sins.

21. Observing fast on the eleventh day in the bright half of the lunar month and worshipping *Janārdana* on the twelfth day he shall be freed from great sins.

22. Austerity, recital of prayers, visit to holy places and worship of gods and brahmins on the occasion of eclipses, etc. are destructive of great sins.

23. Even though a person is guilty of all sins, if he were to die in holy places after due performance of rites, he shall be freed from all sins.

24. A woman can redeem her husband guilty of slaughter of a brahmin, or any other great sin, ingratitude, etc. if she ascends the funeral pyre of her husband.

24. If a woman is chaste and is devotedly attached to her husband, she has no sin whatsoever here in this world or hereafter.

26. As it is said that Sītā, celebrated in the three worlds, wife of Rāma the son of Daśaratha, subjugated even the lord of Rākṣasas.

27. Persons taking a dip in the holy river "Phalgu"[1] (in Gayā), etc., shall reap the fruit of all good actions. Thus did Lord Viṣṇu speak to me, O sages observing due rites !

1. This river flows through the town of Gayā.

CHAPTER FIFTYTHREE

Eight nidhis[1]

Sūta said:

1. After hearing from Hari, Brahmā described the eight *Nidhis.*[1] [These nidhis or treasures belong to Kubera. In the *Tāntrika* system they are described as attendants on Lakṣmī]. They are *Padma* (Lotus), *Mahāpadma, Makara,* (Crocodile), *Kacchapa,* (Tortoise),

2. *Mukunda, Nanda,*[2] *Nila* and *Śakṅha.*[3] These *Nidhis* are conducive to the flourishing of qualities *Sattva,* etc. I shall now describe their special characteristics.

3. A man bearing the marks of *Padma* shall be *Sāttvika* in quality. He shall be chivalrous. He will gather together gold,

4. Silver, etc., and will be offering the same to gods, ascetics and sacrificial priests. A person having the marks of *Mahāpadma* will be liberal in giving wealth and other things to the pious.

5. The two nidhis *Padma and Mahāpaama* are *Sāttvika* in characteristics. A person having the marks of *makara* gathers together swords, arrows, javelins, etc.

6. He will be a donor unto well-read persons and friendly with kings. He will be wasting his wealth and his enemies will kill him in battle.

7. *Makara* and *Kacchapa* — these two *nidhis* are supposed to be *tāmasika* in characteristics. A person having the marks of *Kacchapa* does not have faith in any person. He neither enjoys his wealth nor gives it to anybody.

8. He will keep his wealth boarded in a deep pit in the ground. He will remain a single person (without any friend). The *nidhi Mukunda* is *rājasika* in characteristics. A person having the marks thereof collects realms.

9. He enjoys all good things in life and distributes wealth among musicians and courtesans. A person having the marks of

1. Treasures of Kubera, the god of Wealth. *Nidhis* are said to be nine also.

2. A lute. (*SSED*, p. 279).

3. Conch.

Nanda — both *tāmasika* and *rājasika* shall be the vital support of his family.

10. He will be pleased by flattery: He will have many wives. He will lose interest in old friends and contract friendship with others.

11. A person having the marks of the *nidhi Nīla* shall have *sāttvika* splendour. He will gather together garments, grains, etc.

12. He has the manliness and power of three persons. He will be making mango groves, tanks, etc. The *nidhi Śaṅkha* indicates selfcentredness. He spends all his wealth in his own enjoyment.

13. His servants and kinsmen eat wretched food and do not wear good garments. The *Śaṅkhin* (one bearing the marks of *Śaṅkha*) is assiduous in nourishing himself. If, ever he gives anything to anybody it shall go in vain.

14. When the markings of different *nidhis* are present the results are mixed. Lord Hari had thus expounded to Hara and others the characteristics of the *nidhis*. I am expounding now as Hari had expounded them previously.

CHAPTER FIFTYFOUR

Bhuvana-Kośa

Hari said :

1. Priyavrata[1] had ten sons. They were Agnīdhra, Agnibāhu, Vapuṣmān, Dyutimān, Medhā, Medhātithi[2], Bhavya, Śabala, Putra,

2. And Jyotiṣmān. Of these ten, the three, viz., Medhā, Agnibāhu and Putra indulged in yogic pursuits.

1. One of the two sons of Brahmā and Śatarūpā, or a son of Manu. (*CDHM* p. 244).

2. He is mentioned in the Veda as a sage. (*CDHM* p. 207).

3. They never cared for the realm. They were *Jātismaras* (i.e. they could know their previous births). The king (Priyavrata) gave seven islands to the seven other sons.

4. The earth is situated like a boat floating on water. It is fifty crores of Yojanas in extent (i.e. 6000000000 kilometres).

5. The seven islands are Jambu,[1] Plakṣa,[2] Śālmala,[3] Kuśa,[4] Krauñca,[5] Śāka,[6] and Puṣkara.[7]

6. Each of these islands is surrounded by seven oceans; those of (1) Lavaṇa (salt) (2) Ikṣu (sugarcane juice), (3) Surā (wine), (4) Sarpis (ghee), (5) Dadhi (curd), (6) Dugdha (milk) and (7) Jala (water)

7. The ocean is twice the island in area it encircles. The mountain Meru[8] extending to a hundred thousand *Yojanas* (i.e. one million two hundred thousand kilometres) is in Jambūdvīpa.

8. Its height is eighty-four thousand Yojanas (one million and eight thousand kilometres). It goes sixteen thousand *Yojanas* underneath and the upper ridge is thirty-two thousand *Yojanas* in girth.

9. It is in the form of the pericarp of a lotus. The *Varṣaparvatas*—boundary mountains Himavān,[9] Hemakūṭa[10] and Niṣadha[11] are towards the south of Meru.

10-11. And Nīla[12], Śveta[13] and Śṛṅgin[14] are in the north. O Śaṅkara, there is no division of *Yugas* (Ages) among the people living in Plakṣa and other islands. Agnīdhra, the king of Jambūdvīpa had nine sons:

1. The island having Meru at its centre. It includes Bhāratavarṣa
2. Not identifiable.
3. Not identifiable.
4. Not identifiable.
5. Not identifiable.
6. Not identifiable.
7. Not identifiable. But, for the probable identfication of the islands see S.M. Ali : Geography of the Purāṇas.
8. The modern Pāmīr-knot in Central Asia.
9. The Himalayas.
10. Not identifiable.
11. Not identifiable.
12. Not identifiable.
13. Not identifiable.
14. Not identifiable. But, for the probable identification of the mountains see S.M. Ali, Op. cit.

12. Nābhi, Kimpuruṣa, Harivarṣa, Ilāvṛta, Ramya, Hiraṇvān, Kuru, Bhadrāśva.

13. And Ketumāla the king gave each of his sons a division of the island which later on were known after them. Nābhi married Merudevī and had a son known Ṛṣabha[1].

14. His son was Bharata[2] who performed sacred rites in *Śālagrāma*. Bharata's son was Sumati and his son was Tejasa.

15. His son was Indradyumna. His son was Parameṣṭhin. His son was Pratīhāra and his son Pratihartṛ.

16. His son was Prastāra. His son was Vibhu. His son was Pṛthu. Next was Nakta. Nakta had a son Gaya.

17. Nara was the son of Gaya. His son was Buddhirāṭ. He had four sons very intelligent Dhīmān, Bhauvana,

18. Tvaṣṭṛ and Viraja. Rajas was his son. Śatajit was Raja's son and his son was Viśvakjyoti.

CHAPTER FIFTYFIVE

Bhuvana-Kośa

Hari said :

1. The Ilāvṛta-Varṣa is situated in the middle. Bhadrāśva is in the East. The *Hiraṇvān*-Varṣa is in the South-East.

2. Then Kimpuruṣa-Varṣa is to the South of Meru. Bhārata is also in the South. Harivarṣa is in the South-West.

3. Ketumāla-Varṣa is in the West and Ramyaka in the North-West. Kuruvarṣa is in the North. It is covered with *Kalpa* trees.

4-5. Except in Bhārata Varṣa *siddhi* (achievement) is natural everywhere. The nine islands surrounded by ocean

1. According to the legend, Ṛṣabha gave his Kingdom to his son Bharata and himself led a life of penance.

2. According to the legend, he was a great devotee of Viṣṇu. Intent on devotion he abdicated his throne (*CDHM*, pp. 46-7).

are — Indradvīpa, Kaśerumān, Tāmravarṇa, Gabhastimān Nāgadvīpa, Kaṭāha, Siṁhala,[1] Vāruṇā[2] and this the ninth one.

6. In its Eastern parts are the *Kirātas*, the *Yavanas*[3] are in the West, the *Āndhras*[4] live in the South and the *Turuṣkas*[5] in the North.

7. Brāhmaṇas, *Kṣatriyas*, *Vaiśyas* and *Śūdras* live in the middle. Mahendra[6], Malava[7], Sahya[8], Śūktimān[9], Ṛkṣa[10].

8. Vindhya and Pāriyātra[11] are the seven *Kulaparvatas*. The sacred rivers are Veda-smṛti[12], Narmadā[13] Varadā[14] Surasā[15] Śivā,[16]

9. Tāpī[17], Payoṣṇī[18], Sarayū[19] Kāverī[20], Gomatī[21], Godāvarī[22], Bhīmarathī[23], Kṛṣṇavarṇā[24], Mahânadī,[26].

1. Modern Ceylon.
2. Modern Borneo.
3. Represents Greeks and other Europeans.
4. Modern Āndhras, perhaps here they represent the Dravidians.
5. The inhabitants of Central and South-Western Asia.
6. Modern Mahendra mountain in eastern coast of India and allied mountains.
7. Modern Nilgiri Hills in the South India.
8. The Western Ghats on the western sea-coast of India.
9. Not identifiable.
10. It is situated on the bank of Narmadā, according to Mallinātha (Raghuvaṁśa, 5.44). Most probably it represents the modern Satpura-mountain in Central India.
11. The modern Vindhya-ranges.
12. Not identifiable.
13. Not identifiable.
14. Modern Narmadā.
15. Modern Wardha river in Vidarbha.
16. Not identifiable.
17. Modern Śivanātha river in Chhattisgarh in Madhya Pradesh.
18. Modern Tāpti river in Central India. It falls in the Arabian Sea.
19. Not identifiable.
20. Modern Sarayū in Uttara Pradesh.
21. Modern Kāveri.
22. Modern Gomati in Uttara Pradesh.
23. Modern Godāvarī.
24. Modern Bhīmā.
25. Modern Kṛṣṇā.
26. Modern Mahānadī in Central Eastern India.

10. Ketumālā[1], Tāmraparṇī[2], Candrabhāgā[3], Sarasvatī, Ṛṣikulyā[4], Kāverī, Mattagaṅgā[5], Payasvinī[6].

11. Vidarbhā[7], and Śatadrū.[8] They are auspicious and they destroy sins. People in the central states drink the waters of these rivers.

12. The races that inhabit the central states are—Pāñcālas[9], Kurus[10], Matsyas[11], Yaudheyas[12], Paṭaccaras[13], Kuntis[14], and Śūrasenas[15].

13. O *Vṛṣadhvaja* (Śiva) the people living in the east are Padmas[16], Sūtas[17], Māgadhas[18], Cedis[19], Kāṣāyas[20], Videhas,[21] and Kosalas[22].

1. Not identifiable.
2. Modern Tambervari in South India.
3. Modern Chenab in the Punjab.
4. Modern Ṛṣikulyā in Orissa.
5. Not identifiable.
6. Modern Payasvinī, a tributary of the Yamunā.
7. Not identifiable.
8. Modern Sutlaj in the Panjab.
9. Pāñcālas were the people who inhabited a region which roughly corresponds to the modern Rohilkhanda-division of Uttara Pradesh and also the region south of it. Later on, the region north of the Gaṅgā was called North Pāñcāla and its capital was Ahicchatra. The one to the South of the Gaṅgā was South Pāñcāla and its capital was Kāmpilya.
10. The Kurus inhabited roughly the region around Delhi on the west of the Yamunā, generally covered by the modern province of Haryana. Their two capitals Hastināpura and Indraprastha are well known.
11. The people who inhabited the modern territory around Alwar Jaipur and Bharatpur.
12. Not identifiable.
13. Not identifiable.
14. Perhaps the people who inhabited the territory north of Cambala.
15. The people who lived in the region around Mathura.
16. Perhaps those who lived around Padma-river in the East-Bengal.
17. Not identifiable.
18. Modern South Bihar.
19. The people inhabiting the central or the eastern Vindhya-ranges.
20. The people inhabiting the region around Kāśī, modern Vārāṇasī.
21. Modern North Bihar.
22. The people living around Ayodhyā.

14. People living in the South-East are Kaliṅgas[1], Vaṅgas[2], Puṇḍras[3], Aṅgas[4], Vaidarbhas[5] Mūlakas[6], and those who stay in the Vindhya ranges.

15. The people living in Dakṣiṇā-patha are those of Pulinda[7], Aśmaka[8], and Jīmūta[9], Naya[10], rāṣtra regions as well as Karṇāṭas[11], Kāmbojas[12] and Ghāṭas.[13]

16. The people in the South-West are Ambaṣṭhas,[14] Draviḍas[15], Lāṭas[16], Kambojas[17], Strīmukhas[18], Śakas[19] and the people of Ānarta[20].

17. The people in the West are Strīrājyas[21] (governed by women) Saindhavas[22], Mlecchas[23], Atheists[24], Yavanas[25] Māthuras[26] and Naiṣadhas.[27]

1. Modern Orissa.
2. Modern Bengal.
3. Not identifiable.
4. Modern North Bengal.
5. Modern Vidarbha (Berar).
6. Not identifiable.
7. Modern Chhatisgarh in Madhya Pradesh.
8. The region around modern Aurangabad-Hyderabad.
9. Not identifiable.
10. Not identifiable.
11. Modern Mysore.
12. Not identifiable.
13. The people inhabiting the sea-coast.
14. Not identifiable.
15. In modern days, the people believed to be of non-Aryan origin inhabiting the South India are called Draviḍas. The specific reference is perhaps to the modern Tamilnadu.
16. Modern Khandesh area of Mahārāṣṭra.
17. Not identifiable.
18. Not identifiable.
19. Not identifiable.
20. Modern Eastern Gujrata.
21. Not identifiable.
22. Modern Sindh.
23. Non-Hindus of the Western India.
24. Non-Hindus of the Western India.
25. Non-Hindus of the Western India.
26. The people inhabiting the region West of Mathurā. Śūrasenas have been mentioned before.
27. The region around modern Gwalior.

18. The regions in the North-West are Māṇḍavyas[1] Tuṣāras[2], Mūlikas[3], Aśvamukhas[4], Khaśas[5], Mahākeśas[6], and Mahānāsas.[7]

19. The people occupying the Northern region are Lambakas[8] Stananāgas[9], Mādras[10], Gāndhāras[11], Bāhlikas[12], and the Mlecchas occupying the Himālayan ranges.

20. The people living in the North East are Trigartas[13] Nīlakola[14] Brahmaputras[15], Sataṅkaṇas[16], Abhīṣāhas[17] and Kāśmīras.[18]

CHAPTER FIFTYSIX

Bhuvana-Kośa

Hari said :

1. Medhātithi, the king of Plakṣa-dvīpa, had seven sons :—They are :—the eldest Śāntabhava, Śiśira.

2. Sukhodaya, Nanda, Śiva, Kṣemaka and Dhruva. They ruled over Plakṣa-dvīpa.

3. The seven mountains are Gomeda, Candra, Nārada, Dundubhi, Somaka, Sumanas and Vaibhrāja.

1. Not identifiable.
2. The people of Central Asia adjoining North-Western India.
3. Not identifiable.
4. Not identifiable.
5. The region North of Kashmir.
6. Not identifiable.
7. Not identifiable.
8. The modern Lamgan.
9. Not identifiable.
10. The region around modern Peshawar.
11. The region around modern Kandhar.
12. The region around modern Balakh.
13. Not identifiable.
14. Not identifiable.
15. The valley of the Brahmaputra.
16. Not identifiable.
17. Not identifiable.
18. Modern Kashmir.

4. The seven rivers there are Anutaptā, Śikhī, Vipāśā, Tridivā, Kramu, Amṛtā and Sukṛtā.

5. Vapuṣmān, the king of Śālmala-dvīpa hads even sons. They are Śveta, Harita, Jīmūta, Rohita,

6. Vaidyuta, Mānasa and Saprabha. (The divisions over which they ruled are known after their names, Śvetavarṣa, Haritavarṣa etc). The seven mountains are :—Kumuda, Unnata, Droṇa, Mahiṣa, Balāhaka,

7. Krauñca and Kakudmān. The seven rivers removing sins are :—Yoni, Toyā, Vitṛṣṇā, Candrā, Śuklā, Vimocanī,

8. And Vidhṛti. Jyotiṣmān, the king of Kuśa-dvīpa, had seven sons. They are :—

9. Udbhida, Veṇumān, Dvairatha, Lambana, Dhṛti, Prabhākara and Kapila. (Here also the divisions ruled over by each is called respectively Udbhidavarṣa, Dvairathavarṣa, etc.).

10. The seven mountains are :—Vidruma, Hemaśaila, Dyutimān, Puṣpavān, Kuśeśaya, Hari and Mandarācala.

11. The seven sacred rivers removing sins are :—Dhūtapāpā, Śivā, Pavitrā, Sanmati, Vidyudabhrā, Mahī and Kāśā.

12. The noble-minded king of Krauñca-dvīpa, Dyutimān had seven sons. They are :—Kuśala, Mandaga, Uṣṇa, Pīvara, Andhakāraka,

13. Muni and Dundubhi. The seven mountains are Krauñca, Vāmana, Andhakāraka,

14. Divāvṛt, Mahāśaila, Dundubhi and Puṇḍarīkavān. The seven rivers in the seven divisions are :—Gaurī, Kumudvatī, Sandhyā, Rātri, Manojavā,

15. Khyāti and Puṇḍarīkā. The king of Śākadvīpa Bhavya had seven sons.

16. They are :—Jalada, Kumāra, Sukumāra, Maśīvaka, Kusumoda, Samodārki and Mahādruma.

17. The seven rivers are :—Sukumārī, Kumārī, Nalinī, Dhenukā, Ikṣu, Veṇukā and Gabhastī.

18. The king of Puṣkara, Śabala, had two sons Mahāvīra and Dhātaki. These are two Varṣas (divisions), one to the north of Mānasa and the other to the east.

19. This dvīpa is a high land fifty thousand *yojanas* high and as much wide too. (It was circular in shape, diameter being fifty thousand *yojanas*).

20. The Puṣkara-dvīpa is encircled by an ocean of sweet water known as Svādūdaka. In front of it are seen the people living.

21. The ground has golden colour twice as bright (as the gold here). It is devoid of all sorts of animals. Beyond that is the mountain Lokāloka, ten thousand *yojanas* wide. The mountain is pervaded by darkness which is on the side of Aṇḍakaṭāha.

CHAPTER FIFTYSEVEN

Bhuvana-Kośa

Hari Said :

1. The height of the earth (from Pātāla) is said to be seventy thousand *yojanas* (about 840,000, Kilometres) and the seven nether worlds are each ten thousand *yojanas* from the other below.

2. The seven nether worlds are Atala, Vitala, Nitala Gabhastimat, Mahākhya, Sutala and the last Pātāla.

3. The grounds are respectively black, white, crimson, yellow, (in colour) and stony, rocky, and golden coloured [seven in order]. There Rākṣasas and Serpents live.

4. In the terrific Puskaradvīpa there are the hells. Their names are :— Raurava, Śūkara, Rodha, Tāla, Vinaśana,

5. Mahājvāla, Taptakumbha, Lavaṇa, Vimohita, Rudhira, Vaitaraṇī, Kṛmiśa, Kṛmibhojana,

6. Asipatravana, Kṛṣṇa, Nānābhakṣa, Dāruṇa, Pūyavaha, Pāpa, Vahnijvālodbhava, Aśiva.

7. Sadaṁśa, Kṛṣṇasūtra, Tama, Avīci, Śvabhojana, Apratiṣtha, and Uṣṇavīci.

8. Sinners guilty of poisoning, inflicting injuries with weapons and arson are cooked and roasted here. O Rudra, the upper regions *Bhūḥ*, etc. are situated one above the other.

9. The *Aṇḍa* or the cosmic egg is encircled by water, fire, wind and ether. It is then encircled by *Mahat* (the great principle) and *Pradhāna* (the *mūla-prakṛti*).

10. Lord Nārāyaṇa pervades ten times the space occupied by the *Aṇḍa*.

CHAPTER FIFTYEIGHT

Description of the planets

Hari said :

1. I shall now expound the measurements and situation of the Sun and other planets. The chariot of the sun is nine thousand *yojanas* in length.

2-3. O Vṛṣabhadhvaja (Śiva), its shaft is twice that much long. The axle of the wheel is one and a half crores and seven million *yojanas* long. The wheel is fitted to it. It has three central joints (*Nābhi*), five spokes (*Ara*) and six *nemis* (encircling rims).

4. All these constitute one year (when the wheel takes one round). The second axle of the sun is forty thousand *yojanas* long.

5. The five other axles are sixty thousand *yojanas* long, each. The length of the axle is in proportion to that of the two ends of the yoke.

6. The short axle is fixed to the pole of the circular wheel along with the end of the yoke. The second axle is fixed in the *Mānasa* mountain.

7. The seven horses of the Sun are the seven metres (*chandas*) *Gāyatrī*, *Bṛhatī*[1] *Uṣṇik*[2], *Jagatī*[3], *Triṣṭup*[4], *Anuṣṭup*[5] and *Paṅkti*.[6]

1. A metre with nine syllables in a quarter.
2. A metre with twentyeight syllables (total).
3. A metre with twelve syllables in a quarter.
4. A metre with eleven syllables in a quarter.
5. A metre with eight syllables in a quarter.
6. A metre with five syllables in a quarter.

8. In the month of *Caitra Dhātā*, (*Āditya*) *Kratusthalā*, (*Apsaras*) *Pulastya* (*Ṛṣi*) *Vāsuki* (Serpent), *Rathakṛt* (*Yakṣa*), *Grāmaṇī*, *Heti* (*Rākṣasagaṇa*) and *Tumburu* (*Gandharva*) reside in the solar zone.

9. In the month of *Mādhava* (*Vaiśākha*), *Aryaman* (Sun) *Pulaha* (*Ṛṣi*), *Rathañjas* (*Yakṣa*), *Puñjikāsthalā* (*Apsaras*), *Praheti* (*Rākṣasagaṇa*) *Kacchanīra* (Serpent) and *Nārada* (*Gandharva*) (reside in the solar zone).

10. In the month of *Jyeṣṭha*, *Mitra* (Sun), *Atri* (Sage), *Takṣaka* (Serpent), *Pauruṣeya* (*Rākṣasagaṇa*) *Menakā* (*Apsaras*), *Hāhā* (*Gandharva*) an *Rathasvana* (*Yakṣa*) reside in the chariot of the sun.

11. In the month of *Āṣāḍha Varuṇa* (Sun), *Vasiṣṭha* (Sage) *Rambhā Sahajanyā* (*Apsaras*), *Kuhu* (*Gandharva*), *Budha* (*Bhāskara*), *Rathacitra* (*Yakṣa*) and *Śukra* (*Rākṣasagaṇa*) reside in the solar zone.

12. In the month of *Śrāvaṇa*, *Indra* (Sun), *Viśvāvasu* (*Gandharva*), Srota (*Yakṣa*), *Elāpatra* (*Bhāskara*), *Aṅgiras* (Sage) *Pramlocā* (*Apsaras*) and the serpents reside in the solar zone.

13. In the month of *Bhādrapada*, *Vivasvān* (Sun), *Ugraṣena* (*Gandharva*), *Bhṛgu* (Sage), *Āpūraṇa* (*Yakṣa*), *Anumlocā* (Apsaras), *Śaṅkhapāla* (Serpent) and *Vyāghra* (*Rākṣasagaṇa*) reside in the solar zone.

14. In the month of *Āśvayuj* (*Āśvina*), *Pūṣan* (Sun), *Suruci* (*Gandharva*), *Dhātṛ* (*Rākṣasagaṇa*), *Gautama* (Sage), *Dhanañjaya* (Serpent), *Suṣeṇa* (*Yakṣa*), and *Ghṛtācī* (*Apsaras*) reside in the sun.

15. In the month of *Kārttika*, *Viśvāvasu*, (*Gandharva*), *Bharadvāja* (Sage), *Parjanya* (Sun), *Airāvata* (Serpent), *Viśvācī* (*Apsaras*), *Senāji* (*Yakṣa*) and *Āpaḥ* (*Rākṣasagaṇa*) are rightful residents of the solar zone.

16. The rightful possessors of the *Mārgaśirṣa* month are *Aṁśu* (Sun), *Kāśyapa* (Sage), *Tārkṣya* (*Yakṣa*), *Mahāpadma* (Serpent), *Urvaśī*, (*Apsaras*) *Citrasena* (Gandharva) and *Vidyut* (*Rākṣasagaṇa*).

17. In the month of Pauṣa *Kratu* (Sage), *Bharga* (Sun), *Ūrṇāyu* (Gandharva), *Sphūrja* (*Rākṣasagaṇa*), *Karkoṭaka* (Serpent), *Ariṣṭanemi* (*Yakṣa*) and the excellent celestial damsel *Pūrvacitti* (*Apsaras*) these seven, reside in the solar zone.

18. In the month of *Māgha* *Tvaṣṭṛ* (Sun), *Jamadagni* (Sage), *Kambala* (Serpent), *Tilottamā*, (Apsaras), *Brahmāpeta* (*Rākṣasagaṇa*), *Ṛtajit* (*Yakṣa*) and *Dhṛtarāṣṭra* (*Gandharva*)—these seven reside in the solar zone.

19. In the month of *Phālguna*, *Viṣṇu* (Sun), *Aśvatara* (Serpent), *Rambhā* (*Apsaras*), *Sūryavarcas* (*Gandharva*), *Satyajit* (*Yakṣa*), *Viśvāmitra* (Sage) and *Yajñāpeta* (*Rākṣasagaṇa*) reside in the solar zone.

20. O Brahman, in the solar zone the sages (mentioned above), whose power has been enhanced by Viṣṇu's *Śakti*, pray to the sun. The *Gandharvas* sing songs in front.

21. The celestial damsels dance. The demons walk behind the sun. The serpents bear the yoke. The *Yakṣas* catch hold of the reins.

22. The *Vālakhilyas*[1] sit surrounding him. The chariot of the Moon has three wheels. His horses are as white as the *Kunda* flower.

23. Five horses are yoked to the left and five to the right. The Moon moves about by this. The chariot of the son of the Moon (*Budha*—Mercury) is evolved out of the substances-wind and fire.

24-25. He has eight tawny-coloured horses as fast as the wind. *Śukra's* great chariot has the fender and bottom pole. It is yoked with horses born of earth. It is adorned with banners. The chariot of the son of earth (Mars) is like heated gold in colour.

26. It has eight horses. It is huge in size.

27-29. The horses are crimson-coloured like *Padmarāga*-gem. They are evolved out of fire. *Bṛhaspati* (Jupiter) stays in each Zodiac for a year. His gold-coloured chariot is fitted with eight grey horses. Saturn moves very slowly seated on a chariot fitted with horses of variegated colours evolved out of the ether. The horses of *Rāhu* are eight. They are bee-coloured. The chariot is grey-coloured.

1. They are said to be pigmy in size and 60,000 in number. According to the legends they were born from the hair of Prajāpati or from Sumati, the wife of Kratu. They move with the sun.

30. They are yoked only once and they move constantly, O Śiva. The horses fitted to the chariot of *Ketu* are eight in number. They are as fast as the wind.

31. Some are smoke-coloured, some straw-coloured, and some as crimson as the lac-juice. The islands, rivers, mountains and the ocean, nay the whole universe (consisting of many worlds) is the body of Lord Viṣṇu.

CHAPTER FIFTYNINE

Astrology

Sūta said :

1. After having expounded the dimensions of the different planets, Lord Keśava explained the essence of Astrology that has fourfold aims, to Rudra, the giver of everything that he is.

Hari said :

2. *Kṛttikā* (Alcyone) (A group of six stars) has Fire-god as the Presiding Deity. *Rohiṇi* (Aldebarem) has *Brahmā*. *Ilvalā*—otherwise known as *Mṛgaśiras* (Orionis) has the moon as the presiding deity; *Ardrā* (Betelguese) has *Rudra*.

3. *Punarvasu* (Pollux) has *Aditi*, *Tiṣya* (Puṣya) (Cameri) has *Guru* (Jupiter), *Āśleṣa* (Hydrae) has *Sarpa* (Rāhu); *Maghā* (Regulus) has *Pitṛs* (Manes).

4. *Pūrvaphālguni* (Lenis) has *Bhaga* (Śiva); *Uttaraphālgunī* (Denebola) has *Aryaman*; *Hasta* (Spica) has *Savitṛ* (Sun); *Citra* (Corvi) has *Tvaṣṭṛ*.

5. *Svāti* (Arcturus) has *Vāyu* (wind); *Viśākhā* (Libra) has *Indra* and fire.

6. *Anurādhā* (Scorpia) has *Mitra* (Sun); *Jyeṣṭhā* (Antares) has *Śakra* (Indra); the presiding deity of *Mūla* (Scorpia) is *Nirṛti* as explained by those who know it.

7. *Pūrvāṣāḍhā* (Sagittari) has *Apaḥ* (water); *Uttarāṣāḍhā* (Sagittari) has *Viśvedevas*. *Abhijit* has *Brahmā*, *Śravaṇa* (Affair) has *Viṣṇu*.

8. *Dhaniṣṭhā* (Delphini) *has Vāsava* (Indra), as mentioned by scholars: *Śatabhiṣak* (Aquarii) has *Varuṇa.*

9. *Pūravabhādrapada* (Monkele) has *Aja* (*Brahmā*): *Uttarabhādrapada* (Pegasi) has *Ahirbudhna*. *Revati* (Piscium) has *Pūṣan*. *Aśvini* (Arietis) has *Aśvinīdevas.*

10. *Bharaṇi* (Arietis) has *Yama.* Thus I have mentioned the different presiding deities of the different stars. *Brahmāṇī* stands in the east on the first and ninth day of the lunar fortnight.

11. *Maheśvarī* stands in the north on the second and tenth day. *Vārāhī* stands in the south on the fifth and thirteenth day.

12. *Indrāṇī* stands in the west on the sixth and the fourteenth. Cāmuṇḍā in the north-west on the seventh day and Full moon day.

13. *Mahālakṣmī in* the north-east on the eighth day and the new moon day. Vaiṣṇavī stands in the south-east on the third and eleventh day.

14. *Kaumārī* in the south-west on the fourth and twelfth days. No one shall travel in the direction of the *Yoginis.*

15. The following stars are auspicious for undertaking journeys :—*Aśvini, Revati, Mṛgaśiras, Mūla, Punarvasu, Puṣya, Hasta*, and *Jyeṣṭhā.*

16-18. For wearing new garments the following stars are auspicious:—*Hasta, Citrā, Svāti, Viśākhā, Anurādhā, Uttarāphālguni, Uttarāṣāḍhā, Uttarabhādrapada, Aśvinī, Rohiṇī, Puṣya, Dhaniṣṭhā* and *Punarvasu.* The following stars are said to be *Adhovaktras* (face turned down) : *Kṛttikā, Bharaṇi, Āśleṣā, Maghā, Mūlā, Viśākhā, Pūrvāṣāḍhā, Pūrvāphālguni,* and *Pūrvabhādrapadā.* All activities involving going down the earth such as digging tanks, wells, lakes,

19. Laying foundations of temples, digging treasures, going into mines, digging grass, ploughing can be done during these stars.

20-21. Other activities such as the study of Mathematics, Astrology etc. can also be undertaken. The following stars are said to be *Pārśvamukha* (face sideways) *Revati, Aśvini, Citrā, Svāti, Hasta, Punarvasu, Anurādhā, Mṛgaśiras* and *Jyeṣṭhā.*

22. Taming of elephants, camels, horses, bullocks and buffaloes, sowing of seeds, paying visits, making of wheels, chariots and machines, floating of boats,

23-24. Can be done during these stars. The following nine stars are said to be *Ūrdhvamukha* :— *Rohiṇī*, *Ārdrā*, *Puṣya*, *Dhaniṣṭhā*, *Uttarāphālgunī*, *Uttarāṣāḍhā*, *Uttarabhādrapada*, *Śatabhiṣak* and *Śravaṇa*. During these stars a king can be crowned, and silk clothes can be worn.

25. All activities involving going up and all noble actions can be pursued. The following days of the lunar fortnight are inauspicious : fourth, sixth, eighth, ninth,

26. Twelfth, fourteenth, new moon and full moon. The following days are auspicious :—first day of the dark fortnight, second day of either fortnight if it is on Wednesday.

27. Third day on Tuesday; fourth day on Saturday; fifth day on Thursday, sixth day on Tuesday and Friday.

28. Seventh day on Wednesday; eighth day on Tuesday and Sunday; ninth day on Monday; tenth day *on* Thursday.

29. Eleventh day on Thursday and Friday; twelfth day on Wednesday; thirteenth day on Friday and Tuesday; fourteenth day on Saturday.

30. Full Moon and new Moon on Thursday are good. The sun burns the twelfth day of the lunar fortnight [*Dvādaśī* falling on a Sunday is burnt (*dagdha*)]. The moon burns the eleventh day.

31. Mars burns the tenth day [*Daśamī* on *Tuesday*]; Budha (Mercury) (Wednesday) burns the ninth day; Jupiter (Thursday) burns the eighth day; Bhārgava (Friday) burns the seventh day.

32-33. The Sun's son (Saturn) burns the sixth day. During these burnt days, one shall not travel. The undertaking of long journeys shall be avoided on the first, eighth, ninth and the fourteenth days of the lunar fortnight and on Wednesdays. The sixth day when the *lagna* (Ascendent) is *Meṣa* (Aries) or *Karkaṭaka* (Cancer); the eighth day with the *lagna Kanyā* (Virgo) or *Mithuna* (Gemini).

34. The fourth day when the *Lagna* is *Vṛṣa* (Taurus) or *Kumbha* (Aquaris) ; the twelfth day when the *lagna* is *Makara* (Capricorn) or *Tulā* (Libra) ; the tenth day, when the *lagna* is

Vṛścika (Scorpio) or *Siṁha* (Leo) and the fourteenth day when *the lagna* is *Dhanuṣ* (Sagittarius) or *Mīna* (Pisces).

Hari said :

35-37. Times are also *dagdha* (burnt) and hence inauspicious for undertaking journeys. The following conjunctions are *Autpātika* (harmful). They may cause death, sickness, etc.: that of the Sun (Sunday) with *Viśākhā, Anurādhā or Jyeṣṭhā*; that of the Moon (Monday) with *Pūrvāṣāḍhā, Uttarāṣāḍhā or Śravaṇa*; that of Mars (Tuesday) with *Śatabhiṣak, Dhaniṣṭhā*, or *Purvabhādrapada*; that of Mercury (Wednesday) with *Revatī, Aśvinī or Bharaṇī*; that of Jupiter (Thursday) with *Rohiṇī Mṛgaśiras or Ārdrā*; that of Venus (Friday) with *Puṣya, Āśleṣā* or *Maghā* and that of Saturn with *Uttarāphālgunī, Hasta or Chitrā.*

38-39. The following conjunctions are *Amṛtayogas* (Nectar-like) and hence conducive to the fulfilment of tasks undertaken:—The sun in *Mūla*, the moon in *Śravaṇa*, Mars in *Uttarabhādrapada*, Mercury in *Kṛttikā*; Jupiter in *Punarvasu*; Venus in *Pūrvāphālgunī*, and *Svāti* in Saturn.

40. Add together the letters in the names of husband and wife. Divide by three. If two is the remainder, wife is harmed; if one or zero, husband is harmed.

41-43. There are certain *yogas* (conjunctions) bringing death. All auspicious activities shall be avoided then. In *Viṣkambha*—five *hours*; in *Śūla*—seven *hours*; in *Gaṇḍa*—six *hours*; in *Atigaṇḍa* — six *hours*; in *Vyāghāta* and *Vajra* nine *hours*. In *Vyatīpāta, Parigha* and *Vaidhṛta* the whole day.

44-45. The following are *Siddha yogas* — auspicious conjunctions when all evils are destroyed — the *Sun* and *Hasta* Jupiter and *Puṣya, Anurādhā* and Mercury, *Rohiṇī* and Saturn, *Mṛgaśiras* and Moon, *Revatī* and Venus, *Aśvinī* and Mars.

46-47. The following are *Viṣayogas* — poisonous conjunctions. *Bharaṇī* with Venus; *Citrā* with Moon, *Uttarāṣāḍhā* with Mars, *Dhaniṣṭhā* with Mercury, *Śatabhiṣak* with Jupiter; *Rohiṇī* with Venus and *Revatī* with Saturn.

48-49. The stars auspicious for the performance of post-natal religious rites are:—*Puṣya, Punarvasu, Revatī, Citrā, Śravaṇā, Dhaniṣṭhā, Hasta, Aśvinī, Mṛgaśiras* and *Śatabhiṣak*. The following stars are very inauspicious for journey and if journey is undertaken at that time it will result in death : *Viśākhā*, *Uttarāphālguni*, *Uttarāṣāḍhā*, *Uttarabhādrapadā*, *Maghā*, *Ārdrā*, *Bharaṇī*, *Āśleṣā* and *Kṛttikā*.

CHAPTER SIXTY

Astrology

Hari said :

1. The *daśā* (duration of the period of special influence) of the Sun is for six years; that of the Moon fifteen years; that of the Mars eight years; that of Mercury seventeen years.

2. That of Saturn ten years; that of the Jupiter nineteen years; that of Rāhu twelve years and that of Venus twenty-one years.

3. The *daśā* of Sun yields misery and heart-burn and destroys kings. Moon's *daśā* yields prosperity, happiness and sumptuous food.

4. The *daśā* of Mars is miserable. It may cause deposition from the kingdom, etc. The *daśā* of Mercury gives women of divine charms and flourishing kingdom with ample treasury.

5. The *daśā* of saturn destroys kingdom and yields misery to kinsmen. The *daśā* of Jupiter provides happiness, virtue and flourishing kingdom.

6. The *daśā* of Rāhu causes destruction of kingdoms and produces sickness and misery. The *daśā* of Venus provides elephants, horses, flourishing kingdom and women.

7. *Meṣa Rāśi* is the house of Mars; *Vṛṣa* that of Venus; *Mithuna* that of Mercury; *Karkaṭaka* that of Moon.

8. *Siṁha* is the house of sun. *Kanyā* that of Mercury; *Tulā* that of Venus; *Vṛścika* that of Mars;

9. *Dhanus* that of Jupiter; *Makara* and *Kumbha* both of Saturn and *Mīna* that of Jupiter. Thus I have explained the houses of the planets.

10. If in the month, of *Āṣāḍha* there are two full moons and two *pūrvāṣāḍhās*, it is called *Dvirāṣāḍha* (having two *Āṣāḍhas*). Viṣṇu sleeps in Cancer then.

11-13. Auspicious stars for wearing ornaments are *Aśvinī*, *Revatī*, *Citrā* and *Dhaniṣṭhā*. At the time of starting on a journey the following animals seen on the right are auspicious :—deer, serpent, monkey, cat, dog, boar, birds, mungoose, and mouse. Seeing a Brahmin girl, dead body, conch, bugle, earth, bamboo, woman, and a pot full of water, at the time of starting on a journey is auspicious. A jackal, a camel, a mule, etc. when seen on the left side while proceeding on a journey are auspicious.

14. Seeing cotton, medicine, oil, burning embers, snakes, a woman with dishevelled hair, a garland of red flowers and a nude person is inauspicious.

15. I shall explain the implication of *Hikkā* (the sound of hiccough when heard). If it is heard from the east it produces great results from the south-east—sorrow and anxiety; from the south—loss.

16. From the south-west—sorrow and anxiety; from the west—sumptuous feast: from the north-west —money; from the north—quarrel.

17. From the north-east—death. Draw the solar circle and inscribe in it the picture of the sun in the form of a man.

18-20. Find out the asterism on which the Sun presides (at the time of the birth of a child). Write the names of the three stars beginning with that star on the head. The next three stars shall be assigned to the mouth; assign one star to each of the shoulders, arms, and palms. Assign five stars to the heart; one to the navel; one to the genital; one to each of the knees The remaining six stars to the feet.

21-23 If the star at the time of birth is one of those assigned to the feet, the child dies young; if it is one of those assigned to the knees—foreign travel; one at the genital—adulterer; one at the navel—he will be satisfied with what little he gets; one at the heart—he shall be a great lord; one at the palms—a thief; one at the arms he falls from high position; one at the shoulders—very wealthy; one in the mouth—gets sumptuous feast; one at the head—he gets silk-clothes.

CHAPTER SIXTYONE

Astrology

Hari said :

1. When the moon is on the ascendency after the seventh day in the bright half it is always favourable. Similarly the second, fifth and ninth days are also auspicious.

2. Being honoured by the world like Jupiter it is considered (also like him). There are twelve Avasthās (stages) of the moon. Hear them.

3-6. I shall explain them as they are situated in sets of three stars beginning with *Aśvinī* [2¼ *Nakṣatras* for each *Avasthā.*] The results are :—*Pravāsa* (exile), *Punarnaṣṭa* (repeated loss), *Mṛtyu* (death), *Jaya* (success), *Hāsa* (being laughed at), *Krīḍā* (sexual sport) *Pramoda* (happiness), *Viṣāda* (sorrow), *Bhoga* (enjoyment), *Jvara* (fever and debility), *Kampa* (trembling), *Svastha* (being at ease). If the moon is in *Janma Rāśi* (the sign of zodiac at the time of birth) it gives satisfaction; in the second, absense of mental satisfaction.

7. In the third—royal honour, in the fourth—quarrels with others; in the fifth—acquisition of wife.

8. In the sixth—acquisition of wealth and grains; in the seventh—enjoyment of sexual pleasure and praise of others; in the eighth—risk of life, in the ninth—accumulation of wealth.

9. In the tenth—successful fulfilment of activities; in the eleventh—sure success; in the twelfth—death is certain.

10. Making a journey to the east during the seven stars from Kṛttikā is fruitful; journey to the south can be made during the seven stars from Maghā, making journey to the west during the six stars from Anurādhā is good.

11. And journey to the north during the seven stars from Dhaniṣṭhā is good. The stars Aśvinī, Revatī, Citrā, and Dhaniṣṭhā are auspicious for wearing ornaments.

12. For the performance of marriage, journey, installation of idols, etc. the auspicious stars are Mṛgaśiras, Aśvinī, Citrā, Puṣya, Mūla and Hasta.

13. Venus and Moon are auspicious when they are in the

Janma Rāśī or in the second house; Moon, Mercury, Venus and Jupiter in the third house are good.

14. Mars, Saturn, Moon, Sun and Mercury in the fourth house are good; Venus and Jupiter in the fifth house aspected by Moon and Ketu are good.

15. Saturn, Sun and Mars in the sixth; Jupiter and Moon in the seventh; Mercury and Venus in the eighth are good. Jupiter in the ninth is good.

16. Sun, Saturn and Moon in the tenth; All the planets in the eleventh; Mercury and Venus in twelfth are beneficent.

17-18. The ṣaḍṣṭaka (being in the sixth and eighth mutually) is conducive to pleasure such as :—Siṁha with Makara, Kanyā with Meṣa, Tulā with Mīna, Kumbha with Karkaṭaka, Dhanuṣ with Vṛṣabha, Mithuna with Vṛścika.

CHAPTER SIXTYTWO

Astrology

Hari said :—

1. At sunrise every day the sun is in his own *Rāśi.* Then he begins his transit to the other *Rāśis* (signs of zodiac). He covers six *Rāśis* in the day-time and six in the night.

2. In *Mina-lagna* and *Meṣa-lagna* he spends five *ghatikās* each (5+24=120 minutes=2 Hrs.) In *Vṛṣa-lagna* and *Kumbha-lagna* he spends four ghaṭikās each (96 mts). In *Makara-lagna* and *Mithuna-lagna* he spends three *ghaṭikās* each (1 Hr.—12 mts.); In *Dhanur-lagna* and *Karkaṭaka-lagna* he spends five *ghaṭikāṣ* each (2 Hrs.)

3. In *Siṁha* and *Vṛścika-lagnas* he spends six *ghaṭikās* each (2 Hrs. 24 mts.) and in *Kanyā-lagna* and *Tulā-lagna* he spends seven *ghaṭikās* each (2 Hrs. 48 mts.) Thus I explained the time spent in *lagnas.*

4. Meṣa and Mīna lagnas have six *ghaṭikās*; other lagnas have six or four ghaṭikās. Each and every lagna is circumscribed by its own ghaṭikās. [The second part is not clear.]

5. A woman born in *Meṣa-lagna* becomes barren; in *Vṛṣa-lagna* very passionate; in *Mithuna-lagna*—fortunate; in *Karakaṭa-lagna*—a prostitute.

6. In *Siṁha-lagna*—she will have very few children, in *Kanyā-lagna*—very beautiful and comely; in *Tulā-lagna*—beauty and prosperity; in *Vṛścika-lagna*—harsh of speech.

7. In *Dhanur-lagna*—endowed with good luck; in *Makara-lagna*—she will marry a baseborn; in *Kumbha-lagna*—very few children; and in *Mīna-lagna*—detachment from the world.

8. The *Rāśis Tulā, Karkaṭaka, Meṣa* and *Makara* are called *Cara rāśis* (moving).

9. The *Rāśis—Siṁha, Vṛṣa, Kumbha* and *Vṛścika* are *Sthira*; *Kanyā, Dhanus, Mīna* and *Mithuna* are of both characteristics.

10. Undertaking a journey and other activities involving motion are to be in the *Cara Rāśis*. Entering a house and other affairs involving stabilisation are to be in *Sthira Rāśis*.

11. Installation of idols, marriage and other activities involving motion and stabilization are to be in *Dvisvabhāva Rāśis*. The first, sixth and the eleventh days of lunar fortnight are called *Nandā*.

12. The second, seventh and the twelfth are called *Bhadrā*; the eighth, third and the thirteenth are called *Jayā*.

13. The fourth, ninth and the fourteenth are called *Riktā*, they are to be avoided; the fifth, the tenth and the full moon are called *Pūrṇā* and they are auspicious.

14. Mercury is called *Cara* (moving); Jupiter—*Kṣipra* (quick); Śukra—*Mṛdu* (soft); Sun—*Dhruva* (fixed); Saturn—*Dāruṇa* (terrific); Mars—*Ugra* (fierce); Moon—*Sama* (having equanimity).

15. Journey should be undertaken when *Cara* and *Kṣipra* planets are ascendant. Entry of house, etc. when *Mṛdu* and *Dhruva* planets are ascendant; war should be undertaken when *Dāruṇa* and *Ugra* planets are ascendant, if victory is wished for.

16. The anointing of a king and activities with fire should be performed on Monday. House-building activities can be started in the ascendancy of Soma and Tulā.

17. When Mars is ascendant, leading an army, war, practising of weapons can be undertaken; activities involving practice for yogic or mantra-siddhis and journeys can be undertaken when Mercury is ascendant.

18. When Jupiter is ascendant, study, worship of gods, wearing of garments and ornaments can be undertaken; marriage, riding an elephant, contract with women can be undertaken when Venus is ascendant.

19. An installation of idols, entry to a house, binding elephants, etc., are auspicious when *Saturn* is ascendant.

CHAPTER SIXTYTHREE

Physiogonomy

Hari said :

1. I shall now describe in brief the prominent characteristic features of men and women, O Śaṅkara. If the palms are soft like the inner portion of a lotus and do not perspire.

2. If the fingers are close together; if the nails are copper-coloured, if the ankles are well shaped and free from protruding nerves: if the feet are plump and shaped like the back of a tortoise—the man is bound to become a king.

3. Rough and yellow-coloured nails, face lifted up with protruding nerves, feet shaped like winnowing sieves, toes dry and fleshless.

4. All these indicate sorrow and poverty. There is no doubt about it. The calf resembling the trunk of an elephant with sparsely grown hairs—is an excellent sign.

5. To those who are destined to become great men or kings each pore has a hair growing out of it. To those who are destined to become great scholars and Vedic interpreters, two hairs grow out of each pore.

6. To those who are destined to become poor three hairs grow out of each pore. A sickly person has knee caps

devoid of flesh. A man with a small penis is destined to be rich but without issues.

7. A man with a stout penis shall be poor. A man having a single scrotum will be miserable. A man having scrotums of different sizes shall become lecherous. If the scrotums are of equal size he shall be a king.

8. A man having scrotums hanging lose will not live long. A man having badly shaped scrotum shall be poor. Men become happy if the scrotums are pale coloured and dirty in appearance.

9. The man passing urine with a loud noise shall suffer from poverty. Men destined to become kings pass urine steadily without noise. Those destined to enjoy pleasures have even bellies. Pot-bellied persons are penurious.

10. A man destined to be poor has serpentine belly. Lines indicate the age of men. A man in whose forehead three straight parallel lines are seen,

11. Shall be happy with children and will live upto sixty years. Two lines indicate life-expectation upto forty years.

12. A single line extending upto the ears indicates a short life, say upto twenty years. Three lines extending upto the ears indicate a life expectation upto a hundred years.

13. A man having two such lines (extending upto ears) shall live upto seventy years. If the three lines are partly distinct and partly indistinct he shall live upto sixty years.

14. If the number of lines decreases, twenty years shall be reduced from the previous. If the lines are broken in the middle premature death is the result.

15. If the figure of a trident or a broad-edged spear appears on the forehead the man shall be endowed with children and wealth and shall live upto hundred years.

16. If the line of longevity comes upto the centre of the middle finger and index finger the man lives upto hundred years.

17. The first line from the thumb is the line of knowledge. The middle line goes upto the root (bottom) of the palm. Beyond that is the line of longevity.

18. If that line extends upto the little finger, broken or unbroken, he shall live a hundred years.

19. O Rudra, the line on the palm indicates the longevity as also the enjoyment of pleasures. There is no doubt.

20. Based on the little finger if the line of life reaches upto the middle finger the man shall live upto sixty years.

CHAPTER SIXTYFOUR

Physiognomy

Hari said:

1. The girl whose locks are curly, face circular in shape and the navel curling to the right makes the family flourish.

2. She whose complexion is golden and whose hands resemble red lotus is one in a thousand women famous for chastity.

3. The woman with uneven hair and rotund eyes shall be unhappy everywhere and becomes widowed soon.

4. A girl with a face like the full moon and shining like the rising sun, having wide eyes and lips red like the *Bimba* fruit shall always be happy.

5. If a woman has many linear marks over her body she will suffer much; a few lines like that indicate poverty; red linear marks indicate happiness in life and black lines denote slavery.

6. A real wife is like a minister for the personal affairs of her husband; a friend in executing his tasks; in affectionate dealings she is like his mother and in his bed she is like a courtesan to him. Such a wife is auspicious.

7. The woman having lines in her palm resembling a goad, a circle or a wheel marries a king and gives birth to a son.

8. If the sides of a woman or her breasts contain plenty of hair and if her lips are high the husband dies soon.

9. If the lines on the palm of a woman resemble a fort-wall or the entrance, she is destined to become a queen even if she is born of a poor family.

10. If a woman has brown hairs curling upwards over her body, she is destined to become a slave even if she is born a princess.

11. If the little finger and the thumb of a woman placed on the ground do not rest there, she is destined to be a widow and a woman of ill-repute.

12. A woman, who shakes the ground as she treads, kills her husband quickly and lives like a *mleccha* woman.

13. Smooth oily eyes indicate happy married life ; oily teeth denote pleasure of food; oily skin indicates sexual pleasure and oily foot denotes possession of conveyances.

14. If the feet are beautiful and raised up with copper-coloured nails; if the soles have the lines resembling fish, goad and lotus, wheel and ploughshare.

15. And they do not perspire, the woman leads a happy life. The calves shall be free from hair, the thighs shall resemble the elephant's trunk.

16. The vagina shall be broad like the leaf of an *Aśvattha* tree, the navel shall be deep curling to the right, the three curls of hair curling to the right, the chest and breasts shall be free from hair. These are all auspicious signs.

CHAPTER SIXTYFIVE

Physiognomy

Hari said :

1. I shall now describe the auspicious characteristics of men and women as narrated by Samudra[1] (the sage who originally propounded this) by knowing which one can understand the past and future without difficulty.

2. If the feet rarely perspire, have the soles as soft as the inner surface of a lotus, the toes adjoin one another, nails are copper-coloured, have sufficient warmth, are free from protruding nerves,

1. A legendary personality said to be the originator of *sāmudrika* śāstra (palmistry).

3. The instep is arched like the back of a tortoise, the ankles are concealed, and the heels are fine, the man is destined to be a king. If the feet are flat and spreading like a winnowing fan, harsh of surface, uneven, have many protruding nerves,

4. Dry, the nails are greyish and the toes are detached too much, the man is destined to be poor. If the feet have the ridges lifted up, the man is destined to be a wanderer; if the feet are reddish brown,

5. The man brings about split in the family; if they are dart-like the man may slay even a brahmin. If both the calves are of equal length and have soft sparsely grown hair,

6. The thighs are like the trunk of an elephant and the knees are fleshy and even, the man is destined to be a king.

7. If the calves are like those of a fox and there is only a single hair growing from each pore the man is destined to be poor. If there are two hairs growing from each pore the man is destined to be a king or a great scholar and very prosperous.

8. If there are three or more hairs growing from each pore the man is destined to be poor, miserable and despised. Persons with curly hair are likely to die in exile.

9. If the knee has no flesh at all he will be lucky; if there is a little of flesh and that is depressed he is loved by women; if the knee is deformed, the man becomes poor and if it is plump and fleshy he will win a kingdom.

10. Great men say that a man with a short penis lives long and becomes rich; the man with a stout penis has no son and will be devoid of wealth.

11. If the penis is slanting to the left the man shall be devoid of sons and wealthy; if it is a bit curved he shall have sons;if it is depressed below, he will be poor.

12. If the penis is small, the man will not beget sons; if it has protruding nerves he shall be happy; if the bulb of the penis is stout, he will be blessed with sons, etc.

13. If the scrotum is well-hidden he becomes a king; if it is long and curved he is devoid of wealth; a man with a short penis will be strong and spirited in fight.

14. A man with a single scrotum is weak; if the two scrotums are unequal in size, he will be running after girls; if

the scrotums are of equal size, he shall be a king; if the scrotums hang loose, he will live hundred years.

15. If the scrotums are lifted up the man shall be long-lived; if they are rough the man becomes a lord; if they are grey the man is poor; if they are dirty in appearance, the man enjoys happiness.

16. If the urine comes out noisily and silently by turns, the man becomes poor; if the urine comes out evenly, or in two. three, four, five or six spurts

17. Or if the urine comes out curling to the right, the man becomes a king;If the urine comes out in scattered drops, he is poor; if it comes out in a single continous flow, it indicates happiness.

18. Persons passing urine in a single flow will enjoy women, persons having high, equal and oily scrotum will possess good women and riches; persons with scrotum depressed in the middle will beget daughters.

19. If the semen is very dry the man is destined to be poor and miserable; if the semen is fragrant like flowers, the man becomes a king; if the semen has the smell of honey the man will have plenty of wealth.

20. If the semen has the smell of fish the man begets sons; if the semen has no smell the man begets daughters; if the semen has the smell of meat the man will enjoy sexual pleasure: if the semen smells of ichor the man becomes a performer of sacrifices.

21. If the semen emits a salty smell the man is destined to be poor. A man who finishes coitus quickly, enjoys longevity; a man of prolonged coitus is short-lived; a man with stout buttocks is destined to be poor.

22. A man with fleshy buttocks is ever happy; a person with a lion's buttocks is destined to be a king. Similarly, if the hips are leonine the man becomes a king; a man with monkey-like *hips* is destined to be poor.

23. Persons with serpentine, pan-like or pot-like bellies are destined to be poor. Persons with broad sides are rich and those with depressed sides reddish in hue are poor.

24. Persons having arm-pits of equal size enjoy various objects of life; those with too depressed armpits are destined to

be poor; those of elevated arm-pits become kings and those of unequal armpits are crooked in character.

25. Persons having fishlike bellies are destined to be wealthy; those with large and capacious navel are destined to be happy; if the navel is depressed the man will lead a miserable life.

26. If the navel is within a curly wrinkle, the man will suffer much; if the wrinkle is curling to the left, the man will achieve something; if to the right he will be intelligent.

27. If the wrinkle is long and spreads on either side, the man shall be longlived; if it is above the ground, the man is destined to be wealthy; if it goes downwards, the man will possess cows; if it has the shape of the pericarp of a lotus he shall become a king.

28. A man with a single wrinkle lives for hundred years; with two wrinkles enjoys prosperity; with three wrinkles he becomes a king or a preceptor; if the wrinkles are straight he enjoys happiness.

29. If the wrinkles are awry he will have illicit union with women of base character. If the sides are fleshy, soft and of equal size with curly locks of hair turning right, the man is destined to be a king.

30. If otherwise, he will be a slave to others, devoid of wealth and happiness. If the nipples are not protruding up, men become lucky.

31. If they are uneven or long or yellow in hue, they are destined to be poor. If the chest is stout and fleshy, of *even* height and unmoving.

32. He is destined to be a king; if full of hard hair and protruding nerves, the man is destined to be base. If both the sides of the chest are equal, stout and firm, the man becomes rich.

33. If of unequal size, he becomes poor and is doomed to die by means of a weapon. If the clavicle is rugged or inter-woven by bones, the man is destined to be poor.

34. If it is raised up, the man will enjoy life; if it is depressed the man becomes poor; if it is thick he becomes rich. If the neck is thin and flat the man is poor; if the throat is dry and nerves protrude, the man becomes happy.

35. If a man is buffalo-necked, he is destined to be a warrior; if he has the neck of a deer, he masters sacred literature. A man with a conch-like neck becomes a king and he with a long neck becomes a glutton.

36. A back devoid of hair and not stooping indicates auspiciousness; otherwise it is inauspicious. The armpit shaped like the leaf of the *Aśvattha* (Holy fig) tree emitting sweet smell and having hair like those of a deer is an excellent sign.

37-38. Otherwise it indicates poverty. Plump, curling a little, and well joined hands are good. Well-rounded thick and long coming upto the knees indicate royalty. In poor people the hands are short and covered with hair. Good hands resemble the trunk of an elephant.

39. Fingers having ventilators are auspicious. Those of an intelligent person are short; those of servants are flat.

40. If the fingers are stout, the man is bound to be poor; if the fingers are very lean the man is sure to be humble. Persons with hands resembling those of a monkey are poor; with hands like those of a tiger are strong.

41. If the palm is depressed the ancestral property is doomed to be destroyed. If the wrists are well hidden and well knit, emitting sweet smell, the man is destined to be,

42. A king; persons destined to be poor have wrists that are noisy on being twisted. Persons destined to be rich have wrists depressed and well covered (with flesh).

43. If they are streched the man pays taxes always; if the wrists are unequal they are not good indications. If the palms and hands have the colour of the lac (red), the man is bound to be a lord.

44. If they are yellow, he is sure to be an adulterer; if they are rough he will be poor. If the nails resemble husks, the man is sure to be impotent, if the nails are split, he is bound to be crooked.

45. With nails of stunted growth, he is sure to be indigent; if the nails are pale the man is bound to be fond of verbal disputes. If the thumb has lines in the form of a barley grain and is copper-coloured he is destined to be a king.

46. If the marks of barley grain are at the root of the thumb, be will beget sons; if the joints of the fingers are well

apart he will enjoy longevity and will be fortunate; if the fingers stand apart he will be indigent.

47. If they are close together he will be rich. If three lines start from the wrist and go up to the palm he will become a king.

48. If pictures of a yoke or a fish are formed by the lines in the palm, the man will perform sacrifices; lines resembling thunderbolt indicate wealth; those like the tail of a fish indicate scholarship.

49. Lines resembling *Śaṅkha,* umbrella, tent, elephant or lotus indicate royal glory; those resembling pot, goad, banner or lotus stalk indicate affluence.

50. Lines resembling rope indicate possession of cows and cattle; those like the *Svastika* indicate royalty and lordship and lines in the shape of a wheel, sword iron club, bow or lance indicate royalty.

51. Lines in the shape of a mortar indicate performance of sacrifices; those resembling altar indicate the performance of *Agnihotra*;[1] lines in the form of tank, temple or a triangle indicate virtuousness.

52. Lines at the foot of the thumb foretell happiness and birth of sons, small ones indicate wives. One starting from the foot of the little finger and going upto the index finger,

53. Indicates longevity for a hundred years; if it is broken in the middle the man over-comes danger.[2] Having many lines indicates poverty. If the chin is thin the man becomes devoid of possessions.

54. If the chin is fleshy and plump the man becomes wealthy. If the lips are red the man becomes a king. The lips of a king resemble the *Bimba*[3] fruit. If the lips are split, rough,

55. And uneven, the man becomes poor. Oily (smooth and shining) adjoining teeth are auspicious. Sharp teeth of equal size are good; tongue reddish in colour is auspicious.

1. Maintenance of the sacred fire and offering oblations to it. *SSED* p. 4.
2. Variant : *chinnayā taruto bhayam.*
3. The same as Coccinia indica, (*GVDB* p. 274)

56. A long and fine tongue is also auspicious. A white palate indicates destruction of riches. If the palate is rough and dark in colour and if the mouth is finely shaped,

57-58. It indicates royalty; the opposite indicates misery. A round face indicates prosperity; if it is of a lady she will beget a son; a long face indicates poverty, misfortune and great sorrow. A square face indicates that he is a coward, sinner and a rogue.

59-60. A depressed face indicates issuelessness; a short face indicates miserliness. Persons with shining moustache enjoy all luxuries; smooth soft thickly grown moustache is auspicious, if its tip is not broken. A man with a reddish moustache is a thief. Persons with slightly red rough moustache may be like *Karṇa*[1] (very liberal) but may have tragic sinful death.

61. If the ears are flat and less fleshy he will enjoy all luxuries; misers will have short ears; kings will have spear-shaped ears; ears covered with hair indicate shortage of the span of life.

62. Persons with big ears become kings or rich men; ears smooth, hanging down, fleshy and not firm indicate royalty.

63. A man with depressed cheeks enjoys all luxuries; well-formed plump cheeks indicate that the man will become a minister. A man with nose like that of a parrot is happy, a man of dry nose lives long.

64. A person with a nasal edge looking as if chiselled and deep nostrils will have intercourse with unworthy women. Good luck is indicated by a long nose. A thief has a curved nose.

65. Flat nose indicates death and misfortune; a long straight nose with small nostrils and well defined curvature at the tip indicates royalty.

66. The nose bent towards the right indicates cruelty. A sudden spasm of sneeze indicates strength; if it is continual it indicates delight and if resonant it indicates long life.

1. The well known character of the Mahābhārata. He was born to Kuntī before she was married to Pāṇḍu : Indra, disguised as a *brāhmaṇa*, begged for his armour which he readily gave it to him. Hence he is known as a great donor.

67. If the eyes resemble petals of a lotus and are a little curved at the corners the men will be happy; A sinner has cat-like eyes and a wicked man has eyes tawny like honey.

68. Squint-eyed persons are ruthless; green-eyed men are sinful; valorous persons have oblique dim eyes and commanders of armies have eyes like those of an elephant.

69. Lordly persons have grave eyes, ministers have thick fleshy eyes; scholars have eyes like the blue lotus; good fortune is indicated by dark eyes.

70. Dark pupils and pupils protruding out and round eyes indicate a sinner, persons destined to be poor will have pitiable eyes.

71. Oily smooth skin indicates vast enjoyment of luxuries.[1] If the navel is elevated the man is short-lived. Persons having wide elevated eyebrows are happy; persons with uneven eyebrows are indigent.

72. Long unattached eyebrows indicate wealth, beautiful crescent-shaped eyebrows indicate richness; persons with broken eye-brows and with those depressed in the middle,

73. Are devoted to unworthy women and become devoid of children and wealth. If the forehead is high, wide conchlike and rugged,

74. The man becomes poor and those with crescent shaped foreheads become wealthy. Persons with foreheads wide like oystershells become preceptors; those with sinewy foreheads are sinful.

75. Persons with high foreheads with *Svastika*-shaped sinews become rich. Persons with depressed foreheads are fond of cruel deeds and deserve imprisonment.

76. Persons with foreheads covered (by hair on the head) are misers; high foreheads indicate royalty. Tearless gentle cry without piteous toes is auspicious.

77. Shrill cry with profuse perspiration is inauspicious. Untrembling mild laughter is excellent; laughter with the eyes closed indicates sin.

78. Frequent laughter indicates defect and the onset of madness. Three lines along the forehead indicate longevity upto hundred years.

1. The second part is not very clear.

79. If there are four lines, the man will become a king and live upto ninety-five years. If there is no line on the forehead, the man lives upto ninety years. If the lines are broken, the man will be guilty of sodomy.

80. If the lines reach the hair on the head, the man lives upto eighty years. If there are five, six, seven or more lines, the span of life is fifty years.

81. If there are curved lines, the man lives upto forty years; if the lines go to the eyebrows the span of life is thirty years; if the lines are curved towards the left the span of life is for twenty years; if the lines are short the man is short-lived.

82. If the head is umbrella-shaped, the man becomes rich or a king. A flat head indicates father's death; a circular head indicates richness.

83. A man having a pot-like head takes delight in sinful activities and is devoid of wealth. Black smooth slightly curled hairs,

84. Not too thickly grown with the ends, not snapped indicate royalty. Hairs having many roots, uneven in length, with gross tips, tawny-coloured,

85. Thickly grown, bent down, dark-blue in colour, indicate poverty. Whatever may be the limb, if it is very rough, sinewy and lacks in flesh,

86. It is a very inauspicious sign; otherwise it is auspicious. Persons destined to be kings have three which shall be wide, grave and long; five which are very fine; six which shall be high; four which shall be short,

87. Four which shall be red and seven which shall be even. Navel, voice and understanding—these shall be deep and grave.

88. Forehead, face and chest—these three shall be wide for a man. Eyes, sides, teeth, nose, mouth and back of the neck—these six shall be elevated.

89. Calves, neck, penis and back—these four shall be short. The hand, palate, lips and nails—these four shall be red.

90. The corners of the eyes, feet, tongue and lips shall be short. There are five which shall be fine—teeth, knots of fingers, nail, hair and skin.

91. There shall be long—the space between the nipples, hands, teeth, eyes and nose. I have mentioned the characteristic signs of men. I shall now describe those of women.

92. The queen's feet are smooth and even, the soles and nails are red; the toes are adjoining one another, the tips are raised; he who marries her shall surely be a king.

93. The heels shall be well hidden and plump. The soles shall have the lustre of lotus; they shall rarely perspire, are smooth and contain the lines of fish, goad or banner.

94. Thunderbolt, lotus and ploughshare—these signs indicate that a woman is destined to be a queen; otherwise not. The calves are devoid of hair, well-rounded and devoid of sinews—these are auspicious.

95. The joints shall not be manifestly clear and the knees are even. The thighs resemble the trunk of an elephant and are devoid of hair.

96. The vagina is of the shape of the figleaf and is very wide. Loins, forehead and thigh shall be high and arched like the back of a tortoise.

97-98. The clitoris shall be hidden. The hips shall be big and heavy. All the above limbs shall be large. The navel shall be fleshy, and curling to the right. The middle portion shall be bedecked by three circular wrinkles. The breasts shall be equally developed, devoid of hair and well-grown and firm.

99. The neck shall be firm, overgrown with hair soft and resembling conch. Red lips are auspicious; so also a circular fleshy plump face,

100. Teeth like the *Kunda*-flower (white) and a sweet voice like that of a cuckoo. Simplicity and consideration for others and absence of stubbornness in the speech pleasant to hear like that of a swan.

101. And a nose beautiful in appearance with symmetrical curves at the tip—all these are auspicious in women. The eyes shall be like the blue lotus close to the nose.

102. The brows should not be very thick. They must resemble the crescent moon. The forehead shall not be high.

It should resemble the semi-circular moon and be devoid of hairs.

103. The ears shall not be fleshy. They must be smooth and of equal size. The hair shall be glossy, dark-blue and soft and slightly curling.

104. Symmetrical well-formed head is auspicious for women. The following marks should be present either in the palm or soles—horse, elephant, *Śrīvṛkṣa* (the Sacred fig tree), sacrificial pole, arrow, barley grain, iron club.

105. Banner, *Chowri*[1], garland, a mount, earring, altar, *Śaṅkha*, umbrella, lotus, fish, *Svastika*, a good chariot,

106. Goad etc. Women with these signs shall become consorts of princes. The wrists shall be well-formed and well-hidden (by flesh), the hands shall be soft like the inner part of a lotus.

107. The palms shall neither be depressed nor elevated. Linear marks (as hereinafter mentioned) shall indicate continued matrimonial bliss in women. The line starting from the wrist and going upto the middle finger

108. Or in the palm or in the upper part of the instep is auspicious. The husband shall be very happy and even win a kingdom.

109. The line arising from the foot of the little finger shall make her live upto hundred years. If there is a line between the index finger and the middle finger it indicates chastity in women.

110. The line from the foot of the thumb, if short, makes the woman short-lived; if long, blesses the woman with sons; if faded the woman shall be proud.

111. If that line is broken in many places the woman is shortlived; if it is long and unbroken the woman enjoys longevity; all auspicious marks of woman have been mentioned; contrary signs are inauspicious.

112. If the palm is placed on the ground and the little finger and the ring finger do not touch the ground, she is

1. Bushy tail of Cāmara (Bos Grunniens) used as a fly-flap or fan, and reckoned as one of the insignia of royalty. *SSED* p. 206.

surely a whore. If the thumb goes beyond the root of the index finger that too is inauspicious similarly.

113. If the calves are elevated or have protruding sinews and are hairy and fleshy; if the belly resembles a pot.

114. And the private parts are curved to the left and a bit depressed the woman becomes unhappy. If the neck is short it indicates poverty; if it is very long—destruction of the family.

115. If it is very stout the woman becomes very fierce, there is no doubt about this. Squint in the eyes, dark blue or tawny in the eyes, roving eyes—these indicate absence of chastity.

116. If when she smiles two dimples are seen in the cheeks, she is surely one adultress. If the forehead hangs down the woman kills her brother-in-law.

117. If the belly hangs down she kills her father-in-law; and if the buttocks hang down, she kills her husband. A moustache-like growth of hair above the upper lip is inauspicious for the husband.

118. Hairy breasts are inauspicious and uneven ears too are inauspicious. Sharp and uneven teeth indicate misery.

119. If the gum is dark blue, she is a thief, if the teeth are long, she will bring about the death of her husband. If the hands resemble those of *Rākṣasas*, wolves or crows,

120. If they are sinewy, uneven and dry (wrinkled), the woman becomes poor. An elevated upper lip indicates quarrelsome nature and harshness in speech.

121. These defects are very great in ugly women. If there is beauty some of these defects can be ignored. I have mentioned the characteristics of men and women. Now I shall mention something informative.

CHAPTER SIXTYSIX

Astrology

Hari said :

1. An image without characteristic marks is better than worshipping one with circular signs thereon. The first image is *Sudarśana*; The next one is *Lakṣmī Nārāyaṇa.*

2. The image of *Acyuta* has three *Cakras*; *Caturbhuja* (four armed) image has four *Cakras*; the fifth, sixth and the seventh are *Vāsudeva*, *Pradyumna* and *Saṅkarṣaṇa.*

3. *Puruṣottama* is the eighth. Then *Navavyūha* and *Daśātmaka*. The eleventh is *Aniruddha* and *Dvādaśātmaka* is the twelfth.

4. Beyond that is *Ananta.* These characteristics are the number of lines in the *Cakra* in order. If these *Sudarśanas* are duly worshipped they give all desires.

5. Where there is *Śālagrāma* stone, there Lord of *Dvāravatī* (Viṣṇu) is also present. The coexistence of these two is conducive to salvation.

6. *Śālagrāma*, *Dvārakā*, *Naimiṣa*, *Puṣkara*[1], *Gayā*, *Vārāṇasi*, *Prayāga*, *Kurukṣetra*[2], *Śūkara.*

7. *Gaṅgā*, *Narmadā*, *Candrabhāgā*[3], *Sarasvati*, *Puruṣottama* and *Mahākāla*[4] are the sacred places, O Śaṅkara,

8. That remove all sins and yield enjoyment and emancipation. 1. *Prabhava*, 2. *Vibhava*, 3. *Śukra* (*Śukla*), 4. *Pramoda*, 5. *Prajāpati.*

9. 6. *Aṅgiras*, 7. *Śrīmukha*, 8. *Bhāva* (*Bhava*), 9. *Pūṣā*, 10. *Dhātṛ* (*Dhātu*), 11. *Īśvara*, 12. *Bahudhānya*, 13. *Pramāthī*, 14. *Vikrama*, 15. *Vidhu* (*Viṣu*).

10. 16. *Citrabhānu*, 17. *Svarbhānu* (*Svabhānu*), 18. *Dāruṇa* (*Tāraṇa*), 19. *Pārthiva*, 20. *Vyaya*, 21. *Sarvajit*, 22. *Sarvadhārī*, 23. *Virodhī*, 24. *Vikṛta* (*Vikṛtī*), 25. *Khara*,

1. A town about six miles to the north of Ajmer in Rajasthan. It has a lake considered to be very ancient and sacred. It is a place of pilgrimage.

2. The site of the Mahābhārata-war.

3. Modern Chenab.

4. The temple of Mahākāla at Ujjayinī (modern Ujjain in Madhya Pradesh).

11. 26. *Nandana*, 27. *Vijaya*, 28. *Jaya*, 29. *Manmatha*, 30. *Durmukha* (*Durmukhī*), 31. *Hemalamba* (*Hemalambi*), 32. *Vilamba*, 33. *Vikāra*, 34. *Śarvarī*, 35. *Plava*.

12. 36. *Śubhakṛt*, 37. *Śobhana*, 38. *Krodha*, 39. *Viśvāvasu*, 40. *Parābhava*, 41. *Plavaṅga*, 42. *Kīlaka*, 43. *Saumya*, 44. *Sādhāraṇa*, 45. *Virodhakṛt*,

13. 46. *Parıdhārī* (*Paritapī*), 47. *Pramādi*, 48. *Ānandī* 49. *Rākṣasa*, 50. *Nala*, 51. *Piṅgala*, 52. *Kāla* (*Kālayukti*), 53. *Siddhārtha*, 54. *Durmati*, 55. *Sumati* (*Raudrī*).

14. 56. *Dundubhi*, 57. *Rudhirodgārī*, 58. *Raktākṣa*, 59. *Krodhana*, and 60. *Akṣaya*. These are the names of the sixty-years according to Hindu calender. Whether they are auspicious or inauspicious can be inferred from their names. (There are some differences in the traditionally accepted names. They are given in brackets).

15. O Rudra, I shall now describe time for the sake of success by the rise of the *Pañcasvara* (five vowels). They are *Rājā*, *Sājā*, *Udāsā*, *Pīḍā* and *Mṛtyu*.

16. With six lines drawn horizontally and vertically, make five squares of five rows. The vowels *Ā*, *Ī*, *Ū*, *AI* and *AU* are to be written in five squares in order. They are called *Agnikoṣṭhakas*.

17. The *Tithis* (days of the lunar fortnight) three in number, *Rājā*, *Sājā*, *Udāsā*, *Pīḍā* and *Mṛtyu*, Mars, Mercury,

18. Jupiter, Venus, Saturn, Sun and Moon, the six stars from *Revatī* to *Mṛgaśiras*—all these are written in order.

19. Then five stars are written in each square. The months *Caitra*, etc. are also written with their first letters, two months in one square.

20. The *Kalā*, *Liṅga* whatever stands fifth, it is his death. The time, *tithi*, day of the week, the star and the month,

21. Shall be before the rise of the name, not otherwise. *Oṁ Kṣaum* obeisance to *Śiva*,

22. *Kṣāmā Dyaṅga Śivāmīkṣa* is the mystic mantra, O Hara, of this *Viṣagrahamati*. The *bija* in the *Padma* which enchants the three worlds belongs to *Nṛsiṁha*.

23. The names of *Mṛtyuñjaya* (Śiva), *Gaṇa* and *Lakṣmī* shall be written with *Gorocanā* (yellow pigment) on the *Bhūrjā*[1] leaf. This shall be worn round the neck or on the arm. It yields success.

CHAPTER SIXTYSEVEN

Svarodaya or Pavana-vijaya

Sūta said :

1. After hearing it from Hari, Hara told Gaurī the knowledge of planets, etc. stationed in the body.

2. The planets Mars, Sun, Earth and the gods fire, Śauri and water god and *Rāhu*—all these permeate the body of a man through the vital airs and manifest through the pores on the right side.

3. Jupiter, Venus, Mercury and the Moon are stationed in the middle of the left *Nāḍi's* (nerves)

4. When the *Cāra* or movement is through the *Nāḍī Iḍā* auspicious actions shall be initiated such as occupying a resort, meditation, trade, visit to a king, etc.

5. When the right *Nāḍī* functions *Śani* (Saturn), Mars, and *Rāhu* reign supreme.

6. And at that time inauspicious actions are started. Finding out the auspicious and the inauspicious is based on the *Svarodaya*.

7-8. The *Nāḍis* or nerves functioning in the body are numerous and are of various forms. From the nerve-ganglion beneath the navel seventy-two thousand nerve-shoots come out and are coiled in the middle of the umbilicus. They carry the very vital existence of man.

9. Of them the one on the left, the one on the right and the one in the middle—these three are important. The one

1. Betula attilis *GVDB*, p. 287.

in the left is presided over by the moon and the one in the right resembles the sun.

10. The middle one is fire itself and is a great agent of destruction. The left one is nectar itself and saves the whole world.

11. The nerve on the right with the essence of *Rudra* dries up the whole world. If both the *Nāḍis* function death will result, all activities will be destroyed.

12. Activities involving going out are influenced by the left one and those involving entry are influenced by the one in the right. When the *Iḍā* or the left nerve presided over by Mercury, the moon and the sun is permeated by the Vital Air all auspicious activities are undertaken.

13. Cruel deeds are done when the vital air permeates the *Piṅgalā* or the right nerve. In journeys, big undertakings, removal of poison, etc. *Iḍā* is preferable.

14. In dinner, coitus, battle, etc. *Piṅgalā* is fruitful. In acts of ostracism, killing and other activities *Piṅgalā* is to be used.

15. In cohabitation, battle and dinner *Piṅgalā* is beneficent. In auspicious actions, journeys, poison undertakings,

16. Achievement of peace, salvation, etc. *Iḍā* should be followed by kings. If both the nerves function simultaneously both ruthless and gentle actions are avoided.

17. It shall be considered *Viṣuva* the equinox. A cautious man shall remember this. In gentle and auspicious activities in undertakings of profit and success in life,

18-19. In shifting, etc. the left nerve *is always favoured*. In war, etc., dinner, killing and sexual intercourse with women, the right nerve is good. In entries and minor activities too this is *favoured*. If one were to ask about auspicious and the inauspicious actions, profit and loss, success and failure, life and death,

20. The answer will not be correct, if the middle *nāḍi* is predominant. If the enquirer asks when the leader is in the *cāra* of the left or the right nerve,

21. There is no doubt about the *siddhi* (achievement). When the *nāḍīs Vaicchanda* or *Vāmadeva* flow in the body,

22. The *siddhi* is fruitless. If the *Śivā nāḍī* flows either into the left or into the right,

23. The ruthless actions are fulfilled if the *nāḍī* is terrific and the results are neither good nor bad if it is gentle. If the *Haṁsa nāḍī* proceeds partially through the two *nāḍis* it is called *svaravāhinī*.

24-25. A yogin who is an expert in *yoga* shall understand that death will take place then. If the enquirer stands to the left and asks, the rise of the wind is from the left. If to the right, the rise of the wind is from the right. The left side is excellent if the enquiry is frontal and the right side is excellent if the enquiry is from behind.

26. When from the left, it is called Vāmā; when from the right, Dakṣiṇā. Vāmā is auspicious at left, Dakṣiṇā at right.

27. A life sustains itself by Jupiter. If any thing is devoid of its influence it is called Svara. If good signs of victory, etc. are aimed at,

28. They can be achieved in the Pūrṇanāḍī without exception. With respect to other nāḍīs three alternatives are possible.

29. If the enquiry is on the sixth day or a pūrnātithi of the lunar fortnight the first man will be victorious. If it is on a riktā-tithi, the second man will be victorious. This can be mentioned unhesitatingly.

30. The wind on par with the movement of the left nerve yields success in actions. If it begins to blow along the path to the right, which is uneven, it brings about uneven result.

31. If it blows elsewhere to the left, it brings about uneven result. Then the warrior who is in the middle of the battlefield, becomes victorious.

32. In the movement of the wind to the right if it results in even results then there is no doubt it can be traced to the middle of the nāḍī.

33. If the vital air permeates Piṅgalā, he shall be victorious in the war that is to be tranquilised. If the movement is as long as the rise of the nāḍī, it shall be taken so far as that direction.

34. He will not be competent to give. No hesitation is

to be felt here. In the middle of a battle, where the nāḍī flows continuously,

35. That party shall be victorious. If it is void he can point out defeat. If the cāra (movement) has taken place success can be known; if it is extinct he can be pointed out as dead.

36-37. He who knows victory and defeat is a real scholar. To the right or to the left wherever the nāḍī moves, stepping in that direction one obtains benefit. His journey is always auspicious. A battle shall be fought when the nāḍī presided over by the sun and the moon flows.

38. If the person therein enquires, he shall be surely successful. Where the wind blows there success is sure,

39. Even if Indra were to stand opposite. The ten nāḍīs Meṣī, etc. are situated on the left and right.

40. If they are situated on a Cara (mobile) path they are also Cara. If they are situated on a Sthira (fixed) path they are also Sthira. If it comes out the nāḍī too comes out. If it is squeezed in, the nāḍī too is squeezed in.

41. After hearing the words of the enquirer, the diviner shall point out by means of the shape of the bell. O Gaurī, the five elements too are situated either to the left or to the right.

42. The fire element is above; the water element is below; the wind element is sideways; the earth element is to be known stationed in the middle; the ether element is everywhere and always.

43. If (the nāḍī) goes up, death is the result; if it is below—peace; if it is sideways—the scholar shall avoid it; if it is in the middle—it shall be understood as a stunning situation; if it goes everywhere there is salvation always.

CHAPTER SIXTYEIGHT

On the test of gems—Diamond

Sūta said :

1. I shall now expound the process of testing gems. There was a demon *Bala.* He conquered Indra and other gods. They could not reconquer him.

2. Under the pretext of choosing a boon the gods requested Bala to be the animal at sacrifice, and he conceded their request. Though very powerful, he was killed as the sacrificial animal.

3-4. Since he was bound by his pledged words, he had suffered himself to be tied to the sacrificial column. For the benefit of the world and for doing good unto the gods his limbs became seeds of gems. This was due to his meritorious deeds as he was pure with *Sāttvika* virtues.

5. A great tussle took place among gods, *yakṣas*, *siddhas* and serpents over the seeds of gems.

6-8. When they were speeding in their aerial chariots in the sky here and there the seeds fell in the oceans, rivers, mountains or jungles. Wherever the seed fell, those places became the storehouses of gems. On account of their intrinsic merit some of them imbibed the power of quelling obstacles accruing from the influence of demons, poison, serpents and sickness, and others were devoid of any quality.

9-10. These are the different kinds of gems :—*Vajra* (diamond); *Muktā* (pearl), *Maṇi* (gems), *Padmarāga* (ruby) *Marakata* (Emerald), *Indranīla* (sapphire) *Vaiḍūrya* (Lapis Lazuli), *Puṣparāga* (Topaz), *Karketana* (?) *Pulaka*, *Rudhira* (Blood red stone), *Sphaṭika* (crystal) and *Vidruma* (coral). Persons who know gems have classified them thus.

11. First the shape and the colour are to be tested; then its merits and defects are to be understood; its influence must then be known; after consultation with experts in gems who have studied technical literature on them the price shall be decided on.

12. Gems bought or first used in a bad *lagna* or inauspicious day become defective and lose even their merits.

13. Collection or wearing of only well-tested gems should be undertaken by a king who wishes for prosperity.

14. Only those who have studied the technical literature concerning them, and who habitually deal in them can be deemed to be the proper persons to know the price and quality of gems.

15. Experts have spoken of diamond as highly influential, hence our description also starts with a detailed description of diamond.

16. Indra wielding thunderbolt while moving about dropped little particles of bones from his weapon. These particles acquired various shapes in the various places as they fell.

17. Diamond is found in eight different places. They are :—*Himālayas*, *Mātaṅga*[1] territory *Saurāṣṭra*, *Pauṇḍra*[2], *Kaliṅga*, *Kosala*[3], *Sauvīra*[4] and the banks of the river *Veṇvā*[5].

18. Diamonds found in the *Himālayan* region are slightly copper-coloured; those found on the banks of the river *Veṇvā* have the lustre of the moon; those from *Sauvīra* land resemble blue lotus and cloud; diamonds found in *Saurāṣṭra* are light copper-coloured; those from *Kaliṅga* have the brilliant colour of gold; diamonds from Kosala are deep yellow in colour; diamonds from the Puṇḍra territory are dark-blue and the diamonds found in Mātaṅga land are not too deep yellow in colour.

19. Really the deities will grace it with their presence if anywhere in the world even if a bit of a diamond with very sharp edges can be seen, which has a clear light shade and the usual good features, which is quite light, symmetrical in the sides and is free from the defects, such as scratches, patches, dark spots, crows, foot and Trāsa (atom of dust found in a gem).

20. Idols of gods are prepared from diamonds of various colours. For different castes different colours in diamonds are

1. A *janapada* in eastern India.
2. The region around modern Santal Parganas.
3. The ancient region around Ayodhyā, the capital in the Rāmāyaṇa age.
4. The region around modern Multan.
5. Either the Bīnā river, or the Waingaṅgā river in Central India, or Veṇā river in South India.

assigned. Diamonds are classified also according to their colours.

21. Green diamonds are assigned to Lord Viṣṇu; white diamonds to Varuṇa; yellow diamonds to Indra; brown diamonds to Agni; blue diamonds to Yama and copper-coloured ones to the Maruts. All these colours are naturally beautiful.

22. Brāhmaṇas shall use diamonds white like Śaṅkha, Kumuda[1] flower and crystal; Kṣatriyas shall use diamonds brown like the eyes of a rabbit; Vaiśyas shall use diamonds shining like the green leaves of a plantain tree and the Śūdras shall use diamonds refulgent like the fresh sharpened sword.

23. Two colours of diamonds are specially assigned to kings. They are not for the general public. One is the crimson colour of the Javā flower (China Rose) or freshly cut coral and the other yellow like the turmeric juice.

24. In his capacity as the lord of all castes a king can wear good diamonds of any colour as he pleases but not the others.

25. The improper use of colours in diamonds by the different castes is more baneful than the mixture of castes resulting from the improper pursuit of one another's avocation.

26. A scholar shall not wear a diamond merely because it is assigned to him in view of the path chosen by him. A diamond having good qualities yields weal and wealth; otherwise it becomes the source of sorrow.

27. A diamond with even one of its horns (angles) broken or withered, scratched or shattered shall not be retained in the house by people wishing for prosperity even though it may have all other good qualities.

28. The diamond of which the apex is mutilated or withered by fire and the centre is vitiated by dirty spots and marks will induce the goddess of fortune to resort to others even if it happens to be the diamond of Indra.

29. The diamond that has impressions of scratches in any part or is painted with stripes of red will bring about the destruction of a person even if he has attained mastery over death.

1. Nymphaea alba.

30. The qualities of a diamond springing from the place of its origin are as follows. It must have six elevated tips, eight equal sides and twelve sharp edges.

31. A perfect diamond with these features is not easy of access. It has six fine tips, it is pure, the edges are clear and sharp. It has fine colour. It is light. Its sides are well smoothed. It has no defects. It sheds lustre all around like the thunderbolt[1] of Indra.

32. He who, pure in body, wears a faultless diamond, bright and sharp-edged, shall flourish in life, blessed with wife, children, wealth, foodgrains and herds of cattle.

33. All sorts of fears arising from serpents, fires, poison, tigers, thieves and imprecatory and maledictory actions, the sorcery of the enemies shall not harass him.

34. Persons who know the science of diamonds and gems say that a man shall wear a diamond free from all flaws weighing twenty Taṇḍulas (rice grains). Its characteristic, features and price are twofold.

35-36. The price of a diamond weighing twelve Taṇḍulas is taken as the standard. When the weight is reduced by two Taṇḍulas the price is reduced by one third. For further reduction in weight the reduction in price is gradually by 1/13, 1/30, 1/80, 1/100 and 1/1000 upto a weight of one Taṇḍula.

37. Diamonds are not weighed only by rice grains. Eight white mustard seeds constitute one Taṇḍula.

38. If a diamond possesses all other qualities and floats in water, a man shall wear that alone although he may have all other precious gems in possession.

39. If a diamond is vitiated by a small defect visible or invisible to the eye, one shall get only one-tenth of its price.

40. If there are many defects small or great, not even one hundredth of its price need be offered.

41. A diamond, the defect of which is clearly seen is valued very low even if set in an ornament of gold.

1. As the legends record, it was fashioned out of the bones of the sage Dadhīci.

42. A diamond may be flawless at the beginning; but while setting in an ornament it may acquire defects. A king shall not wear such an ornament. Defective diamonds are not to be used even in ornaments.

43. If a woman desires sons, she shall not wear even a flawless diamond. Otherwise she can wear elongated, flat and short ones, even devoid of good qualities.

44-45. Experts prepare imitation diamonds by using iron, Puṣparāga (topaz), Gomedaka, Vaiḍūrya (Lapis lazuli), Sphaṭika (crystal) and different kinds of glasses. They must be tested well by means of alkaline solutions and emery-wheel, etc.

46. A diamond can scratch all other gems and metals but it cannot be scratched by other gems or metals.

47. Weight is a criterion in the appraisal of other gems; but scholars say that in diamonds contrary is the case.

48. Vajra (diamond) and Kuruvinda (cyprus rotundus) can scratch similar or dissimilar materials. But Vajra alone can scratch another Vajra, nothing else.

49-50. Diamonds and pearls set in ornaments do not shed lustre upwards. If laterally cut, some diamonds may emit lustre upwards but then they do not emit lustre sideways.

51. A diamond scintillating with flashes of rain-bow blesses the wearer with wealth, food grain, and good children although the tip may be mutilated, or the diamond may have faded colour or may contain dots and scratches.

52. A king wearing a diamond dazzling with lightning flashes will surely enjoy the whole earth asserting his sway over the vassal kings and over-powering his enemies by means of his exploits.

CHAPTER SIXTYNINE

On the test of Gems — pearls

Sūta said :

1. Pearls are found in lordly elephants, clouds, wild boars, shells, fishes, cobras, oysters and the bamboos. Pearls in oysters are more abundant.

2. Only these are valued as gems and only these and not the other ones can be bored through entirely—say the experts.

3. Pearls found in bamboos, elephants, whales, and wild boars are usually devoid of lustre though reputed to be auspicious.

4. Of the eight varieties of pearls as the experts say those obtained from shells and temples of elephants are the poorest in quality.

5. Pearls found in shells have the same colour as the central portion of shells. They have big angles and weigh about a pala. Pearls from the temple of elephants have a slight yellowish colour without lustre.

6. The well-known conch (of Viṣṇu) rendered yellow by its clash with Śārṅga (the bow of Viṣṇu) and elephants of good breed are the sources of yellowish circular pearls devoid of lustre.

7. Small light pearls are found in the mouths of the Pāṭhīna fish that usually frequent the middle of the vast ocean. They have the same colour as their back.

8. Pearls obtained from the curved teeth of wild boars having the same colour as their source are very rare and are prized like the Divine Boar (Viṣṇu).

9. Pearls found in the joints of bamboos resembling the hail stone in colour are very rare since these bamboos grow only in those places which noble virtuous men frequent and not in wild forests or public places.

10. Pearls found from the hoods of cobras are perfectly round like fish and have brilliant colour and lustre like a sword frequently sharpened and polished.

11. Only meritorious persons will have access to the cobra-pearl. Then they can get other gems of great brilliance, wealth, kingdom and grow brilliant.

12-13. The man possessing cobra-pearl should invite persons well-versed in sacred rites and perform Rakṣāvidhāna (Protection rites) during an auspicious hour and place it on the top of the mansion. Then the whole sky will be enveloped by rainbearing clouds hanging low. Sounds of thunder will be heard as resonant as the sound of drums. Flashes of lightning will illuminate the quarters.

14. He who has a cobra pearl in his treasury is never harassed by serpents, evil demons, foul diseases and defects of evil associations.

15. The Pearl with cloud as its origin rarely comes to the earth. Gods take it away from the sky. By the lustre it emits all round it illuminates the quarters. No one can gaze at its dazzling brilliance as no one can gaze at the disc of the sun.

16. This pearl outshines the brilliance of fire, moon, stars and planets. It is equally brilliant in the day as in the night enveloped by pitch darkness.

17. I am sure that the whole earth surrounded by four oceans overflowing with waters sparkling like gems is not an adequate price for this pearl even if the earth, the most beautiful of all worlds, is filled with gold.

18. Even if an indigent man were to obtain it as a result of his previous merits he will enjoy unrivalled lordship as long as the pearl remains in his possession.

19. It is capable of bestowing good fortune not only upon the meritorious king but also upon the subjects as well. It is capable of dispelling evil thousands of yojanas all round.

20. Scattered all round from heaven, the rows of teeth of the great demon Bala shining with its pure colour like the milky way, fell into the waters of the ocean of various colours.

21. The seed of the pure gem of great quality, having the lustre of full moon, found a place in the oyster where other seeds born of other sources also were present.

22. Where the seeds of beautiful pearl fell, the water from the clouds too fell and both together entered the oyster shell and were converted into pearls.

23. Pearls found at eight different places are called (1) Saiṁhalika (of Ceylon), (2) Pāralaukika (Heavenly), (3) Saurāṣṭrika (of Gujarat), (4) Tāmraparṇa, (5) Pāraśava (of Persian gulf), (6) Kaubera, (7) Pāṇḍyahāṭaka (of the Pāṇḍya country in South India), and (8) Hemaka.

24. In size, shape quality and lustre, the oyster pearls from Vardhana, Pārasīka, Pātāla and other worlds and Siṁhala are not inferior to any other pearl.

25. In the matter of pearls (from oyster) the source need not be taken into consideration. An expert shall note the features and the size. Pearls of all sizes and shapes can be found everywhere.

26. An oyster pearl ground well on the emery wheel can be priced five thousand three hundred silver pieces.

27. A pearl weighing half a Māṣaka[1] less shall be priced two fifths less ($5300 \times 2/5 = 2120$ i.e. 3180 silver pieces). The pearl weighing three Māṣakas is priced 2000 silver pieces as the maximum.

28. If the pearl weighs two and a half Māṣakas, its price is one thousand three hundred silver pieces. A pearl weighing two Māṣakas (if its quality is good) is priced 800 silver pieces.

29. A pearl weighing a Māṣaka and a half is priced three hundred and twenty five silver pieces. A pearl weighing six Guñjās[2] has the maximum price of two hundred silver pieces, thus say the experts. If it is ground well and has all merits, the price can be increased by a hundred and fifty silver pieces.

30. If there are not less than sixteen pearls in a Dharaṇa (ten palas) it is called Dārvika. Even a child will be paid a hundred and ten silver pieces for it.

31. If there are not less than twenty pearls in a Dharaṇa (ten palas) experts call it Bhavaka. It can fetch seventy nine silver pieces if the pearls are not deficient in quality.

32. If a Dharaṇa is complete with thirty pearls it is called Śikya. Its maximum price shall be forty.

33. Forty pearls together weighing a Dharaṇa can be termed Śiktha. Its price is thirty. Sixty pearls together weighing a dharaṇa can be termed Nikaraśīrṣa. Its price is fourteen.

34. Eighty or ninety pearls in a Dharaṇa is called a Kūpyā. Its price is eleven and nine.

35. Gather together the pearls in a rice bowl and cook them well in the juice of Lemon. Rub them well with finely chopped carrot. Now the pearls can be bored quickly.

1. A measurement for weight. Twelve *māṣakas* make one *tolā* and 86 *tolās* make one kilogram.

2. The fruits of Abrus precatorius used for weighing in ancient India.

36-37. Make a Matsyapuṭa covering the pearls with clay. [A puṭa is baking anything in a crucible]. Heat it well by means of the process Vitānapatti (covering the crucible, etc. with a canopy). Then cook the pearls, in milk first, then in water and then in lime water. Finally cook them in condensed milk, then rub them with a clean cloth. Now the pearls will begin to shine brilliantly. Vyāḍi[1], the great sage of wonderful powers, has mentioned this process of cleaning pearls out of consideration for the world and experts in gems.

38. A white pearl shining like glass together with gold one hundredth of it by weight shall be put in mercury for some time before using it as an ornament. Experts in Siṁhala do like this.

39-40. If there is a doubt to the artificiality of a pearl, put it in hot oil with a pinch of common salt. Then take it out and soak it in water for a whole night. The next day cover it with a dry cloth and rub it with grains of paddy. If the colour does not fade the pearl is genuine not artificial.

41. A white pearl of proper size smooth and heavy, pure and clean, circular in shape and brilliant is of good quality.

42. If a pearl delights even a person who does not want to buy it, if it is of proper size, if it sheds white rays, if it is white and circular, if the hole is of uniform width throughout we can say that it is of good quality.

43. If such a fine pearl with commendable features as described above is in one's possession he will be free from all evils and faults.

CHAPTER SEVENTY

On the test of Gems—Ruby

Sūta said :

1. Taking the blood of the mighty demon Bala, which contained seeds of excellent gems, the sun traversedt he sky and shone blue like a sword.

1. He is also reputed as a grammarian somewhat later than Pāṇinī.

2. He was thwarted suddenly half way by Rāvaṇa, King of Laṅkā, who appeared like another Rāhu, and was proud of his exploits such as the conquest of deities in battles many times before.

3. Thereupon the sun dropped the blood in the excellent river whose banks were overgrown with Areca-palms and whose deep pools are constantly agitated by the beautiful thighs of the Siṁhala maidens.

4. Thenceforward the river became famous as Rāvaṇa Gaṅgā[1] since it acquired the same merits as the divine Gaṅgā.

5. Ever since, its banks are strewn over with precious gems during nights and they appear as though they are pierced by shafts of gold, blazing inside as well as outside.

6. On its banks and waters, rubies began to appear resembling those found in Saugandhika, Kuruvinda, and Sphātika territories. All of them had great merits.

7. Some of these rubies have the colours of the Bandhūka[2] flower, Guñjā, Indragopa (glowworm), Javā flower (China Rose) blood, pomegranate seeds and the Kiṁśuka[3] flower. All of them have a shining lustre.

8. Some of the rubies have the colour of vermillion, red lotus and Saffron; some have the colour of Lākṣā juice; although the red colour is uniform throughout; their centre has a special manifest brilliance; the rubies are self-luminous.

9. Some of these rubies of the Sphaṭika (crystal) variety, endowed with all good qualities, reflect and refract the rays of the sun illuminating all the surrounding objects.

10. Some of these rubies of the brilliance of the fresh blown red lotus have a mixture of blue colour like that of Kusumbha[4]; others have the lustre of Aruṣkara[5] and Kaṇṭakāri[6] flower and still others have the colour of Hiṅgula (Asafoetida).

11. Some of the rubies have the colour of the eyes of the

1. Not identifiable.
2. Pentapetes phoenicea.
3. Butea monosperma.
4. Carthamus tinctorius.
5. Semecarpus omacardium.
6. Solanum xanthocarpum.

birds Cakora[1], Cuckoo or Sārasa;[2] others have the lustre of the Kokanada (Red Lotus) in full bloom.

12. In their influence, firmness and weight Saugandhika rubies are similar to crystalline rubies; but they have the colour of the fine red lotus with a slight bluish tinge.

13. The Kuruvindaja variety of rubies are red no doubt, but that redness is not akin to that of the crystalline variety. They are dull hued and the lustre remains within. Their influence too is not on par with that of the crystals.

14-15. In the beds of Rāvaṇagaṅgā some Kuruvindaka variety of rubies are produced which have the deep red hue of other varieties of rubies, but they have crystalline rays; in Āndhra they are not usually found; if at all some of them have the ruby colour they fetch only a less price.

16. Similarly, in the Tumburu[3] territory too, some rubies akin to the crystalline variety are found but are priced very low.

17. In brief, the good features of gems are profusion of colour, heaviness, smoothness, evenness, transparency, iridiscence and greatness.

18. Gems are not good if they are sandy, cracked within, and stained, if they are lustreless, rough and dull although they may have all the characteristic features of their family.

19. If any one wears a gem of many flaws out of ignorance, then grief, anxiety, sickness, death, loss of wealth and other evils torment him.

20. Inferior alien varieties of gems are usually substituted for the five genuine ones. The intelligent shall note this well.

21. The spurious ones alien to genuine rubies but akin to one another are (1) Kalaśapurodbhava, (2) Siṁhala, (3) Tumburudeśottha, (4) Muktapāṇīya and (5) Śrīpūrṇaka.

22-25. The first variety of Kalaśa has the peculiarity of husky aspect. The second Siṁhala variety can be detected by its darkness. The third variety of Tumburudeśottha has the tinge

1. The Greek Partridge. *SSED*, p. 200.
2. The Indian crane.
3. Probably the Vindhya-region. *GP.*, p. 158.

of copper colour. The Muktapāṇīya type has the tinge of the sky and the Śrīpūrṇaka variety is devoid of lustre and brilliance. These characteristics show that they are alien. If one is called upon to distinguish between a genuine and a spurious ruby one shall note whether it has the copper tinge or husky aspect; whether it appears to be smeared with oil; whether on being rubbed it loses its lustre; or whether on placing two fingers on the top it casts dark shade on either side; or whether on being tossed up and caught hold of retains all the qualities. Of two gems put to test the one with more weight is genuine.

26. If the doubt is not removed, it shall be put on the emery-wheel or scratched with a similar gem and tested.

27. On ruby and sapphire no gem except diamond and Kuruvinda can make a scratch mark.

28. There are many spurious ones alien to the genuine ruby but of similar colour. Still here some are mentioned only to indicate their names and difference.

29. A gem belonging to an alien group devoid of virtue shall not be worn along with a genuine one endowed with all good points. Even with Kaustubha (the divine gem of Viṣṇu) an alien variety should not be worn by a scholar.

30. Even one Cāṇḍāla[1] can attack and kill a number of brahmins. Similarly a spurious alien gem can nullify the potency of many gems endowed with good qualities.

31. No evil can even touch the wearer of a Padmarāga of great potency even if he is caught amidst his deadly enemies or even if he errs habitually.

32. He who is mentally and bodily pure and wears Padmarāga whose crimson colour is heightened by its good qualities is never sullied by any sort of evil.

33. The price of a Taṇḍula of well-cut, well-polished diamond is equal to that of a Māṣaka of purified Padmarāga of great potency.

34. A gem is prized for its colour and brilliancy. Hence any defect in these two qualities lowers the value.

1. A low-caste person, a person doing wicked deeds.

CHAPTER SEVENTYONE

On the test of Gems—Emerald

Sūta said :

1. Taking away the bile of the chief of demons, Bala, Vāsuki the king of Serpents was speeding across the sky as though he was cutting it into two.

2. He appeared like a bridge of silver across the sky illumined by the gem on his head.

3. Then Garuḍa began to attack the Serpent-king by his wings as if eager to destroy heaven and earth.

4. Suddenly the Serpent dropped it on the ridge of the excellent Māṇikya mountain, which is rendered fragrant by the Nalikā forest and where the Turuṣka[1] trees of good oozing juice grew abundantly.

5. The fallen bile immediately after the fall crossed the mountain Māṇikya and reached the shore of the ocean near Ramā (Goddess Lakṣmī) because of its faith in her and became the source of Marakata (Emerald).

6. Garuḍa caught hold of some of the falling bile but became unconscious. He then let out the stuff through his nostrils.

7. Emeralds that got their line and lustre from the tender neck of parrots, Śirīṣa[2] flower, back of the glow-worm, grassy plain, moss, Kalhāra[3] flower, grass-blade and the wings of Garuḍa are auspicious.

8. The place on the mountain where the bile let loose by the Serpent-chief fell is inaccessible though endowed with all virtues.

9. In the place of Marakata (i.e. near the sea where

1. 'Storax is the Turuṣka of Ayurveda, which is a balsam obtained from foreign trees of *Ligendamber* (L. *Orientalis* Miller and L. *Styraciflua* Linn. A similar sort of inferior quality of balsam is found from an Indian species *Attingia excelsa* Naronha.'. *GVDB*, p. 188.

2. Albizzia lebbeck *GVDB*, p. 399.

3. A variety of *utpala*.

it finally came to) many things grow. Whatever is grown there is efficacious in subduing poison and sickness.

10. What cannot be cured by any mantras and medicinal herbs—the poison from tbe fangs of great cobras—is quelled by that.

11. Whatever grows there free from defects is considered to be the holiest of holy things.

12-15. Experts in gems are inclined to say that the following types of emeralds are of good potency : Emerald that has dark green colour, a soft glow, that is highly complicated, hewn in different ways and appears to be stufled with gold dust; emerald that is endowed with qualities of shape, even shade all over it, sufficient heaviness and shoots diffusion of light when sun's rays fall on it; emerald the interior of which changes its natural shade and a dazling light becomes infused making it appear like a green meadow where lightning flashes spread and emerald that delights the mind at the very sight.

16-17. The emerald within which a sheet of transparent rays appears to spread on account of the profusion of colour; the sheet of rays is of the hue of the tender feathers of a peacock, pure, smooth and thick set and seems to be a great diffusion of light—this emerald is not as virtuous as the preceding one.

18. The emerald of variegated hues, very firm and rough, stained and sand-grained and encrusted with Śilājatu (Bitumen) is of inferior quality.

19. The remnant of any gem other than emerald left over after fixture shall never be worn nor bought by those who wish for welfare.

20. Two spurious emeralds Bhallātaki and Putrikā have the colour of emerald but they are really alien to it.

21. The Putrikā substitute loses its brilliance when rubbed with a silken cloth. Glass substitute can be detected by its lightness alone.

22. The Bhallātaka is a very close imitation of emerald in features, qualities and colour but its colour fades and changes when air is blown over it.

23. Diamonds, pearls and other gems of the alien species do not shoot up rays upward when not set in an ornament.

24. Some of them do shoot upwards if kept straight but when held horizontally the rays disappear.

25-27. Emerald devoid of flaws and endowed with potency shall be worn after setting it in gold at the following specified occasions :—At the time of bath, Ācamana, recital of prayers, when charms and mantras are invoked; by those who give gifts of cow and gold; by those who practise austerities; when sacrificial rites are performed to gods, manes or special guests; when the preceptor is specially honoured; when the Tridoṣas (wind, bile and phlegm) are upset; when poisoned and when engaged in war.

28. An emerald endowed with virtues fetches more price than a ruby of equal weight.

29. Similarly, in case of defects, the depreciation in value of an emerald is more than that of ruby.

CHAPTER SEVENTYTWO

On the test of Gems—Sapphire

Sūta said :

1. Both the eyes of the demon Bala resplendent like the full blown lotus fell in a place where the Siṁhala maidens were busy culling the tender shoots and flowers of the creeper Lavalī (Phyllanthus Longifoluis) with their tender fingers resembling tender shoots.

2. The marshy foreshore of the ocean hedged by the plant Ketaka[1] on which waves from either side lash shines brilliantly due to the abundance of Sapphires.

3. There the sapphire gems of bluish shades are found, just as :—the blue lotus, ploughshare section, honey bee,

1. Pandanus tectorius.

Viṣṇu's body, Śiva's neck, Kaṣāya flower and the flowers of Girikarṇikā[1] (those which are not white).

4. Some have the colour of the waters of the clear blue sea; others resemble a flock of peacocks; some have the refulgence of bubbles coming from blue juice of indigo plant; and some have the colour of the neck of intoxicated cuckoo.

5. There many sapphire gems of great potency can be found; they are of uniform size, clear lustre and fine colour.

6. Defective sapphires are those encrusted with clay, rockbits and gravels, those with holes, those having the flaw of Trāsa (tremulousness), and those impregnated with traces of mica. Some are defective in their colour.

7. Poets well versed in the sacred technical literature praise the genuine gems found there (Siṁhala).

8. Virtues resulting from wearing sapphire are the same as in the case of rubies.

9. Three types of Rubies have been enumerated before based on their sources. The same applies to sapphires also without any difference.

10. The modes of testing the genuineness of sapphire are the same as those in the case of Rubies.

11. The sapphire stands the test of fire of a longer duration than the ruby. It can withstand a greater quantity of heat.

12. Still, under no circumstances, should any gem be subjected to the test of fire seeking more brilliancy.

13. While the test is being carried out some new defects due to the process of burning may enter the gems. This brings ill-luck to the owner, the man who conducts the test and the man who induced him to conduct it.

14. Spurious sapphires are akin to the genuine ones in colour but actually alien are glass, marble, Karavīra and crystals.

15. Heaviness and firmness increase in glass, etc. in order. This should be noted.

16. If a sapphire has a tinge of copper colour in it, it shall be preserved. So also Karavīra and Upala marble if they have the copper tinge.

1. Probably symphorema polyandrum, *GVDB*, p. 138.

17. That sapphire which has a brilliant flash like the thunderbolt in its centre is of great potency and very rare. It is the real Indranīla.

18. The sapphire that turns milk hundred times its weight entirely blue is called Mahānīla. This is because of the profusion of the colour.

19. The price of a Māṣa of ruby is the same as that of four Māṣās of sapphire of great virtue.

CHAPTER SEVENTYTHREE

On the test of Gems—Lapis Lazuli

Sūta said :

1. The test of Vaidūrya (Lapis Lazuli) and Puṣparāga (Topaz), Karketana and Bhīṣmaka was first expounded by Brahmā and then repeated by Vyāsa.

2. From the loud shout of the demon Bala resonant like the shout of the ocean agitated at the end of a Kalpa[1] (the final dissolution after many a deluge[2]) Vaidūrya (Lapis Lazuli) was produced. It is of many colours and the brilliance of the different colours is pleasing and delightful.

3. Not far from the lofty mountain of Vidūra and very near the frontiers of Kāmabhūtika can be found the mine of the lapis lazuli gems.

4. Raised aloft by the loud shout of the demon, the mine of great virtues has virtually become an ornament for the three worlds.

5. Emitting the fine colours of the clouds of rainy season, lapis lazuli gems shot off flames as it were in tune with the shrill cry of the demon.

1. *ŚP* (*AITM*), p. 2163.

2. According to the Purāṇas, the universe is destroyed at the end of a *Kalpa*, and a new creation starts. References to such a Deluge we find in the story of Manu and Fish in the Śatapatha Brāhmaṇa. The Bible also refers to the story of the Deluge and the Noah's Ark.

6. Lapis lazuli has the colours of all gems available on the earth, beginning from Ruby.

7. The chief of them is the blue one resembling the neck of a peacock or that which has the colour of the leaf of bamboo. Lapis lazuli gems that have the colour of the outer feathers of the Cāṣa (Blue jay) bird are not approved of by the experts in the technical literature of gems.

8 A lapis lazuli gem of commendable virtues brings good luck to its owner; if it has defects it brings ill-luck. Hence, it must be tested well (before buying and wearing).

9. There are spurious gems resembling lapis lazuli, such as Girikāca, Śiśupāla, and glass crystals affected by smoky colour.

10. A glass piece can be detected by its inability to scratch; a Śiśupāla by its light weight; a Girikāca by its lack of brilliance and a crystal by its great brilliance.

11. The price of two palas of lapis lazuli is equal to that of Sapphire of two gold pieces in weight and of very commendable virtues.

12. Although there are many spurious imitations of a gem of excellent quality, here some names can be indicated from which the varieties can be inferred.

13. An intelligent man can easily see the difference. A universal characteristic of alienness is glossy surface, lightness and softness of touch.

14. The price of lapis lazuli set in ornaments varies inasmuch as the purification and setting is executed by an expert or an incompetent person instilling it with virtue or defect as the case may be.

15. These gems set carefully by the jeweller, if free from defects, will outlive the present value and fetch even six times their price.

16. The price which the gems fresh from the mine or in towns on the sea-coast fetch is not current in other parts of the world.

17-19. According to Manu a Suvarṇa weight is equivalent to sixteen Māṣakas. One seventh of it is called a Sañjñā.

A Śāṇa is four Māṣas and a Māṣaka is five Kṛṣṇalas. A tenth of a Pala is Dharaṇa [According to others 10 palas make a Dharaṇa]. Thus the process of arriving at the price of gems has been explained.

CHAPTER SEVENTYFOUR

On the test of Gems—Topaz

Sūta said :

1. From the particles of the skin of demon Bala that fell on the top of the Himālaya mountain Puṣparāga (Topaz) gems of great virtue have come up.

2. A gem of this variety, yellowish grey in colour, is called Padmarāga (Ruby). If it is crimson-yellow it is called Kauruṇḍaka.

3. A transparent variety slightly red and yellow is called Kāṣāyaka; slightly blue and white in colour, glossy and commendable is called Somānaka.

4. That which is of deep red colour is indeed Padmarāga (Ruby) ; if it is of deep blue colour, it is called Indranīla (Sapphire).

5. The price of this gem is fixed like that of Vaidūrya (Lapis Lazuli) by experts in Gems. The result is also similar but it blesses women with sons.

CHAPTER SEVENTYFIVE

On the test of Gems—Karketana

Sūta said:

1. The wind in his delight gathered together the nails of the king of demons Bala and scattered them amid clusters of lotuses. Thereafter, Karketana[1] which is prized very much in the world cropped up.

1. What sort of gem it might be is not clear.

2. The best variety of Karketana has the copper colour of blood, the yellowish tinge of the moon, and burning fiery brilliance of honey. The other variety of rough surface bluish white in colour is not approved of since it brings about evils such as sickness, etc.

3. Those Karketanas are very auspicious which are glossy, pure, of uniform reddish hue, of yellowish tinge, heavy, of diverse colours and free from defects, such as Trāsa, cracks, snakelike scratches, etc.

4. If, when it is set in an ornament of gold, it sheds brilliant rays as if heated in fire, Karketana removes sickness, dispels Kali defects and is conducive to longevity, flourishing family and general happiness.

5. Those who wear Karketana of auspicious and commendable virtues for the sake of embellishments are highly honoured, rich, surrounded by many kinsmen and they prosper always enjoying all kinds of happiness.

6. Some spurious Karketana gems of distorted untied aspect and pale blue colour and affected by pale red hue appear to have the shape of the genuine Karketana though devoid of brilliance and colourful effect.

7. If Karketana is scrupulously tested for its colour and features and found to be bright and brilliant like the rising sun, it is to be priced in accordance with its greatness. The price is based on weight, as expounded by experts in Gem-literature.

CHAPTER SEVENTYSIX

On the test of Gems—Bhīṣmamaṇi

Sūta said :

1. The Semen of the demon fell in the northern region of the Himālayas which became the source of the gems called Bhīṣma.

2. Bhīṣma stones, white like Śaṅkha and lilies or Syonāka[1] (the white fruit of the tree of that name) are lustrous. There are some Bhīṣma stones similar to a fairly big-sized diamond.

3. The man who wears a pure Bhīṣma stone with reverence and faith round his neck after setting it in gold acquires wealth.

4. Wild leopards, wolves, Śarabhas (the fabulous eight-footed monsters), elephants, lions, tigers, fly from him at the very sight.

5-6. He need not fear any one. He can wander like an unfettered elephant. Wearing this stone in the ring if one performs Pitṛtarpaṇa the manes will be satisfied for many years. Poisons of snakes, birds, mice and scorpion are ineffective. He has no fear from floods, fire, enemies or thieves.

7. An intelligent man must shun spurious Bhīṣma stones of the colour of moss or clouds, rough of surface, lustreless or yellowish in tinge, or faded and dirty-coloured.

8. Scholars shall fix the price of Bhīṣma stones after observing the place of origin and according to the reason. If the stone comes from far, its price is more than that of one of local origin.

CHAPTER SEVENTYSEVEN

On the test of Gems—Pulaka

Sūta said:

1. The Serpents publicly worshipped the chief of demons, Bala, in a famous place and scattered his claws over various holy mountains, and other places and in rivers flowing in the northern region.

1. Oroxylum indicum.

2. These famous Pulaka gems originated from those nails and claws in the territories : Dāśārṇa[1] (Eastern part of modern Mālvā), Vāgadava, Mekala[2], Kālaga. They have the colours of Guñja (a red-black berry), Añjana (collyrium), honey and lotus-stalk. They are brilliant like the musk-deer, fire and the plantain tree.

3. Pulakas of variegated colours of shell, lotus, honeybee and the Arka[3] (Sun-plant) flowers free from scratches and lines are very holy and auspicious. They are conducive to increasing prosperity.

4. Pulaka stones carried here and there by crows, dogs, donkeys, jackals and fierce vultures in their mouths wet with blood and flesh bring about death and hence should be avoided. The price of a perfect Pulaka stone a pala in weight is five hundred silver pieces.

CHAPTER SEVENTYEIGHT

On the test of Gems—Bloodstone

Sūta said :

1. The fire god carried the features of the demon Bala and deposited the same in the low-lyingmarshes of the river Narmada.

2. From that did originate the gem Blood-stone of various forms and sizes, with colours like that of a glowworm, the beak of a parrot, etc, but of manifest uniform thickness throughout.

3. The Blood-stone which is grey like the moon in the centre is of the purest type with the same merits as those of Indranīla (sapphire). It is productive of prosperity and munificence, when boiled it assumes the colour of the lightning flash.

1. The region around Dhasāna in Central India.

2. The region around Mount Mekalā the source of the Narmadā river also called Mekala-sutā.

3. Calotropis procera and C. gigantea. *GVDB*, p. 23.

CHAPTER SEVENTYNINE

On the test of Gems — Crystal

Sūta said :

1. Balarāma exerted himself and scattered the fat of the demon Bala over the mountains Kavera and Vindhya and the lands of Yavana, Chīna and Nepal.

2. Sphaṭika (crystals) of different types originated therefrom: Ākāśaśuddha (as clear as the sky), Tailākhya (having the brilliance of oil) Mṛṇālaśaṅkhadhavala (white as lotus stalk and Śaṅkha) and others of various colours.

3. A gem destructive of sins, like Sphaṭika, does not exist. Cut and polished well, it will fetch a little tidy sum immediately.

CHAPTER EIGHTY

On the test of Gems — Coral

Sūta said :

1. Śeṣa (the Serpent king) carried the entrails of the demon Bala and deposited the same in Kerala and other places; there corals of great virtue are produced.

2. The most important of them is the one coloured like the blood of a hare, the Guñjā-berry or the China-rose. The foreign lands where corals abound are Sunīlaka, Devaka and Romaka.[1] Corals found there are of deep crimson colour. Corals found elsewhere are not so important. The price of coral depends upon the efficiency of the artisan.

3. A coral of pleasing colour, soft and glossy, possessing deep crimson colour,

4. Is productive of wealth and food-grain in the world and dispels the fear of poison and sorrow. O Śaunaka, knowledge of crystals and corals is necessary for the knowledge of gems.

1. Modern Rome.

CHAPTER EIGHTYONE

Sacred Places

Sūta said :

1-2. I shall enumerate the holy places and sacred rivers. Gaṅgā is the holiest of the holy rivers. Gaṅgā is easy of access everywhere but in three places it is of very difficult access, viz., in Haridvāra[1] (at the source), Prayāga (at the confluence with Yamunā) and Gaṅgāsāgarasaṅgama (where it falls into the sea). Prayāga is a very holy place conducive of worldly enjoyments and salvation to those who die there.

3. By resorting to it (by taking a dip therein) it dispels sins; those to whom oblations are offered there enjoy all desires. Vārāṇasī is the holy place where Lord Keśava has taken the form of Viśveśa (Lord Śiva).

4. Kurukṣetra is a holy place. By acts of charity at this place it is conducive to worldly enjoyment and salvation. Prabhāsa[2] is a very holy place. Lord Somanātha is installed there.

5. Dvārakā is a beautiful city. It affords worldly pleasures and salvation. The eastern Sarasvatī is holy. The surrounding territories known as Saptasārasvata are very holy.

6. Kedāra[3] dispels all sins. Śambhala[4] village is an excellent holy place. Nārāyaṇa is a great holy place. For salvation Badarikāśrama is the most suitable place.

7. Śvetadvīpa, city of Māyānaimiṣa and Puṣkara are all great holy places. Ayodhyā, Āryatīrtha, Citrakūṭa[5] and Gomatī are all holy.

8. The holy place of Vaināyaka, and Rāmagiri-Āśrama[6]

1. Spelt Haradvāra now-a-days.
2. Prabhāsapattana in Gujrata. Recently the Somanātha temple has been re-built here.
3. Modern Kedāranātha in the Himālayas.
4. Modern Sambala in Uttara Pradesh.
5. A town in the Banda district of Uttara Pradesh.
6. The Ramtek-hill near Nagpur in the Maharastra State.

are sacred most places. The city of Kāñcī[1], the river Tuṅgabhadrā, Śrīśailam[2] and Setubandhana are holy places.

9. Rāmeśvara is a great holy place, similarly Kārttikeya is an excellent holy place. Bhṛgutuṅga, Kāmatīrtha, and Amarakaṇṭaka[3] are equally holy places.

10. Mahākāla (Lord Śiva) is the deity in Ujjain; (Lord Hari in the form of Śrīdhara is the deity in Kubjaka[4]; Kubjāmraka is a great holy place; Kālasarpi[5] yields all desires.

11. Mahākeśī[6], Kāverī, Candrabhāgā along with Vipāśa are great holy rivers. Ekāmra[7], Brahmatīrtha[8], Devakoṭaka[9] are all great holy places.

12. Mathura is a beautiful city; Śoṇa is a great holy river. Jambūsaras[10] is a great holy pool;

13. Wherever the idols of Sun, Śiva, Gaṇeśa, goddess and Lord Viṣṇu are installed shall be considered sacred places. In all these and other similar sacred places, performance of holy dip, giving of gifts, recital of prayers, austerities,

14. Worship, Śrāddha and food oblations become everlasting in their efficacy. Śālagrāma is a holy place yielding everything; Paśupati's (Lord Śiva's) Tīrtha[11] is a holy place.

15. Similarly, the Tīrthas of Kokāmukha[12], Vārāha[13], Bhāṇḍīra[14] and Svāmitīrtha[15] are holy places. Mahāviṣṇu in Mohadaṇḍa[16] and Madhusūdana in Mandāra[17] are holy installations.

1. Modern Kanjeevaram in South India.
2. A sacred hill near Karnal, on the bank of Kṛṣṇā.
3. A place in Madhya Pradesh, the source of Narmadā river.
4. Modern Kannauja in Uttara Pradesh.
5. Not identifiable.
6. Not identifiable.
7. Not identifiable
8. Not identifiable.
9. Not identifiable.
10. Not identifiable.
11. Not identifiable.
12. Not identifiable.
13. Not identifiable.
14. Not identifiable
15. Not identifiable.
16. Not identifiable.
17. Not identifiable.

16. Kāmarūpa[1] is a holy place where goddess Kāmākhyā is the presiding deity. Puṇḍravardhanaka is a holy place where Kārttikeya is installed.

17. Virajas[2] is a great Tīrtha as well as Śrīpuruṣottama.[3] Mahendra is a holy mountain and Kāverī is a holy river.

18. Godāvarī is a holy river; Payoṣṇī is a river that accords boons. Vindhya is holy mountain dispelling sins; Narmadā is an excellent holy river.

19. Gokarṇa[4] is a holy place; so is the city of Māhiṣmatī[5] a holy place; Kālañjara[6] is a great Tīrtha; Śukratīrtha[7] is a holy place than which there is no other more sacred place.

20. Lord Viṣṇu abides nearby, hence the place affords salvation even if a person defiles it. Viraja[8] is a holy place that accords everything; Svarṇākṣa[9] is an excellent Tīrtha.

21. Nanditīrtha[10] accords salvation yielding fruits of a crore of holy places. Nāsikya[11] is a holy place and Govardhana[12] is beyond that.

22. Kṛṣṇā, Veṇī, Bhīmarathā, Gaṇḍakī[13], Irāvatī[14] are holy rivers. Bindusaras[15] is a sacred pool where water from Lord Viṣṇu's feet flows.

23. The meditation on Brahman is on a par with sacred places; control of sense organs, subjugation of mind and purity of thought have also on a par with these places.

1. Modern Assam.
2. Not identifiable.
3. Modern Puri in Orissa.
4. A place in the North-Kanara district of Karnataka.
5. Identified in north Onkar Mandhata on the bank of Narmada river. Some identify it in north Maheśvara, south of Indore in Madhya Pradesh.
6. There is a hill and a fort of this name in Central India.
7. Not identifiable.
8. Not identifiable.
9. Not identifiable.
10. Probably the same as the famous Nandigrāma of the Rāmāyaṇa. It is now known as Nandgaon, South of Fyzabad in Uttara Pradesh.
11. Modern Nāsika in Maharastra.
12. Most probably some other Govardhana than the one near Mathura.
13. Modern Gaṇḍaka.
14. Modern Ravi.
15. Not identifiable.

24. He who takes a holy dip in the Tīrtha of Mānasa that has the eddy of Jñāna (pure knowledge) and the pure water of Dhyāna (meditation) that removes the dirt of Rāga (passion) and Dveṣa (hatred) attains the supreme goal.

25. The demarcation of places particularly holy or otherwise is for only those people who differentiate things and places saying "This is a holy place; this is not." He who identifies everything with Brahman will not find a place not holy.

26. All rivers and all mountains are holy places frequented by gods and others. Taking a holy dip, making gifts and performance of Srāddha and Piṇḍadāna in these places have endless benefit.

27. Śrīraṅga[1] is a holy place of Lord Viṣṇu; Tāpī is an excellent pious river. Territories surrounding Godāvarī called Saptagodāvara are holy places and Koṇagiri[2] is a great sacred place.

28. The great river Praṇītā flowing from Sahyādri with the shrines of Mahālakṣmī[3], Ekavīra[4], the lord of lords and Sureśvarī[5], are the holiest of holy.

29. He who takes a holy dip in Gaṅgādvāra[6], Kuśāvarta[7] and Kanakhala[8], in the mountains of Vindhya and Nīlaparvata[9] is not born again.

Sūta said :

30. After hearing the details of the Tīrthas from Lord Hari, Brahmā addressed Vyāsa, Dakṣa and others.

31. After mentioning the Tīrthas he spoke about Gayā the foremost among Tīrthas which affords to the devotee the attainment of Brahmaloka for ever.

1. The same as Shri-ranga-patanam near Tirichinapalli in Tamilnadu.
2. Probably the place known as Koṇārka in Orissa.
3. Probably the temple of Mahālakṣmī in Kolhāpur in Maharastra.
4. The temple of the Goddess in Goa.
5. Not identifiable.
6. Modern Haridvār.
7. Not identifiable.
8. Situated in Saharanpur District of Uttara Pradesh.
9. Modern Nilgiri.

CHAPTER EIGHTYTWO

Greatness of Gayā

Brahmā said :

1. O Vyāsa, listen. I shall narrate, in brief, the details of the greatness of Gayā.

2. There was a demon Gaya of great vitality. Once, he performed a terrible penance which scorched all living beings.

3-5. Devas, scorched extremely by his austerity, took refuge in Lord Viṣṇu.

Lord Viṣṇu said :

"When my great body is felled, all of you shall be experiencing welfare within." The gods said "So be it." Thereafter, one day, he culled lotuses for worship of Śiva from the Milk-ocean and brought them to Kīkaṭa. The demon was deluded by Viṣṇu's Māyā and instead of proceeding with his worship he lay down and slept. Then Viṣṇu killed him with the mace.

6-7. Thenceforward, Lord Viṣṇu has been staying there with the mace lifted up, ready to offer salvation. Over the purified mortal remains of that demon, Lord Śiva, in the form of a liṅga (phallic emblem) and Viṣṇu and Brahmā too presided there. Lord Viṣṇu the primordial deity demarcated the boundaries of the place and proclaimed that it would be a holy place.

8. A man who performs sacrifices, Śrāddha, Piṇḍadāna and ceremonial baths there will attain heaven and the world of Brahmā, never the hell.

9. Understanding the holy character of Gayā, Brahmā himself performed a sacrifice there and honoured the brahmins who came there as Ṛtviks.

10. The Lord created a great stream of juice (of milk and milk products), ponds, etc. and different types of foodstuffs fruits, etc. He then created the divine Kāmadhenu[1].

11. The land 15 kilometres all round constituting the holy site of Gayā was given as gift to the Brahmins.

1. The divine cow who fulfils all desires.

12. The easy acquisition of the land gift made the brahmins complacent. Then the brahmins were cursed.

13. Your learning will not extend even to three generations. Your riches will not survive your successive third heir. The river will flow with water not milk. The mountains will be mere rocks (not fruits and other edibles).

14. The cursed brahmins pleaded and the lord relented and said : "Those who perform Śrāddha here, will attain holy worlds and Brahmā's abode. I will consider myself worshipped if they worship you."

15. Knowledge of the supreme Brahman, performance of Śrāddha at Gayā, death in a cowshed and residence in Kurukṣetra—these are the four ways of attaining salvation.

16. Holy oceans, rivers, sacred ponds, wells and eddies go unto Gayātīrtha for a holy dip. There is no doubt about this.

17. The five great sins, viz. the murder of a brahmin, drinking wine, stealing, illicit intercourse with the preceptor's wife and association with sinners are removed by performing Śrāddha at Gayā.

18. Those who die and are not cremated duly, those who are killed by animals and dacoits, and those who die due to snake-bite attain salvation if Gayāśrāddha is performed unto them.

19. It is difficult to explain in detail the greatness of the benefits accruing from offering food oblations at Gayā even in twenty crores of years.

CHAPTER EIGHTYTHREE

Greatness of Gayā

Brahmā said :

1. In the land of Kīkaṭa, Gayā is a great holy place: the forest of Rājagṛha and the places frequently watered by the river are very holy.

2-3. To the east of Gayā is the place Muṇḍapṛṣṭha. In the west, south and north it extends to 4½ kilometres. The whole expanse of Gayākṣetra is 15 kilometres. The gift of oblations to the manes satiates as well as grants salvation. Even a visit to this place frees a person from the obligation to the manes. The Gayaśiras (the head of Gayā) is three kilometres long.

4. From the mount Janārdana and the well known mānasa is Gayāśiras. It is called Phalgu-tīrtha.

5. By offering piṇḍa there, the manes are freed. Simply by going to Gayā one is freed of mane's debt.

6. The lord of lords Viṣṇu presides over Gayā in the form of Manes. By visiting his shrine one is freed of three debts (to gods, manes, sages and guests).

7. Seeing the main highway at Gayā and visiting the shrines of Rudra, Kāleśvara and Kedāra a man becomes free from the debts to the manes.

8. By visiting the shrine of Brahmā one becomes free from all sins. By seeing the Prapitāmaha (the primordial deity) one attains region free of sickness.

9. After kneeling devoutly before the lord Gadādhara, Mādhava and Puruṣottama, the man is not born again.

10. O Brahmin Sage (Vyāsa)! By visiting silently the shrines of Maunāditya and Kanakārka the noble, a man becomes free from debts to the manes. By worshipping Brahmā one attains Brahmā's world.

11. Getting up early in the morning if one performs Sandhyā and visits the shrine of Gāyatrī, one gets the fruit of visiting the shrines of all gods.

12. By visiting the shrine of Sāvitrī in the midday, one gets the fruit of all sacrifices.

13. By visiting the shrine of Sarasvatī in the evening one gets the fruits of charitable gifts. By visiting the shrine of Īśvara on the top of the mountain, one becomes free from debts to the manes.

14. By visiting lord Dharma in Dharmāraṇya the material debts are wiped off. Who is not freed from bondage by visiting the shrine of lord Gṛdhreśvara?

15. By visiting the shrine of Cow in Dhenuvana one enables one's ancestors to attain Brahmaloka. By visiting lord Prabhāseśa in the shrine Prabhāsa one attains the highest goal.

16. By visiting the shrines of Koṭīśvara and Aśvamedha the material debts are wiped off. By visiting the shrine of Svargadvāreśvara one is freed from the bondage of worldly existence.

17. By visiting the lord with the mace in the shrine of Rāmeśvara one attains to heaven. By visiting the shrine of Brahmeśvara one is freed from the sin of murdering a Brahmin.

18. By visiting the shrine of Mahācaṇḍī in the mountain Muṇḍapṛṣṭha one attains all desires. By visiting the shrines of Phalgvīśa, Phalgucaṇḍī, Gaurī, Maṅgalā, Gomaka and lord Gopati one becomes free from debts to the manes.

19. Similarly, by visiting the shrines of Aṅgāreśa, Siddheśa, Gayāditya, Gaja and Mārkaṇḍeyeśvara one becomes free from debts to the manes.

20. A ceremonial bath in the holy pond of Phalgutīrtha and a visit to the shrine of Gadādhara,

21. Are these not sufficient for men of meritorious deeds? He makes his ancestors upto the twentyfirst remove attain Brahmaloka.

22. The holy rivers, oceans and lakes of the world will be coming to Phalgutīrtha, once every day.

23. In the whole world, Gayā is the holiest; in Gayā, Gayāśıras is the holiest spot and in gayāśiras the Phalgutīrtha is the holiest since it constitutes the mouth of gods.

24. To the north of Kanaka river is Nābhitīrtha and in its middle is the holy Tīrtha called Brahmasadas. A bath therein enables one to attain Brahmaloka.

25. After offering Piṇḍa (food-balls) etc. in the well one becomes free from indebtedness to the manes. Śrāddha at Akṣayavaṭa takes ancestors to Brahmaloka.

26. By taking the ceremonial bath in Haṁsatīrtha a man becomes free from all sins. A person who performs Śrāddha in Koṭitīrtha, Gayāloka, Vaitaraṇī and in Gomaka takes ancestors upto the twenty first remove to the Brahmaloka.

27. A person who performs Śrāddha in Brahmatīrtha, Rāmatīrtha, Āgneyatīrtha, Somatīrtha or in Rāmahrada takes all ancestors to Brahmaloka.

28. A man who performs Śrāddha in the Uttara-Mānasa is not born again; and in the Dakṣiṇa Mānasa takes his ancestors to the Brahmaloka.

29. A man who performs Tarpaṇa on the top of the hill Bhīṣma makes the manes cross hell. A person who performs Śrāddha in Gṛdhreśvara becomes free from debts to the manes.

30. A person who after taking his bath, gifts away gingelly seeds and cows, visits the shrine of cow and performs Śrāddha in Dhenukāraṇya, takes his ancestors to the Brahmaloka.

31. A person who performs Śrāddha in the Tīrthas Aindra, Nara, Vāsava and Vaiṣṇava and also in Mahānadī takes his ancestors to the Brahmaloka.

32. A person who performs ceremonial bath, Sandhyā, Tarpaṇa and Śrāddha in the Tīrthas—Gāyatra, Sāvitra and Sārasvata takes his ancestors upto the hundred and first remove to the Brahmaloka.

33. With the mind absorbed in contemplating his ancestors the devotee shall pass through the cleft Brahmayoni. Then by performing Tarpaṇa to the manes and gods he will be freed from the pangs of birth (i.e. he will not be born again).

34. By performing Tarpaṇa in the Tīrtha Kākajaṅghā he satiates manes forever. A person who performs Śrāddha in the holy pond of Mataṅga in Dharmāraṇya attains heaven.

35. By performing Śrāddha, etc. in Dharmayūpa and Kūpa one becomes free from debts to the manes.

36. He shall invoke gods by saying "O Gods ! ye be the witness unto this. I have performed Śrāddha for my ancestors today."

37. By taking the ceremonial bath in Rāmatīrtha and performing Śrāddha on a rock in Prabhāsa, the manes though long departed can be made liberated.

38. A person who performs Śrāddha in the holy Tīrtha Svapuṣṭā shall uplift his ancestors upto the twentyfirst remove. A person who performs Śrāddha on the hill Muṇḍapṛṣṭha shall lead his ancestors to the Brahmaloka.

39. There is no spot in Gayā which is not a holy Tīrtha. A person who offers Piṇḍa anywhere in Gayākṣetra, shall reap everlasting benefit and take his ancestors to Brahmaloka.

40. The pilgrim shall place the Piṇḍa in the hand of Janārdana (the idol) saying

41. "O Janārdana, I have offered the Piṇḍa in thy hand. When I go to the other world let everlasting liberation bless me."

42. It is certain that he will attain Brahmaloka along with his manes. The oblations offered to the manes in Dharmapṛṣṭha, and Brahmasaras, in Gayā and in

43. Akṣayavaṭa in Gayāśīrṣa shall be everlasting. The act of visiting Tīrthas, Dharmāraṇya, Dharmapṛṣṭha and Dhenukāraṇya,

44. And performing Arghya to the manes uplifts twenty generations. Brahmāraṇya is to the west of the river Maya while in the east are Brahmasadas, Nāgādri and Bharatāśrama.

45-47. Śrāddha shall be performed in the region of Mataṅga in the Āśrama of Bharata. There is the holy place called Campakavana to the south of Gayāśira and to the west of Mahānadī. There Pāṇḍuśilā is situated. If one performs Śrāddha there in the zone of Niścirā on the third day of the lunar fortnight or in the sacred eddy of Kauśikī everlasting benefit is secured.

48. To the north of Vaitaraṇī is the sacred pond called Tṛtīya. There the sacred spot Krauñcapāda is situated. One who performs Śrāddha there shall take his ancestors to the Heaven.

49. To the north of Krauñcapāda is the sacred pond Niścirā. Even a single visit to Gayā and offering of Piṇḍa once is rarely secured, then what of those who stay there permanently?

50. If the pilgrim performs Tarpaṇa in Mahānadī for the manes and gods he shall attain everlasting worlds and uplift his family.

51. If Sandhyā is performed in the Sāvitratīrtha the benefit of performing the same for twelve years shall be acquired.

52. He who stays for two fortnights (the bright and the

dark) in Gayā purifies his family upto the seventh generation. There is no doubt in this.

53. By seeing the three mountains Muṇḍapṛṣṭha, Aravinda and Krauñcapāda, the pilgrim is freed from all sins.

54. When solar or lunar eclipse occurs in the month of Makara (January—February) Piṇḍa shall be offered in Gayā. It bestows rare merits and is highly beneficent to the people.

55. A Śrāddha performed in Mahāhrada (great-eddy) of Kauśikī, in Mūlakṣetra and in the cave of Gṛdhrakūṭa is seven times fruitful.

56. A person who performs Śrāddha where the river Māheśvarī flows shall be freed from material debts. By visiting the holy river Viśālā famous in the three worlds a man obtains the fruits of Agniṣṭoma sacrifice. By performing Śrāddha he shall go to heaven.

57. A person who takes bath and performs Śrāddha in Somapada shall derive the fruits of Vājapeya sacrifice.

58. By offering Piṇḍas in Ravipāda the fallen souls shall be uplifted. The manes consider themselves blessed with a son if he goes to Gayā and offers food oblations.

59. Fathers desire for sons in their fear of falling into Hell thinking, "One of them will go to Gayā and uplift us". On seeing the son who has reached Gayā the manes are excessively jubilant.

60. They will think like this : "Either the son or some one else at some time or other shall offer us water at least by wading through it in Gayākūpa."

61. A pilgrim takes any one with that name to the eternal Brahman by repeating which he offers the Piṇḍa. A person who visits Koṭitīrtha shall attain the Viṣṇuloka called Puṇḍarīka.

62. The river which is renowned in the three worlds as Vaitaraṇī has incarnated in Gayākṣetra for the uplift of the manes.

63. There is no doubt in this that a person who performs Śrāddha, offers Piṇḍa and makes a gift of a cow uplifts his ancestors to twenty one generations.

64. If a son goes to Gayā sometime (after the death of

his father) he shall feed the local brahmins who had been allotted that right by Brahmā.

65. Their post is Brahmasadas. The same is the post of Somapas (drinkers of Soma juice).

66. The worship, Śrāddha, etc. shall be in the place assigned by Brahmā and the Brahmins also shall be those mentioned by Brahmā. If they are honoured, honoured shall all the deities be along with the manes.

67. The pilgrim shall propitiate the Brahmins at Gayā according to Śāstraic injunctions by means of Havyas and Kavyas (sacrificial foodstuffs). The best place for shedding the mortal body is Gayā.

68. There is no doubt in this that he who makes the gift of a bull in Gayākṣetra, the unrivalled holy place, derives the merit of a hundred Agniṣṭomas.

69. An intelligent man can offer Piṇḍa unto himself as unto others at Gayā but without using gingelly seeds.

70. O Vyāsa, Piṇḍas shall be offered to all at Gayā, whether cousins, ancestors kinsmen or friends in accordance with Śāstras.

71. By taking the ceremonial bath at Rāmatīrtha a man obtains the benefit of a gift of hundred cows. By taking the bath at Mataṅga pond he shall get the benefit of the gift of a thousand cows.

72. By taking the ceremonial bath at the confluence of Niścirā a man takes his ancestors to Brahmaloka; at Vasiṣṭha's hermitage — the benefit of Vājapeya.

73. And by staying in Mahākośī for a year he gets the fruit of Aśvamedha (Horse sacrifice).

74. There is a holy river flowing from Brahmasaras which sanctifies the whole world. It is famous as Agnidhārā and is on a par with Kapilā (the divine cow that grants all boons). A person performing Śrāddha here derives the fruit of Agniṣṭoma and by taking bath here one feels as if one has fulfilled all tasks.

75. By performing Śrāddha in Kumāradhārā one gets the fruit of Aśvamedha. Having reached Lord Subrahmaṇya he will attain salvation.

76. By taking the ceremonial bath in Somakuṇḍa a man goes to the moon's world. A person giving Piṇḍas in the sacred pond of Saṁvarta shall be highly lucky.

77-78. A man offering Piṇḍas in Pretakuṇḍa shall wash off all his sins. Those who offer Piṇḍas in the Tīrthas, Devanadī, Lelihāna, Mathana, Jānugartaka and others shall uplift all ancestors. By bowing to lord Vasiṣtheśa all accumulated material debts shall be liquidated.

CHAPTER EIGHTYFOUR

Greatness of Gayā

Brahmā said :

1-2. If a person wishes to proceed to Gayā, he shall first perform Śrāddha according to Śāstraic injunctions. He shall then disguise himself and go round his village. Then proceeding to another village he shall take in only what is left over after Śrāddha. He shall go round that village as well. During his journey to Gayā he shall never take Pratigraha (money by way of charity).

3-4. Every step that he takes after leaving his house towards Gayā enables his ancestors to ascend a step towards heaven. With regard to other holy places the injunction of tonsure and fasting holds good; but in the case of Kurukṣetra, Viśālā, Virajā and Gayā it does not. Śrāddha can be performed at Gayā during the day or night.

5-6. A person performing Śrāddha in Vārāṇasī, Śoṇanada and frequently in Mahānadī shall take his ancestors to heaven.

7. By going to Uttaramānasa unrivalled achievement is acquired. The pilgrim who takes bath and performs Śrāddha there shall acquire all his desires mundane and divine and also the means to achieve salvation.

8. After reaching the Dakṣiṇamānasa he shall offer Piṇḍa, etc. silently. At that place he shall wipe off the threefold debts.

9-10. To the north of Muṇḍapṛṣṭha there is the holy place named Kanakhala famous in the three worlds, frequented by devas and sages and infested by illustrious serpents pleasing to the Siddhas and terrific to the sinners, horrible in appearance and putting out their unsplit tongues.

11. By taking bath there one goes to heaven; the Śrāddha performed there is everlasting. After bowing to the Sun and performing Piṇḍadāna and other holy rites he shall say like this :

12-13. "O ye deities of manes, Kavyavāha, Agniṣvāttas, Barhiṣads, Somapas, Soma, Yama and Aryaman, do come, you noble Sirs; with your protection I have come here to Gayā desiring to offer Piṇḍas to all of my ancestors and to all kinsmen born in the family."

14. After offering Piṇḍas in Phalgutīrtha he shall visit lord Pitāmaha and then Gadādhara. He shall be freed from indebtedness to the manes.

15. By taking bath in Phalgutīrtha and visiting lord Gadādhara the devotee shall immediately save himself, ten generations gone before and ten generations yet to come.

16. I have mentioned the programme for the first day. On the second day he shall go to Dharmāraṇya and perform Piṇḍadāna, etc. in the sacred pond of Mataṅga.

17. By visiting Dharmāraṇya he will derive the fruit of Vājapeya.

18. In the holy Tīrtha of Brahmā he will derive the fruit of Rājasūya and Aśvamedha.

19. Śrāddha and Piṇḍodaka in the middle of Kūpa and Yūpa shall be done with the water of the well. What is offered to the manes shall be endless.

20. On the third day he shall go to Brahmasadas, take bath and perform Tarpaṇa, Śrāddha and Piṇḍadāna in the middle of Kūpa (well) and Yūpa (Sacrificial stake).

21. The brahmins ordained by Brahmā are staying near Gopracāra. By honouring and serving them the manes shall

attain salvation. After going round the sacrificial stake he shall derive the fruit of Vājapeya.

22-23. On the fourth day he shall take bath, perform Tarpaṇa and Śrāddha in Gayāśira in the temple of Lord Rudra etc. Then O Vyāsa, he shall offer Piṇḍas in Pañcāgni (five fires) and worship the three gods Sūrya, (Sun) Indu (Moon) and Kārttikeya. The Śrāddha thus performed shall be everlasting.

24-25. The Śrāddha may be for nine deities or twelve deities. During the Anvaṣṭakā days (i. e. the ninth day of the lunar fortnights in Pauṣa, Māgha and Phālguna months), during Vṛddhi (i. e. in the bright fortnights) or on the day of death separate Śrāddha is performed here for the mother. At other places the Śrāddha has to be performed alongwith father's.

26. By taking bath in Daśāśvamedha and visiting Lord Pitāmaha and touching the feet of Rudra a man is not born again.

27. By performing Śrāddha in Gayāśira a man obtains the same as obtained by making a gift of a land endowed with the three kinds of wealth (fertility, nearness to water, and good soil).

28. At Gayāśira, the balls of oblation shall be of the size of a Śamīpatra (the leaf of Śamī tree). Then the manes become gods. No one need worry about this.

29. Lord Mahādeva of great intellect has set foot on the hill Muṇḍapṛṣṭha. By performing even a small penance he shall acquire great merit.

30. Those who are in hell will go to heaven and those in heaven attain liberation if he names them and offers Piṇḍas in Gayāśira.

31. On the fifth day he shall take his bath in Gadālola and offer Piṇḍas at the foot of the Banyan tree. He shall thereby enable the entire family of his ancestors to cross hell.

32. At the root of the Banyan tree even if a single brahmin is fed with vegetable dishes and hot water it is as good as feeding a crore.

33. At Akṣayavaṭa he shall perform Śrāddha and see the

Primordial deity. He shall attain everlasting worlds and uplift a hundred generations.

34. Many sons are to be wished for. At least one of them may go to Gayā or perform Aśvamedha or make a gift of a dark bull.

35. A ghost once addressed a certain merchant—"Please ffer Piṇḍas in my name at Gayāśira. I shall be liberated from the state of a ghost and the giver of the Piṇḍas shall attain heaven."

36. The merchant on hearing that offered Piṇḍa to the chief of ghosts and thereafter offered the same to his manes alongwith the younger brothers.

37. All of them were liberated and Viśāla the offerer of Piṇḍas was blessed with a son. There was a prince in the country of Viśālā named Viśāla. He addressed the Brahmins.

38. "How can I have sons ?" The brahmins replied, "By offering Piṇḍas in Gayā you will have sons". The prince Viśāla offered Piṇḍas in Gayā and was blessed with sons.

39. He saw in the sky three human shapes white, red and black in colour and said "Who are you ?". The white one from among them replied to Viśāla.

40. "I am the white one, your father. I attained Indraloka due to meritorious deeds. My son, this red one is my father. He is a great sinner, a murderer of a Brahmin.

41. This black one is my grandfather. Some sages had been killed by him. Both of them had fallen into the hell Avīci (Rayless). Now that you have offered the Piṇḍas both of them have been liberated.

42. Now that we have been liberated, we are proceeding to Heaven." Viśāla who was satisfied ruled the kingdom (for some time) and attained heaven.

43-48. [The devotee shall repeat thus]. "Let all the manes in our family who had been deprived of Piṇḍa and Udaka (water) rites, who died in infancy without the rite of Cūḍā (ceremonial cutting of forelocks), who had been still born, who had not been duly cremated and who had died in flames, be satisfied with the Piṇḍas offered in the Earth and attain salvation. Let these Piṇḍas deliver everlastingly all these :— Father, grandfather, great grandfather, mother, paternal grand mother, paternal great-grand mother maternal grand-father, maternal great grandfather maternal great-great grand father, maternal grand mother, maternal great grandmother, maternal great great grandmother and other kinsmen.

CHAPTER EIGHTYFIVE

Greatness of Gayā

Brahmā said :

1. After taking bath in Pretaśilā, etc., with the nectar (holy water) of Varuṇatīrtha the pilgrim shall invoke the manes with the following mantras and offer Piṇḍas.

2. "With gingelly seeds and holy water, I invoke on this Darbha grass all those in our family who have not attained salvation after death.

3. I offer this Piṇḍa to uplift all those who died in my father's family and mother's family.

4. I offer this Piṇḍa to uplift all those in my maternal grandfather's family who have not attained salvation.

5. I offer this Piṇḍa to uplift all those who died in infancy without cutting the first tooth or who were still born.

6. This Piṇḍa is assigned to those kinsmen whose names and Gotra (spiritual clan) are forgotten whether in my gotra or others.

7. I offer this Piṇḍa to those who committed suicide by hanging themselves or by other means or poisoned to death or killed with any weapon.

8. I offer this Piṇḍa to those who died in an incident of arson, or were killed by lions or tigers or sharp-teethed animals or horned beasts.

9. I offer this Piṇḍa to those who were cremated or not, who were electrocuted or killed by dacoits.

10. I offer this Piṇḍa to uplift those who have been consigned to the hells—Raurava, Andhatāmisra and Kālasūtra after death.

11. I offer this Piṇḍa to uplift those who have been confined to the terrible hells Asipatravana and Kumbhīpāka after death.

12. I offer this Piṇḍa to uplift those who are being tortured and tormented (by Yama) in the Pretaloka (Infernal region).

13. I offer this Piṇḍa to those who have been born as beasts, birds, worms, reptiles or trees.

14. I offer this Piṇḍa to uplift those who are being tortured and tormented in innumerable ways at the bidding of Yama.

15. I offer this Piṇḍa to those to whom birth in human society has become difficult of access due to their actions and who are born and reborn in countless other species.

16. Let all those be satiated with this offer of Piṇḍa forever whether kinsmen or not or whether they were kinsmen in my previous birth or not.

17. Let all those ancestors of mine be satiated forever by this offer of Piṇḍa and those who are still in the state of Ghosts.

18-20. Let this Piṇḍa offered by me go for endless benefit unto all those who were born in my father's family, mother's family or those of preceptor's, father-in-law or kinsmen or other kinsmen who are dead, those who have been deprived of Piṇḍadāna, those who had no sons or wives, those who had not performed any rites, those who had been born blind, those who were lame, those who were deformed or those who died in the womb whether known to me or not.

21-22. Let Devas bear witness, let Brahmā, Īśāna and others bear witness. I have come to Gayā and have performed the obsequies. O Gadādhara, for performing the rites for manes I have come to Gayā. Be my witness today. I am now absolved of my three debts."

23. In Gayā, the sanctity of Mahānadī, Brahmasaras Akṣayavaṭa Prabhāsa, Gayāśiras, Sarasvatī, Dharmāraṇya, Dhenupṛṣṭha, of all these holy spots, is equal to that of Kurukṣetra.

CHAPTER EIGHTYSIX

Greatness of Gayā

Brahmā said :

1-2. The spot famous as Pretaśilā has three sections in Prabhāsa, Pretakuṇḍa and Gayāsuraśiras. This rocky promontory is held aloft by Dharma and is called Pretaśilā because it is conducive to the prosperity and uplift of those men, their friends or kinsmen who become ghosts. It is presided over by all devas.

3. Hence, here sages, kings and queens perform Śrāddha on that rock. They have attained Brahmaloka too.

4. The rock at the place where the skull of the demon Gayāsura fell is known as Muṇḍapṛṣṭha. It is also presided over by all devas.

5. At the foot of the mountain Muṇḍapṛṣṭha there are ponds Brahmasaras etc. overgrown and partially hidden by Aravinda forest.

6. The hill in Aravinda forest marked by the feet of a Krauñcā bird (akin to heron) is called Krauñcapāda which enables the pilgrim to attain Brahmaloka.

7. The primordial deities Gadādhara and others are latent in the stone idols. Hence, the rock is saturated with divine presence.

8-9. The idol of Gadādhara buried under its heavy weight the head of the demon Gaya and gradually the beginningless and endless lord Hari in the company of Mahārudra and other devas became manifest in it for the preservation of virtue and destruction of evil.

10-11. The Lord Viṣṇu took the incarnations of Matsya (fish), Kūrma (tortoise), Varāha (boar) Nṛhari (Man-lion), Vāmana (Dwarf) the powerful Paraśurāma, Rāma son of Daśaratha Kṛṣṇa, Buddha and Kalki for the destruction of demons and ogres. In the same way the manifest and unmanifest form of the primordial Gadādhara.

12. The deity Gadādhara is called Ādi (primordial) because he had been worshipped by lords Brahmā and others with Pādya, fragrant flowers in the beginning.

13-18. He who, after visiting the shrine of the primordial Gadādhara along with the other gods, makes an offering of Arghya, Pādya, fragrant flowers, incense, lamp, Naivedya (food offerings) of the highest sort, different sorts of garlands, clothes, crown, bell, chowries, mirrors, ornaments, Piṇḍa and various foodstuffs, is sure to get wealth, grains, longevity, health, blessings of sons and children, all kinds of riches, learning, all desires, good wife, enjoyment in heaven and after the return from heaven a flourishing kingdom, nobility of birth, Sāttvika qualities, defeat of enemies in the battle, freedom from murder and bondage and finally will attain liberation. Those who perform Śrāddha and offer Piṇḍa will go to Brahmaloka along with their ancestors.

19. Those who worship Balabhadra and Subhadrā shall acquire strength, welfare, knowledge, wealth and children and attain Puruṣottama.

20. Offering of Piṇḍa to the manes in front of Puruṣottamarāja, the Sun and Gaṇeśa yields Brahmaloka to the ancestors.

21. By bowing down to Kapardin (Śiva), and Vighneśa (Gaṇeśa) one is freed from all obstacles. By worshipping Kārttikeya he shall attain Brahmaloka.

22. By worshipping twelve suns one is freed from all sickness. By worshipping Vaiśvānara one gets an excellent brilliance.

23. By adoring Revanta the pilgrim obtains excellent horses; by worshipping Indra—great riches and by worshipping Gaurī—good fortune.

24. By worshipping learning, Sarasvatī, Lakṣmī, Śrī and Garuḍa one is extricated from numerous obstacles.

25. By worshipping Kṣetrapāla one is freed from evil planets and by worshipping Muṇḍapṛṣṭha one shall obtain all desires.

26. By worshipping the eight serpents one will not be affected by serpent bite; by worshipping Brahmā one shall attain Brahmaloka.

27. By worshipping Balabhadra one shall get strength and health: by worshipping Subhadrā one gets good luck.

28. By worshipping Puruṣottama one obtains all desires. By worshipping Nārāyaṇa one becomes lord of men.

29. By touching the idol of Narasiṁha and worshipping it one becomes victorious in battle. By worshipping Varāha (the divine Boar) one acquires suzerainty over the whole Earth.

30. By touching idols of two Vidyādharas whoever one may be, becomes a Vidyādhara. By worshipping the primordial Gadādhara one attains all desires.

31. By worshipping Somanātha one obtains Śivaloka. By bowing Rudreśvara one is honoured in Rudraloka.

32. By bowing to Rāmeśvara a man becomes delightful to others like Lord Rāma. By worshipping Brahmeśvara and reciting prayers one becomes competent to be in Brahmaloka.

33. By worshipping Kāleśvara a man conquers the god of death; by worshipping Kedāra one is honoured in Śivaloka. By worshipping Siddheśvara one shall become a Siddha and go to Brahmapura.

34. By visiting the Primordial Gadādhara along with the primordial Rudra and others a man is able to uplift a hundred generations and lead them to Brahmapura.

35-36. By worshipping the primordial Gadādhara a man desirous of Dharma (virtue) shall acquire it; a man desirous of wealth shall acquire wealth; a passionate man shall acquire love; a man desirous of salvation shall acquire salvation; a man desirous of a kingdom shall acquire a realm and a man desirous of tranquillity shall acquire it.

37. By approaching and worshipping the primordial Gadādhara a woman desirous of sons shall get sons; a woman desirous of blissful married life shall acquire it and a woman desirous of a flourishing family shall attain it.

38. By worshipping the primordial Gadādhara one obtains the Brahmaloka even as by Śrāddha, Piṇḍadāna, gift of food and gift of cool water.

39-40. Just as Gayāpurī is the most excellent of all Tīrthas in the world so also Gadādhara is the most excellent of all sacred idols. Since Gadādhara is the entire world if Gadādhara is seen the entire sacred spot and all idols are virtually seen.

CHAPTER EIGHTYSEVEN

The fourteen Manus

Hari said:

1. I shall enumerate the fourteen Manus and their sons such as Śuka. Svāyambhuva Manu is the first among the Manus. Agnīdhra and others are his sons.

2. The seven sages are Marīci, Atri, Āṅgiras, Pulastya, Pulaha, Kratu and the brilliant Vasiṣṭha.

3. These four are called Somapāyins (drinkers of Soma juice) : Jaya, Amita, Śuka and Yāma. The foregoing twelve are collectively called Dvādaśaka Gaṇa.

4. Vāmadeva who enjoyed the entire universe was elected Indra (during this Manvantara i.e. period of regime of Manu and his dynasty). The demon Bāṣkali was his enemy. He was killed by Viṣṇu with his Sudarśana discus.

5-7. The second Manu was Svārociṣa. His sons were Maṇḍaleśvara, Caitraka, Vinata, Karṇānta, Vidyuta, Ravi, Bṛhadguṇa, and Nabha of great strength and exploit. The seven sages were Ūrja, Stamba, Prāṇa, Ṛṣabha, Nicula, Dambholi and Arvavīra. The Tuṣitas and Pārāvatas together constituted the Dvādaśaka Gaṇa.

8. Vipaścit was elected as Indra of the devas. His enemy was the demon Purukṛtsara whom Lord Madhusūdana killed in the guise of an elephant.

9. The sons of the third Manu, Auttama were : Āja Paraśu, Vinīta, Suketu, Sumitra, Subala, Śuci, Deva, Devāvṛdha, Mahotsāha and Ajita, O Rudra.

10. The seven sages during his regime were : Rathaujas, Ūrdhvabāhu, Śaraṇa, Anagha, Muni, Sutapas and Śaṅku.

11. The Five Deva gaṇas were Vaśavarti, Svadhāmans, Śivas, Satyas and Pratardanas. These with the seven sages constituted the Dvādaśaka Gaṇa.

12. Svaśānti was elected Indra during this regime and his enemy was the demon Pralamba. Lord Viṣṇu in his incarnation as fish killed him.

13-16. The sons of the fourth Manu named Tāmasa were :—Jānujaṅgha, Nirbhaya, Navakhyāti, Naya, Priyabhṛtya,

Vivikṣipa, Havuṣkadhi, Prastalākṣa, Kṛtabandhu and Kṛta. The seven sages were Jyotirdhārā, Dhṛṣṭakāvya, Caitra, Cetāgni, Hemaka, Surāga and Svadhiya. The four Haris together with others constituted the twentyfive Devatāgaṇas. Śibi was elected Indra and his enemy was the giant Bhīmaratha. This giant Bhīmaratha was killed by Lord Viṣṇu in His incarnation as Tortoise.

17-18. The sons of the fifth Manu Raivata were Mahāprāṇa, Sādhaka, Vanabandhu, Niramitra, Pratyaṅga, Parahā, Śuci, Dṛḍhavrata and Ketuśṛṅga.

19. The seven sages were Vedaśrī, Vedabāhu, Ūrdhvabāhu, Hiraṇyaroman, Parjanya, Satyanāman and Svadhāman.

20-21. The four Devatā gaṇas were Abhūtarajas, Devāśvamedhas, Vaikuṇṭha and Amṛta. These were altogether fourteen in the Gaṇa. Vibhu of great exploits was elected Indra. The demon Śāntaśatru was killed by Viṣṇu in the guise of a Swan.

22-23. The sons of the sixth Manu Cākṣuṣa were :—Ūru, Pūru of great strength, Śatadyumna who performed penances, Satyabāhu, Kṛti, Agniṣṇu, Atirātra, Sudyumna and Nara. The seven sages were: Haviṣmān, Sutanu the glorious, Svadhāman, Viraja, Abhimana, Sahiṣṇu and Madhuśrī.

24. There were five gaṇas each with eight deities. They were — Āryas, Prasūtas, Bhāvyas, Lekhas and Pṛthukas.

25. Manojava was elected Indra and his enemy was Mahākāla of long arms. He was killed by Lord Viṣṇu in the guise of a horse.

26-28. The sons of the seventh Manu Vaivasvata who were great devotees of Viṣṇu were : Ikṣvāku, Nābha, Viṣṭi, Śaryāti, Haviṣyanta, Pāṁśu, Nabhas, Nediṣṭha, Karūṣa, Pṛṣadhra and Sudyumna. The seven sages were Atri, Vasiṣṭha the dignified, Jamadagni, Kaśyapa,

29. Gautama, Bharadvāja and Viśvāmitra. There were fortynine Maruts.

30. The Ādityas, Vasus and Sādhyas together constituted the Dvādaśaka Gaṇa.

31. The Rudras were eleven in number, Vasus were eight; the Aśvins are stipulated as two and Viśvedevas were ten in number. The Āngiras were also ten and nine Devagaṇas.

32. Tejasvin was elected Indra. Hiraṇyākṣa was his enemy. This demon was killed by Lord Viṣṇu in His incarnation as the Boar.

33. I shall now enumerate the future Manus (and their sons and followers). The sons of the eighth Manu named Sāvarṇi will be Vijaya, Arvavīra, Nirdeha, Satyavāk, Kṛti, Variṣṭha, Gariṣṭha, Vāca and Saṅgati.

34. The seven sages will be : Aśvatthāmā, Kṛpa, Vyāsa, Gālava, Dīptimān, Ṛṣyaśṛṅga and Rāma.

35. The chief deities will be Sutapas and Amṛtābhas; their gaṇas are twenty in each.

36. Virocana's son Bali will be elected Indra.

37. After giving his realm to Viṣṇu who will be begging for three steps, he will forsake his Indra-hood and achieve salvation.

38. Listen to the names of the sons of Dakṣasāvarṇi descendant of Varuṇa. He will be the ninth of Manus. The sons will be : Dhṛṣṭiketu, Dīptiketu, Pañcahasta, Nirākṛti, Pṛthuśravas, Bṛhaddyumna, Ṛcīka, Bṛhata and Guṇa.

39-40. The seven sages will be — Medhātithi, Dyuti, Sabala, Vasu, Jyotiṣmān, Havya and Kavya. Vibhu, Marīci and Garbha will be elected Indra. The three will be strictly observing their duties. Kālakākṣa will be the enemy of gods. Lord Padmanābha will kill him.

41-42. Listen to the names of the sons of the tenth Manu, Dharmaputra. They will be Sukṣetra, Uttamaujas, Bhūriśreṇya the virile, Śatānīka who will have no enemies, Vṛṣasena, Jayadratha, Bhūridyumna and Suvarcas. Śānti will be elected Indra. He will be valorous.

43. The seven sages will be :—Apomūrti, Haviṣmān, Sukṛta, Avyaya, Lābhaga, Apratima and Saurabha.

44. The hundred Prāṇas will constitute the Devatāgaṇas. Bali will be the enemy whom lord Hari will kill with his mace.

45-48. I shall tell you the names of the sons of Rudraputra the eleventh Manu. They will be — Sarvatraga, Suśarman, Devānīka, Puru, Guru, Kṣetravarṇa, Dṛḍheṣu, Ārdraka and Putraka. The sages will be — Haviṣmān, Haviṣya, Varuṇa, Viśva, Vistara, Viṣṇu and Agnitejas. Vihaṅgamas (skywanderers) Kāmagamas (Going as they pleased) Nirmāṇarucis and

Ekaikarucis will constitute the Gaṇas. Vṛṣa will be elected as Indra. Daśagrīva will be the enemy. The lord Śrīrūpin will kill him.

49-50. Listen to the names of the sons of Dakṣaputra, the twelfth Manu. They will be Devavān, Upadeva, Devaśreṣṭha, Vidūratha, Mitravān, Mitradeva, Mitrabindu the virile, Mitravāha and Pravāha.

51. The seven sages will be Tapasvin, Sutapas, Tapomūrti, Taporati, Tapodhṛti, Tapodyuti and Tapodhana.

52. Sutapas who will be observing the duties, Harita, Rohita, and Suràris constitute the gaṇas each consisting of ten.

53. Ṛtadhāman will be elected as their noble Indra. Tāraka will be their enemy. Lord Hari assuming the form of a eunuch will kill him, O Śaṅkara.

54-57. Know from me the names of the sons of Raucya the thirteenth Manu. They will be Citrasena, Vicitra, Tapodharmarata, Dhṛti, Sunetra and Kṣetravṛtti. The seven sages will be Dharmapa the firm or steady, Dhṛtimān, Avyaya, Niśārūpa, Nirutsuka, Nirmāṇa, and Tattvadarśin. The gaṇas will be constituted by Svaromans, Svadharmans, Svakarmans and Amaras consisting of thirtythree sections. Divaspati will be elected Indra and the enemy will be Iṣṭibha the great demon.

58. Lord Mādhava will kill him in the guise of a peacock. Listen to the names of the sons of Bhautya the fourteenth Manu from me.

59. They will be :—Ūru, Gabhīra, Dhṛṣṭa, Tarasvin, Grāha, Abhimānin, Pravīra, Jiṣṇu, Saṁkrandana, Tejasvin, and Durlabha.

60. The seven sages will be :—Agnīdhra, Agnibāhu, Māgadha, Śuci, Ajita, Mukta and Śukra.

61. These five constitute the gaṇas Cākṣuṣas, Karmaniṣṭhas, Pavitras, Bhrājins and Vācāvṛthas, each having seven sections.

62-64. Śuci will be elected Indra. His enemy will be the demon Mahādaitya. Lord Hari will Himself kill him. Lord Viṣṇu though single by Himself will assume the form as Vyāsa and write the Purāṇas and propagate them. Eighteen lores constitute the six Aṅgas, the four Vedas, Mimāṁsā, Nyāyavistara, Purāṇas, Dharmaśāstras, Āyurveda, Arthaśāstra, Dhanurveda and Gāndharva (musicology).

CHAPTER EIGHTYEIGHT

Story of Ruci

Sūta said :

1. Lord Hari narrated the Manvantaras to Lord Śiva, Brahmā and others. The sage Mārkaṇḍeya narrated to Krauñcuki the hymn of the Manes. Listen to that.

Mārkaṇḍeya said :

2. Formerly, Ruci, an elderly sage, free from attachment to the world, devoid of egotism and for whom Māyā (Ignorance) was well-nigh put to rest, was roaming about in the world here and there.

3. Seeing the sage not nursing the sacrificial fires, not staying in a permanent abode, not fulfilling the duties of (householder's) Āśrama (stage in life) and satisfied with a single meal (anywhere), his ancestors addressed him.

The Manes said :

4-5. "Dear Son, wherefore has the holy wedlock not been entered into by you ? Of course it is a binding fetter since it is the bridge that unites Heaven and earth. Hence, a householder performing due and deserving hospitality to deities, manes, sages and suppliants without meat, shall attain the higher worlds.

6. By repeating Svāhā, the householder propitiates the deities; by repeating Svadhā he propitiates the manes, by gifts of food he propitiates servants and guests.

7. O mortal Sage ! You too have fallen into a bondage by incurring debts to gods, to us and to all living beings day after day.

8. Without begetting sons, without performing Tarpaṇas to the manes and without shaving off your head (in Sannyāsa) how can you wish for heaven ?

9. O son, know that only pain will befall you and that too by your unjustifiable act. If you die, either you go to hell or suffer pain in the next birth.

Ruci said :

10. Wedlock is conducive to greater distress, sin or fall. Hence I did not marry sire.

11. One is held in suspense by a momentary consultation; there seems to be no way out for salvation; this will be the result if I enter into matrimony.

12-13. The soul which is tarnished by the multifarious acts of innumerable births has to be washed by the water of knowledge of reality with a full curb on the sense-organs. A soul free from the ties of wedlock may still be tainted with the feeling of "my-ness"—an obsession of possession. Yet it is better and easier to wash it off by the water of learning.

The Manes said :

14. "Dear son, no doubt, the soul has to be scrubbed of its impurities by curbing the sense-organs. Yet the path you have chosen as the remedy is not the suitable one.

15-16. Dispelling the effects of good and bad actions of the previous births by means of five sacrifices (Pañca-yajñas) austerities and charitable gifts and performing the duties (enjoined by sacred circles) one is not fettered by that action like the one resulting from transgressing the same. There will never be any obstacle.

17. Dear son, sin, or merit accumulated by previous actions is wasted away steadily when one experiences the fruits thereof whether pleasure or sorrow.

18. It is thus that intelligent men wash off their souls and save them from bondage. If they protect themselves with discretion they are not sullied by the taint of sin.

Ruci said :

19. Noble sires ! The paths of activities are condemned in the Vedas as the sequel of ignorance. Still, wherefore do you enjoin the same on me ?

The Manes said :

20. It is wrong to say that everything is the result of ignorance and actions constitute the cause of the same. But there is no doubt that action is the cause of extension of learning (or true knowledge).

21. The good never invite trouble by not doing the rites mandatorily enjoined. A self-restraint coupled with it is conducive to salvation, otherwise it leads to fall.

22. What you consider to be the excellent way out with the attitude "O I am washing off" (is wrong); you will be burnt by the sins of dereliction of duty.

23. Even the illusion, like poison (which nullifies other poisons and helps) is conducive to good; as a means for the performance of duties it is not fettering though capable of it.

24. Hence, dear son, find out a suitable girl and marry her. Let not your life be in vain without the assurance of attaining the other world and its benefit.

Ruci said :

25. O sires, I am now an old man. Who will provide me with a wife ? It is difficult for a poor wretch to go in for marriage.

The Manes said :

26. O son, If you do not appreciate our advice, our degradation and your fall is certain. You should render our advice into practice.

27. After saying this, O noble sage (Krauñcuki), the manes suddenly vanished like lamps blown out by the wind, even as Ruci stood gazing at them.

28. Thus Mārkaṇḍeya narrated to Krauñcuki the entire episode of Ruci involving his conversation with the manes.

CHAPTER EIGHTYNINE

Story of Ruci

Sūta said :

1-2. When requested by Krauñcuki Mārkaṇḍeya continued the story : Ruci became worried and anxious on hearing the last utterance of the Manes. In his search for a wife the brahmin sage wandered over the world. He could not get any girl. The utterance of the manes kindled him. He became agitated and excited and began to ruminate.

3. "O what shall I do ? Where shall I go ? How can I secure a wife ? How is it possible to uplift myself and my ancestors quickly ?"

4. Thus ruminating he thought of an idea. "O I shall propitiate Brahmā the lotus-born god by means of penance !"

5. He stayed in a forest for a long time leading a disciplined life and propitiating (Brahmā). With a concentrated mind he performed divine austerities for full one hundred years.

6. Brahmā the patriarch of worlds revealed himself to the sage and said—"I am pleased. Let me hear what you desire."

7. Thereupon the sage bowed down and told Brahmā the ultimate refuge of the universe what he was desirous of doing at the bidding of the manes.

Brahmā said :

8-9. You shall be a Prajāpati (a progenitor of children). O Brahmin, after begetting children and performing sacred rites, you shall achieve the desired results. Hence, go ahead in your attempt to secure a wife as advised by the manes.

10. With desire in your mind worship the manes who being duly propitiated, will bestow upon you what you desire. Won't they, your grandfathers when propitiated provide you with a wife and sons ?

Mārkaṇḍeya said :

11. After hearing the words of Brahmā born of the un-

manifest, the sage Ruci performed Tarpaṇa unto the manes on the sacred banks of a river.

12. With reverence he thought of the manes with pure and concentrated mind and stooping his shoulders with due devotion the brahmin adored the manes by means of the following verses in prayer.

Ruci said :

13. "I bow unto the manes with devotion—the manes who reside amidst the deities and who are propitiated by the deities during Śrāddhas, with mantras ending with 'Svadhā.'

14. I bow unto the manes who are propitiated by the sages in the heaven desirous of devotion and salvation by Śrāddha performed mentally with great devotion.

15. I bow unto the manes whom the Siddhas in heaven propitiate during Śrāddhas by means of unrivalled divine offerings.

16. I bow unto the manes who are worshipped with devotion by the Guhyakas[1] in heaven who desire an identical prosperity that is the utmost possible.

17. I bow unto the manes who are worshipped by men in the world during Śrāddhas with perfect faith and who bestow full nourishment of the desired world.

18. I bow unto the manes who are worshipped by the brahmins in the world for the acquisition of the object of desire as they are the bestowers of Prājāpatya (State of being a Progenitor).

19. I bow unto the manes who are propitiated by the dwellers in the forest who exercise full control over their diet and who have dispelled their sins by penance, in their Śrāddhas with articles produced in the forest.

20. I bow unto the manes who are propitiated by Samādhis (mystic trances) by brahmins of great self discipline, righteous activities and self-control over the senses.

21. I bow unto the manes whom the great kings propitiate during Śrāddhas with every kind of Kavyas (food oblations) as they are the bestowers of fruits of both the worlds.

1. Attendants of Kubera and guards of his treasury.

22. I bow unto the manes who are worshipped by Vaiśyas devoted to their special functions and who use flowers, incense, foodstuffs and water for the worship.

23. I bow unto the manes famous throughout the world as Sukālins and worshipped by even Śūdras with great devotion.

24. I bow unto the manes who have nectar for their diet and who are propitiated in Pātāla by the demons who have forsaken their haughtiness and pride.

25. I bow unto the manes who are worshipped in Rasātala during Śrāddhas by the Nāgas desirous of attaining cherished wishes, by means of offerings not leaving anything.

26. I bow unto the manes who are duly propitiated there itself (in Rasātala) by Sarpas (Serpents) fully equipped with riches, mantras and all food offerings.

27. I bow unto the manes directly who reside either in heaven or on the Earth or in Ether worthy of being worshipped even by Rākṣasas. Let them accept what is offered by me.

28. I bow unto the manes who retain their reality and who stay in their aerial chariots in airy unembodied forms and whom the Yogīśvaras (great yogins) worship in their unsullied minds — the manes who cause the removal of all pains.

29. I bow unto the manes in heaven the Svadhā-dieted embodied ones, who are capable of bestowing all wishes in case the devotee has any charished desire and who are competent to bestow salvation if the devotee has no special desire.

30. Let the manes be propitiated with the Tarpaṇa ceremony. The manes bestow the desired objects upon those who desire the lordship of deities, devahood or even greater things or elephants, horses, gems or great mansions.

31. Those who stay in the rays of the moon, or in the disc of the sun or in a white aerial chariot for ever shall be propitiated by this. Let those manes be nourished by the food oblations, water and fragrance.

32. May the manes be propitiated by food and water in sacred rite — the manes who are satiated when the Havis is offered in the fire, who take in food by staying in the bodies of the brahmins and who are delighted by the offerings of Piṇḍa.

33. By this sacred rite delighted may the manes be who are sought to be pleased by gods with the flesh of the Rhinoceros, the black gingelly seeds, of divine origin and pleasing appearance, and by great sages with Kāla Śāka (Black vegetable).

34. Let those Kavyas (food offerings) which delight the manes worthy of my respect, be present, in their entirety, in these flowers, fragrant water and food offerings prepared by me.

35. Let this sacred rite offer satisfaction to the different manes — who receive worship daily, who are to be worshipped at the end of every month, or on Aṣṭakās (the 7th, 8th and 9th days of the lunar fortnight), or at the end of a year or on special occasions of prosperity or victory.

36-37. Some manes white like the moon or the Kunda flower are to be worshipped by brahmins; the manes coloured like the fire and the Sun are to be worshipped by the Kṣatriyas; the manes of golden hue are to be worshipped by the Vaiśyas and the manes coloured like the indigo are to be worshipped by the Śūdras. Let these manes be delighted and satiated by my offerings of flowers, incense, water and foodstuffs as well as by Agnihoma. I bow unto those manes always.

38. Let those manes be delighted with this rite — the manes who partake of the Kavyas, auspiciously offered for their satiation after giving precedence to the deities and who when delighted create prosperity. I bow unto them.

39. Let the primordial manes of the deities worthy of worship even by Indra, be satisfied with this sacred rite and let them remove all evil spirits, bad ghosts, goblins of fierce type and miseries of the people. I bow unto them.

40. Let the different types of manes, viz. — Agniṣvāttas, Barhiṣads, Ājyapas and Somapas be propitiated by this Śrāddha. I have offered Tarpaṇa unto them.

41. Let the groups of manes Agniṣvāttas, protect the eastern side; let the manes, Barhiṣads, protect the southern side; Ājyapas — west and Somapas — the north.

42. Let the manes accord me protection from evil spirits, ghosts, geni, goblins, all round.

43-48. Let the thirty one sets of manes by whom the entire universe is pervaded be satisfied with what I have offered. The sets are as follows :—The nine sets are these :—Viśvas, Viśvabhuks, Ārādhyas, Dharmas, Dhanyas, Śubhānanas Bhūtidas, Bhūtikṛts and Bhūtis. The six sets are these :—Kalyāṇas, Kalyadas, Kartṛs, Kalyas, Kalyatarāśrayas and the sinless Kalyatāhetus. The seven sets are these :—Varas, Vareṇyas, Varadas, Tuṣṭidas, Puṣṭidas, Viśvapātṛs, and Dhātṛs. The five sets dispelling sins are :—Mahāns, Mahātmans, Mahitas, Mahimāvāns and Mahābalas. The four sets are :—Sukhadas, Dhanadas."

Mārkaṇḍeya said :

49. As he (Ruci) was repeating this prayer, a high column of brilliant light came into view suddenly spreading over the sky.

50. On seeing that column of brilliant light enveloping the world, Ruci knelt on the ground and sang this hymn.

Ruci said :

51. I offer my salutations to the manes who are worshipped, disembodied, of brilliant splendour, endowed with divine vision and engaged in meditation.

52. I offer my salutations to the manes who bestow cherished desires and who are the leaders of Indra and other gods, Dakṣa and Mārīca and of the seven sages and others.

53. I offer my salutations to the manes who are the leaders of Manu and others, the sun and the moon. He (Manu) uplifted even the manes ?

54. With palms joined together I offer my salutations to the manes of stars, planets, wind, fire, sky, heaven and Earth.

55. With joined palms I offer salutations unto Kaśyapa Prajāpati, Soma, Varuṇa and all Yogeśvaras.

56. I make obeisance to the seven gaṇas in the seven worlds. I offer salutations to Brahman the self-originated and endowed with yogic vision.

57. I offer salutations to the groups of manes called Somādhāras, Yogamūrtidharas, and the moon the father of worlds.

58. I make obeisance to the manes who have assumed the form of fire and others as well. The universe is permeated by fire and the moon and it is meet that I make my obeisance to them.

59-60. Those who are in the Cosmic fire, those who have assumed the forms of the moon, sun and fire, those who have assumed the form of the Universe and those who have assumed the form of Brahman — obeisance, obeisance, obeisance unto all those Yogins and manes. I have purified my mind. Let manes, whose diet is Svadhā, be delighted."

Mārkaṇḍeya said :

61. Thus glorified by him (Ruci) those excellent sages, the manes, came out of that brilliant column of light illuminating the quarters.

62. He saw them standing in front smeared and embellished with flowers and fragrant unguents offered by him.

63. Kneeling and then with palms joined in reverence the devout Ruci said like this with respect "Obeisance to you all, obeisance to you all."

64. The delighted manes said to the sage, "Choose your boon". Ruci with stooping shoulders said :

Ruci said :

65. "Brahmā has entrusted me with the task of initiating the creation of a new set of people. I wish for a wife satisfactory in every respect, divine in origin and capable of conceiving."

The manes said:

66. "O noble sage, presently, here itself a very comely maiden shall be your wife. You will beget of her a son too.

67. O Ruci, he will be renowned as Raucya. He will be the founder of a Manvantara named after him.

68. Many sons will be born to him who will be endowed with strength and valour. They will be noble souls reigning over the world.

69. You will become a Prajāpati and create four sorts of people. When your power wanes you will achieve the final goal, well versed in Dharma that you are.

70-71. We will be pleased with the man who will adore us with devotion with this hymn. We will bestow on him the gift of sons, enjoyments, interest in meditation, longevity, health, wealth and a flourishing family. Hence, we are to be adored with this hymn for ever by those who wish for these.

72-73. If any one recites this hymn that delights us in Śrāddhas in front of excellent Brahmins taking food we shall be present there delighted by hearing this hymn. Then, undoubtedly the Śrāddha shall be everlasting in benefits.

74-76. Even if a Śrāddha were to be Aśrotriya (not presided over by a Vedic Scholar), even if it be defective, or performed with the money acquired by illegal means, even if the materials used are unworthy of Śrāddha, if it is performed untimely, if it is performed in an unworthy place, if it is performed breaking the rules and canons, if it is performed without faith or if the persons performing it are haughty (in spite of all these defects) the Śrāddha shall be delightful to us if this hymn is recited.

77. Our satisfaction will last for twelve years if in a Śrāddha this hymn pleasing to us is recited.

78-79. This hymn will delight us for twelve years if the Śrāddha is in the season of Hemanta (early winter) and for twentyfour years—in Śiśira (late winter). It will give us satisfaction for sixteen years if the recitation is in Vasanta or Grīṣma (spring and summer).

80. O Ruci! even if the Śrāddha is incomplete our satisfaction will be endless if in the rainy season this hymn is recited.

81. If this hymn is read by men at the time of Śrāddha in the season of Śarad (autumn) it will give us delight lasting for fifteen years.

82. We will grace with our presence that house in which this hymn is written and preserved, whenever Śrāddha is performed.

83. Hence you, O fortunate one, shall recite this hymn elevating us, at the time of Śrāddha, in front of brahmins taking food there."

CHAPTER NINETY

Story of Ruci

Mārkaṇḍeya said :

1. Then from the middle of the river rose up Manoramā (a comely maiden). The celestial damsel Pramlocā was nearby.

2. Making obeisance to Ruci again and again the celestial damsel Pramlocā addressed Ruci the noble soul in sweet words.

3. The noble soul Puṣkara, son of Varuṇa, begot a beautiful girl due to my favour.

4. Accept this beautiful girl for wife. Your son will be born of her who will become a Manu of great intellect.

Mārkaṇḍeya said :

5. Ruci accepted the offer by saying "so be it" and it was as it were he lifted up a woman of good body and mind out of the river.

6. On the banks of that river the noble sage took the hand of the girl duly.

7. The son of Ruci was born of that lady. He became famous as Raucya as narrated by me before.

CHAPTER NINETYONE

Worship of Hari

Sūta said :

1. Sages Svāyambhuva Manu and others meditated on Hari. They became devoted to regular rituals, worship, good conduct, meditation, prayer and recital of names.

2. Hari who is devoid of body, sense organs, mind, intellect, vital breath, ego. (Hari) who is devoid of Ether and fiery essence.

3. Free from water and its attributes, free from Earth, devoid of all living beings.

4. The presiding deity of all living beings, the enlightened, the controller, the lord, the extensive, the sentient, presiding deity of everything, the unsullied.

5. Free from attachment, the great lord, worshipped by all deities, the brilliant, free from Sattva quality, devoid of Tamas quality.

6. Free from Rajas; aloof from three qualities, devoid of all colours, devoid of Kartṛtva (the state of being the doer) etc.

7. Free from Vāsanās (impressions and evil propensities) the pure, free from all defects devoid of thirst, free from sorrow and delusion.

8. Free from old age and death, the steady, devoid of delusions, having no birth, having no dissolution.

9. Devoid of all conduct of life, the true, the untainted, the supreme lord, free from the states of wakefulness, dream, sound slumber, devoid of names.

10. Presiding deity of the states of wakefulness, of tranquil form, lord of gods, stationed in wakefulness, the everlasting, free from causes and effects.

11-12. Observed by all, the embodied, the subtle, still subtler, endowed with the vision of knowledge, knowing through the ears, the blissful in form, free from the three cosmic forms of Viśva, Taijasa and Prājña, the fourth imperishable entity.

13. Protector of all, destroyer of all, having the form of the soul of all living beings, free from the attributes of intellect, devoid of support identical with Śiva and Hari.

14. Free from disintegration, known and realised through Vedānta (metaphysics), of the form of Vedas, the supreme living being, the auspicious beyond the sense organs.

15-16. Devoid of primary attributes of Sound, Taste, Touch, Colour essence, Colour and Smell, the beginningless, the Brahman, the end of the hole — I am the Brahman.

17. O Mahādeva, a man of controlled sense-organs shall meditate thus. He who meditates thus becomes identical with Brahman.

18. O Vṛṣadhvaja, thus I have expounded the meditation of the supreme god, what else shall I expound to you now ?

CHAPTER NINETYTWO

Meditation on Viṣṇu

Rudra said :

1. O the bearer of Śaṅkha, Cakra and Gadā, please expound again the process of meditation of Viṣṇu, a knowledge whereof makes a man happy in having fulfilled his task.

Hari said :

2. I shall expound the meditation on Hari that suppresses the machinations of Māyā. O Hara, the meditation is of two kinds, one on the embodied and the other on the unembodied.

3-4. The one on the unembodied has already been explained. I shall expound the one on the embodied. By those who seek salvation Hari has to be meditated as refulgent like a crore of suns, the victorious, uniformly resplendent, white as the Kunda flower and cow's milk, endowed with the large gentle Śaṅkha.

5. Endowed with the discus resembling a thousand suns, fierce with a series of shooting flames, the tranquil, of auspicious face, having the mace in his hand.

6. Equipped with the priceless crown brilliant with gems, having weapons, the omnipresent, the shining, holding the lotus.

7. Wearing the garland of wild flowers, the pure, of even shoulders, having golden ornaments, good garments, of pure body, having good ears, stationed in the lotus.

8. Of golden body having good necklaces, good bracelets, the armlet, equipped with the garland of wild flowers.

9. Having the mark Śrīvatsa and the gem Kaustubha, Lakṣmī's eyes fixed on him, equipped with the qualities such as Aṇimā, the originator and the destroyer.

10. Worthy of meditation of the sages, the deities and the asuras, extremely beautiful, stationed in the hearts of living beings from Brahmā to a blade of grass.

11. The eternal, the imperishable, the pure, the lord blessing all, Nārāyaṇa the great God with his earrings shaped like the Makara fish shining profusely.

12. Destroyer of all harassments, worthy of worship, the auspicious, destroyer of the wicked, the immanent soul of all, omniformed, omnipresent, destroyer of evil influence of planets.

13. Having beautiful rings, and shining nails, worthy of being approached as refuge, the pleasing, of gentle form, the great lord.

14. Having all ornaments, smeared with sweet sandal paste, accompanied by all Devas, the doer of what is pleasant to the gods.

15. Seeking the benefit of all worlds, the lord of all, conceiver of all, stationed in the sphere of the Sun, Fire, and Water.

16. Vāsudeva, the sole meditator of the universe, should be meditated upon by those who seek salvation "I am Vāsudeva", thus shall the soul be meditated upon Hari.

17-18. Those who meditate like this on Viṣṇu attain the final goal. Formerly, the sage Yājñavalkya meditated on the supreme lord of gods Viṣṇu, attained the position of the law-giver and finally the supreme region. O Śaṅkara, lord of gods, you also contemplate over Viṣṇu.

19. Those who recite this Viṣṇudhyāna attain the final goal, viz., liberation

CHAPTER NINETYTHREE

Teachings of Yājñavalkya[1]

Maheśvara said :

1. O Hari, the destroyer of Keśin, how was virtue expounded by Yājñavalkya formerly. Please explain to me as the facts are, O Mādhava.

Hari said :

2. After making obeisance to Yājñavalkya who was staying in Mithilā, the sages asked him about the various duties of different castes. With due meditation on Viṣṇu the sage of controlled senses expounded the same to them.

Yājñavalkya said :

3-6. The virtue expounded hereafter is current in that country where the black deer roam about fearlessly. The Vedas in addition to Purāṇas, Nyāya, Mīmāṁsā, Dharmaśāstra, etc. are the basic lore for all kinds of learning and virtue. They are fourteen in number. The expounders of law are :—Manu, Viṣṇu[2], Yama[3], Aṅgiras[4], Vasiṣṭha[5], Dakṣa, Saṁvarta, Śātātapa[6],

1. A famous personality in Indian Literature. He is said to be a sage present in the court of King Janaka of Mithilā. He is also mentioned in the Mahābhārata. His name is closely connected with the Śukla-Yajurveda. Some hold that the Vājasaneyi Saṁhitā of the Śukla Yajurveda is known after his surname Vājasaneya. The Yājñavalkya-Smṛti is also known after his name. This Smṛti seems to be later than Manusmṛti. but is widely acknowledged as a Code of Hindu Law. The interpretation of the Mitākṣarā commentary by Vijñāneśvara on this Smṛti, is generally accepted by Indian Law Courts.

2. Author of Viṣṇu-Dharma-Sūtra.

3. Author of Yama-smṛti.

4. Author of Aṅgirasa-smṛti or Bṛhad-aṅgirasa-smṛti.

5. Author of the Vasiṣṭha-dharma-sūtra.

6. Author of several smṛti-works, Karma-vipāka, etc.

Parāśara[1], Āpastamba[2], Uśanas[3], Vyāsa[4], Kātyāyana[5], Bṛhaspati[6], Gautama[7], Śaṅkha[8], Likhita[9], Hārīta[10], and Atri[11]. All these ever engaged in meditation of Viṣṇu have become expounders of law.

7. Whatever material or wealth is given at the proper time and place with due faith to the deserving is conducive to virtue.

8. Acting in a way pleasing to others, control of mind, non-violence, charity, self-study of the Vedas, realisation of Ātman by means of Yoga—all these are Dharmas.

9. Scholars in Vedic lore enumerate four and some say three. Whatever that may be those who are engaged in the worship of devas and have realised the soul maintain their own duties.

10. The four castes are Brahmins, Kṣatriyas, Vaiśyas and Śūdras. The first three are Dvijas (Twice born). The rites from Niṣeka (sprinkling) to the cremation ground are performed with mantras.

11. The Garbhādhāna[12] rite (conception) is after the menstruation; Puṁsavana[13] rite before the throbbing of the child in the womb; Sīmanta[14] in the sixth or eighth month. The Prasava (delivery) and Jātakarma[15] (birth) and

1. Author of Parāśara-smṛti.
2. Author of Āpastamba-dharma-sūtra.
3. Author of Auśanasa-dharmaśāstra
4. Author of Vyāsa-siddhānta.
5. Various references to him are found in Sanskrit Literature.
6. And profusely quoted as the author of a Smṛti. Mentioned by Kauṭilya.
7. Author of Gautama-dharma-sūtra.
8. Author of Śaṅkha-smṛti. Also mentioned in the Mahābhārata.
9. According to the Mahābhārata, the brother of Śaṅkha. The co-author of Śaṅkha Likhita smṛti.
10. An oft-quoted author, who flourished before 600 A.D.
11. Author of Ātreya-dharma-śāstra. Also mentioned in Manu-smṛti.
12. Authorities hold different views about its time.
13. The aim is to beget a male child.
14. Literally means parting (the child's) hair.
15. This rite is performed to ensure the child's welfare.

12-13. Nāmakaraṇa (naming) rites the eleventh day. Niṣkrama[1] (coming out of the house) in the fourth month. The Annaprāśana[2] (feeding with solid food) in the sixth month and Cūdākaraṇa[3] (ceremonial cutting of the forelock) as per practice in the family. Thus the sin of seed and conception is nullified. To girls these rites are performed without reciting the mantras) but marriage is performed by reciting the mantras.

CHAPTER NINETYFOUR

Teachings of Yājñavalkya

Yājñavalkya said :

1. The sacred thread investiture of a brahmin shall be performed in the eighth year from conception or nativity; that of a Kṣatriya in the eleventh year and that of Vaiśya in the twelfth year or according to some, as is the convention in the family.

2. After duly investing the disciple with the holy thread the preceptor shall teach him the Vedas along with the Mahāvyāhṛti. He shall duly instruct him in the rules of hygiene and good behaviour.

3. He shall pass urine and evacuate his bowels with the sacred thread turned round his right ear facing the north if it is during the day or in the Sandhyās i.e. dawn, midday and dusk or facing the south if it is during the night.

4. The brahmin or others strictly adhering to the sacred rites shall hold the penis and stand up and wash it with earth and water till the bad smell and stickiness are removed.

5-7. A twice-born shall perform the purificatory ceremony thus. He shall sit on a clean ground facing

1. In this rite , the child is taken out of the house for the first time.
2. In this rite the child is fed for the first time with solid food.
3. In this rite, for the first time the child's hair is cut, but *cūḍā* (a tuft of hair) is left on the head; hence the name *cūḍākaraṇa*.

north or east and perform Upasparśa (ceremonial touching) with the Brāhmatīrtha (pure water) between his knees. He shall touch the roots of the little finger, index finger, and the thumb and the tip of the hand respectively called Prajāpatitīrtha, Pitṛtīrtha, Brahmatīrtha and Daivatīrtha. He shall perform Ācamana thrice and Unmārjana (wiping off) twice. He shall touch mouth, etc. ritualistically. The water shall be undisturbed and free from bubbles.

8. The brahmin shall be pure if the water reaches the heart; the Kṣatriya if it reaches the throat and the Vaiśya if it reaches the palate. A woman and a Śūdra shall become pure if the water touches the inner parts once.

9. Bath, Mārjanam with the divine mantras, Prāṇāyāma, Sūryopasthāna (worship of the sun) and Gāyatrījapa shall be performed every day.

10. Gāyatrī should always be recited with its Śiras (head) and with the Vyāhṛti prefixed. Prāṇāyāma with the Praṇava is for three times (for every unit of japa).

11-12. The purity of Prāṇāyāma is in the three Ṛks that constitute the mantra and its deity. In the evening the Sāvitrī shall be recited squatting down till the rise of stars. In the morning the Gāyatrī shall be recited standing facing the east till the sun rises. Thereafter both in the morning and evening sacrificial rites in fire shall be performed.

13. Then elders shall be bowed to saying "asau aham," etc. He shall then with great concentration and faith approach the preceptor for the study of Vedas.

14. He shall recite the Vedas when called upon to do so. He shall give the preceptor whatever he has and serve him with mind, body and speech activities.

15. The sacred staff, deer skin, thread and girdle shall be worn. For sustenance let him beg alms of worthy brahmins.

16. In the morning, midday and the evening the alms shall be sought from brahmins, Kṣatriyas and Śūdras.

17. After performing the rites in fine he shell take his food with the permission of the preceptor, duly taking in water in the ritualistic way. He shall never find fault with the food served.

18. A student observing Brahmacarya shall take varieties of food if there is no risk. At the time of a Śrāddha, a brahmin can eat as he pleases but without prejudice to his Vrata.

19. He shall avoid wine and meat and steam cooked food, etc.

He is called a preceptor who makes him do all rites and teaches him Veda.

20. He is Ācārya who initiates him with the investiture of sacred thread. He who teaches a portion of Vedas is Upādhyāya. The performer of sacrifice is called Ṛtvik.

21. All these people are to be honoured duly. One's own mother is superior to all these. For each Veda, the duration of study is for five or twelve years.

22-23. Some hold that the study shall continue till full comprehension. The Keśānta (cutting off hair) is at sixteen. The time limit for the investiture with the sacred thread is sixteen years for brahmins, twentytwo for Kṣatriyas and twentyfour for Vaiśyas. If it is not performed during this period they become deprived of all virtues. The persons who become degraded by non-observance of Sāvitrī are called Vrātyas. Sacrifices are to be performed without including the Vrātyas.

24. The first three castes are called Dvijas (twice born) because after the first birth from mother they are born again with the sacred girdle girting round their body.

25. Vedas alone are indispensable for sacrifices, penances and sacred rites. They are conducive to the highest salvation.

26-27. The twice-born shall propitiate the deities with honey and milk and the manes with honey and ghee. Every day, the twiceborn shall recite the ṛk mantras, yajus, sāman and atharvāṅgiras mantras. With ghee and holy water he shall propitiate the manes and the deities.

28-29. The reciters shall not decry the Vedic passages or Purāṇas. Those who read and study the Vedas and epics every day according to capacity and propitiate the deities and manes shall be blessed with all desired objects when they are satisfied.

30. The regular study of different portions in the Vedas dealing with the diverse sacrifices shall bless him with the fruits thereof. The twice-born will reap the fruits of gifts of land and penances by study alone.

31-32. The Naiṣṭhika (life-long) Brahmacārin shall remain by the side of the preceptor or in his absence, of his son, wife or the sacrificial fire. He shall control his sense organs and lead a pure life finally attaining Brahmaloka never to be born again.

CHAPTER NINETYFIVE

Teachings of Yājñavalkya

Yājñavalkya said :

1-3. O sages, listen to the various duties of the householder. After giving fees to the preceptor and taking the ritualistic bath with his permission and concluding his student stage he shall marry a girl endowed with good characteristics. She shall be a virgin, younger in age, not sickly, having brothers not of the same ṛṣi, lineage or Gotra[1], beyond the fifth remove on the mother's side, and the seventh remove on the father's and hence asapiṇḍa (unrelated).

4. A brahmin bridegroom must belong to the reputed ninety families of great Vedic Scholars or their own relation, a scholar without defects.

5. I do not approve of a brahmin's marriage with a Śūdra girl, for virtually he is born again of her (when he begets a son).

6. A brahmin can marry a girl belonging to any of the first three castes; a kṣatriya can marry a girl belonging to two

1. Generally the Hindus trace their descent to a common male ancestor. Such a descent is called gotra. The prominent *gotras* were eight but they multiplied later on. "*Gotra* occurs several times in the Ṛgveda in the account of the mythic exploits of Indra. Roth interprets the word as 'cowstall', while Geldner thinks that 'herd' is meant. The latter sense seems to explain best the employment which the term shows in the later literature as denoting the 'family' or 'clan', and which is found in the Chāndogya Upaniṣad. In the Gṛhya Sūtras stress is laid on the prohibition of marriage within a *Gotra*, or with a *Sapiṇḍa* of the mother of the bridegroom—that is to say, roughly, with agnates and cognates." (*VINS*, p. 235-6).

castes and a vaiśya only one, a śūdra girl shall never be married by any of these.

7. There are many types of marriages among them; the Brāhma type is that in which the bridegroom is invited and a girl bedecked according to capacity is given in marriage. A son born of that girl sanctifies twentyone generations on either side.

8. The Daiva type of marriage is that in which the Ṛtvik in a sacrifice is chosen as the bridegroom. A son born of that wedlock sanctifies fourteen generations. If two cows are taken along with the bride the type of marriage is Ārṣa, the son born of that wedlock sanctifies six generations.

9. A marriage in which the advice, "both of you carry on your sacred duties together" is given, is called Sakāma (with love) marriage. A son born of that wedlock sanctifies six generations including himself.

10. In the Āsura form of marriage, money is taken; in the Gāndharva marriage, mutual love and consent is the criterion; in the Rākṣasa marriage, the bride is taken forcibly after a fight and in the Paiśāca marriage, the girl is duped and married.

11. The first four types of marriage are recommended for brahmins; the Gāndharva and the Rākṣasa type for kings; the Āsura type for vaiśyas and the despicable last type for the śūdras.

12. If a brahmin marries a brahmin girl, the hands are clasped together; if a kṣatriya girl, she catches hold of an arrow the other end of which is held by the bridegroom; the vaiśya girl holds a goad.

13. The father, the grandfather, brother, a kinsman or the mother gives away the girl in marriage; the latter in case the former is not available.

14. A father not giving a daughter in marriage, incurs the sin of Bhrūṇahatyā (murder of the foetus) at every menstrual period. If no one gives her away in marriage, the girl is at liberty to choose her own lover.

15. A girl can be given in marriage only once; a person who abducts a girl should be punished like a thief; if an unsullied girl is forsaken he should be punished. A fallen girl should be forsaken at once.

16-17. For producing a son and a heir in the family the brother-in-law or a cousin or a person of the same clan can have intercourse with an issueless widow till she conceives. If he touches her after that he becomes degraded. The son born thus is the legitimate son of the deceased husband.

18. A wife found guilty of adultery shall be compelled to wear dirty garments, shall be given only a single morsel daily, shall be rebuked and forced to lie on the bare ground.

19. The moon god has blessed women with purity; Gandharva has blessed them with sweet speech. Fire is always pure and women are always pure.

20. If a woman subjects herself to abortion, except in the case of adultery and for purposes of expiation, she becomes guilty of two great sins the murder of the foetus and the murder of her husband.

21. A wife addicted to wine, suffering from incurable diseases or inimically inclined can be forsaken. A wife of sweet speech should be maintained. Otherwise, O sages, great sin will result.

22-23. If there is no discord or dispute between the husband and wife, virtue, love and wealth flourish there. If the wife survives the husband but remains unmarried, she is praised in the world. After death she becomes delighted with goddess Umā. If a man divorces a chaste virtuous woman he shall give her a third of her ornaments back.

24-26. The highest duty of a woman is to carry out the behests of her husband. Sixteen nights subsequent to the monthly menstrual flow are the nights of rut for women. The husband shall restrain himself during the parvan (full moon-new moon days) when the stars maghā and Mūlā are ascendant and on the first four nights. Thereafter, on even nights, he can have intercourse with her. Thereby, he will be able to beget a healthy son of auspicious traits. If the woman is in a mood to receive him on any night he should satisfy her remembering that lust in women is terrible.

27-28. The husband should be loyal to his wife. Since women are to be well protected the husband, his brothers, father, mother or kinsmen should honour her with ornaments, raiments and foodstuffs. The wife should be able to maintain the household with a modicum of requisite things. She should be skilful, pleased with the minimum and reluctant to spend lavishly.

29-31. She should pay respects to her mother-in-law and father-in-law by touching their feet. A woman whose husband is away shall forsake sports, decoration of the body, attending festivities, boisterous laughter, visits to other people's house. During childhood the father shall protect the girl; during her youth the husband shall do so and during old age the son. If these are not available, kinsmen shall protect her. Whether during day or during night, a woman shall not stay outside her house without her husband.

32-33. Only the senior wife is entitled to take part in religious rites not the junior ones. If the wife had been of good conduct she should be cremated duly by the husband with Agnihotra rites. He can remarry duly for the preservation of Agnihotra. A woman who had been dutiful shall earn good name here and repair to heaven after death.

CHAPTER NINETYSIX

Teachings of Yājñavalkya

Yājñavalkya said :

1-5. I shall enumerate the mixed castes and also the duties of the householders. A brahmin father and a kṣatriya mother beget a Mūrdhābhiṣikta. Similarly

Brahmin father	+	Vaiśyā mother	>	Ambaṣṭha
,, ,,	+	Śūdrā ,,	>	Niṣāda, Parvata
Kṣatriya father	+	Vaiśyā ,,	>	Māhiṣya
,, ,,	+	Śūdrā ,,	>	Mleccha
Vaiśya father	+	Śudrā ,,	>	Karaṇa
Kṣatriya ,,	+	Brahmin ,,	>	Sūta
Vaiśya ,,	+	,, ,,	>	Vaidehaka
Śūdra ,,	+	,, ,,	>	Cāṇḍāla (Lowliest of all)

Vaiśya Father + Kṣatriyā Mother > Māgadha
Śūdra ,, + ,, ,, > Kṣattṛ
Śūdra ,, + Vaiśyā ,, > Āyogava
Māhiṣya ,, + Karaṇī ,, > Rathakāra

6-7. These mixed castes are unprivileged ones whether Anulomaja (higher caste father and lower caste mother) or Pratilomaja (higher caste mother and lower caste father). On account of the intrinsic loftiness, they will have the rights of their original caste in the seventh generation if the duty has undergone change or in the fifth generation if the duty is the same. A householder shall perform everyday the rites according to the Smṛtis in the fire first lighted on the occasion of marriage.

8-9. All rites laid down in the Vedas, except that of charitable gifts, shall also be performed in the marital fire. After answering the calls of nature and observing the requisite toilet and washing the teeth he should perform Sandhyā in the morning. After the fire sacrifice he should recite the Sūrya mantras with due faith.

10. He should understand the meaning of Vedic passages and the various Śāstras. He should go to the temple of God for the acquisition and preservation of his desired objects.

11-13. After taking bath he should perform Tarpaṇa and worship the gods and the manes. According to capacity he shall read Vedas, Purāṇas and Itihāsas. In order to achieve the full result of Japas and Yajñas (sacrifice) spiritual Vidyā shall be practised. Oblations, Svadhāhoma, study of Vedas and reception of guests should be duly observed. The great sacrifices for ghosts, manes, Brahman and human beings shall be duly performed.

14. For Cāṇḍālas and crows, cooked rice should be strewn on the ground. Cooked rice should be offered with water every day to the manes and human beings.

15-16. Vedic study shall be invariably pursued every day. Food shall not be cooked for one's own use exclusively. All children, elderly people, pregnant women, invalids, girls shall be fed duly and thereafter guests should be fed. Then the couple should partake of what is left over. With Prāṇāgnihoma (ritualistic taking in of a few grains) he should take his meal without finding fault with the food served.

17. Only after feeding the boys should he take in moderate quantities wholesome food after due digestion. The earlier part of the meal and the later one should be taken after drinking water.

18. The food should be taken in relishingly in a covered place. Charity should be given according to capacity to the guests and to people of all castes.

19. No such thought shall be entertained as "This guest is not worthy of bowing to", "This is the same as that one" with regard to guests. Even by reducing other expenses, alms should be given to mendicants and persons of good rites.

20-21. Whoever happens to come should be fed. A great bull should be consecrated and a Vedic scholar shall be fed thereby once in a year. Snātakas (those who perform ritualistic ablutions after sacrifices) preceptors, kings, friends, boys eligible for marriage, persons in anguish—all these shall be honoured and respected. All wayfarers are guests. A Śrotriya is a person who has mastered the Vedas.

22. These two (the guest and Vedic Scholar) should be honoured if a householder wishes to attain Brahmaloka. A householder shall never yearn for another man's food unless invited and unless it is what is not censurable.

23. He shall avoid the misuse of speech, hands and feet and over-eating. When the guest and the Vedic Scholar are fully satiated he shall accompany them up to the boundary of the village.

24-25. The remaining part of the day he shall spend in the company of good men, friends and relations. After performing the evening prayer, offering of ghee in the fire, etc., he should take food. Consulting the learned he should decide what is to be done for his own progress. He must get up in the Brāhma muhūrta (before sunrise). A brahmin should be honoured with money, gifts, etc.

26-27. To the aged, grief-stricken and burden-bearers he should be a support leading the way. The common duties of the twice-born, the brahmins, vaiśyas and kṣatriyas are sacrifice, study of the Vedas, charity, etc. The additional duties of a brahmin are acceptance of fees, presiding over sacrifices and teaching of the Vedas. The special duties of a kṣatriya are the administration of kingdom and the protection of the people.

28. Usury, agriculture, trading and cattle-breeding are the duties of a vaiśya. The duties of a śūdra are service to the twice-born. A twice-born shall never neglect sacrifice.

29. The common qualities of the castes for the preservation of virtue constitute non-violence, truthfulness, non-stealing, purity, control of sense-organs, control of the mind, patience, straightforwardness, liberal-mindedness, equality and activities devoid of crookedness or deceit (roguery).

30. Those who have food-grains in stock lasting for more than three years can perform the Soma sacrifice and drink the Soma juice. Those who have in stock food-grains lasting for a year shall perform the preliminary rites of Soma sacrifice.

31. Every year, he shall perform the rites of Soma Sacrifice as well as Paśupratyayana, Grahaṇeṣṭi and Cāturmāsya[1] rites carefully.

32. If these rites are not possible, the twice-born shall perform the sacrifice Vaiśvānarī. No sacrifice shall be performed with deficiency in the materials used. If the full complement of the materials are duly used, the sacrifice becomes fruitful.

33. If a sacrifice is performed utilising the money begged of a Śūdra, the sacrificer becomes a Cāṇḍāla. A person pilfering articles gathered for a sacrifice becomes a crow or a vulture.

34. A person sustaining himself by gleaning rice grains has a better spiritual life than the one with a day's supply. He in turn is better than one with three days' supply. He is still better than one with a pot, full of grain who is himself better than one with a granary under his command.

35. A brahmin never craves for wealth that would interfere with his daily study of the Vedas. He should not seek it

1. Name of the three sacrifices, viz., *Vaiśvadeva*, *Varuṇapraghāsa* and *Śākamedha*, performed in the beginning of the three seasons of four months each. (*CSL*, p. 422).

from any and every place. If he is terribly harassed by hunger he can seek money from a king, his pupil or a person of his clan. He should not earn by resorting to haughtiness, hypocrisy or cunning.

36. A householder should preferably wear a white cloth. Hair, moustache and nails shall be kept always clean. He should not take food unless supervised by his wife.

37. He should never speak unpleasant words. He should always be humble with the sacred thread on. While going round the idols in a temple he should hold the holy staff and water pot.

38. He should never pass urine in riverbeds, shady groves, ashes, cowsheds, running water, facing fire, sun, moon, cows, water, women and brahmins, or at the evening hours.

39. He should never gaze at fire, sun, a nude woman, a woman engaged in the sexual act, wine, faeces, etc. He should never sleep with his head to the west.

40. He should never spit in water nor pour blood, urine, faeces or poison in water. Feet should not be shown to fire for warming, nor should be jump across fire.

41. He should not drink water off his cupped palms nor should be waken up a sleeping person. He should not gamble with dishonest gamblers nor should he share the bed with a sick person.

42. All adverse activities should be eschewed. So also the smoke from a funeral pyre, river banks, the burning hair and husk and its ashes. He should never sit on a broken jar.

43. He should never pull a suckling cow, never enter a place except by the proper door. He should never accept bees from a miserly king decrying scriptures.

44-45. The annual Upākarma rite (Revising of Vedic study and expiatory rites) should be performed on the full moon day in the month of Śrāvaṇa, on Hasta asterism or fifth day of the bright fortnight, or on Rohiṇī asterism in the month of Pauṣa or on Aṣṭakā (7th, 8th or 9th) days. The Utsarga rite should be duly performed outside near a place where there is natural water.

46. (There are thirty seven Anadhyāya days (Holidays for Vedic Study) when any one of these—a disciple, a precep-

tor, a kinsman or a Ṛtvik dies three days are Anadhyāya, so also after the Upākarma and Utsarga rites, when a Vedic scholar of one's own branch of Veda dies.

47. At the Sandhyā hours, when thunder rumbles, when there is an earthquake, fall of a comet or a meteor, Vedic recital should be stopped and Āraṇyaka portion is read.

48. The eighth, fourteenth and fifteenth days of the lunar half month, the eclipse days, the junctions of Ṛtus (seasons) and after taking a meal or accepting fees in a Śrāddha,

49. When any animal—frog, mungoose, dog, snake, cat or pig walks between the teacher and the pupil, when the owl falls or flies up (Anadhyāya for the day).

50. When the sound of the barking dogs, howling jackals, braying asses, hooting owls, crying children or groaning sick patients is heard (Vedic Study is stopped). Where there is excreta, dead body or a Śūdra nearby or cremation ground or a fallen sinner (cessation of Vedic study).

51. In an unclean place, on the highway, when there is thunder and lightning, when the man is having the hand still wet after taking meals, in the middle of two watery places, in the middle of the night or when there is a sandstorm (Anadhyāya).

52. When the quarters burn (when the sun blazes), when dust is raised during snowfall, when the preceptor is running, when there is foul smell of something rotting, when a "very important person" visits the house,

53. When mounting a mule, camel, cart, elephant, horse, boat, tree or a hill. These are the thirty seven Anadhyāyas or cessation of Vedic Study for special reasons for the nonce.

54. What is prohibited by the Vedas should not be performed. The preceptor's or king's shadow shall not be treaded on. Another man's wife should not be transgressed. Blood, faeces, urine, spit or vomited matter, etc. should not be treaded on.

55. Brahmins Serpents, Kṣatriyas and the Ātman should never be slighted. Leavings of food partaken, excreta, etc. should be kept far even from the extremity of the foot.

56. The acts enjoined by Vedas and Smṛtis should be performed in faith. No one should be hit in vulnerable parts. No one should be censured or beaten. Only a son and a disciple can be beaten.

57. All virtues should be practised; nothing contrary to them. A householder should never have verbal disputes with his mother, father or a guest.

58. Without offering the five piṇḍas he shall not take bath in another man's pond or well. A bath is better taken in a river, fountains and natural puddles and eddies.

59. The use of another man's bed and personal belongings should be avoided. Unless there is danger to life, food offered by a miser, enemy or a man without sacred fire should be refused.

60-64. Food offered by these people should never be eaten :—a bamboo-worker, a calumniated person, a person practising usury, a person acting as priest of prostitutes and their flock, physicians to the low class people, eunuchs, professional stagers of plays, cruel, fierce, fallen Vrātyas, haughty people, persons partaking of other people's leavings after food, persons who misuse sacred texts, henpecked husbands, village priests, wicked kings, washermen, ungrateful, hangsmen, liars, backbiters, wine-merchants, bards, goldsmiths, etc. Meat should not be taken without consecration. Food mixed with hair or germs should not be taken. Food cooked more than twelve hours before, partaken by another, sniffed at by a dog, sprinkled over by a sinner, touched by a woman in her monthly-course, squeezed or kneaded by others should be avoided. Insufficient food should also be avoided [or unlimited quantity of food should also be avoided]. Similarly, food sniffed at by a cow or a bird or trampled by anyone should be avoided.

65. Among Śūdras, these persons can serve food :—Dāsas[1], Gopālas[2], Kulamitras, Ardhasīrins, Nāpita[3] and one who has dedicated himself to the task.

66. Food cooked a day before can be taken if it has

1. Perhaps a fisherman.
2. A cowherd.
3. A barber.

been seasoned with oil or ghee. No food prepared with wheat or barley should be taken after the lapse of a day unless it is fried in oil or ghee.

67. Milk of a camel, a single-hoofed animal (such as mare) and that of women should be avoided. The flesh of carnivorous animals, birds, Dātyūha (gallinule), and parrots should be avoided.

68-71. After eating Sārasas, single-hoofed animal's flesh, swans, cranes, storks, swallows, unconsecrated Kṛsaras, Saṁyāvas, Pāyasas [all puddings], Apūpas, Śaṣkulis (fried macaronis)[1] the flesh of Kurara Jālapāda, Khañjarīṭa, Cāṣa (Jay) and other birds, fish, red-footed animals, the man should atone for the sin by fasting three days.

72. By eating garlic and onion one becomes sinful and as atonement one should perform Cāndrāyaṇa. If one takes meat after worshipping deities and manes in Śrāddha one does not acquire sin.

73. If one kills animals otherwise (and eats their flesh) he will fall into hell and remain there for as many days as there are hairs on that animal. Eschewing flesh a devotee attains God Hari after due prayer.

CHAPTER NINETYSEVEN

Teachings of Yājñavalkya

Yājñavalkya said :

1. O good Sirs, I shall now expound the process of cleaning articles. Articles such as gold, silver, pearls, Śaṅkha, ropes, leather (?) seats (wooden) and vessels are cleaned with water.

2-3. The purification of sacrificial ladles is by hot water; that of grains by mere sprinkling; that of wooden and horn articles by paring and that of sacrificial vessel by scrubbing. Woollen or silken stuff is purified by a mixture of

1. A wag-tail.

fresh cow's urine and hot water. Articles received as alms become pure when the mendicant sees his wife's face. A mud pot becomes pure by keeping it over fire.

4. If food is defiled by a cow sniffing at it or by hair, flies or worms it can be purified by sprinkling holy ashes over it. The ground is purified by sweeping or scrubbing.

5. Vessels made of brass, lead and copper are cleaned by acid solution or tamarind water. Iron and bell metel vessels are cleaned by ashes and water. A vessel not known to be impure is pure.

6. If a vessel is contaminated by faeces it shall be cleaned by clay and water till the bad smell and stickiness are removed. Natural water gladly drunk by cows is pure.

7. A piece of flesh dropped down by a dog, a caṇḍāla or a carnivorous animal is naturally pure. The sun's rays, fire, the shadow of a goat or a cow, the ground—all these are naturally pure.

8-10. The foam and froth of horses and goats are pure, their dung is also pure. After bath or a drink, after sneezing, sleep, taking food, traversing a street, and changing clothes one should perform Ācamana twice. After sneezing, spitting, sleeping, shedding tears or changing clothes, if he does not perform Ācamana he should touch his right ear. Gods of Fire, etc. stay in the right ear of a brahmin.

CHAPTER NINETYEIGHT

Teachings of Yājñavalkya

Yājñavalkya said :

1-2. I shall now expound the process of making gifts. Please listen, O noble sirs of excellent rites. Brahmins are superior to others and those who regularly observe rituals are still better. The person who has realised Brahman is superior to them. Know him to be the deserving person as he is endowed with penance. Cows, plots of land, gold, etc. should be given to deserving persons after duly honouring them.

3. A gift should never be taken by a person devoid of learning and austerity. By taking it he degrades the giver as well as himself.

4. Every day, gifts should be given to deserving persons particularly on festive or special occasions; when request is made, a gift should be given with reverence and according to one's ability.

5. A milch cow with its horns cased in gold, hoofs in silver, should be given along with clothes, a bell-metal vessel and sufficient money.

6. Each horn is to be cased in a pala weight of gold; and each of the hoofs in seven pala weights of silver; the bell-metal vessel should be fifty palas in weight. The details of the calf are as mentioned before.

7. The calf may be a bull or a cow-calf. It should be given with a gold or silver vessel. The calf should be that of the cow itself and free from sickness.

8. The giver remains in heaven for as many years as there are hairs on the body of that cow. If the cow is tawny, it enables his seven generations to cross hell.

9. A cow in the act of delivery with two feet and the face of the calf protruding from the vagina is on a par with Earth.

10. A person who gives a cow free from sickness whether yielding milk or not, with or without the articles. should be honoured in heaven.

11. The massaging of the feet of a weary wayfarer, nursing a sick person, worship of god, washing the feet of brahmins, and scrubbing the place where brahmins have taken food—all these are on a par with the gift of a cow.

12. By giving a brahmin what he desires one attains heaven. By giving grounds, lamps, food, raiments and butter one attains prosperity.

13. By giving house,-grains, umbrella, necklace, trees, carts, butter, cool water, bed, and unguents, one is honoured in heaven.

14. The giver of the Vedas (in Manuscript) attains the region of Brahmā not accessible even to the gods. Those who transcribe the Vedas with meanings, yajña śāstras, Dharma Śāstras, on payment, also, attain the region of Brahmā.

15. Since God has created the universe with Vedas as the basis, collection of Vedic texts with bhāṣyas (commentories) should be done with effort.

16. He who transcribes Itihāsas[1] (Epics) or Purāṇas or makes a gift of them,

17. Attains merit equal to that of gifting Vedic text or even twice the fruit.

18. A twice-born shall never listen to materialistic discourses, false arguments, speeches in prakrit[2] or foreign[3] tongues, since these degrade him.

19. A deserving person who desists from accepting gifts attains the world of the giver of gifts. An offering of Kuśa grass, water, vegetables, milk and fragrant unguents shall never be refused.

20. For the propitiation of gods or guests or the manes whatever one gets without solicitation should be accepted even from a man of evil deeds except a prostitute, an impotent person, a fallen man or an enemy.

CHAPTER NINETYNINE

Teachings of Yājñavalkya

Yājñavalkya said :

1-2. I shall expound Śrāddha, the performance of which removes sins. The opportune time for Śrāddha is any of the following :—The New moon day, Aṣṭakā days (7th, 8th, 9th days in Pauṣa, Māgha and Phālguna) any special prosperous occasion

1. The term is especially applied to the Mahābhārata. *CDHM*, p. 128.
2. *Prākṛtas* generally meant the regional dialects.
3. The reference is perhaps to the foreign languages.

of windfall, the Pretapakṣa (dark half of Bhādrapada) the two Saṅkrānti days (when the sun transits to capricorn and cancer) when one has sufficient wealth, when deserving brahmins are available, the equinoxes, the Vyatīpāta (deviation of planets), Gajacchāyā (thirteenth day in the dark half combined with Maghā star), solar eclipse, lunar eclipse, and a desire to perform Śrāddha.

3-5. The brahmins constituting the deities of Śrāddha should be from among these. A Great Śrotriya (Vedic Scholar) young man, a good astrologer, a man of Trimadhus, a Trisavarṇika, a sister's son, Ṛtvik, son-in-law, preceptor, father-in-law, maternal uncle, a Triṇāciketa, daughter's son, a disciple, relatives, kinsmen, Brahmins scrupulously observing rituals, the Pañcāgni Brahmacārins and persons devoted to their mothers and fathers.

6-7. The following should not be entertained. A sickly person, a person deficient in limbs or having additional appendages, a one-eyed man, son of a widow after remarriage, a fallen sinner like Avakīrṇa and those who do not conform to conventions, and an a-Vaiṣṇava (non-believer in Viṣṇu). These are not worthy of being invited for Śrāddha. They (the deserving brahmins) shall be invited the day before when they shall observe celibacy.

8. On the day of Śrāddha early in the morning they should perform Ācamana and sit in their respective seats called Daiva and Pitrya. If it is not possible to provide seats, on the ground itself.

9. In the Daiva (divine) seats two brahmins shall be seated facing east. In the Pitrya seats (of the manes) three brahmins shall be seated facing north.

10. The arrangement for maternal grandfathers also is the same but the mantras will be the same as in Vaiśvadeva Śrāddha. Water should be given for washing hands and Kuśa grass for seats.

11. Āvāhana—Invocation and Anujñā (permission) with the Ṛk mantras of Viśvedevas shall be performed.

12-14. In the vessel tied with Pavitra (Kuśa grass twisted in a peculiar way) he should strew barley grains. With the mantra *Śanno Devi*, water should be sprinkled. With the mantra *Yavosi* barley grains shall be strewn. With the mantra *Yā divyā* they should be given in the hands. Similarly, scents, water, Pavitra and incense should be given. To the manes the offerings shall be made from right to left and water shall be sprinkled anticlockwise. Twice the number of Kuśa blades shall then be given. Pitṛs (manes) shall be invoked with the Ṛk *Uśantas tvā*. With the permission of the brahmins the householder should repeat the mantra *Āyantu naḥ*. The purpose of barley grains can be served with gingelly seeds. Arghya and other things shall be performed as before.

15. After giving Arghya he should duly make promise to the brahmins. With the mantra *Pitṛbhyaḥ sthānam asi* he should bend the vessel.

16-20. He should hold the cooked food soaked in butter and reciting the mantra *Agnau kariṣye* he shall obtain the permission and place it in fire. He shall then recite *Gāyatrī*[1] with Vyāhṛti and Ṛks *Madhu vātā*, etc. and say *Yathāsukham* (as convenient to you). They should take food silently. Whatever food and Haviṣya they require shall be served them without anger.

21-23. Till the brahmins are fully satiated he shall be reciting holy mantras and the previous japas. He shall ask the brahmins *Tṛptāḥ stha* (are you fully satiated?) The brahmins shall reply : *Tṛptāḥ smaḥ* we are fully satiated. The cooked rice left over should be strewn on the ground slowly. After taking cooked rice with, gingelly seeds he shall face the south and offer Piṇḍas near the place where the brahmins took their food. To maternal grandfathers also the same procedure gives Ācamana after that.

24. Then *Svasti* (hail thee) should be mentioned. Then the Akṣayya Udaka (ever fruitful water) shall be offered to the brahmins along with the fee according to capacity. After that he shall proceed for Svadhākāra.

25. When the brahmins permit by saying *Vācyatām* (let it be recited) he shall say *Pitṛbhyaḥ Svadhā* (svadhā unto the manes) when the brahmins repeat it he should sprinkle water on the ground.

1. ṚV. 1.90.6.

26-27. He shall say *Viśve devāḥ priyantām* (Let all devas be pleased) and offer water. "May those who give us flourish. Let Vedas flourish. Let not faith forsake us. Let us have much to give." Thus addressed by the brahmins he should bid them farewell with sweet words and salutation.

28. While bidding farewell he should recite *Vāje Vāje*. The Arghya pātra in which the promise had been invoked before should be placed in proper position and the brahmins should be formally dismissed.

29. After going round in Pradakṣiṇā and prayer he should partake of the leavings of Pitṛs along with his wife.

30. He shall remain celibate that night. At the ceremony of attaining prosperity the rites as well as fee are similar but with Nāndī rites in addition the Piṇḍas will be mixed with barley grains and Karkandhu[1] (cucumber) fruits.

31. The Ekoddiṣṭa form of Śrāddha performed for a single mane in view has no seat assigned for *Daiva*. Only Pavitra is used. One dish is prepared.

32. It is devoid of Āvāhana (invocation) and Agnīkaraṇa (placing the Haviṣya in fire). There also the procedure is anticlockwise. In the place of ever fruitful water *Upatiṣṭhatām* (may you approach) is used at the time of farewell. *Abhiramyatām* (may you be delighted) is also said when they reply *Abhiratāḥ smaḥ* (we are delighted).

33-34. In Sapiṇḍīkaraṇa ceremony four vessels with scents, water and gingelly seeds shall be used. For Arghya the Pitṛpātra is kept covered with Pretapātra. Two mantras beginning with *Ye samānā*, etc. shall be recited. The other items are as in the previous.

35. The Ekoddiṣṭa can be performed for the deceased women also. If Sapiṇḍīkaraṇa is performed, a year after death,

36. Cooked rice with water pot (sodakumbha) should be offered at the end of the year. The Piṇḍas can be given to cows, goats or brahmins or deposited in fire or water.

37-38. In that annual Srāddha in the first month let him offer Haviṣyānna (rice cooked with vegetables and soaked

1. Zizyphus nummularia.

in ghee), in the second month milk pudding and in the succeeding month he should offer fish, or the flesh of deer, goats, bird, Ram, Pṛṣata, Eṇa, Ruru, boar or rabbit. The grandfathers shall be satisfied with this offer with increasing relish every month.

39-42. In the rainy month on the thirteenth day when there is Maghā star also, if any one dies being wounded by an arrow Śrāddha is performed from the first to the fourteenth day. He will obtain daughters, gold, children, valour, fields, strength prosperity, excellent sons, health, fame, freedom from sorrow, salvation, wealth, learning, fluency of speech, metallic wealth, cattle horses, if he duly performs the Śrāddha.

43-45. Similarly, when the manes of a brāhmaṇa or a twice born are gratified under the stars Kṛttikā to Bharaṇī they give to him long life, progeny, wealth, learning, heaven or salvation or kingdom on earth.

CHAPTER ONE HUNDRED

Teachings of Yājñavalkya

Yājñavalkya said :

1-3. Please listen and understand the symptoms of a person harassed by Vināyaka (Lord of impediments and obstacles]. The Victim suffers from hallucinations and dreams as if he or she plunges into deep waters and sees headless trunks and shaven heads. All enterprises being impeded and fruitless he becomes morose and exhausted without any apparent reason. The king is not restored to his kingdom, the virgin does not get a husband, and the pregnant woman does not get a son. The atonement and remedy is thus :— On an auspicious day he should be bathed duly. White mustard seeds and sandal paste should be ground together and kneaded with ghee. All medicinal herbs and fragrant essences should be mixed and the admixture smeared over the patient's head.

4-5. The patient is seated on an auspicious soft leather cushion red in colour. Brahmins are requested to recite Svastivācana mantras. Four pitchers of the same shape and colour are filled with water from the same pool. Clay, Rocanā (yellow pigment), sandal paste, and Guggulu (gum resin) are respectively put into them.

6-9. The brahmins then recite thus :—"The thousand-eyed, hundred-currented flow which the sages drank deep is being poured over you. May the Pāvamānī (purificatory) hymns sanctify you. Let God Varuṇa the king Soma (moon) the sun, the planet Jupiter, the god Indra, the wind god and the seven sages resuscitate your lost splendour. Let ill luck sticking to your locks of hair, the line of parting hair, the head, the forehead, the ears, and the eyes be dispelled for ever."

10. After the ablution, Kuśa grass soaked in ghee shall be held round his head, and mustard oil be poured into his ears and over his forehead drop by drop.

11. With fire ignited in the public road invoked by Svāhā mantras, the evil spirits of Kūṣmāṇḍa[1] and Rājaputra shall be measured and bound.

12-14. In the Catuṣpatha (where four roads meet) Kuśa grass shall be spread on the ground. Various kinds of cooked and uncooked food, flowers of various colours, sweet scents, wine of three kinds, curd, milk pudding, cooked food, ghee, jaggery sweets shall be placed on the ground. The preceptor then prays to the goddess Ambikā and offers the food offering with joined palms.

15. With Dūrvā grass and mustard seeds he shall perform "Svastyayana" (Bon-voyage) rites and pray to Ambikā for the birth of sons.

16. "Give me beauty. Give me fame, O Goddess, give me good luck. Give me sons, give me wealth. Give me all desired objects."

17. He shall delight the brahmins with white cloth and unguents. The preceptor shall be given a pair of cloths. The planets are then to be worshipped.

1. Gucurbita pepo.

CHAPTER ONE HUNDRED AND ONE

Teachings of Yājñavalkya

Yājñavalkya said :

1. A person desirous of wealth and splendour, or a person wishing for peace and tranquillity or a person affected by the malignant aspect of the planets shall perform the Planetary Sacrifice (Grahayāga). These are the planets as enumerated by learned men.

2. The Sun, Moon, Mars, Mercury, Jupiter, Venus, Saturn, Rāhu and Ketu.

3. The malignant aspect is countermanded respectively by wearing copper, bellmetal, crystal, the red sandal wood, gold, silver, iron, lead and bell metal on their bodies.

4. O sages, know their respective colours to be red, white, red, yellow, yellow, white black, black and black.

5. By the articles favourite to the planets the affected persons shall be asked to perform Homa after due ablution. Gold pieces should be given as gifts together with the clothes and flowers.

6. Libations with sweet smelling substances, incense and gum resin shall be offered with their respective mantras for the principal as well as subordinate deities.

7-8. The Homa shall be performed reciting these Ṛks in order.

Mantra	Planet
Ā kṛṣṇena[1]	Sun
Imaṁ devā[2]	Moon
Agnir mūrdhā[3]	Mars
Udbuddhyasva[4]	Mercury
Bṛhaspate paridīye[5]	Jupiter

1. ṚV. I.35.2.
2. VSK 11.3.2.
3. ṚV. 8.44.16.
4. VS. 15.54.
5. ṚV. 10.103.4.

Annāt parisruto rasam[1]	Venus
Śanno devī[2]	Saturn
Kayā naścitrā[3]	Rāhu
Ketuṁ kṛṇvan[4]	Ketu

9. Sacrificial twigs shall be soaked in honey, ghee and curd and offered in the fire. The twigs for the different planets shall be of the following trees as in the previous order :—Arka, Palāśa, Khadira Apāmārga[5], Pippala, Udumbara, Śamī[6], Dūrvā[7] and Kuśa grass.

10-12. Naivedya and Dakṣiṇā to be offered as below.

	Planet	*Naivedya*	*Dakṣiṇā*
1.	Sun	treacle rice	cow
2.	Moon	milk pudding	Śaṅkha
3.	Mars	Haviṣya	bull
4.	Mercury	ṣaṣṭika-rice in milk	gold
5.	Jupiter	rice with curd	cloth
6.	Venus	havis	horse
7.	Saturn	pies	black cow
8.	Rāhu	meat	iron
9.	Ketu	mixed Pulao	goat

Planets are to be worshipped by all. Even the kings reap the fruits of their worship.

1. VS. 19.75.
2. 10.9.4.
3. ṚV. 4.31.1.
4. *Ibid.* 1.6.3.
5. Achyranthes aspera.
6. Prospis apicigera.
7. Cynodon dactylon.

CHAPTER ONE HUNDRED AND TWO

Teachings of Yājñavalkya

Yājñavalkya said :

1. O sages, I shall expound the Vānaprastha (Retired life in Hermitage). The person who wishes to take to it shall go to the forest either alone or with his wife. If he goes alone he leaves his wife to the care of his son.

2. A Vānaprastha observes celibacy, fosters the sacred fire, exercises control over mind and sense-organs, is patient, honours brahmins who keep sacred fire as also the manes, deities and guests.

3. He shall gratify even the servants. He shall grow long hair, beard and moustaches. He shall be perfectly self-controlled. He shall take three baths a day. He should not accept money charities.

4. He shall continue Vedic studies. He shall regularly meditate. He shall be engaged in what is beneficent to all living beings. He shall attend to his personal needs once or twice a month.

5-6. He shall lie on the bare ground. He shall do everything without worrying over the results. In summer he shall stand in the midst of five fires and in the rainy season he shall lie on the bare ground. In the winter he shall wear wet clothes. During the day he shall perform Yogic Exercises. He shall not be angry with anyone. He shall be contented with himself.

CHAPTER ONE HUNDRED AND THREE

Teachings of Yājñavalkya

Yājñavalkya said :

1-2. I shall mention the duties of mendicants. O Noble Sirs, know them. After returning from the forest he shall first perform the sacrifice Sarva-Veda-Pradakṣiṇā and then the Prājāpatya Vrata. At the end of the rites he shall assimilate the fiery splendour in himself. He shall wish good for all living beings and be tranquil. Bearing three staffs and holding the water pot he shall resort to the village seeking alms and discard all physical labour for remuneration.

3. Without erring he shall continue seeking alms. He should not be seen in the evening along with other mendicants roaming about in the village, or he may do simple journeys without being ever ambitious.

4. He should become a Paramahaṁsa (great saint) with a single staff and self control. When he finally achieves the yogic accomplishment and sheds the mortal body he will attain immortality.

5. By a regular practice of yogic exercises and taking food in small quantities he will have the great achievement. A donor, a person fond of guests, a householder who performs Śrāddha and knower (Jñānin) becomes liberated.

CHAPTER ONE HUNDRED AND FOUR

Teachings of Yājñavalkya

Yājñavalkya said :

1. A person who murders a Brahmin first falls into hell. When his sin has all but vanished he is born as a dog, a mule, a camel, etc., and finally when he is born as a man he is bound to become dumb.

2. The person who steals gold becomes a germ and a worm and a blade of grass. The person who sleeps with his preceptor's wife becomes a tuberculosis patient or one with black teeth and swollen nails or a leper. These bad results shall befall the children of the murderer.

3. The person who steals food grain becomes one who cannot eat at all. A person who steals the musical notes and instruments becomes a dumb man. A person who steals money has a surplus appendage of limbs. A back-biter becomes one whose nostrils begin to rot and putrefy.

4. A person who steals oil becomes one who drinks the same.

5-6. One who purchases a girl, becomes a demon in the forest; who steals a gem, becomes a base-born; who steals vegetables, becomes a peacock; thief of pearl-necklace becomes a strew; of grains, a rat; of fruit, a monkey; of animals, a goat; of water, a crow; of meat, an eagle; of cloth, a leper; and of salt, a ragged one.

7-9. A malicious person becomes one whose mouth is putrid or he is born devoid of good traits, poor, or base man. Persons with good conduct are born wealthy and endowed with food grains.

CHAPTER ONE HUNDRED AND FIVE

Teachings of Yājñavalkya

Yājñavalkya said :

1. A person is degraded when he fails to do what he is enjoined to do and does what is forbidden and also by not curbing his sense organs.

2. Hence expiatory acts have to be performed with great care for purification. Thereby his conscience becomes clear and the world he attains becomes pure.

3-6. The whole world becomes happy if he performs atonement whereby his sins are dispelled. Those who never do atonement and repent fall into hell, according to the gravity of sins. The names of different hells are :—Tāmisra, Lohaśaṅku (Iron bolted), Pūtigandha Samākula (agitated by putrefying smell), Haṁsābha, Lohitoda, Sañjīvana, Nadīpatha, Mahānilaya, Kākolam, Andhatāmisra, Avīcī and Kumbha Pāka, a murderer of brahmins, a wine-drinker, a stealer of gold, a defiler of preceptor's bed and a person who associates with any of these—these and similar sinners fall into hell.

7-8. Decrying Vedas and despising preceptors are equivalent to the sin of murdering a brahmin in gravity. Taking food prohibited, low and base acts, and drinking the honey off the lips of a maiden in her monthly course are all akin to drinking of wine. Stealing of a horse is on a par with stealing of gold.

9. Coitus with a friend's wife, a virgin, a woman of a low caste, a woman of the same clan or one who gave birth to oneself-all these are sins akin to defiling of preceptor's wife.

10-12. Illegitimate intimacy with father's sister, mother's sister, aunt, one's own sister, mother's co-wife, her sister, preceptor's daughter and wife and one's own daughter—all these, are on a par with defiling preceptor's bed. The guilty man's penis should be cut off and he should be killed. The woman too shall be killed if she had been a willing partner in the illegal intercourse.

13-20. There are many Upapātakas (minor sins and turpitudes). They are :—slaughtering of a cow, stealing a brahmin's personal effects, non payment of debts, not maintaining sacred fires, trading, the younger brother's marrying when the elder brother is still a bachelor, learning from a servant, teaching a boss, adultery, abetment of Parivedana, Usury, sale of salt, killing of a good Śūdra, Vaiśya or Kṣatriya, infamous livelihood, misappropriation of a deposit, breaking of a vow, sale of meet, sale of a cow, abandonment of father, mother or a friend, sale of tanks and parks, selling of daughter's ornaments, giving the post of the presiding priest in a sacrifice to a man guilty of Parivedana, giving one's daughter to such a man, crookedness, causing break in the vow of others, selfish ventures, cohabitation with a wine-drinking woman, forsaking of one's study of Vedas, sacred fires, son, and kinsmen, perusal of illegal and unholy literature, selling of oneself or one's own wife, all these are Upapātakas. Now know the process of atonement. A brahmin-slayer shall hold a broken skull over his head, loudly proclaim his guilt, beg for alms for sustenance and roam about for twelve years taking only very little food. He will thus be purified. Or in the alternative he shall perform some sacrifice or Graha Homa with the respective mantras—"Somebhyaḥ Svāhā," "Lobhavān," etc. Thus also a sin of slaying a brahmin can be atoned for.

21-22. If a brahmin or a cow was killed for the sake of a brahmin, without much cruelty, the murderer shall read Vedasaṁhitā three times residing in a forest in a holy atmosphere. Or he shall pray to Goddess Sarasvatī and deposit a pot of coins in the river Sarasvatī. If one kills a Kṣatriya or a Vaiśya in the act of performing a sacrifice, he too shall perform the expiatory rites of a brahmin-slayer.

23-25. The man guilty of abortion shall perform the Vrata "Trayīniṣūdana" according to the caste of the child killed. If a brahmin engaged in Savana is the victim of an attempted murder the would-be slayer should perform the Vrata twice. The expiatory rite for drinking wine is the drinking of red hot wine, ghee water and cow's urine. If the man does not die by drinking the hot liquid he shall perform the expiatory rite of a brahmin-slayer wearing barks of trees and matted hair, he now becomes pure. But he must have all brahminical rites all over again.

26. A brahmin woman drinking wine should similarly perform expiatory rite by drinking semen, faeces and cow's urine. Otherwise, she becomes fallen from husband's world (Patiloka) and is born as a vulture, pig or bitch.

27. A brahmin stealing gold should hand over a pestle to the king proclaiming his guilt. If the king strikes him with it the brahmin becomes pure. Or he should give the king enough gold equal in weight to himself. He thus becomes pure.

28-29. If a man rapes a woman sleeping in her own bed, his penis and scrotum should be cut off and thrown in the south west quarter.

30. The wicked defiler of the preceptor's bed should perform the Prājāpatya[1] Kṛcchra Vrata[2] or the Cāndrāyaṇa Vrata or should read Veda Saṁhitā for three months.

31. A slayer of cow shall remain celibate for a month, lie down in the cowshed for the night and during the day he

1. An expiation of four periods of three days.
2. Bodily mortification.

should serve the cow following it like a shadow and finally make a gift of it. He shall be pure.

32. Expiation for all Upapātakas is by Cāndrāyaṇa Vrata. Or he should live on milk alone for a month or perform Parāka (Twelve days' fast) rite.

33. The killer of a Kṣatriya should make a gift of one bull or a thousand cows. Or he should perform the expiatory rite of a brahmin-slayer for three years.

34. The slayer of a Vaiśya should perform it for a year or make a gift of a hundred cows. A slayer of a Śūdra should perform the rite for six months or make a gift of ten cows. A slayer of an undefiled woman shall perform the expiatory rite of a slayer of a Śūdra.

35. A slayer of a cat, mungoose, alligator, a frog or any other animal shall drink only milk for three days and perform Kṛcchra Vrata.

36. A slayer of an elephant should atone for it by making a gift of five blue bulls and a calf white in colour and two years old. If a mule goat or sheep is killed a bull should be given. If a Krauñca bird is killed a three year old bull should be given.

37-38. For felling and cutting down trees, hedges and creepers the expiation is the recital of a hundred Ṛks. A Brahmacārin embracing a woman will become the breaker of vows. If he touches an ass he should recite a Nairṛta mantra. For the sin of taking wine and meat the rites of Kṛcchra Śesa shall be performed.

39. If the disciple dies running an errand the preceptor should perform the Kṛcchra rite. If the disciple acts, contrary to the interests of the preceptor, he should propitiate him and crave forgiveness. He will be free from sin.

40. If the enemy is wounded he shall be taken care of by giving food and affectionate treatment. If a brahmin dies when being treated there is no sin.

41. After committing a major sin or a minor turpitude if a person utters falsehood he should expiate by remaining in exile for a month without begging anyone and exercising self-control.

42. Without the formal sanction of the elders, if a younger brother indulges in sexual intercourse with the wife of the elder brother he shall perform Cāndrāyaṇa. To expiate for the sin of cohabiting with a woman in her menses he should drink ghee at the end of three days' fast.

43. To expiate for the sin of accepting a gift from an undeserving person, he should stay in a cowshed for a month drinking milk, leading a celibate life and chanting Gāyatrī mantra. He should be free from the sin.

44. For the sin of not sheltering a person seeking refuge the atonement is reading the Vedas upto capacity. If a Vrātya is employed in sacrifice both shall expiate by performing the Kṛcchra rite thrice.

45. If a man is forced to travel in a mule cart or a camel cart he should do Prāṇāyāma thrice. If a man indulges in sexual intercourse with his wife during the day, he shall bathe naked to atone for the sin.

46. O sages, the sin resulting from being rude or using abusive language to the preceptor or by defeating a brahmin in an argument shall be wiped off by craving his indulgence and observing fast for a day.

47. For the sin of brandishing a staff at a brahmin the expiation is Kṛcchra; for the sin of beating, the atonement is Atikṛcchra. Whenever atonement is mentioned the facts of time, place, age, strength and the gravity of the sin should be taken into consideration before deciding the way of expiation.

48. Wilful abortion and hatred of the husband are great sins in women without any expiation. Hence, she shall be shunned from a distance.

49. If the guilt has become public the expiation shall be done as prescribed by the preceptor, in public view. If it is not publicised the Vrata shall be performed secretly.

50. A slayer of a brahmin shall give a milch cow after fasting for three days.

51-52. And he shall repeat Aghamarṣaṇa mantra standing in water. He shall stand in water for a day, only breathing (i.e. without taking food) and performing homa with the mantra "Somebhyaḥ Svāhā" for forty times using ghee. A drinker of wine or a stealer of gold shall remain standing in water reciting

"Rudra" mantras and shall afterwards perform homa with ghee with the "Kūṣmāṇḍa" mantra and observe fast for three days.

53. A defiler of preceptor's bed shall be expiated by reciting *Sahasraśīrṣā*[1] mantra.

54. To expiate for any sin committed, one shall perform Prāṇāyāma a hundred times.

55. By unwittingly swallowing faeces, semen and wine a brahmin incurs impurity, which shall be wiped off by fasting for the day and drinking water in the evening with Oṅkāra.

56. O Brahmins, the destruction of all sins inadvertently committed is possible when Sandhyā prayers are offered thrice in the day. All sins should be dispelled if Rudra mantra is recited eleven times.

57. No sin defiles a brahmin regularly studying Vedas and performing the five sacrifices. Excepting the sin of slaying a brahmin all sins are removed by reciting Gāyatrī, a thousand times.

58. The Yamas (restraints) are :—Celibacy, mercy, patience, meditation, truthfulness, contentment, nonviolence, non stealing, sweetness, and mental control.

59. The Niyamas (Suppressions) are bathing, silence, fasting, sacrifices Vedic study, control of sense organs, austerity, non-furiousness, devotion to the preceptor, and physical purity.

60. O Brahmins, the Pañcagavya consists of cow's milk, ghee, curd, urine and dung. The expiator should swallow these and fast for the next day. This is called Sāntapana Kṛcchra.

61. Six days' fast after taking in one of the articles constituting the Sāntapana and Kṛcchra for the seventh day. This is called Mahāsāntapana.

62. The leaves of Udumbara, Rājīva (lotus) Bilva and water from Kuśa Grass—each of these is taken once every day. This is Parṇakṛcchra.

63. Boiled milk, water, curd—either of these is taken every day and fasting for the night. This is the holy Taptakṛcchra.

1. ṚV. 10.90.1.

64. One unsolicited morsel one night, and fast for the next—This is called Pādakṛcchra.

65. Any of the above practised three times is called Prājāpatya. If one takes only a palmcupful of water along with the previous, it is called Atikṛcchra.

66. Kṛcchra and Atikṛcchra alternatively for twenty one days and fast for twelve days—This is called Parāka.

67. One morsel of Piṇyāka (oil cake), whey, and powdered barley is taken one day and fasting for the next—This is called Kṛcchrasāma.

68. The rite for fifteen days when each one of the Kṛcchras mentioned above is practised for three days, is called Tulāpuruṣa.

69. In the bright half of the lunar month on the first day, a morsel of food of the size of a peacock's egg is taken; on the second day two morsels are taken. Thus the number is increased upto fifteen. In the dark half the number is gradually reduced. This is called Cāndrāyaṇa.

70. Another type of Cāndrāyaṇa is taking in two hundred and forty morsels of food in the course of a month without any stipulation on the number for any day.

71. This Piṇḍa Cāndrāyaṇa is to be performed after Triṣavaṇasnāna (plunging into water for three times). Gāyatrī mantra shall be repeated over the piṇḍas.

72-73. In sins known or unknown there is purification by Cāndrāyaṇa. Those who practise this only for the sake of virtue attain to Candraloka. Those who practise Kṛcchra similarly attain great prosperity.

CHAPTER ONE HUNDRED AND SIX

Teachings of Yājñavalkya

Yājñavalkya said :

1. O noble Sirs, maintaining Vratas, I shall now describe the Pretāśauca, i.e. the obsequies and the impurity subsequent to the death of persons. If a child who has not completed its two

years dies, the corpse is simply buried (not cremated). No Udaka rites (offering of water, etc.) in that case.

2. The corpse shall be borne upto the cremation ground by kinsmen reciting Yamasūkta. For ordinary men ordinary fire may be used. If the dead man is an Āhitāgni (person regularly maintaining sacred fires) the same shall be used for cremation.

3. Kinsmen upto the seventh or tenth degree shall perform Udakakriyā facing the south and reciting the mantra *apa naḥ śośucadagham*[1], etc.

4. The Udakakriyā for maternal grandfather, preceptor and one's own wife is also the same. In the case of sons, friends, sister's sons, father-in-law (all being brahmins) the water is sprinkled once proclaiming the name of the dead man and his Gotra but otherwise remaining silent.

5. No water-offering is made to the heretics, sinful persons, Vrātyas (persons not duly invested with sacred thread, etc. Brahmacārins, and wives without fidelity.

6. Those addicted to drinking of wine and those who had committed suicide need not be honoured with the water offering or observation of Āśauca. A dead man shall not be bewailed after the water-offering. Indeed, the existence of all living beings in the world is never permanent.

7-8. All rites are to be performed upto the utmost extent of one's ability. Thereafter, they shall proceed homeward. At the door of the stallion, torn leaves of the Nimba[2] tree (Margosa) shall be strewn. They shall step slowly on a rock first and perform Ācamana and touch fire, water, cowdung and white mustard seeds before entering the house formally.

9. Those who have touched the corpse must purify themselves by these rites and the final formal entry into the house. Those who had merely witnessed the rites do not require any formal purificatory rites. They are pure at the close of the rites. Others become pure after bath. They should remain celibate for the next three days.

10. There should be no cooking of food in the house. They shall take food bought or received from others. They

1. ṚV. 1.97.1.
2. Azadirachta indica.

shall sleep on the ground away from one another. To the departed soul a rice-ball (piṇḍa) is given for three days.

11. Milk and water should be kept in a mud pot out in the open. Sacrificial rites enjoined by the Vedas should also be performed.

12. If a child dies before cutting its first tooth there is no impurity; if a child dies before the tonsure (cutting of the forelocks) rite is performed, the impurity is for a night only; if a child dies before the sacred thread investiture, the impurity is for three days; thereafter the impurity lasts for ten days.

13. In brief, the impurity due to death lasts for three or ten days. If two children die not two years old, the impurity is for the mother alone. If two impurities due to birth and death overlap, at the close of the latter, everyone becomes pure.

14. The impurity due to death has to be observed by the four castes for ten days, twelve days, fifteen days and thirty days respectively.

15-16. If a girl dies before being given in marriage or a son, a preceptor, a disciple, person continuing Vedic studies, an uncle, a Vedic Scholar, a son not one's own but of the wife who has had intercourse with others, or if an unpopular king dies, the impurity is for a day only.

17. There is no impurity at all on the death due to king's orders, attack of a cow or a brahmin or due to suicide in secret, or due to poison.

18-20. On the death of a sacrificer, a person performing Vratas, Brahmacārins, donors and those who have realised Brahman there is no impurity. In the case of those who die at the time of charity, marriage, sacrifice, battle, civic commotion or any other calamity there is no impurity at all. Lapse of time, rites in fire, lump of clay, wind, mind, knowledge austerities, recital of prayers, repentence, fasting—all these are agents for purification. Charity purifies a person committing an unworthy act and the current itself purifies the river.

21-23. In cases of emergency a brahmin shall pursue a kṣatriya's duties (taking part in wars) or a vaiśya's activities. But these articles he shall not sell :—Fruits, soma, silk, medicinal creepers, curd, milk, ghee, water, gingelly seeds, cooked rice, mercury, acids and alkalis, honey, lac, requisites of homas, cloth, stone, utensils flowers, vegetables, clay, leather shoes, deer-skin, silk, salt, meat, oil cakes, roots and perfumes. If it is for the purpose of religious observances, some of the articles mentioned above can be sold along with gingelly seeds and grains.

24. Even in dire necessity a brahmin should not sell salt, etc. He should rather pursue cultivation. Horses should never be sold.

25. A brahmin oppressed by great poverty shall fast for three days (and approach the king for help). The king on seeing the brahmin devoid of a means of support shall provide him with one.

CHAPTER ONE HUNDRED AND SEVEN

Teachings of Parāśara

Sūta said :

1. Parāśara[1] narrated to Vyāsa the various duties of the different castes and stages in life. At the end of every Kalpa there is dissolution and a new creation. But the unborn god does not perish.

2. Śrutis (Vedas), Smṛtis and the conduct of the good not repugnant to the Vedas (are to be followed by all). At first Brahmā remembered the Vedas (and taught Manu and others). Manu and others propagated Dharma through their Smṛtis.

3. In the Kali age charity is the main virtue. Other virtues are likely to forsake the doer. Sinful deeds are perpetrated only in the Kali age. A curse uttered bears fruit in a year.

1. Parāśara is known as the author of some hymns in the Ṛgveda. He is also said to have taught Viṣṇu Purāṇa. According to the statement of the Mahābhārata, he is known as the father of Kṛṣṇa Dvaipāyana Vyāsa. His writings on Dharma are often quoted in Hindu law-texts.

4. By strictly adhering to the performance of six rites every day man obtains everything. They are—taking bath, sandhyā prayers, recital of mantras, homas, worship of gods and hospitality to guests.

5. Brahmins observing all rites properly will be rare then (in the Kali age); sages will be rare. A kṣatriya shall conquer the enemie's army and protect the earth. Business transactions and agriculture shall be the duties of vaiśyas and devotion to the twice-born that of the Śūdras.

6. By eating forbidden food, by stealing, and by approaching unworthy women a man becomes degraded. A twice-born engaged in cultivation shall not employ tired bullocks in ploughing,

7. Upto midday one shall be engaged in religious rites such as bathing, yogic rites and then feed brahmins. The five sacrifices shall be performed. The cruel shall be treated with contempt.

8. A brahmin shall not sell gingelly seeds and clarified butter. He shall become sinful if sūnāyajña is performed. A man engaged in agriculture shall not be sullied if he gives a sixth of the produce to the king, one-twentieth to the gods and one-thirtythird to the brahmins.

9. A kṣatriya, a vaiśya and a śūdra engaged in agriculture shall be considered a thief if he does not give the tax mentioned before. A pure brahmin shall be cleansed of the impurity of death in three days.

10. A kṣatriya becomes pure in ten days, a vaiśya in twelve days and a śūdra in a month. If proper rites are not maintained a brahmin shall become pure in ten days and a kṣatriya in twelve days.

11. A vaiśya shall be pure in fifteen days and a śūdra in a month. Some kinsmen living separately have a single rice-ball in common.

12. In the event of birth and death such kinsmen shall observe inpurity. If the kinsmen are removed to the fourth degree the impurity lasts for ten days; if they are of the fifth remove the impurity is for six days.

13. If they are removed to the sixth degree the impurity is for four days; if they are of the seventh remove the impurity

is for three days. If a person dies in a foreign land or if an ascetic dies, there is no impurity.

14-15. No cremation, no offering of rice-ball and no offering of water for children dying before cutting teeth or still born. In regard to still-birth and abortion the impurity is for as many days as the number of months of pregnancy.

16. If the child dies before the naming ceremony, there is no impurity; if it dies before the rite of first cutting of the forelock, the impurity is for one day and night; if he dies before the holy rite of investiture with the sacred thread, the impurity is for three days, beyond that the impurity is for ten days only.

17. Abortion usually occurs within four months and miscarriage and still births in the fifth and sixth months. No impurity in case these are observed strictly—celibacy rites in fire and abstention from evil association.

18. Artisans, craftsmen, physicians, servants, a Vedic scholar maintaining holy fire, the king—all these are of immediate purity (i.e. no impurity is observed on their death).

19. After the birth of a child the mother becomes pure after ten days and the father by taking bath. The impurity due to birth is removed by touching water.

20. In the rites of marriage, festivals and sacrifices, interrupted by the impurity of death or birth, all further rites shall be given up except what had been already undertaken.

21. If a child dies within the period of impurity, both the impurities cease with the former. If anyone dies in a cowshed the impurity is only for a day.

22. By carrying the corpse of an unknown person the impurity incurred is very little and that very little is removed by Prāṇāyāma. If the dead man is a Śūdra, the impurity is for three nights.

23. No purificatory rite is necessary in case the death is due to self-immolation, poison, hanging or insect bite. The man who touches a person killed by a cow or bitten by an insect becomes pure by means of kṛcchravrata.

24. If a person forsakes an undefiled undegraded wife in the prime of her youth he shall be born as a woman in seven successive births and suffer widowhood over and over again.

25. If a man does not cohabit with his wife after the fourth day from menstruation he shall incur the sin of infanticide. A woman not allowing her husband to have intercourse during those days shall be born as a sow. Unworthy women though they perform Vratas have no right for a rice-ball or water-offerings.

26. The son legitimately born or after Niyoga[1] in one's wife through another, shall offer a rice-ball to the legal father. A person committing the minor sin of Parivedana[2] shall perform Kṛcchra and the girl who marries him too shall perform Kṛcchra.

27. The man who gives his daughter in a Parivedana marriage and the priest who officiates in the same shall perform Atikṛcchra and Cāndrāyaṇa respectively. If the elder brother is dwarfish, hunch-backed, stammerer, idiotic, blind, deaf or dumb, Parivedana is no offence at all.

28. If the husband is untraceable, dead, or has renounced the world or is impotent or degraded—in these cases of emergency a woman can remarry.

29. A wife who dies in the company of her husband shall remain in heaven as many years as there are hairs on his person.

30. If a person is bit by a dog he shall become pure by reciting Gāyatrī mantra. A brahmin killed by a cāṇḍāla or others shall be cremated with ordinary fire. If he has maintained sacrificial fires his corpse shall be bathed in milk and cremated with those sacred fires with mantras.

31-35. If a man dies in a foreign land the obsequies are done as follows :—On a deer skin six hundred Palāśa twigs are spread making the contours of a human body. A Śamī twig is placed in the spot where penis should be, the Araṇi wood is placed in the spot of scrotum; a pot is placed at the right hand and a sacrificial pitcher at the left; mortar at the sides, a threshing rod at the back, the sacrificial slab at the thighs, rice

1. This term is used to denote the legally permitted intercourse of a married woman to obtain a son with a male other than her husband, generally her brother-in-law i.e. her husband's younger brother.

2. The act of one's marrying before one's elder brother. *CSL*, p. 445.

grains, ghee and gingelly seeds in the mouth, the vessel of holy water at the ears and the vessel for ghee at the eyes; small bits of gold shall be dropped into the ears, eyes, mouth and nostrils. An effigy of the man made of kuśa grass is placed over this and burnt. The Āhuti is offered with the mantra *Asau svargāya lokāya svāhā* slowly once. Since all the requisites of an Agnihotra are used he will surely attain Brahmaloka.

36. A person who kills Swans, Sārasas, Krauñcas, Cakravākas, hens, peacocks and sheep becomes pure in a day and night.

37. The killer of any bird becomes pure in a day and night. After killing quadrupeds one shall observe fast for a day and night and perform Japa.

38. After killing a śūdra, the rite of Kṛcchra shall be performed; if a vaiśya is killed atikṛcchra shall be performed. If a kṣatriya is killed Cāndrāyaṇa shall be performed twenty times and if a brahmin is killed it is performed thirty times.

CHAPTER ONE HUNDRED AND EIGHT

Bṛhaspati-nīti-Sāra

Sūta said :

1. Now I shall explain the essence of Polity based on Economics for the benefit of kings and others. It is holy and conducive to longevity, heavenly bliss, etc.

2. A person wishing for success and achievement should always associate with good men: never with the wicked; it is good neither for this nor for the other world.

3. One should always avoid arguments with mean-minded base people and shun even the very sight of the wicked. He should avoid enmity with friends and intimacy with persons serving the enemy.

4. Even a scholar comes to grief by trying to advise a foolish disciple, by supporting a wicked wife and by keeping the company of wicked men.

5. One should keep aloof from a brahmin foolishly puerile, a kṣatriya averse to fighting, a vaiśya sluggish and inactive and a śūdra hot-headed and vain due to complete, defective study.

6. Alliance with an enemy or estrangement with a friend should be indulged in at proper time. A true scholar bides his time after a careful consideration of causes and effects.

7. Time allows all living beings to mature, time brings the dissolution of all people. Even when people are asleep, time is watchful and awake, it is difficult to transgress time.

8. The semen virile flows out at proper time and develops itself in the womb. It is time that causes creation and it is time again that effects the dissolution.

9. The passage of time is incomprehensible. It has twofold functions, an apparent gross movement at one place and a subtle invisible movement at another.

10. The divine preceptor Bṛhaspati expounded the essence of polity to god Indra which got him omniscience and heavenly glory after killing the asuras.

11. The worship of gods, brahmins, etc. should be performed by saintly kings and brahmins. They should also perform the horse-sacrifice to wipe off their sins both small and great.

12. A person never comes to grief if he associates with good people, conducts discourses with scholars and contracts intimate friendship with persons devoid of greed.

13. Illicit contact with or gay revelries in the company of another man's wife, desire for another man's wealth or residence in another man's house shall never be pursued.

14. A well-intentioned enemy is actually a kinsman and a kinsman acting against one's interests is an enemy. Sickness in the body is inimical and a herb in the forest is friendly and beneficial.

15. He is a kinsman who works to our benefit; he is the real father who nurtures and nourishes us; he is a friend where confidence can be placed; it is the native land where sustenance is available.

16. He is the true servant who is loyal and obedient; it is the real seed that germinates well; she is the real wife who

speaks pleasantly and he is the real son who lives to the family tradition.

17. His life is perfect who has virtues and good qualities; fruitless, indeed, is the life of a man devoid of these two.

18. A true wife manages the household affairs skilfully, speaks sweet pleasant words, solely dedicates herself to her husband and is loyally devoted to him.

19-21. The man who has a wife endowed with these qualities is no less than Indra the lord of heaven. He is no ordinary man. The good wife takes her daily bath, applies sweet scents to her body, speaks sweetly, is satisfied with limited quantity of food, is not garrulous, has always auspicious things around her, is very scrupulous in virtuous activities, exhibits her love to her husband by every action and is pleased to surrender herself to his dalliance after the four days of the menstrual flow. She enhances the good luck of everyone.

22-23. What we call old age is not so dispiriting as a wife devoid of good qualities and possessing all bad traits—ugly-eyed, slovenly, quarrelsome, argumentative, visiting other people's house frequently, depending on other people's help, evil in actions and devoid of shame.

24. A wife who appreciates good qualities, devoted to her husband, and satisfied with the minimum in everything is the real beloved.

25. It is death indeed if one has a wicked wife, a rogue as a friend, a servant who answers back and serpents infesting his house.

26. Forsake the contact with wicked people, resort to the assembly of the good; do meritorious acts day and night and remember the unstability of everything.

27. A woman devoid of love, terrific in appearance, ferocious by nature, more horrible than a serpent round the neck, tigerlike in having ruddy eyes, appearing to spit fire desirous of visiting other houses and cities should never be approached.

28. Devotion in the son, good deed in the ungrateful, coldness in the fire may occur sometime by God's grace; but love in a prostitute is never come across.

29. Who can be complacent and carefree if serpents infest the house wherever we cast our eyes, if sickness cannot be cured with all appliances of treatment and if death is ever ready to pounce on the body at every age from infancy to old age ?

CHAPTER ONE HUNDRED AND NINE

Bṛhaspati-nīti-sāra

Sūta said :

1. Money should be saved for emergency; wife should be protected by spending hoarded wealth and one's own self should be saved even at the risk of preserved assets and wife.

2. One should sacrifice oneself to save the family; a family should be sacrificed to save the village; a village should be secrificed for the safety of the land and the land should be sacrificed to save one's soul.

3. The residence in hell is better than that in a house of evil conduct. By the former, one's sins are washed away whereas there is no redemption from the latter.

4. The intelligent man fixes one foot firmly and moves with the other. Without testing the new place well, the old place of resort should not be abandoned.

5. One should unhesitatingly abandon a country infested with men of evil conduct, a residence of harassing environment, a king of miserly temperament, and a friend of deceptive disposition.

6. What purpose can be served by the riches in the hands of a miser ? Of what avail to men can that knowledge be that is tarnished by a roguish disposition ? Of what avail is beauty bereft of good qualities and valour ? Of what value is a friend who turns his face away at the time of misfortune ?

7. Many persons unknown to him before will flock round a person occupying a high post as his friends and assistants.

Time being adverse, if he loses his wealth and is dismissed from his post even his kinsmen become his enemies.

8. A friend can be found out if he is genuine or otherwise in times of danger; the test of valour is the battlefield; the test of purity of a man is his conduct in isolated places. Loss of wealth puts fidelity of the wife to a test and famine provides an opportunity to test whether a man is fond of entertaining a guest or otherwise.

9. Birds leave off the tree when the fruits are exhausted; the Sārasa quits the lake when it is dried up; the courtesan turns out the man who has no money in his pockets; ministers bid good-bye to the king who has lost his throne; honeybees never touch the flower that is faded and withered; the deer flee the forest consumed by fire—So, it is evident that people take delight in things that delight them. Who takes interest in others otherwise ?

10. One should propitiate a greedy man by giving him money; a praiseworthy man by reverence with joined palms; a fool by allowing him to do as he pleases and the scholar by a clear statement of facts.

11. Devas, good people and brahmins are pleased with genuine good nature; the ordinary vulgar people by an offer of something to eat or drink and the learned scholars by due honour and fitting rewards.

12. The noblest can be won over by humility and submission; the rogue with a threat; the vulgar with small gifts and concessions and men of equal status by exhibiting an equal strength and valour.

13. An intelligent man must penetrate deep into the innermost recesses of every one's heart and speak and act befitting his nature and inclination and win him over to his side.

14. Implicit trust in rivers, clawed beasts, horned animals, armed men, women and scions of royal families is never to be encouraged.

15. Men of sense will never disclose loss of wealth, mental anguish, illicit actions in the house, deception (of which they had been the victim) and disrespect.

16. The following are the activities that bring about the destruction of chastity and good conduct in women :— Association with base and wicked people, a long separation from the husband, too much of consideration and love shown to them (by the would-be defiler) and residence in another man's house.

17. Which family is devoid of defects ? Who is not distressed by sickness ? Who is not oppressed by vices and calamities ? Who enjoys continuous blessings of the goddess of fortune ?

18. Who is the man in the wide world who does not become haughty on attaining wealth ? Who has escaped miseries in his life ? Whose mind is not ripped asunder by maidens ? Who has been a favourite of kings for ever ? Who is it that has remained out of sight of the god of Death ? Who is that suppliant who has won honour and respect ? Who is that fortunate fellow who has escaped unscathed after having once fallen into the wily nets of the wicked ?

19. He who has no friends, relatives or kinsmen to advise him and he who has no intrinsic intellect in himself suffers certainly. How can a wise man pursue that activity which does not produce any tangible result even when completed successfully but which necessarily ushers in great sorrow when left incomplete ?

20. One should leave off that land where no one honours him or loves him; where there is no kinsman, and where there are no amenities for higher learning.

21. Earn that wealth to which there is no danger from kings or robbers and which does not leave you even after your death.

22. The wealth that a man acquires by putting in exertions risking his own life is divided among themselves by his successors after his death. Only the sin that he commits in his eagerness to earn remains his exclusive property.

23. Amassed and deposited wealth of the miser is ransacked by others frequently like that of the mouse and is conducive to sorrow.

24. Beggars roaming the streets, naked, grief-stricken,

rough and armed with broken bowls point out to the world that the fruits the non-charitable persons reap are like these.

25. O misers ! the beggars who request you saying "Please give" really teach you that this is the result of not giving. Do not become like them.

26. A miser's hoarded wealth is not being employed in hundreds of sacrifices (i.e. for good purposes) nor is it being given in charity to the deserving; but in the end, it is utilised in the houses of robbers or put in the king's treasury.

27. The wealth of the miser does not go unto the deities, brahmins, relatives or to himself but it goes unto the robbers or kings or is consumed by fire.

28. Let those riches be not thine—the riches acquired with great deal of toil, by transgressing the curbs of virtue or by falling at the feet of the enemy.

29. A blow of destruction to learning is absence of practice; wearing rags is a blow unto the goddess of wealth; eating after digestion is a blow to sickness; and craftiness is a blow to the enemy.

30. A fitting punishment to the thief is the death sentence; being reserved is the best punishment for a false friend; lying on a separate bed is a punishment for women, and non invitation in sacrifice is a punishment for brahmins.

31. Wicked persons, artisans, slaves, defiled ones, drums and women are softened by being beaten; they do not deserve gentle handling.

32. By sending them on errands the ability of servants can be known; sincerity of kinsmen can be known by their behaviour during our adversity; the genuine friendship can be understood when some mishap occurs and the fidelity of the wife is known when one's fortune dwindles.

33. The diet of a woman is twice as much as that of a man; shrewdness four times, energy is six times and amorousness is eight times as much as that of a man.

34. It is impossible to overcome sleep by sleeping it off; to overpower a woman by loving her; to smother a flame by adding fuel and to quench thirst by drinking wine.

35. A delicious fatty meat diet, pleasing dress, glowing

wine, fragrant scented pastes, and sweet smelling flowers kindle passion in women.

36. It can be said with certainty that even during the period of celibacy the god of love is busily active. On seeing a man pleasing to her heart the vagina of a woman becomes wet with profuse secretion.

37. O Śaunaka, it is true, definitely true that the vaginal passage of a woman begins to secrete profusely on seeing a well dressed man whether a brother or a son.

38. Rivers and women are of similar nature in their love of freedom to choose their own course. The rivers erode the banks and the women undermine their own families.

39. The river undermines the banks and the woman causes the fall of the family. The course of rivers and women is wayward and cannot be checked.

40. A blazing fire cannot be satiated with sufficient supply of fuel; the ocean can never be filled to satiety by rivers flowing into it; the god of death is never satiated by the living beings (whom he smites) and a passionate woman is never satiated with man.

41. It is impossible to be satiated with the company of good men, friends, men of delightful conversation, and pleasures, sons, life and boons.

42. A king is never gratified with his ambitious activity of amassing wealth; a sea is never gratified with a perennial flow of water into it; a scholar is never satiated with the talks and speeches given by him; no layman's eye is satiated with the glimpses of the king that he gets.

43. They maintain themselves by what they earn by doing their duties; they are devoted to the sacred scriptures; they are fond of their own wives; they have subjugated the unreasonable wanderings of the sense-organs; they are delighted in serving guests; they attain salvation at their very doors; they are the excellent among men.

44. If the wife is after your heart, if she is attractive, well bedecked and delightful, if you live in your own house it is heaven indeed which can be obtained only by good deeds performed in previous birth.

45. Women are incorrigible; they can never be brought round by making a gift, or offering respect, or a straight forward dealing, or repeated service. They can neither be threatened with a weapon nor asked to be quiet by citing scriptural codes.

46. Five things should be pursued slowly and cautiously. Learning, riches, ascending the mountain, amorous approach to women, and assimilation of virtuous conduct.

47. Worship to gods is of permanent benefit; a present to a brahmin leaves a permanent blessing behind; a thoroughly good learning has an everlasting beneficent result and a good bosom friend is a permanent asset.

48. Those who have not acquired enough learning during studentship and those who have not secured a decent wife and sufficient wealth during youth are to be pitied for ever. They are no better than beasts, but have a human form.

49. A person devoted to the scriptural codes shall not worry over the meal. He must ponder over a regular study. A man seeking knowledge must be prepared to go a long way with the speed of Garuḍa.

50. Those who had been unmindful of studies during studentship and those who had wasted their wealth during youth in pursuit of lust fall into a miserable plight during old age slighted by others and burning within like the lotuses in the winter season.

51. Arguments are never stable and irrefutable; Vedas are wide and varied; there is no sage who has not mentioned something different from others. Still the central theme of virtue is hidden in a cave, as it were. Hence, the path traversed by great men should be taken as the correct one.

52. The inner workings of a man's mind should be inferred from his facial reflexes, behaviour, gestures, movements, speech and the contractions and distortions of his eyes and lips.

53. A spoken word is understood by even a beast. Horses and elephants carry out the orders given. But a scholar infers what is not expressly stated. Intellect is fruitful in being able to comprehend other's gestures.

54. Deprived of wealth one should go on a pilgrimage; going astray from truth one cannot but fall into the hell Raurava; though failing in the initial attempt in the Yogic practice one shall continue to be strictly truthful; a king divested of his royal splendour has no other alternative but go ahunting.

CHAPTER ONE HUNDRED AND TEN

Bṛhaspati-nīti-sāra

Sūta said :

1. If a person forsakes things of sure results in his pursuit of things of uncertain results he loses both—the certain as well as the uncertain.

2. No thrilling pleasure is felt by a man bereft of the mechanism of speech though he may be learned as in the case of a coward holding the sword in his hand or of a blind man wedded to a beautiful wife.

3. It is the fruit of no small penance to possess both delicious foodstuffs and good appetite; sexual virility and healthy as well as handsome wives, extensive wealth and desire to give it to others.

4. The aim of the study of Vedas is the ability to perform Agnihotra; everything auspicious should have the invariable results of good conduct and purposeful life; a good wife must yield perfect sexual pleasure and good offsprings and wealth is for both charity and personal enjoyment.

5. An intelligent man should marry a girl of noble family though not very beautiful; he shall not marry a girl of low descent though she may be beautiful and have developed hips.

6. Of what avail is the wealth which brings disaster in its wake? Who will dare to remove the crest-jewel of a serpent embedded in its hood?

7. Butter for sacrificial purposes can be taken even from the family of wicked persons; a wise saying uttered by even a

child shall be listened to; gold can be taken even from the heap of rubbish and a jewel of a girl can be brought even from a mean family.

8. Nectar may be taken from even a poison-infested spot; gold can be taken even from a heap of rubbish; good learning may be received even from a mean-minded person and a girl of low parentage can be wedded if she has good qualities.

9. Friendship with a king is an impossibility; a serpent devoid of poison is unheard of; a household cannot remain pure if too many women flock there together.

10. A devoted servant should be engaged in household duties; a son should be engaged in study; an enemy should be employed in acts of vice and a friend in virtuous acts.

11. Servants and ornaments should be put in proper places; a crest-jewel worn on the foot will never shine.

12. Crest-jewel, ocean, fire, bell, the vast expanse of the firmament and a king—these have to be at the head; it is wrong to keep them at the foot.

13. A man of stuff will have access to one of the two goals like a bunch of flowers. Either he is at the head of everyone or he fades in a forest.

14. If a fine jewel worthy of being set in a fine earring is worn on the foot it will not take away the brilliance. It is only the wearer who will be criticised by others.

15. Great is the difference between any two members of each of these :—horses, elephants, iron, wood, stone, cloth, women, men and water.

16. It is impossible to deprive a courageous man of his good qualities though he may be tortured and tormented. Even if it is suppressed by a rogue the flame of a fire does not shoot downwards.

17. A horse of good breed does not brook a cut from the whip; a lion cannot bear to hear the trumpeting sound of an elephant. A true hero does not coolly listen to the loud boasts of his enemy.

18. None shall deign to serve the wicked or the base even if unfortunately deprived of wealth or fallen from a high position. Even though oppressed by hunger the lion does not

stoop to graze the grass. It is satisfied only when it drinks the hot blood of elephants.

19. He who tries to cultivate again the friendship of one who has once deceived him really seeks his own death like the she-mule that conceives.

20. The children of an enemy shall never be neglected or treated with indifference by sane men in spite of the fact that they may be speaking sweet words. After the lapse of some time they may be very dangerous and terrible like vessels of poison.

21. If a thorn pricks the foot, another thorn is held in the hand with which the former one is removed. Similarly, an enemy should be wiped off by another enemy whose help for the nonce can be secured by an act of gratification.

22. None need worry about a man who constantly harasses him. Such people will fall off themselves like the trees on the banks of rivers.

23. When fate is adverse, disastrous harmful things may seem to be auspicious and vice versa. This attitude shall eventually bring destruction too.

24. If the fate is favourable, naturally, good fruitful thoughts befitting the matter on hand occur to everyone everywhere.

25. Unnecessary bashfulness and reserve need not be felt in monetary transactions, acquisition of knowledge, taking food and dealings (with the wife in the bed chamber).

26. None shall stay in a place where these five do not live, viz :—rich men, Vedic scholar, king, river and a physician.

27. Even a day's stay shall be avoided in places where means of livelihood, fear of law, sense of shame, courteousness and liberal-mindedness are not available.

28. One shall not think of staying permanently in a place where these five are not available :—An astrologer, a Vedic scholar, a king, a river and a saint.

29. O Śaunaka, knowledge is not the monopoly of any one. All do not know everything; there is no omniscient being anywhere.

30. In this world we cannot find an omniscient man nor a person utterly foolish. A man can be considered base, middling, or highly intelligent in accordance with the type of knowledge he possesses.

CHAPTER ONE HUNDRED AND ELEVEN

Bṛhaspati's nītisāra

Sūta said :

1. I should now mention the characteristic features of the king as well as the servants. A king should examine the following carefully.

2. He should protect the kingdom with devotion to truth and virtue. He should righteously rule over the earth after conquering the enemy.

3. A florist collects flower after flower but does not uproot the plant. The king should also do likewise but not like the maker of charcoal who burns the entire tree in the forest.

4. Those who milk the cow and drink milk do not do so if it is turned sour. So also the king should not defile the kingdom of the enemy which is expected to be enjoyed.

5. The man who wants cow's milk does not cut off its udders. He draws the milk no doubt. Similarly, the king who wants to tap the resources of a kingdom shall avoid injury to the same.

6. Hence, the king should rule over the earth with care and exertion. In that case the earth, the fame, longevity, renown and strength shall all be truly his.

7. The king of well controlled sense-organs will be able to protect the subjects only if his rule is righteous and if he worships Lord Viṣṇu and is eager to render service to cows and brahmins.

8. After acquiring prosperity which is not permanent it is essential that a king should turn his attention to virtue. All riches will perish in a moment but not the wealth of the soul.

9. Indeed, it is pleasing to gratify the lust. It is true that riches are highly pleasant. But life is as fickle as the roving glances of a winsome maiden.

10 Threatening us like the tigress, old age is waiting for an attack on us. Diseases like enemies crop up all over the body. Life flows out like water from a broken pot. Still no one in the world does ever think of redeeming the soul.

11. O Men ! do service unto others. Do what will be beneficent, later on. Why do you rejoice now, without any suspicion whatsoever, along with the bevy of beautiful damsels, smitten by the arrows of Cupid, with your eyes very slow (to see what is in store for you) ? Do not commit sins. Taking brahmins and Lord Viṣṇu as your refuge begin worship. Your life is slowly coming to an end like water in a pot. In the guise of death a great spirit will pounce upon you.

12. He is a wise man who regards another man's wife as his mother, another man's wealth as a lump of clay and all living beings like himself.

13. It is for this that brahmins wish their kings to be rich, that in all their rites their words should be heeded and never slighted.

14. It is for this that kings board wealth that after serving themselves they shall give unto the brahmins what is left over.

15. The king in whose realm the sound of Om uttered by the brahmins is resonant, flourishes. Getting whatever he wants he is never tormented by sickness.

16. Even the apparently incompetent sages can gather riches and articles of daily use. Then why cannot a king who protects his subjects like his children ?

17. He who has riches has many friends. He who has riches has many kins. People consider him who has riches fit to be called a Man and a Scholar.

18. Friends, sons, wives and relatives abandon a man devoid of wealth. When he regains his lost wealth they come back to him. Hence, wealth alone is a man's kith and kin and none other.

19. The king who has discarded the Sacred Code is no

better than a blind man. A blind man may well see through spies but not so a man devoid of sacred codes.

20. The kingdom of that king is indeed unstable whose sons, servants, ministers, priests and sense-organs are not active and alert but always asleep.

21. He who has acquired the valuable support of the three sons, servants and kins has actually conquered the earth girdled by the four oceans along with the kings.

22. The king who transgresses the injunctions of scriptures and the dictates of reason perishes here in this world and forfeits the right to Heaven.

23. A king surrounded by calamities should not lose heart. He should maintain equanimity both in happiness and sorrow and should never lose enlightened delight of the soul.

24. Courageous souls never become grief-stricken when mishaps occur. Does not the moon rise again though gobbled up by Rāhu?

25. Fie, Fie upon men who yearn for the pleasures of body. Do not grieve over the thinness of body or loss of wealth. It is well known that the sons of Pāṇḍu[1] and their wife suffered poverty for some time but came unscathed through it and were happy for ever.

26. A king should maintain teams of courtesans and patronize their arts of music and dance. He should give sufficient protection to the science of archery and Economics too.

27. The king who becomes angry with his servants without sufficient cause actually takes in the poison vomited by a black serpent.

28. A king should avoid fickleness and false utterances towards all men and especially to Vedic Scholars and his personal attendants.

29. Proud of his servants and kinsmen, if a king remains complacent and begins sports and dalliance he is sure to be outwitted by the enemy.

1. The son of Vicitra-Vīrya and the brother of Dhṛtarāṣṭra. His five sons are known as Pāṇḍavas—Yudhiṣṭhira, Bhīma, Arjuna, Nakula and Sahadeva.

30. It is despicable on his part to fret and fume without faults in others. He who punishes servants unjustifiably becomes a victim of the enemie's attack.

31. A king should abandon sensuous enjoyments and pleasures. Such people become easy targets of enemies who are always on the alert.

32. Enterprise, adventurousness, courage, intellect, prowess and valour—he who possesses these six is viewed with suspicious awe even by Devas.

33. Where results are not remarkable even after energetic exertion it is due to an adverse fate. Still man should put up endeavour and take resort to fruitful activities.

CHAPTER ONE HUNDRED AND TWELVE

Bṛhaspati's nītisāra

Sūta said :

1. Servants are of various types—the excellent, the middling and the base. They should be employed befittingly in the three types of jobs.

2. I shall narrate the mode of test for servants and the qualities necessary for different jobs as narrated by authorities on them.

3. Just as gold is tested in the four ways by rubbing on the touchstone, cutting, beating and melting, so also a servant is tested by his appearance, conduct, parentage and activities.

4. A man of noble family, endowed with good character and qualities, truthful and virtuous, handsome and pleasant-mannered should be appointed as the officer-in-charge of the Treasury.

5. He who can appraise the value, shape and size, (of gold, gems, etc.) should be appointed as the chief jeweller. A man who can understand strength and weakness of the soldiers should be appointed as the Commander-in-Chief.

6. The chief of watch and ward should be a mind-reader who can understand each and every gesture, is strong, comely to look at, unerring and competent to strike a timely blow.

7. The chief secretary to the king should be intelligent, clever in conversation shrewd, truthful in speech, with sense-organs under his control, and acquainted with all Śāstras.

8. The chief Ambassador should be intelligent, sensible, a reader of others' minds, ruthless and blunt in speaking facts.

9. The officer-in-charge virtue should be well versed in Smṛti texts, a scholar of great erudition, with good control over his sense-organs and equipped with the qualities of heroism, valour and other good qualities.

10. The Head Cook should be a man whose father and grandfather had served in a similar capacity. He should be skilful, truthful and acquainted with Śāstras. He should be clean in person and capable of hard work.

11. The Royal physician shall be well-versed in Āyurveda[1] with enough practical experience. He should have all the qualities of a decent man and look comely in appearance.

12. The Royal Priest should be a great scholar in Vedas and their ancillaries. He should be observing Japas and Homas. He should readily bless everyone.

13. Whether he is a writer, or a reciter, an accountant or a chief executive, if any one is found to be lazy, he should at once be dismissed.

14. The mouths of a wicked man and a serpent are sources of distress—since they are double-tongued, causing pain, ruthless and terrific.

15. A wicked man should be avoided even if he happens to be a scholar. Is not a serpent terrific though its head is bedecked with a precious gem ?

16. Who is not afraid of the wicked ? Who is furious without provocation ? It is the wicked from whose mouth the poison of a great serpent in the form of unbearable words flows out continuously.

17. If a salaried servant of the king becomes so rich as to vie with him, is of equal competency, who knows his inner

1. The ancient Indian medical science propagated and practised by Caraka, Suśruta, Vāgbhaṭa and others is still recognized by Indian Government and put to use by the people in India.

secrets and vulnerable points, who is very industrious and puts up a claim to half of his kingdom there is no harm if the king puts him to death.

18. Those servants are not to be retained who were at first valorous, slow and gentle of speech, truthful and self-controlled but later on proved to be otherwise.

19. Servants of this type are very rare—servants who are not lazy, who are satisfied, who can be easily roused from sleep in emergency, who have the equanimity in happiness and sorrow and who are courageous.

20. A servant suffering from all these bad points or from any one of them should be summarily dismissed—devoid of patience, dishonest, cruel-tempered, speaking ill of others, haughty, gluttonous, roguish, greedy inefficient and cowardly.

21. The king shall keep in his fort strong weapons of all types and then try to conquer his enemies.

22. If he is not well-equipped he should make peace with his enemy for a period of six months or a year and when he is well equipped he shall attack the enemy.

23. If a king engages foolish persons in various offices the results will be ignominy, loss of wealth and hell after death.

24. Whatever the king does himself or whatever his servants do meritorious or sinful acts, the king has to reap the fruits thereof. He will flourish or fall as the case may be.

25. Hence, a king should employ intelligent and capable men in offices of virtue or wealth for the welfare of cows and brahmins in the State.

CHAPTER ONE HUNDRED AND THIRTEEN

Bṛhaspati's nītisāra

Sūta said :

1. One should employ only the capable servant and not the inefficient. All good qualities can be found in a scholar and all faults in a fool.

2. One should always sit in the company of the good and associate with them. Discussions and friendship should ever be with the good and not with the wicked.

3. Even in a prison one should associate only with the learned, the humble, the virtuous and the truthful. Outside, he should never associate with the wicked.

4. Completing all works left unfinished he shall become wealthy. He should make it a point to complete un-finished tasks.

5. Like the honey bee that sucks honey but does not cause the fall of the flower the king should take revenue from the realm without harming it. The cowherd leaves something for the calf and milks the rest. Similarly, the king should milk the earth but leave plenty for the calves i. e. the subjects.

6. Just as the honeybee collects honey from a number of flowers so the king shall gather wealth taking a little from each.

7. The anthill, honey, the moon in the bright half and alms wax little by little.

8. Seeing that collyrium and ink, used though very little every day, become exhausted after some time, and that the ant-hill flourishes day by day, one should be careful in not wasting one's time. One should engage oneself in activities of charity or self-study.

9. A vicious and lustful man shall find hundreds of obstacles even in a forest; but if he can control his five senses he can practise penance even in his house. He who is engaged in activities not censurable and he who is free from passion can make his house a hermitage.

10. Virtue is protected by truth. Knowledge by further acquisition; a pot by frequent cleaning and a family by good conduct.

11. It is better to stay in the forest of Vindhya, to die without partaking of food; it is better to sleep in a spot infested by serpents or to leap into a well; it is better to plunge into a whirlpool or a dangerous water current, than to say "Please give" or beg for a sum of money from one's own kindred.

12. Riches dwindle when fortune dwindles and not by enjoyment; if merit had been acquired before, riches will never perish.

13. Knowledge is an ornament to a brahmin; a king is the beautifier of the world; the moon is an ornament of the sky; a good conduct is an ornament to every one.

14. Bhīma, Arjuna and others were born as princes, they were pleasing and delightful like the moon; they were valorous, truthful, brilliant like the sun and were kindly protected by Lord Kṛṣṇa. Even they were subjected to abject misery by the influence of evil planets; they had to beg for alms.; if fate is adverse who is capable of what ? The current of previous actions tosses every one about.

15. Obeisance to Karma which forces Brahmā to work like a potter in the bowls of cosmos by which Viṣṇu was cast into distress of ten incarnations; by which Rudra was compelled to beg for alms with a skull in his hand and at the behest of which the sun goes round and round in the sky.

16. The donor was King Bali, the receiver Lord Viṣṇu himself, the gift consisted of whole Earth and that too in the presence of learned brahmins. What did he get in return ? Only bondage. O Fate ! obeisance to Thee—who workest as it pleasest thee.

17. The mother is Goddess Lakṣmī herself; the father is Lord Viṣṇu; still if the son (cupid) were to be of crooked mind, who is to be punished for the same ?

18. Man enjoys only the fruits of his previous actions; whatever he has done in the previous births has its reactions now.

19. The happiness is enjoined by oneself, the sorrow too is enjoined by oneself; even the womb selected by him is in accordance with the action of the previous birth.

20. A man can never forsake the action done by him far into the sky, or deep into the sea or high on the mountain; whether he is held by his mother on her head or kept in her lap.

21. Even Rāvaṇa perished at the hands of Time. Rāvaṇa whose fortress was the mountain Trikūṭa[1], the moat—the very ocean; soldiers—Rākṣasas; the action of the highest order; and the Śāstra propounded by Uśanas.

1. The mountain on which the city of Laṅkā was situated.

22. Everything happens in the age, time, day, night, hour or moment as is ordained beforehand; not otherwise.

23. Whether people go up in the sky, or deep in the nether world; whether they traverse all quarters, they will not get what is not given by Karma.

24. The learning of by-gone-days, the money made over as gift and the actions done before—these run ahead of a person who walks at speed.

25. Actions alone are of consequence. See Jānakī (Sītā), whose marriage was celebrated when the stars and planets were ascendant and the lagna (i.e. auspicious hour) was decided by sage Vasiṣṭha himself, had to undergo miseries.

26. Auspicious signs, characteristic marks are of no avail when Karma comes into clash; for Rāma who had stout muscular calves, Lakṣmaṇa who was as swift as sound and Sītā who had thickly grown glossy hair—all these had to suffer a lot.

27-28. Neither the son with Piṇḍa-dāna and other rites nor the father with various rites for the welfare of the son can ward off the adverse influence of Karma. In the physical bodies born as a result of Karma, different kinds of illness physical or mental fall in quick succession like the shafts discharged by a skilful archer. Hence, a courageous man should view objects in the light of Śāstraic injunctions and not otherwise.

29. In every birth, a man reaps the fruits of his previous merits and demerits in the respective ages of infancy, youth or old age at which the actions had been performed.

30. Just as a gale blows a boat, the Karma drags a man against his wish even from foreign countries to the place where he has to reap the fruits.

31. A man necessarily gets what he is destined to get. Even a god is incapable of stopping it. Hence, I do not bewail or am not surprised at the events. The line of fate cannot be erased.

32. When chased, a serpent escapes into a well; an elephant to the trunk (to which it can be tethered); a mouse to its hole; but who can fly from Karma which is quicker than all these ?

33. A well-assimilated knowledge never diminishes; it

increases on being imparted to others like the water in a well which increases when water is drawn out.

34. Riches acquired virtuously become stable; they flourish still more with virtue. Hence, when you aim at riches, remember this and seek virtue. You thus become great in the world.

35. None becomes miserable if, seeking virtue, he undergoes the same hardships as a poor layman does seeking food.

36. Of all purities, purity of food is excellent. If a man incurs impurity by taking unwholesome food, he cannot be cleansed with clay or water or any other substance of cleanliness.

37. There are five cleansing agents—truthfulness, pure mind, suppression of sense-organs, sympathy with all living beings and water the fifth of the series.

38. He who maintains truthfulness and purity finds an easy access to heaven. Truthfulness is superior to even Horse-sacrifice.

39. A man habitually wicked in deeds, with his conscience benumbed with evil thoughts cannot be cleansed with a thousand lumps of clay or a hundred pots of water.

40. He who keeps his hands and feet clean, his mind under perfect control, and acquires learning penance and fame reaps the fruit of pilgrimage.

41. The characteristics of a saintly man are :—he is not elated much when honoured, he does not become angry when slighted, he does not speak harsh words in anger.

42. No one feels satisfied at the outset on hearing wholesome advice at the proper time from a poor man though intelligent and sweet-voiced.

43. What men are not destined to get cannot be secured by them through mantras, strength, valour, intellect or manliness. What is there to lament over ?

44. I have secured something unsolicited. When I sent it back, it went away from where it had come. What is there to lament over ?

45. During nights birds flock together on a tree for rest.

In the mornings they go to different quarters. What is there to lament over ?

46. All have the same destination. All are proceeding there. If one among them goes more quickly what is there to lament over ?

47. O Śaunaka, the living beings arise from the unmanifest; at their death they dissolve themselves in the unmanifest. In between they remain manifest. What is there to lament over ?

48. If the time of death has not been reached no one dies even if pierced with a hundred arrows. If the same has arrived he does not survive even a slight prick with the tip of a Kuśa grass.

49. A man gets only those things he is destined to get; he goes only to those places where he has to go (at the behest of Karma) and whether misery or pleasure he gets only what he has to get.

50. A man gets things from Karma only. Why should he shout and cry ? Even if prodded, flowers and fruits do not transgress their stipulated time [they do not come out earlier or later]. So is the case with Karma of the previous birth.

51. Neither conduct, nor parentage, neither learning nor knowledge, neither the qualities nor the purity of seed fructifies in man. As in the case of trees, good deeds acquired by austerities fructify in men.

52. A man meets with death where there is a slayer or riches where there is plenty. Goaded by Karma a man goes to the respective places.

53-56. Just as a calf can recognize its mother in the midst of a thousand cows, the previous Karma approaches the doer. Enjoy your merits, O fool ! Why should you feel aggrieved ? What you do now will certainly follow you hereafter whether good or bad.

57. The vicious and the mean observe other's faults, be they so little as the mustard seeds. They see but pretend not to see their own faults as big as Bilva fruits.

58. O Brahmin ! Nowhere can they find happiness, who are defiled by lust and hatred. After careful consideration I see that there is pleasure where there is enlightened bliss.

59. Attachment is a cause of misery; since apprehension follows in the wake of attachment. If, therefore, attachment is eschewed one should be happy.

60. The body is the base for misery and happiness. Life and body are born together.

61. Pleasure and pain can be defined briefly. Whatever goes in the possession of others is misery, whatever remains in one's own possession is pleasure.

62. After pleasure comes the pain and after pain comes the pleasure. Pleasure and pain whirl like wheels in human life.

63. What has passed has gone for ever; if anything is to happen it is still far off. He who minds the present alone is not afflicted by sorrow.

CHAPTER ONE HUNDRED AND FOURTEEN

Bṛhaspati's instructions

Sūta said :

1. None is friend or enemy to any other person by nature. Friendship and enmity arise from special causes.

2. The two syllables "Mitram" (Friend) signify solace in sorrow, freedom from fear and preservation of love and confidence. By whom has this jewel been created?

3. If any one says for once the two letters "Hari" he has everything made ready for his journey to salvation.

4. Men cannot have as much confidence in mothers, wives, brothers or sons as in a friend of kindred nature.

5. If you wish for a prolonged friendship, avoid the following three, gambling with him, monetary transactions with him and seeing his wife in his absence.

6. One should not sit in the same seat with one's mother, sister and daughter in an isolated place. The powerful sense-organs can drag even an erudite man (into the mire of lust). What of common men?

7. God of love compels persons to turn their attention to such spots as provide risks, death, and punishments and not to one's own ? [i.e. People do not love their wives but run after other women risking even death].

8. It is easier to gauge the velocity of the hailstorm at the time of the final dissolution, the speed of the racing horse and the depth of the great ocean than the heart of the person who does not love.

9. O Śaunaka, if there is no opportune moment, if there is no privacy and if there is no one to make overtures women shall preserve chastity.

10. She serves one man but cherishes love for another. In the absence of man a woman can very well be chaste.

11. A mother moved by passion may commit some misdeeds. Though the sons may disapprove of the conduct yet they shall not worry much about them.

12. The body of a courtesan is prized in the world ; the body that is held at stake always with the neck torn by the hoofs of debauches and hence always agitated and anxious. Her sleep is dependent on others' convenience; she has to follow the wishes of others and without a show of sorrow she has to laugh and sport always.

13. Fire, water, women, fools, serpents and Royal households—these are to be resorted to by others always, yet they take away one's life all of a sudden.

14. What is there to wonder at, if a brahmin well versed in grammar becomes a great scholar ? What is there to wonder at if a king well versed in polity and administration becomes a virtuous king ? What is there to wonder at if a young woman endowed with beauty and charms errs from chastity ? What is there to wonder at if a poor man begins to commit sins sometimes.

15. Do not allow others to see your vulnerable points; but note others carefully like a tortoise that keeps all its limbs safe in its shell.

16. Women may be confined to the nether worlds or may be imprisoned with high walls all round. Still if there is no moving glossy tuft of hair who can see them ? [Using her long tresses she will escape from these places].

17. One's own kinsman pursuing the same activities and knowing his vulnerable points is the fiercest foe. Even an enemy standing outside cannot injure so much.

18. He is the real scholar who pleases children with sweets, the good people with humility, the women with wealth, the deities with penance, and people for their welfare.

19. They are not wise who try to win over a friend by deception, to secure virtue through sins, to attain wealth by harassing others, to learn with pleasure, and to secure a lady's love through harshness.

20. Even a pure action may be defiled and defective when the root is cut off. It is only the senseless man who will cut off a tree laden with fruits in order to secure the fruits.

21. O brahmin, I do not believe that a man with necessary things can become a saint even if he tries. How can a woman drinking wine be chaste as well ?

22. One shall not place trust in a person not trustworthy. Even friends are not to be trusted. Some time later if he is angry the friend may publicise his secrets.

23. A general confidence in all living beings is Sāttvika but the main characteristic of a saintly man is to keep his feelings a secret for ever.

24. Whatever action is done it follows the doer. Whatever may be your action, do not leave off your courage and intellect.

25. An intelligent man shall avoid these six : Old women (for sexual purposes), fresh wine, dry meat, carrot, curd in the night and sleep during the day.

26. To a poor man a party of guests is poison (involving expenses); to an old man a woman in the prime of her youth is poison; an ill assimilated knowledge is poison; eating before digestion is poison.

27. To a man of undaunted spirit honour is pleasing ; overthrow of administration is pleasing to the vile; to a poor man a charitable gift is pleasing and a woman in the prime of her youth is pleasing to a young man.

28. The six main reasons for sickness in men are : Excessive drinking of water; eating hard indigestible food-

stuffs; wastage of semen virile ; holding up of faeces and urine (not evacuating them immediately) ; sleep during the day and keeping awake at night.

29. Early morning rays of the sun, excessive indulgence in sexual intercourse, the smoke column rising from the cremation ground, warming of the palms, and the constant sight of the face of a woman in her menses—all these reduce the longevity of a man.

30. The following six take away one's life immediately : dry meat, old women (if cohabited with), the early morning sun, very sour curd, sleeping and having sexual intercourse in the morning.

31. These six things instil more vitality into the human organism : Fresh melted butter, grapes, cohabitation with a woman in the prime of her youth, a milk diet, hot water and the shade of a spreading tree.

32. The water in a well, the shade of a banyan tree and the well-rounded breasts of a young woman—these three are warm in winter and cool in summer.

33. The three instantaneously invigorating things are: a young woman, oil bath and a wholesome food. The three instantaneously debilitating things are : a hazardous journey, sexual intercourse and fever.

34. Dry meat watered down with milk shall not be taken in the company of wife, friends or the king. If taken, an immediate separation from them is inevitable.

35. Goddess of wealth forsakes a man habitually wearing dirty clothes, allowing dirt to accumulate on the teeth, eating too much, habitually speaking harsh words and sleeping at sunrise and sunset, even if he happens to be Viṣṇu.

36. Cutting of grass frequently, writing on the ground with the toes, chafing of the feet, neglect of the cleaning of teeth, wearing dirty clothes, keeping the hair rough, sleeping at dawn and dusk, lying down naked, eating and laughing excessively, drumming on one's own limbs or on the seat—these may destroy the affluence of even Lord Viṣṇu.

37. These six bring back one's wealth long lost : keeping the head cleaned and washed, keeping the feet spotlessly pure, keeping the company of excellent women, taking food in limited

quantities, lying on the bed without stripping, and sexual intercourse excluding the festival nights.

38. Ill luck and misfortune can be warded off by wearing a flower on the head and especially the white one.

39. Ill luck frequently resides in the back shadow of a lamp, the shadow of the cot, the shadow of a seat and the water used by washermen.

40. The rays of the early morning sun, the column of smoke rising from a funeral pyre, intercourse with an old woman, very sour curd and the dust from a broom should not be resorted to by those who wish for longevity.

41. The dust of elephants, horses, chariots, grains and cows is auspicious. That from ass, camel, goat and sheep is inauspicious.

42. The dust of cows, the dust of grains and the dust from the limbs of one's own son—these are very holy, they destroy even the great sins.

43. The dust of a goat, the dust of an ass and the dust from a broom—these are unholy and conducive to great sin.

44. The wind blowing from the winnowing basket, the water dripping from the nails, the water from the cloth and pot used for bathing, the dust from the broom and the water dripping from hair—all these destroy merits previously acquired.

45. One shall never walk between two brahmins, a brahmin and fire, a husband and wife, two masters, two horses and two bulls.

46. What wise man will have confidence in women, kings, fires, serpents, studies, the enemy, worldly enjoyment, etc. ?

47. Do not trust the incredulous ; do not place too much of confidence even in the trust-worthy ; there is a lurking danger in reposing trust; it may uproot one.

48. He who remains complacent after making peace with the enemy has actually gone to sleep atop the tree, he will wake up after his fall.

49. One should never be too soft nor too cruel in action. The soft would be crushed with the soft and the ruthless with the ruthless.

50. One should never be too straightforward nor too soft. Straight trees are cut in a forest and the crooked trees remain as they were.

51. Meritorious persons bow down like the fruit-laden trees. Dry trees and fools would rather break than bend at all.

52. Miseries come unsolicited ; they go away as they come. Just as the cat pounces upon its prey, man seeking things shall pounce on happiness.

53. Riches go before and after the noble but not so in the case of ignoble. You can do as you please.

54. A counsel in six ears (discussed among three persons) is leaked out immediately; that in four ears is kept for some time but the one in two ears cannot be understood even by Brahmā.

55. Of what avail is the cow which neither yields the milk nor becomes pregnant ? Of what purpose is a son who is neither virtuous nor scholarly.

56. The whole family is lit up by a single good son endowed with learning, intelligence and valour like the sky with the moon.

57. The whole forest is rendered fragrant by a single tree in full bloom like the family by a virtuous son.

58. One good son alone is preferable to a hundred ones devoid of good qualities. The moon alone dispels darkness and not the stars in their thousands.

59. The son should be fondled for five years and thrashed for the next ten years ; when he reaches the sixteenth year he should be treated like a friend.

60. You cannot find an enemy like a son—on being born the son takes away one's wife from one [when a son is born mother's attention is more to the son than to her husband] ; while growing up he takes away wealth and if by chance he dies he takes away the life of the father too.

61. In the world some men are like tigers with the mouth of a deer and some like deer with the mouth of a tiger. In order to know them fully distrust at every step is the only way.

62. There is only one fault in men of forbearance and

patience. There is no second fault. People take him to be powerless.

63. All enjoyments are transitory. If this alone is permitted (it would have been better) that the inclinations of the skilful be unaffected towards their friends.

64. O Śaunaka ! when the father passes away, the eldest brother takes his place. He should maintain everyone being a father unto them.

65. He shall be impartial to his younger brothers and give them the same pleasures as they received from their father.

66. The collection of a number of even insignificant things may be terrific in their effect. A number of blades of grass twisted into a rope may be strong enough to bind even an elephant.

67. The man who robs some one though he uses the money to make a charitable gift goes to hell. The fruit of the meritorious deed goes to the original owner of wealth.

68. Families are faced with fall by the destruction of temple property, looting of brahmins and showing them disrespect.

69. Sages have prescribed expiatory rites for the slayer of a brahmin, a drinker of wine, a thief and a breaker of vows ; but there is no atonement for an ungrateful wretch.

70. Gods and manes do not accept oblations of the mean-minded fellow who keeps a woman of low caste as his concubine, who is a slave to his wife and who allows his wife to enjoy the company of a paramour in his own house.

71. An ungrateful fellow, a person of ignoble qualities, a person who nurses a grouse for a long time and a man of crooked nature — these four are the real Cāṇḍālas and the fifth is one born as such.

72. Even an insignificant enemy of evil intentions should not be neglected carelessly. Even a tiny spark of fire, if not put out immediately consumes the entire world.

73. He who is quiet and tranquil in the boisterous age of blooming youth deserves the credit for being tranquil. Who does not become naturally quiet and tranquil when all his vital forces are spent out ?

74. O foremost among brahmins, riches, like the public thoroughfare are common to everyone. Do not be elated and haughty thinking "This is mine."

75. The body that is dependent on the vital secretions is dependent on the mind too. If the mind is disarranged the vital secretions are destroyed. Hence, mind shall be preserved always. If the mind is in perfect order the vital secretions function properly.

CHAPTER ONE HUNDRED AND FIFTEEN

Bṛhaspati's nītisāra

Sūta Said :

1. One should keep oneself far away from a false wife, a deceitful friend, a tyrannous king, a disobedient son, a defiled daughter and a turbulent territory.

2. Alas, life in the Kali age is troublesome indeed. For, virtue has taken to renunciation, penance has started its long sojourn, truth is in exile in a foreign land, earth has become barren, people are fradulent; brahmins have become greedy, men are uxorious, women are fickle and wayward and base men are raised to high position. Blessed indeed are they who ar dead.

3. Blessed are they who do not witness the destruction of their family, ruin of their lands, the sexual dalliance of their wives with other men and the infamous indulgence of their sons in vice.

4. None can be delighted with their vicious sons; how can one feel a thrilling rapture in the company of a disloyal wife ? There is no question of confiding in a deceptive friend and no peaceful life is possible in a trouble-infested land.

5. Food doled out by others, money robbed from others, defiling of another man's bed, sexual dalliance with another man's wife and a residence in another man's house will strip even Indra of his glory.

6. Sin spreads from man to man slowly by conversation, mutual touch, frequent association, taking food together, sitting together, lying together, and travelling together.

7. Women perish due to their beauty, penance due to fury, the way due to an undue length and pious brahmin by taking Śūdra's food.

8. By sitting together, sharing the same bed, taking food together, and jumbling up the row; sin is transmitted from man to man like water from pot to pot.

9. There are many defects in fondling and many benefits in thrashing. Hence, a disciple and the son are to be thrashed, not fondled.

10. A long way is old age to men; water is old age to mountains; abstention from sexual intercourse is old age to women and sunlight is old age to clothes.

11. Base men desire strife, the middling desire reconciliation and the noble desire high honour. Verily, honour is prized by the great as the greatest asset.

12. Honour is at the root of wealth; if honour is secured of what avail is wealth; if one has lost honour and dignity, of what avail is wealth or longevity ?

13. The base and the mean desire for riches; the middling desire for riches and honour and the excellent desire for honour. Verily, honour is an asset of the great.

14. In the forest, the lions do not bend their ears (in supplication); even when they are hungry they do not look to a share. Men of noble birth never stoop to meanness, even when they are deprived of their wealth.

15. The lion is neither anointed nor consecrated. The lordship of animals comes to it naturally as it has inherent valour.

16. No great task can be achieved by any of these :—An erring merchant; a highly proud servant, an easy going mendicant, an impoverished debaucher, a Helan of a girl bitter in speech.

17. Five incongruent things that we meet in the world are :—the poverty of the benevolent, the opulence of the miser, disobedience in a son, compulsion to serve a wicked man and death of persons engaged in helping others.

18. There are five things which burn without fire :—Separation from wife; insult from kins, balance of debt yet to be discharged, service to a low and base master and desertion of friends in poverty.

19. Among the thousand worries that agitate the mind four are very severe—nay, they are the sharp edges of a sword :—Insult at the hands of a low born person, the starving wife, cold reception by the beloved, and harassment from brothers.

20. The five uproot all miseries :—An obedient son, a remunerative knowledge, freedom from sickness, the companionship of the good and a loving wife surrendering herself.

21. The deer, the elephant, the moth, the honeybee and the fish—these five are destroyed due to addiction to their five sense-organs.[1]

22. Five types of brahmins, though as learned as Bṛhaspati are never honoured :—the impatient, the harsh, the haughty, the ill-clad and the uninvited.

23 These five are clearly defined and decided even when a child is born :—Its span of life, its activities in later life, its character, learning and the time of death.

24. Help rendered to those who suffer when climbing a mountain, from imminent drowning in water, attack of cows and bulls, seizure by the wicked and a spiritual fall are very commendable.

1.

Victim	*Sense-Organ*	*Object*
Dear	Ears	Listens to sweet music and gets caught by the hunter.
Elephant	Sense of touch	It is caught through she-elephants.
moth	Eyes	It is attracted by the colour of the flame and is burnt.
honeybee	Nose	Attracted by the fragrance of lotus it gets caught within.
Fish	Sense of taste	It nibbles at the bait and gets caught.

Even one of the sense-organs is destructive. How is it possible that man who uses all the five will escape destruction ?

25. These five are never stable or long-standing :—the shadow of clouds, pleasant attitude of a wicked man; intimacy with another man's wife, youth and riches.

26. Life is unstable in the world, youth and riches are unstable, sons and wives are unstable; but virtue, fame and renown are permanent.

27. Even a life for a hundred years is too short. Half that period is taken up by nights. The remaining half is rendered fruitless by sickness, sorrow, old age and exertions.

28. It is said that man's span of life is a hundred years. It is too short. Half of that period is spent as nights. Half of the remaining half is spent in infancy and childhood or grieving over the separation or death of kinsmen or in service rendered to the king. The remaining period is as fickle as the waves in water. Of what avail is the sense of prestige and dignity ?

29. Days and nights in the garb of old age traverse the earth. Death swallows the living beings like the serpent taking in air.

30. If our activities while walking or standing, waking or sleeping are not for the service of fellow beings they are not different from beastial actions.

31. What is the difference between a beast and a beast in human form with an intellect devoid of discrimination between what is wholesome and what is not; who enters into endless arguments with people in regard to the Vedic expositions, and who remains fully satisfied if he can fill his belly.

32. He who has not earned spotless reputation for valour, austerity, charity, learning or acquisition of wealth is but an excrement of his mother.

33. A good life even for a moment is considered a perfect life by those who know the same—if it is full of perfect knowledge, valour and fame and men are not disrespected. Even a crow lives a long life and partakes of oblations.

34. Of what avail is that life devoid of wealth and honour ? Of what use is that friend who hesitates whether he is to be friendly or not ? O ye, adopt the rite of a lion, do not be grief-stricken. Even a crow lives a long life and partakes of oblations.

35. If a man does not sympathise with and render help to himself, his preceptor, his servants, the poor public and his friends, of what purpose is his life ? Even a crow lives for a long time partaking the oblations.

36. Days come and go to a man devoid of virtue, wealth and love. Although he may breathe, his life is like that of the bellows of the blacksmith.

37. Success is for him who has an independent means of substance and not for him who depends on others. Those who depend on others are no better than dead even though physically alive.

38. Contemptible wretches fulfil their own wants; a mouse's handful is just enough to fill it; a contemptible wretch though dissatisfied will be contented with something small.

39. These six are like bubbles :—the shadow of clouds, fire made with dry grass, service to the base, water on the surface of the road, the love of a prostitute and the pleasant manners of the wicked.

40. The world cannot be pleased by a person who creates a caravan with words. Life is rooted in honour; if honour is slighted how can one derive pleasure ?

41 A king is the support for the weak; crying constitutes the strength of the child; the strength of a fool lies in silence and that of a thief is falsehood.

42. As a man proceeds ahead with his study of Śāstras his intellect becomes sharper and perfect knowledge appeals to him.

43. As a person goes ahead devoting his mind and attention to the welfare of others, everyone becomes attached to him and he becomes popular.

44. A person perishes due to the three—greed, grave error and implicit confidence. Hence, these shall be avoided.

45. Danger is to be dreaded as long as it does not befall. The moment it occurs fear shall be eschewed.

46. Balance of debt undischarged, remnant of fire not put out and sickness partially cured increase steadily. Hence, these remnants shall be avoided.

47. Repay good action by goodness and violence by

violence. I do not find any fault, if a wicked man is met with wickedness.

48. A friend who speaks sweet words in our presence and spoils our work behind our back should be avoided. Avoid an enemy using foul means.

49. Even a good man perishes by his association with the wicked. Even a clear water is rendered muddy by its mixing up with dust.

50. He whose wealth is dedicated to the brahmins enjoys well. Hence, a brahmin shall be honoured by all means.

51. Food taken in, after brahmins have been fed, is the real food; he is intelligent who commits no sin; that is friendship which manifests itself behind our back; that is the real sacred rite which is performed without ostentation.

52. That is no assembly where the aged are not present; they are not the aged who do not expound virtue; that is not virtue which is not backed by truth; that is no truth which is mixed with deception.

53. The best among men is the brahmin; the best among luminaries is the sun; the best among the organs is the head and the best among the sacred rites is the truth.

54. That is auspicious where mind is delighted; that is a real life which does not involve service and slavery; that is the real earning which is shared and enjoyed with one's own kith and kin and that is the real thunder which is made in the battle in the presence of the enemy.

55. She is the real woman who has no vanity; He is really happy who has shunned vain desires; He is the real friend in whom confidence can be placed and he is the real man who has controlled his organs of sense.

56. One should cast off honour and love where love is extinct; Only that is praiseworthy the core of which is held in esteem.

57. No attempt should be made to trace the origin of rivers, Agnihotra worshippers and the family of Bharata. Such an attempt is bound to fail.

58. Rivers end with the sea of salt-water; sexual intercourse ends with the treachery of the woman; back-biting ends

with the news being made public and wealth comes to an end with misery.

59. The prosperity of a kingdom comes to an end with the curse of a brahmin; the spiritual power of a brahmin comes to an end with his sin; all decency in conduct of life comes to an end if residençe is taken near cowsheds; the family is ruined if women rule.

60. All hoarded things end in wastage, rising in power comes to an end in downfall; all contacts and intimacies come to an end in separation and disintegration; life comes to an end with death.

61. If one wishes the return of the guest he shall not be followed very far at the time of farewell. He can be followed upto a pond or well or a tree with plenty of shade and colourful leaves.

62. One shall not reside in a land where there is no leader or where there are many leaders or where the leadership is vested in a woman or in a child.

63. The father protects her in childhood; the husband in youth and the son in old age. A woman is not to be allowed to stay independently.

64. A barren woman shall be abandoned in the eighth year after marriage; a woman whose children die in infancy shall be abandoned in the ninth year; a woman who gives birth only to daughters shall be abandoned in the eleventh year; and a woman who speaks unpleasant words shall be abandoned immediately.

65. Three persons beyond the pale of money stick to their lords. One who is not in want; one who is afraid of men; one who is afraid of servants.

66. An intelligent man must keep aloof from these :—the exhausted horse, the elephant in its rut, cows in their first parturition, and frogs outside water.

67. Those who are mad after money do not have friends or kinsmen; those who are lustful and lecherous know no fear or shame; those who are worried with anxious thoughts have no pleasure or sleep and those who are oppressed by hunger do not want even salt or warmth in the food.

68. How can these have peaceful sleep?—the poor, the slave, the man fond of another man's wife and the wretch who wants to rob another man of his wealth.

69. Blissfully sleeps the man who has no debts to repay and who is free from sickness. He who is not yet married, takes his food leisurely.

70. The height of a lotus is in proportion to the quantity of water in the pond; a servant becomes proud if his master is strong and influential.

71. The sun and Varuṇa (water) befriend the lotus when it stands firm in its place; they make it fade and putrefy if it is uprooted.

72. Those who had been friends of a man in high office become enemies when he steps down from the office. The sun delightfully causes the bloom of the lotus in water but when it is plucked and put on the ground the sun dries it up.

73. Things in their proper places and persons in their respective offices are honoured. Away from their original places neither hair nor the nails, neither the teeth nor men shine or receive consideration.

74. Manners and behaviour indicate parentage; manner of speech and accent indicates the native place; flutter up indicates affection and the physical build indicates the diet accustomed to.

75. A downpour in the ocean is unnecessary; feeding an over-fed and satiated man is superfluous; a charity made over to an affluent man is unnecessary and the meritorious actions of a base man are futile.

76. Even a person who is far off is as good as near if he has a place in the heart; if cast out of the heart a man close at hand is no better than one far off.

77. Contortions in the face, low sunk husky voice, perspiration all over the body and a frightened appearance—these are the signs usually seen at the time of death and in regard to a man out to beg.

78. The life of a worm in the person of the beggar or that of one blown by the wind over his head is better than the life of beggar himself.

79. The lord of the world Viṣṇu himself when he begged suffered dimunition of stature. Who is there superior to him who can be a suppliant and yet not suffer disrespect.

80. The parents by whom children are not educated are no better than enemies. The uneducated can never shine in an assembly of the learned like cranes amidst swans.

81. Learning gives beauty to the ugly; it is a well protected asset; it makes man a saint; it makes him popular; it is revered of the revered; it dispels the sorrow of kinsmen; it is a deity; even kings honour it; a man devoid of learning is no better than a beast.

82-83. Inside the house there are many things which can be taken away by others but not learning. Lord Viṣṇu expounded the essence of polity to Śaunaka, as well as all sacred rites. Lord Śiva heard this. Vyāsa heard from Śiva and we heard it from Vyāsa.

CHAPTER ONE HUNDRED AND SIXTEEN

Sacred Rites (*Vratas*)

Brahmā said :

1. O Vyāsa, I shall expound the sacred rites by which Lord Viṣṇu should be propitiated and which bestow everything. Lord Viṣṇu can be worshipped in any month or day of the lunar fortnight or the week or when any star is ascendant.

2. The devotee fasts completely or takes a single meal at night or mere fruits. With a desire for the birth of a son, victory in battle and acquisition of a kingdom he shall make charitable gifts of cash or foodgrains.

3-4. Vaiśvānara and Kubera worshipped on the first day of the lunar fortnight bestow wealth. If Brahmā is worshipped on the first day of the lunar fortnight after a full fast he bestows wealth and mares. Yama, Nārāyaṇa and goddess Lakṣmī worshipped on the second day bestow wealth. The three deities Gaurī, Vighneśa (*Gaṇeśa*) and Śaṅkara should be worshipped on the third day.

5. Lord Caturvyūha (*Viṣṇu*) worshipped on the fourth day, Lord Viṣṇuw orshipped on the fifth day, Lord Kārttikeya and Lord Sun worshipped on the sixth day, and Bhāskara[1] on the seventh day—all these bestow wealth.

6. Goddess Durgā shall be worshipped on the eighth day. The seven Mothers and the eight quarters worshipped on the ninth day bestow wealth. Yama and the Moon shall be worshipped on the tenth day and the sages shall be worshipped on the eleventh day.

7. Lord Hari shall be worshipped on the twelfth day and Cupid on the thirteenth day; Maheśvara[2] on the fourteenth day and Brahmā and the Pitṛs (Manes) worshipped on the fifteenth day bestow wealth.

8. The presiding deities of the days of the week, Sun and others, shall be worshipped on the new moon day. The presiding deities of the stars and Yogas worshipped shall bestow everything.

CHAPTER ONE HUNDRED AND SEVENTEEN

Sacred Rites (Vratas)

Brahmā said :

1-2. In the month of Mārgaśīrṣa (Oct-Nov.) on the thirteenth day of the bright half, which is called Anaṅga Trayodaśī, Lord Śiva shall be worshipped with Dhattūra[3] flowers and tooth pick twigs of the tree Mallikā,[4] with the Naivedya (food offering) of honey saying that it is for the Cupid. In the month Pauṣa, Yogeśvara should be worshipped with the Bilva flowers; the Kadamba[5] twig is the tooth pick; sandal paste and

1. The sun.
2. Śiva.
3. Perhaps the same as *dhattūra*—datūra, *GVDB*, p. 214.
4. Jasminum sambac.
5. Anthocephalus indicus

Naivedya of Śaṣkuli (rice dough fried in ghee or oil) should be given.

3. In the month of Māgha (Dec-Jan.) Lord Naṭeśvara[1] should be worshipped with Kunda flowers and necklace of pearls. The tooth pick is of Plakṣa tree and the Naivedya, O sage, is fried pancake.

4. In the month of Phālguna (Jan-Feb.) Lord Vīreśvara[2] should be worshipped with Marūvaka[3] flowers. The Naivedya consists of sugar candy, vegetables and rice gruel. The tooth pick is of mango[4] tree.

5. In the month of Caitra (Feb-Mar.) Lord Surūpa[5] shall be worshipped. Flowers of Karpūra[6] plant shall be taken if no fast is undertaken. The tooth pick is of Vaṭa tree and Naivedya is Śaṣkulī (rice dough fried in ghee or oil).

6-8. In the month of Vaiśākha (Mar-April) Lord Śambhu is worshipped with Aśoka[7] flowers and Modakas and the Naivedya of cooked rice with jaggery is offered to Mahārūpa. Jātīphala (nutmeg) too should be offered and the tooth pick is of Udumbara tree. In the month of Jyeṣṭha (Apr-May) Pradyumna should be worshipped with Campaka[8] flowers and Lavaṅga[9] (clove) offered. The tooth pick should be of Bilva twigs. In the month of Āṣāḍha lord Umā-Bhadra should be worshipped with Apāmārga[10] flowers. The tooth pick is of Aguru tree.

9. In the month of Śrāvaṇa (June-July) Lord Śambhu with the trident in his hand should be worshipped with

1. Śiva.
2. Śiva.
3. Perhaps the same as Phaṇijjhaka—Ocimum basilicum. But identity is not certain. (*GVDB*, p. 266).
4. Mangifera indica.
5. Śiva.
6. Either Cinnamomum camphora or D. aromatica, *GVDB*, p. 82.
7. Saraca indica.
8. Michelia champaka.
9. Syzygium aromaticum.
10. Achyranthes aspera.

Karavīra[1] flowers. Fragrant pastes and seat are offered. The Naivedya is ghee, etc. and the tooth pick is of Karavīra tree.

10-12. In the month of Bhādrapada (July-Aug.) lord Sadyojāta[2] should be worshipped with Bakula[3] flowers. Pūpaka (cake) is the naivedya. In the month of Āśvina (Aug-Sep.) the gandharva lord Madanaja and Indra, the lord of the deities should be worshipped in water in a gold pot, with the offerings of Modaka. The tooth pick is of Khadira[3] tree (catechu). In the month of Kārttika (Sep-Oct.) Rudra should be worshipped. The tooth pick should be of Badari[4] tree. The devotee should either fast or take one tenth of the usual food. At the end of the year he should worship Śiva with lotuses offering milk and vegetables as naivedya.

13. Lord Anaṅga accompanied by Rati should be worshipped on a golden throne. Gingelly seeds and rice grains should be offered in the fire ten thousand times.

14. He should keep awake in the night in singing songs or playing on instruments. In the morning worship should again be performed. Bed, vessels, cloth, umbrella and shoes should be given to brahmins.

15. He should feed cows and brahmins with devotion. He should be delighted. This is the concluding rite for all Vratas. The fruit of all these Vratas is prosperity, health, and good fortune.

1. Nerium indicum.
2. Śiva.
3. Mimusops elengi.
4. Zizyphus jujuba.

CHAPTER ONE HUNDRED AND EIGHTEEN

Sacred Rites (Vratas)

Brahmā said :

1-2. I shall expound Akhaṇḍa-Dvādaśī-Vrata that yields salvation: quelling of all evils. In the bright half of the month of Mārgaśīrṣa the devotee should fast on the eleventh day taking in only Pañcagavya. On the twelfth day he should worship Lord Viṣṇu. For four consecutive months he shall give vessels containing the five kinds of food grains to a brahmin and say :—

3-5. "Whatever, O noble sir, I have done in seven previous births shall, by your grace, be unsevered. Just as the entire universe is one complete whole, let all the vratas performed by me be one whole. You are Puruṣottama himself." In the four months from Caitra he should give vessels of flour and in the four months from Śrāvaṇa he shall give vessels of butter. The devotee who performs this Vrata would obtain good wife, sons and attain heaven after death.

CHAPTER ONE HUNDRED AND NINETEEN

Sacred Rites (Vratas)

Brahmā said :

1-2. I should now expound Agastyārghya Vrata which yields worldly enjoyment and salvation. Three days before the transit of the Sun to Kanyārāśi (Virgo), an image of the sage should be made with Kāśa[1] flowers in a vessel and Arghya shall be offered after duly worshipping it. The devotee should keep awake in the night.

3-4. The worship should be with curd, rice grains, flowers and fruits too. The pot should be painted in five colours. It may be of gold or silver. It should contain seven types of

1. Saccharum Spontaneum

grains. It should be smeared with curd and sandal paste. While giving "Arghya" the mantra "Agastyaḥ Khanamānaḥ" etc. shall be recited.

5. While worshipping, the devotee should say :— "O sage Agastya ! obeisance unto thee. Thou art the son of Mitra and Varuṇa. Thou art born of Fire and Wind. Thou art like the Kāśa flower."

6. Śūdras and women should use only this mantra for offering grains, fruits and juice. The devotee shall give the vessel to a brahmin with dakṣiṇās and feed brahmins. By doing so for seven years he will get every thing he wants.

CHAPTER ONE HUNDRED AND TWENTY

Sacred Rites (Vratas)

Brahmā said :

1-2. I shall now expound Rambhā-Tṛtīyā-Vrata that yields good fortune, wealth and sons. In the month of Mārgaśīrṣa, on the third day in the bright half, the devotee should worship Gaurī with the leaves of Bilva after duly fasting. He should wash his hands with water from Kuśa grass. The tooth pick should be of the Kadamba twig. In the same way in the month of Pauṣa he should worship Girisutā[1] with Maruvaka flowers.

3-4. He should take in only the leaves of Karpūra plant. He should offer Kṛśaras (balls of gingelly seeds in treacle). The tooth pick should be of Mallikā twig. In the month of Māgha, the devotee should worship Subhadrā with Kalhāra flowers. He should take only butter. Maṇḍaka should be offered. The tooth pick should be Gītīmaya ? In the month of Phālguna, Gomatī shall be worshipped. The tooth pick should be of Kunda twigs. He should offer Śaṣkulīs and take only just a little food to keep him active.

1. Pārvatī, the daughter of Himālaya.

5. In the month of Caitra, the devotee should take only Curd. "Viśālākṣī should be worshipped with Madanaka flowers offering Kṛśaras. The tooth pick shall be of Tagara twig. In the month of Vaiśākha, Śrīmukhī should be worshipped with Karṇikāra flowers. The tooth pick is of Aśoka twigs and the devotee should take only Aśoka leaves.

6. In the month of Jyeṣṭha, Nārāyaṇī should be worshipped with lotus flowers. Sugar candy should be offered. He should take in only clove. In the month of Āṣāḍha, Mādhavī should be worshipped.

7. The devotee should take only gingelly seeds. The worship should be performed with Bilva leaves. He should offer milk pudding and Vaṭakas (fried pies). The tooth pick shall be either Udumbara twigs or Tagarī. Goddess Śrī should be worshipped in Śrāvaṇa.

8. The tooth pick should be of Mallikā and milk offerings should be made. In the month of Bhādrapada, Uttamā should be worshipped with lotuses. Offerings are jaggery, etc. The devotee should take in Śṛṅgada (aloe wood).

9. In the month of Āśvina, the goddess Rājaputrī should be worshipped with Japā flowers (China rose), the devotee taking only Jīraka in the night. The Naivedya is Kṛśara.

10. In the month of Kārttika, the goddess Padmajā should be worshipped with Jātī flowers. He shall take only Pañcagavya. At the end of the year, he should worship Brahmin couples. He himself should take butter and cooked rice.

11. After worshipping Umāmaheśvara jaggery should be given along with cloth, umbrella, gold, etc. He should keep awake the whole of the night engaged in singing. In the morning he should give cows, etc. The devotee would get everything.

CHAPTER ONE HUNDRED AND TWENTYONE

Sacred Rites (Vratas)

Brahmā said :

1. I shall now mention the Cāturmāsya Vratas These rites can be taken either on the eleventh day or on Full moon day, in the month of Āṣāḍha. The devotee should pray thus at the outset.

2-3. "O Keśava, I have taken up this Vrata before you. If you are pleased may, it be completed without hindrances. Having taken up this rite if I die before completing the same, O Lord, may it be treated as completed through your grace."

4. One should take up the Vrata, Arcana, Japa, etc after praying at the outset like this. The sins of those who even desire to perform Lord Hari's Vrata perish entirely.

5. He who takes his bath daily and worships Viṣṇu continuously for four months taking a single meal every day attains the region of Viṣṇu, free from impurities.

6. The devotee should abstain from taking wine, meat and oil bath and perform the worship of Hari. He should continue his study of Vedas and perform the Kṛcchra rite. He will attain the region of Viṣṇu and become Viṣṇu himself.

7. By fasting for a night the devotee becomes a deity moving about in aerial car. By fasting for three nights or taking only a sixth of his usual diet he attains Śvetadvīpa.

8. A devotee who performs Cāndrāyaṇa attains the region of Hari. He who performs Prājāpatya attains salvation unsolicited. He who performs Parākavrata attains Viṣṇuloka and becomes Hari Himself.

9. The devotee should sustain himself on grain flour, barley, alms, milk, curd, ghee, cow's urine and Pañcagavya; he should avoid vegetables, roots, fruits and juice. He will thus attain Viṣṇu.

CHAPTER ONE HUNDRED AND TWENTYTWO

Sacred Rites (Vratas)

Brahmā said :

1. I shall now mention the Vrata Māsopavāsa that lasts for a month and is the most excellent of all Vratas. This fast for a month should be undertaken by an ascetic in his Vānaprastha stage of life or by an elderly lady.

2. The devotee should inaugurate the fast for a month on the eleventh day in the bright half of the month of Āśvina.

3-4. He should first pray like this :—"From this day onwards O Viṣṇu, I shall worship Thee for thirty days without taking food till Utthāna Dvādaśī" (the day of rising up) in the month of Kārttika. May not there be any sin of cutting Vrata if I were to die in the midst of the bright twelfths of Āśvina and Kārttika."

5-7. Taking three baths every day, the devotee shall worship Hari with sweet scents. He should refrain from taking oil bath and not smear his body with sweet scents within the precincts of the temple. The fasting devotee shall perform the worship on the twelfth day, feed the brahmins and then do the Pāraṇā (taking of food). If in the course of Vrata he falls unconscious he can drink milk. This Vrata is not spoiled by drinking milk. He will enjoy worldly pleasures and salvation.

CHAPTER ONE HUNDRED AND TWENTYTHREE

Sacred Rites (Vratas)

Brahmā said :

1. I shall mention some Vratas in the month of Kārttika. The devotee should worship Viṣṇu after bathing. He should take a single meal a day in the night or live on alms for a whole month.

2. He should take milk, vegetables and fruits or take

fast. Freed from his sin he should attain everyone of his desires and attain Hari.

3. Hari's Vrata is always excellent. In Dakṣiṇāyana it is still more excellent. In the Cāturmāsya the excellence is heightened further and the Bhīṣmapañcaka in the month of Kārttika is better still.

4. Hence, this excellent Vrata should be performed on the eleventh day in the bright half. He shall take three baths. Lord Hari, and the manes should be worshipped with barley grains.

5. While worshipping he should be silent. The idol should be bathed with butter Pañcagavya and water and smeared with camphor.

6-7. During the five days of Vrata, the devotee should burn incense sticks with ghee-smeared Guggulu. The Naivedya is sweet rice porridge. He should recite 'Om obeisance to Vāsudeva' one hundred and eight times and with this same eight-syllabled mantra ending with Svāhā he shall perform Homa with butter, rice grains and gingelly seeds.

8-10. On the first day of the Vrata he should worship Hari's feet with lotus flowers; on the second day he should worship the knees with Bilva leaves; on the third day the navel with scents; on the fourth day the shoulders with water from Bilva leaves and on the fifth day he should worship the head with Mālatī flowers. During these days he should sleep only on the bare ground. The five constituents of Pañcagavya should be taken in order on each day thus:—first day cowdung; second day urine, third day milk, fourth day curd and on the fifth day all five ones. On the night of the fifteenth day (Full Moon) the Vrata shall conclude. He who performs this Vrata attains to worldly pleasures and salvation.

11. Fasting on Ekādaśī days (eleventh day) in both halves of the month shall be observed. It removes all sins and wards off hell—nay it enables one to attain Viṣṇuloka and gives everything desired.

12-13. For authentic fasts, the eleventh and twelfth phases of the moon should cover the full day from sunrise to sunset and the thirteenth phase should be at sunrise. The Pāraṇā should be on the twelfth day. This Vrata can be performed even when there is impurity due to birth or death. If the eleventh phase covers the whole day from sunrise to sunset Lord Hari is present. If part of the day is covered by the tenth phase and part by the eleventh phase, demons permeate that. Fasts shall not be undertaken then.

14. O sage, if the Full moon or New moon phase is mixed with either the fourteenth or the first phase, fast shall be undertaken.

15. Similarly, fast can be undertaken when the third fourth, fifth or the sixth phase gets mixed with each other in the course of the day.

CHAPTER ONE HUNDRED AND TWENTYFOUR

Sacred Rites (Vratas)

Brahmā said :

1. I shall now mention the "Śivarātri-Vrata', and the story connected with the same that yields everything one desires. Goddess Gaurī was told this Vrata by Śiva when she asked him about it.

Īśvara said :

2. The fourteenth phase of the moon in the dark half between the months of Māgha and Phālguna is the day fixed for this Vrata. The devotee shall keep awake for the whole night and worship Lord Rudra. He should attain worldly pleasures and salvation.

3. Lord Śiva should be worshipped in the company of Lord Cupid just as Lord Keśava is worshipped on Dvādaśī days. If after fast, the lord is worshipped he will enable the devotee to cross the Hell.

4. Once Sundara Senaka, the sinful king of Niṣādas went ahunting into a forest along with his dogs.

5. He was unable to bag any game. He became exhausted due to hunger and thirst. He took rest in a bower on the

banks of the lake on a mountain, but could not get even a wink of sleep.

6. In his attempt to balance himself on the tree he let fall a few leaves from the tree on a Liṅga (the phallic emblem of Śiva) at the foot of the tree but he was not aware of the same.

7-8. An arrow fell from his quiver. He jumped down to retrieve it. In his search for the arrow he crawled up to the liṅga and touched it. To wash himself of the dust he brought some water, a few drops of which fell on the liṅga too. Thus all the items in a worship—bathing, worshipping with leaves, prostration and touching the liṅga and keeping awake—had been performed unconsciously.

9. In the morning he returned home and had his food brought by his wife. After some time when he died he was dragged by the soldiers of Yama with a noose.

10. Then my followers fought with them and released him. Thus purified along with his faithful dog of that day he became one of my attendants (Gaṇas).

11. Thus, even without knowing he got the fruits of worship. He who knowingly performs worship will derive everlasting benefit. The devotee shall first worship Śiva on the thirteenth day and pray thus :

12-13. "O God, I shall keep awake on the Caturdaśī night. The worship, charitable gift, penance and Homa shall be performed according to my ability. O Śambhu after fasting for the whole of Caturdaśī (fourteenth) I shall take food only the next day. O Lord, be my refuge and accord me worldly pleasures and salvation."

14. After bathing the liṅga with Pañcagavya and water, at the close of worship, the devotee should approach his preceptor and worship Lord Śiva again with the mantra "Om obeisance, obeisance to Śiva" and offer scents.

15. Then he should perform Homa with gingelly seeds, rice and other grains as well as butter. After Pūrṇāhuti he should listen to songs of prayer and mythological stories.

16. The worship should again be performed at midnight and at the end of third and fourth Yāmas. The concluding

rites should be performed in the morning with the Mūlamantra.

17-19. "O Lord, with your favour I have concluded the rites unhindered. O lord of the universe, forgive me. O lord of the three worlds, O Hara, the merit that I derived today due to the naivedya offering to the lord Rudra is immense. O Lord with thy grace the Vrata has been concluded. O Lord, be pleased. Return to Thy region. I have become purified by "Thy holy sight." The devotee should feed brahmins stable in their contemplation and give clothes, umbrella, etc, to them.

20-21. "O Lord of gods, lord of goblins, the blesser of the world, what I have offered out of faith be delightfully received by Thee", saying this he shall conclude the final rites. If the devotee does this for twelve years he will attain glory, fortune, children, realm as well as Śiva's region.

22-23. This rite can be performed in twelve months by keeping awake at night. He should feed twelve brahmins and make gift of lamps to them. He will attain heaven hereafter.

CHAPTER ONE HUNDRED AND TWENTYFIVE

Sacred Rites (Vratas)

Brahmā said :

1. Māndhātṛ became an emperor by fasting on Ekādaśi days. In both halves of the month none shall take anything on the eleventh day.

2. Gāndhārī fasted on a day when the tenth and eleventh phases of the moon were mixed. Her hundred sons perished. Hence such days shall be avoided for fasting purposes.

3-4. Where the tenth and eleventh phases of the moon are on separate full days, Lord Hari is present there. When there is any doubt about the mixture of Daśamī and Ekādaśī the fast shall be undertaken where the mixture of Ekādaśī and Dvādaśī is present and the Pāraṇā shall be had on Trayodaśī (the thirteenth day).

5. Where Ekādaśī, Dvādaśī and Trayodaśī are mixed, that is a very auspicious occasion.

6. O Brahmin, thus fast can be undertaken when there is full Ekādaśī, or mixture of Ekādaśī and Dvādaśī or mixture of the three but never on the day when there is mixture of the tenth with the eleventh day.

7. King Rukmāṅgada undertook fast on two Ekādaśī days, kept awake during the night listening to Purāṇas and worshipping Gadādhara. He attained Salvation. Others too have attained salvation by undertaking Ekādaśī Vrata.

CHAPTER ONE HUNDRED AND TWENTYSIX

Sacred Rites (Vratas)

Brahmā said :

1. I shall now explain a means of worship by which people attain salvation and which yields worldly enjoyment and salvation together.

2. The usual mystical diagram shall be drawn and Dhātṛ shall be placed at the entrance. So also Vidhātṛ, Gaṅgā, Yamunā and Mahānadī shall be placed at other entrances.

3. Dvāraśrī, Daṇḍa, Pracaṇḍa and Vāstupuruṣa shall be placed at other entrances. In the middle the Ādhāraśakti (the supporting power), Kūrma (the tortoise) and Ananta (Lord Viṣṇu's serpent bed) should be worshipped.

4-6. In the corners the earth, virtue, knowledge, renunciation, prosperity, the four i.e. Adharma, Ajñāna, Avairāgya and Anaiśvarya (opposite of the foregoing four) Kandanāla (the inner stalk) lotus, the petals, Sattva, Rajas, Tamas, the spheres sun, etc., Vimalā and other Śaktis, Durgā, the attendants, Sarasvatī and Kṣetrapāla should be worshipped. The seats should be worshipped and then the idol, Vāsudeva and Bala and Smara should be worshipped.

7-8. Aniruddha and Mahātmā Nārāyaṇa should be worshipped. The limbs, hearts, etc., Śaṅkha and other weapons, Śrī, Puṣṭi, Garuḍa, the preceptor and the preceptor's preceptor should be worshipped. In the quarters Indra and others (fire, etc.) should be worshipped. The Nāga (serpent) should be worshipped below and Brahmā above.

9-10. The worship of Viṣvaksena is in the north-east. The above worship is narrated in the Vedas. He who worships like this even for once duly, has no re-birth in the world. Worship of Puṇḍarīka, Brahmā and Gadādhara is also necessary.

CHAPTER ONE HUNDRED AND TWENTYSEVEN

Sacred Rites (Vratas)

Brahmā said :

1. Bhīma undertook fast for a day on the eleventh day of the bright half of the month of Māgha, when there was the star Hasta too present.

2. After performing this wonderful Vrata he became free from the indebtedness to the Manes. This Bhīmadvādaśī is very famous and makes the merit of every one flourish.

3. Even when the Hasta star is not conjoined with the Ekādaśī, the fast undertaken is so powerful as to remove the sin of slaying a brahmin. It removes all great sins like the bad king destroying his own realm.

4-8. A bad son destroys his family; a bad wife destroys her husband; virtue destroys evil; a bad minister destroys his king; ignorance destroys knowledge, purity destroys impurity, lack of faith destroys Śrāddha; untruths destroy Truth; the heat destroys the effect of snow; hoarded wealth destroys illness, boasting destroys the merit of charity; haughtiness destroys the power of penance; absence of education spoils a boy; too much of walking destroys cattle; anger destroys mental peace, absence of means to increase it spoils wealth; knowledge destroys ignorance and absence of desire and attachment spoils the fruit. This auspicious Vrata is recommended for the destruction of all sins.

9-11. The sins of slaying a brahmin, drinking wine,

stealing gold, illicit intercourse with preceptor's wife acquired simultaneously cannot be wiped off even if one makes pilgrimage to Puṣkara three times (but this Vrata wipes them off). Neither Naimiṣa, Kurukṣetra, Prabhāsa nor Kālindī, Yamunā, Gaṅgā, Sarasvatī nor any of the other holy rivers, can equal this Ekādaśī. Nor charitable gifts nor japa, nor homa nor any other sacred rite can equal this Ekādaśī.

12. If on one pan the merit of making a gift of the whole world is placed and on the other pan the merit of this Vrata the latter alone will be found excellent.

13-14. A golden image of the Boar incarnation of the Lord should be placed in a copper vessel over another vessel. All grain seeds should be placed in it and the vessel shall be covered with a white cloth. With gold (for Dakṣiṇā) lamp, etc. the worship should be performed duly.

15-17. With the mantras specified the respective limbs should be worshipped duly :

Mantra	*Limbs*
Obeisance to Varāha	two feet
Obeisance to Kroḍākṛti	hip
Obeisance to Gabhīraghoṣa	navel
Obeisance to Śrīvatsadhārin	chest
Obeisance to Sahasraśiras	arms
Obeisance to Sarveśvara	neck
Obeisance to Sarvātman	face
Obeisance to Prabhava	forehead
Obeisance to Śatamayūkha	hair

After worshipping duly, the devotee shall keep awake during the night.

18. He should listen to the Purāṇas illustrating the greatness of the lord. In the morning gifts should be given to brahmins and beggars of auspicious nature.

19. Cloth bordered with gold should be given to brahmins. Meals at the completion of the Vrata should then be had but not upto satiety.

20. Even if the devotee does this only once he will not be born again to be suckled at the breasts of a mother. By fasting on Ekādaśī days the devotee is freed from the three debts. He will get everything he desires by this Vrata.

CHAPTER ONE HUNDRED AND TWENTYEIGHT

Sacred Rites (Vratas)

Brahmā said :

1. O Vyāsa I shall mention the rules governing all Vratas by which Lord Hari will be pleased and bestow everything. A Vrata should be performed together with the observation of Niyamas (restraints) mentioned in the scriptures. A Vrata is a form of penance.

2. Yamas (self-restraints) along with Niyamas (External restraints) should be equally observed. He should take three baths every day and lie on the bare ground. He should have perfect control on his sense-organs.

3. He should not speak to women, Śūdras and degraded persons. He should make offering into fire of five sacred articles to the extent of his monetary capacity.

4. Kṛcchra type of Vratas should be performed for mere merit. If the devotee wants preservation of wealth (and similar things) the Vrata should be performed twice.

5. Persons observing fasts should not drink water out of a bell-metal vessel. During other Vratas he should abstain from taking black grain, Masūr Dāla, Bengal grain, and grains of Koradūṣaka variety ; he should avoid vegetables, honey and other's food.

6. Wearing flower garlands, ornaments and gaudy clothes, smearing of scented unguents, washing the teeth and applying Collyrium spoil the fast.

7. Before starting Vrata he should wash his teeth and take in Pañcagavya in the morning. Constant drinking of water, chewing betel leaves, sleeping during the day, gambling and sexual intercourse spoil a Vrata.

8-9. In all Vratas ten virtuous practices should be followed, viz:—forbearance, truthfulness, sympathy, charity, purity control over the sense-organs, worship of gods, sacrificial offering into the fire, contentment and non-stealing.

10-12. Night-meal means taking food after seeing the stars. When a person performs a Brahmakṛcchra Vrata the Pañcagavya is constituted thus:—One pala of cow's urine is taken and consecrated by Gāyatrī, Cowdung of half the size of the thumb and consecrated by the mantra Gandha[1] etc; One pala of ghee consecrated by the mantra "Tejosi"[2] etc; seven palas of milk consecrated by the mantra "Āpyāyasva"[3] etc; three palas of curd consecrated by the mantra "Dadhikrāvṇo"[4] etc; one pala of Kuśa water consecrated by the mantra "Devasya"[5] etc.

13. During Malamāsa or the intercalary month many auspicious rites are not performed e.g. Agnyādhāna (the first kindling of the sacrificial fire); installation of idols, sacrifices, charities, Vratas, Vedic rites, Vṛṣotsarga (setting free of a bull) rites, tonsure ceremony, investiture with the sacred thread, marriages and crowning of kings.

14-17. Sāvana calculation of month consists of thirty days from one New moon to another. Saura calculation of a month is based on the transit of the sun from one zodiac sign to the next. A stellar month consists of twenty seven days. Saura month is taken for the celebration of marriages. For sacrifices etc. Sāvana calculation is followed. Two phases of the moon on the same day are very auspicious such as—second and third; third and fourth and fourth and fifth; sixth and seventh, eighth and ninth; eleventh and twelfth; fourteenth and the full moon and the New moon with the first. The conjunction of Tithis other than these is very frightful destroying all previous merits.

18. When a woman after starting a Vrata menstruates, the Vrata need not be stopped; all physical activities she can continue but charity, etc. shall be performed through proxies.

19. If there is a cessation of a Vrata in the middle due to anger, greed or mistakes, the devotee should observe fast for three days and completely tonsure the head.

20. If there is physical incapacity due to illness the devotee should ask his son to continue the Vrata. If a brahmin becomes unconscious during the Vrata, he can be allowed to drink water.

1. ṚVKh. 5.87.9.
2. AV. 7.89.4.
3. ṚV. 1.91.16.
4. ṚV. 4.39.6.
5. VS. 1.24.

CHAPTER ONE HUNDRED AND TWENTYNINE

Sacred Rites (Vratas)

Brahmā said :

1. I shall mention the Vratas for Pratipad and other days, O Vyāsa. This is called Śikhivrata. He should take one meal on the first day. At the close, he should make a gift of a brown cow. He would attain Vaiśvānara region.

2. This can be performed in the beginning of Caitra too with due worship of Brahmā, due offerings of fragrant flowers, garlands and homas into the fire. The devotee shall attain all desires.

3. A person desirous of beauty shall perform the Vrata on the eighth day of the bright half of the Kārttika month wearing flower garlands and offering flowers, etc. He shall be endowed with beauty.

4-6. Lord Śrīdhara with Śrī shall be worshipped on the third day in the dark half of Śrāvaṇa. Bed, clothes and fruits shall be gifted to Brahmins. When giving bed he shall pray "Obeisance to Śrīdhara and Śrī. In the beginning of Caitra on the third day the devotee shall worship Umā, Śiva and fire god. The naivedya offered shall be Haviṣya (cooked rice soaked in butter) along with Madanaka. He shall reap the fruit as mentioned by Umā to me.

7-8. A three days abstention from salt from the first to the third day in the beginning of Phālguna is a bliss yielding excellent Vrata and the devotee shall attain Gaurīloka. At the end of the Vrata he shall duly worship a brahmin couple and make a gift of a bed and a house with all requisites, saying, "O Bhavāni (Goddess Pārvatī) be pleased".

9-10. The twelve manifestations of the goddess, viz:— Gaurī, Kālī, Umā, Bhadrā, Durgā, Kānti, Sarasvatī, Maṅgalā, Vaiṣṇavī, Lakṣmī, Śivā and Nārāyaṇī shall be worshipped either on twelve successive days from the third day of Mārgaśīrṣa month or in twelve successive months from the said day (taking the third day in every month for the Vrata). He shall never suffer from separation from his beloved.

11. The devotee shall observe fast on the fourth day in the bright half of the month of Māgha and take up the Vrata.

He shall gift away gingelly seeds to a brahmin and shall drink only gingelly water. The Vrata is concluded in two years. He will not be hindered by obstacles in his life.

12-14. The Mūlamantra is "Oṁ Gaḥ Svāhā". The Nyāsa mantra for the heart is Glaum Glām. The nyāsa mantras for head and tuft are "Gāṁ Gīṁ Gūm and Hrūṁ Hrīṁ Hrīm" the nyāsa for Varman is "Gūṁ" "Gom" and for the eye "Gaum" and "Gom". Hence Āvāhana, etc. The oblation and Visarjana (mystical dismissal) are with the mantras "Āgaccholkāya Gandholkaḥ Puṣpolko Dhūpakolkakaḥ Dīpolkāya Maholkāya". The Nyāsa on the thumb etc. is with "Gāyatrī".

15. The Gāyatrī mantra runs thus :—"Om, we realise the huge-eared deity, we meditate upon the deity with bent trunk. May the deity with the tusk goad us (on our path)".

16. Gingelly seeds shall be consigned to the sacrificial fire in the Homa. All his attendant Gaṇas shall be worshipped: "Svāhā unto the Gaṇa and to the lord of Gaṇas. Obeisance to Kūṣmāṇḍaka.

17. Obeisance to Amogholka, obeisance to Ekadanta and obeisance to Tripurāntakarūpin". Om obeisance to the deity with dark tusks and terrific face, the lord of battles.

18. Svāhā unto Padmadaṁṣṭra. The usual Mudrās (mystical signs) are shown. The devotee then dances, laughs and claps his hands. The fruit of this Vrata is Saubhāgya (good fortune).

19. Beginning with the fourth day in the bright half of Mārgaśīrṣa this worship of Gaṇas shall be continued for a year. The devotee shall be blessed with good learning, wealth, fame, longevity and sons.

20. On a Monday when the fourth phase of the moon is also present, Gaṇas can be worshipped after due fast with the usual japas and homas. The devotee shall attain heaven without obstacles.

21. God Vighneśvara shall be worshipped on the fourth day in the bright half of any month with sugar candies, Laḍḍukas (sweet balls of fried flour dough) and sweet meats. He shall attain everything he desires and good fortune.

22. If the worship is done with Madana flowers he

will be blessed with sons. The Caturthī is also called "Madana Caturthī". With the mantras "Om obeisance to Gaṇapati,"

23-24. All the Gaṇas shall be worshipped in any month with homas and japas. He shall attain everything he desires. All obstacles will be destroyed. He who worships Vināyaka in his idol with these names attains the goal of the good, heaven, happiness and final salvation.

25-26. The names are twelve :—Gaṇapūjya (worthy of the worship of the group), Ekadantin (single-tusked), Vakratuṇḍa (Bent Trunk), Tryambaka (Three-eyed), Nīlagrīva (blue-necked), Lambodara (large-bellied), Vikaṭa (the terrific), Vighnarājaka the remover of obstacles), Dhūmravarṇa (smoke-coloured) Bālacandra (pleasing as the crescent moon) Vināyaka, Gaṇapati and Hastimukha (Elephant-faced). The devotee shall attain everything he desires.

27-29. The serpent gods Vāsuki, Takṣaka, Kāliya, Maṇibhadraka, Airāvata, Dhṛtarāṣṭra, Karkoṭaka and Dhanañjaya shall be worshipped after bathing the idols in Ghee on the fifth day in any of the months Śrāvaṇa, Āśvina, Bhādra and Kārttika. The devotee shall be blessed with longevity, health and heavenly bliss.

30-31. The serpents Ananta, Vāsuki, Śaṅkha, Padma, Kambala, Karkoṭaka, Nāga, Dhṛtarāṣṭra, Śaṅkhaka, Kāliya, Takṣaka and Piṅgala shall be worshipped in order in the different months. Or in the bright half of Bhādra the eight serpents mentioned before shall be worshipped. He will attain salvation and heavenly bliss.

32. On the fifth day in the bright half of Śrāvaṇa the pictures of the serpents shall be painted on either side of the main door of the house. They shall be worshipped. Milk and butter constitute the Naivedya. This rite removes all poisons. The serpents shall bestow freedom from fear. This is called Daṣṭoddharaṇapañcamī.

CHAPTER ONE HUNDRED AND THIRTY

Sacred Rites (*Vratas*)

Brahmā said :

1-2. Similarly, God Kārttikeya is to be worshipped in the month of Bhādrapada. The ceremonial bath, charitable gift etc. in this Vrata is of everlasting benefit. On the seventh day, brahmins have to be fed and god sun is to be worshipped with the following mantra—"Svāhā unto Khakkolka. Thou art immortal, let Thy contact be pleasing for ever." The Pāraṇā is on the eighth day with pepper. The devotee shall attain heaven.

Thus Marīcasaptamī is explained.

3-4. On the seventh day of the lunar month the devotee shall take his bath and duly worship the sun-god. With the prayer "May the sun-god be pleased, he shall give fruits to the brahmins. The fruits offered and taken by himself shall be dates, coconuts or pomegranates. While offering the prayer he shall think "May all my desires be fulfilled".

Thus Phalasaptamī is explained:

5-6. After worshipping one's own favourite deity on the Saptamī (seventh) day he shall feed brahmins with milk puddings and shall drink any milk. The word Odana connotes all kinds of foodstuffs chewed, sucked or licked (lambatives). If the devotee is desirous of wealth, sons, etc. he shall remain Anodana (not taking any of the foodstuffs). Brahmins shall be given due Dakṣiṇās as well.

Thus Anodanasaptamī is explained.

7-8. The devotee desirous of victory shall perform Vijaya Saptamī Vrata taking nothing but air, the devotee desirous of love shall eat leaves of the sun plant (Arka) or observe fast. It yields everything he desires. He who abjures wheat, pulses, barley, the Ṣaṣṭika variety of rice, bell metal vessels, stony vessels, wheat flour, honey, wine, meat, sexual intercourse, oil bath, applying collyrium and gingelly seeds on Saptamī (seventh) days is to be considered as having fasted for seven Saptamīs (as explained in this and the next chapter).

CHAPTER ONE HUNDRED AND THIRTYONE

Sacred Rites (Vratas)

Brahmā said :

1-2. On the Aṣṭamī (eighth) day in the bright half of the month of Bhādrapada, the goddesses Dūrvā and Gaurī as well as Gaṇeśa and Śiva are to be worshipped with fruits, grains and flowers reciting the mantra—"Obeisance to Śambhu and Śiva. O Dūrvā, thou art of immortal birth." Only raw food, not cooked in fire, shall be taken by the devotee. He shall attain everything he desires.

Thus Dūrvāṣṭamī is explained:

3. On the eighth day in the dark half mingled with Rohiṇī star Lord Hari is to be worshipped. Even if the seventh phase of the moon remains in the earlier part of the day, there is no objection. This Vrata dispels the sin of three births.

4. The devotee shall observe fast and pray thus—"Obeisance obeisance to Govinda, the lord of Yoga and Yoga itself." The Pāraṇā is to be had when both the Tithi (lunar day) and the star come to a close.

5. The mantra for ceremonial bath is this—"Obeisance, obeisance unto Govinda the god of sacrifices, the lord of sacrifices, the outcome of sacrifices, nay the sacrifice itself." The mantra for worship is as follows :— "Obeisance, obeisance unto Govinda, the god of the universe, the lord of the universe, nay the universe itself"

6. The mantra for laying the deity to sleep is—"obeisance, obeisance to Govinda, the outcome of all, the god of all, the mountain, the All." The lord is to be worshipped on the bare ground. So also the star Rohiṇī accompanied by the moon.

7. The devotee shall take the holy water in the conch shell along with flowers, fruits and sandal paste, kneel on the ground and give Arghya to the moon.

8. O moon God ! born of the milky ocean, originating from the eyes of sage Atri, be pleased to accept this Arghya of mine along with Thy consort Rohiṇī.

9. Similar Arghya offerings shall be made to goddess

Śrī, Yaśodā, Nanda, Vasudeva and Bala, with offerings of fruits.

10-16. The following names of the lord shall be repeated :—Anagha (sinless) Vāmana (the dwarf) Śauri, Vaikuṇṭha, Puruṣottama (best of man), Vāsudeva, Hṛṣīkeśa, Mādhava (consort of Lakṣmī) Madhusūdana (slayer of the demon Madhu) Varāha (the divine Boar), Puṇḍarīkākṣa, (the lotus-eyed), Nṛsiṁha (the manlion), Daityasūdana (destroyer of demons), Dāmodara, Padmanābha, Keśava, Garuḍadhvaja, Govinda, Acyuta, Ananta Deva (Deathless deity) Aparājita (the undefeated), Adhokṣaja, Jagadbīja (the seed of the universe) Sargasthityantakāraṇam (the cause of creation, sustenance and dissolution) Anādinidhana (having neither the beginning nor death), Viṣṇu, Trilokeśa (lord of the three worlds), Trivikrama Nārāyaṇa, Caturbāhu (four-armed), Śaṅkha cakra gadādhara, Pītāmbaradhara (wearing yellow garments) Divya (the divine) Vanamālāvibhūṣita (bedecked with the garlands of wild flowers), Śrīvatsāṅka (having the natural mark on the chest named Śrīvatsa), Jagaddhāma, (the support of the universe), Śrīpati, Śrīdhara, Hari. After repeating these names the devotee shall pray thus:—Obeisance unto the deity in the form of Brahman whom Vasudeva begot of Devakī for the protection of the entire earth.

17. O Lord of lords Hari, save me from the ocean of existence. O destroyer of all sins, save me from the ocean of miseries and sorrow, O Lord !

18-21. O Lord of Śrī, son of Devakī, Hari, Viṣṇu, thou art reputed to be the saviour of even wicked persons who remember Thee but once. O lord, I am the most wicked of all wicked persons, save me from the ocean of sorrow. O Puṣkarākṣa (lotus-eyed), I am deeply immersed in the ocean of ignorance. O God of gods, save me. Save thee there is no other protector. Obeisance unto the self-born Vāsudeva, the benefactor of cows and brahmins and the whole universe. Obeisance, obeisance to Kṛṣṇa, Govinda. Let there be peace. Let there be welfare. Let me be the possessor of wealth, fame, and a vast realm.

CHAPTER ONE HUNDRED AND THIRTYTWO

Sacred Rites (Vratas)

Brahmā said:

1. The devotee shall perform Vrata on the eighth day taking food only in the night. When the Vrata has been performed for a year he shall make a gift of a cow. This is called Sadgativrata and the devotee attains the status of Indra.

2. The same Vrata performed on the eighth day in the bright half of the month of Pauṣa is called Mahārudravrata. The fruit of that Vrata is a hundred thousand times more fruitful, if it is dedicated unto me.

3. If Aṣṭamī (eighth day in either half) and Wednesday coincide, the Vrata is to be performed. Such votaries will never lose their riches as in the story.

4. The devotee shall aspire for salvation alone. He must have perfect devotion and full faith. Only eight handfuls of grains shall be used for food by him and the handfuls shall be with the thumb and the index finger stretched out.

5. The food is taken on the leaves of a mango tree made into a cup and covered with Kuśa grass. The Kalambikā (a kind of green vegetable) cooked in tamarind water is taken along with the food. The fruit of such a Vrata is whatever one desires.

6. In a pond or a river Budha (Mercury) shall be worshipped with the five usual forms of propitiation or articles of worship. Dakṣiṇā in accordance with the capacity of the devotee shall be given. A Karkarī (water jar with small holes in the bottom) full of rice grains shall also be given as gift.

7. The mystic lotus symbol, etc. shall be used. The Bīja mantra is Buṁ Budhāya Svāhā. The god shall be contemplated as armed with arrows and bow and dark in colour. The Aṅgas (limbs) are in the middle.

8. The performer shall hear the story of Budhāṣṭamī narrated by scholars. There was a certain famous brahmin named Vīra in the city of Pāṭaliputra.

9. His wife was Rambhā. They had a virtuous son named Kauśika and a daughter named Vijayā. They had a bullock named Dhanapāla.

10. On a summer day the boy Kauśika took the bullock to the river Gaṅgā and began to play with the cow-herds there. The bullock was stolen by thieves forcibly.

11. The grief-stricken boy left the river bank and wandered through the forest. The daughter Vijayā who came there to fetch water accompanied her brother.

12. The poor boy became thirsty and so in search of lotus stalks came to a lake where he was surprised to see the remnants of the articles of worship used by celestial damsels.

13. He approached the divine damsels and begged them for food for himself and his hungry sister. They directed him to perform the Vrata saying "Practise this Vrata. We shall give you food."

14. The children performed the Vrata, the boy for the sake of recovering the lost bullock Dhanapāla and the girl for securing a suitable husband. The children took two mangoleaf cupfuls of food given by the damsels.

15. The children saw the bullock returned to them by the thieves and reached home by dusk.

16. Vīra had been grief-stricken. The children bowed to him. They spent the night in sound sleep. The father was now worried on seeing his daughter blooming into a young lady. "To whom shall I give my daughter ?" he mused loudly.

17. As is usual, the girl said "To Yama" out of her sorrow, but really on account of the good effects of her Vrata. The parents passed away and Kauśika performed the Vrata again for the sake of kingdom.

18. As a result of the Vrata. Kauśika became the king of Ayodhyā and gave his sister in marriage to Yama. Yama told Vijayā— "Be the lady of my house in my own city."

19. There in Yama's city she saw her mother bound by noose and tortured. The grief-stricken Vijayā remembered that the Vrata had the potentiality of yielding salvation.

20-21. She herself performed the Vrata and the mother attained salvation due to the meritorious potentialities of the Vrata. She went to heaven and stayed there happily.

CHAPTER ONE HUNDRED AND THIRTYTHREE

Sacred Rites (Vratas)

Brahmā said :

1. Those who chew eight buds of the Aśoka tree on the eighth day in the bright half of the month of Caitra with the star Punarvasu will never be tormented by sorrow.

2. O Aśoka, favourite of God Śiva, blossoming in the month of Caitra, I am chewing Thee, grief-stricken that I am. Be pleased to make me free from sorrow.

Thus Aśokāṣṭamī is explained:

3. If the eighth and ninth Phases of the moon in the bright half of the month of Āśvina coincide with Uttarāṣāḍha star it is called Mahānavamī. Ceremonial bath and charity on that day have everlasting benefits.

4. Even if there is no overlapping of Aṣṭamī, but only Navamī, still Durgā can be worshipped. This is a great Vrata of excellent merit performed by even Śaṅkara and others.

5. A king desirous of overthrowing his enemy shall start the Vrata with Japa and Homa on the previous sixth day (Ṣaṣṭhī) itself and shall feed a virgin every day. The Vrata is then called Ayācitādi Vrata. Of course, the concluding rites are only on the Navamī day.

6. In the worship the mantra is "Obeisance to Thee, O Durgā, Durgā the protectress Svāhā." All the nine goddesses are to be worshipped like this with the names ending in long vowel "Ā"

7. The rites of Nyāsa in the heart, etc. are with the six words Namaḥ, Svāhā, Vaṣaṭ, Huṁ, Vauṣaṭ and Phaṭ, and along with the Nyāsas on the fingers beginning with the thumb and ending with the little finger the devotee shall worship goddess Śivā.

8. On the Aṣṭamī itself nine wooden huts (for nine goddesses) or a single wooden house is built in which the golden or silver image of the goddess is installed.

9-11. Instead of idols, a trident, a sword, a book, a cloth or a mystic diagram can be used as the object of worship. Durgā has eighteen hands. In the nine left hands she holds a skull, a club, a bell, a mirror, a threat, a bow, a banner, a drum and a noose. In the nine right hands she holds a Śakti (Javelin) an iron club, a spear, a thunderbolt, a sword, a goad, an arrow, a discus and a Śalākā (a tubelike dart). The remaining goddesses have sixteen hands without Śalākā and Ḍamaru (drum).

12. The eight other goddesses are : — Ugracaṇḍā, Pracaṇḍā, Caṇḍogrā, Caṇḍanāyikā, Caṇḍā, Caṇḍavatī, Caṇḍarūpā and Aticaṇḍikā.

13. The ninth goddess and Ugracaṇḍā are in the middle and are of fiery colour. The others are in order of pigment colour, rosy, dark, blue, smoke-coloured, white, yellow and grey. They stand in the Ālīḍha pose (right knee advanced and left leg retracted).

14. The Mahiṣa (buffalo) demon is being hit by the sword and his fist is in an attitude of trying to catch hold of the tresses. After reciting the ten-syllabled mantra "Obeisance to Mahiṣāsuramardinī" the trident shall be worshipped.

15. The goddess can be worshipped on the phallic emblem too and the sandals in water also. These must be a variegated Pūjā on the Aṣṭamī day and fasting also.

16-18. A well grown buffalo of five years shall be sacrificed at the close of the night. All rites of Kālī must be duly performed. The blood coming out of the buffalo shall be offered to Pūtanā in the south-west, to Pāparākṣasī in the north-west, to Caṇḍikā in the north-east and to Vidārikā in the south-east.

CHAPTER ONE HUNDRED AND THIRTYFOUR

Sacred Rites (Vratas)

Brahmā said :

1. Mahākauśika mantra which is very efficacious is being mentioned—"Oṁ obeisance to Mahākauśika, Oṁ Hūṁ Hūṁ Prasphura Lala Lala Kulva Kulva Culva Culva Khalla Khalla Mulva Mulva Gulva Gulva Tulva Tulva Pulla Pulla

Dhulva Dhulva Dhuma Dhuma Dhama Dhama Māraya Māraya Dhaka Dhaka Vijñāpaya Vijñāpaya Vidāraya Vidāraya Kampa Kampa Kampaya Kampaya Pūraya Pūraya Āveśaya Āveśaya Oṁ Hrīṁ Oṁ Hrīṁ Haṁ Vaṁ Vaṁ Huṁ Taṭa Taṭa Mada Mada Hrīṁ Oṁ Hūṁ obeisance to Nairṛta. A consecrated oblation inspired with Mahākauśika mantra shall be given to Nirṛti.

2. Thereafter, the king shall take his ceremonial bath and make an image of Indra with flour dough and beaten rice. He then severs it into two and gives it to Skanda and Viśākha.

3-4. In the night, Pūjā of the mothers shall be performed. The mothers are :—Brahmāṇī, Māheśī, Kaumārī, Vaiṣṇavī, Vārāhī, Māhendrī, Cāmuṇḍā, Caṇḍikā, Jayantī, Maṅgalā, Kālī, Bhadrakālī, Kapālinī, Durgā, Śivā, Kṣamā and Dhātrī. Svāhā, Svadhā and obeisance unto Thee.

5. The goddess shall be bathed in milk, etc. The devotee shall propitiate Virgins, young women, Brahmins and Pāṣaṇḍas (heretics) with small gifts.

6. Banners, vehicles, festoons, garments shall be used in the ceremonial processions. This worship on the Mahānavamī day shall bless the devotee with victory and flourishing realm.

CHAPTER ONE HUNDRED AND THIRTYFIVE

Sacred Rites (Vratas)

Brahmā said :

1. On the ninth day in the bright half of Āśvina the devotee shall take a single morsel and worship the goddess and brahmins. He shall repeat the Bīja mantra a hundred thousand times.

Thus Vīranavamī is explained.

Brahmā said :

2. On the ninth day in the bright half of Caitra the goddess shall be worshipped with Damana flowers. The

devotee shall be blessed with longevity, health and good fortune. He shall never be vanquished by his enemies.

Thus Damananavamī is explained.

Viṣṇu said :

3. On the tenth day of every month the devotee takes only a single morsel and performs Vrata for a year At the end of the year he makes a gift of ten cows and gold images of the presiding deities of the quarters. He shall eventually attain the lordship of the whole cosmos.

Thus Digdaśamī is explained.

Brahmā said :

4. Worship of the sages with all materials shall be performed. The devotee shall become wealthy and blessed with sons. After death he shall be honoured in the Ṛṣiloka.

5. The sages are Marīci, Atri, Aṅgiras, Pulastya, Pulaha, Kratu, Pracetas, Vasiṣṭha, Bhṛgu and Nārada. The worship is carried out in the beginning of Caitra with garlands of Damana flowers.

6-7. Thus has been explained the Aśokāṣṭamī; the Vīranavamī, the Damananavamī, the Digdaśamī and the (Ṛṣi) Ekādaśī.

CHAPTER ONE HUNDRED AND THIRTYSIX

Sacred Rites (Vratas)

Brahmā said :

1. I shall explain the Śrāvaṇa Dvādaśi Vrata which yields worldly enjoyments and salvation. If the eleventh and twelfth phases of the moon coincide with the star Śravaṇa,

2. That Tithi is called Vijayā. Worship of Lord Hari on this day is of everlasting benefit.

3. If the devotee fasts, takes alms, takes only a single morsel in the day or foodstuff in the night when not solicited by him he does not violate the rules of the Dvādaśī Vrata.

4. The devotee shall avoid on that day the use of bell metal vessels, meat, honey, greed, idle talk, exercise, sexual intercourse, sleep during the day, application of collyrium, flour, etc. ground at the grind stone and Masūra dāla.

5. The twelfth day in the bright half of the month of Bhādrapada with Wednesday and the star Śravaṇa coinciding is called Mahatī Dvādaśī. A fast on this day with ceremonial bath in the confluence of two rivers yields immense benefit.

6. Gems shall be put in golden water pot and the deity Vāmana shall be worshipped. The image is covered with a pair of white cloths. An umbrella and a pair of sandals also accompany the same.

7-9. With the mantras specified the respective limbs are worshipped.

Om obeisance to Vāsudeva—the head
Om obeisance to Śrīdhara—the face
Om obeisance to Kṛṣṇa—the neck
Om obeisance to Śrīpati—the chest
Om obeisance to Sarvāstradhārin—the arms
Om obeisance to Vyāpaka—the belly
Om obeisance to Keśava—the lower stomach
Om obeisance to Trailokyapati—the penis.
Om obeisance to Sarvapati—the calves.
Om obeisance to Sarvātman—the feet

The naivedya to be offered is butter and milk pudding.

10. He shall make gifts of water pots, sweet meats, etc. He shall keep awake at night. After bath, Ācamana and worship by offerings of flowers he shall pray as follows:

11. "Obeisance unto Thee O Govinda, Budha called Śravaṇa, be pleased to destroy all sins and bless me with all comforts."

12. The devotee shall give water pots to brahmins saying—"May the god of gods be pleased". The Vrata can also be performed on the banks of a river. The devotee shall acquire everything he desires.

CHAPTER ONE HUNDRED AND THIRTYSEVEN

Sacred Rites (*Vratas*)

Brahmā said :

1. The worship of the favourite God on the thirteenth day called Kāmadevatrayodaśī with Madana flowers, etc. bestows sexual pleasure, freedom from sorrow and all due respect from everyone.

Thus Madanatrayodaśī is explained.

2. The devotee shall observe fast on the fourteenth day in the bright half and on the eighth day in the dark half for a whole year and worship Śiva. He shall enjoy all worldly pleasures.

Thus Caturdaśyaṣṭamī Vrata is explained.

3. In the month of Kārttika the devotee shall observe fast for three days and make a gift of an excellent house. He shall attain the region of the sun. This excellent Vrata is called Dhāmavrata.

4. On the new moon day if one offers libations of water to the Manes it has immense benefit. If one worships in water in the names of the days of the week (with their presiding deities) taking food only in the night, one shall attain everything.

Thus Vāravratas have been explained.

5. The devotee shall worship well Lord Acyuta in the name of the twelve stars in the twelve months (in accordance with the name).

6. Keśava is worshipped in the month of Mārgaśīrṣa. This worship can be the inaugural one or in the month of Kārttika. For the four months of the Caturmāsa period homa is offered with butter. The Naivedya is Kṛsara (gingelly seeds rounded into balls with treacle).

7. The naivedya in Āṣāḍha, etc. is milk pudding. The brahmins too are to be fed on this. The bath is in Pañcagavya water. The remnant of naivedya constitutes the night food of the devotee.

8. Before Visarjana (the ceremonial dismissal) all usual materials can be used as Naivedya. When Jagannātha is

formally discharged that becomes Nirmālya (remnant of the offerings).

9. All devotees during the Pañcarātra (five nights) take naivedya. Thus the Pūjā shall be continued for a year with special rites.

10. The prayer—"Obeisance, obeisance unto Thee, O Acyuta, let the sins be destroyed; let the Puṇya (merit) flourish. Let prosperity be everlasting. Let my family flourish.

11. O Acyuta, just as Thou art beyond the greatest, Brahman the Supreme, O destroyer of sins, O the unknowable, make my desire too undegraded; make my actions undegraded.

12. O Acyuta, O Ānanda, O Govinda, O Puruṣottama, let my desire be of everlasting benefit. Make it so O, Unknowable !"

13-14. If this Vrata is performed for seven years the devotee obtains longevity, prosperity and the goal of the good. Observing fast on the eleventh, eighth, fourteenth and seventh days for a year and worshipping Viṣṇu, Durgā, Śambhu, and Ravi (sun) in the order, the devotee attains their respective regions. He becomes pure and gets everything he desires.

15. By taking a single morsel, by taking food received unsolicited at night, by fasting or by taking only vegetables all deities can be worshipped in all the Tithis. The devotee shall attain worldly pleasures and salvation.

16-19. Kubera, Agni and the two Aśvinī gods are to be worshipped on the first day. Śrī and Yama on the second; Pārvatī and Śrī on the fifth; Nāgas and Kārttikeya on the sixth, the sun on the seventh; Durgā and Mothers on the eighth; Takṣaka on the Ninth; Indra and Kubera on the tenth; the sages on the eleventh; Hari on the twelfth; Kāma and Maheśvara on the thirteenth; Brahmā on the fourteenth and the manes on New Moon and Full moon.

CHAPTER ONE HUNDRED AND THIRTYEIGHT

The Solar Dynasty

Hari said :

1. I shall describe the lineage of kings and their exploits. From the lotus coming out of the navel of Viṣṇu arose Brahmā. From Brahmā's thumb rose Dakṣa.

2-3. Dakṣa's daughter was Aditi. Aditi's son was Vivasvān. Vivasvān's son was Manu. Manu had nine sons— Ikṣvāku, Śaryāti, Mṛga, Dhṛṣṭa Pṛṣadhra, Nariṣyanta, Nābhāga, Diṣṭa and Śaśaka.

4. Manu had a daughter Ilā of whom Budha (Mercury) begot three sons: Rajas, Rudra and Purūravas. Ilā was transformed into a man named Sudyumna. Sudyumna begot three sons—Utkala, Vinata and Gaya.

5. Manu's son Pṛṣadhra became a Śūdra due to cow-slaughter. His descendant Karūṣa became a Kṣatriya and a line of Kṣatriya kings called Kārūṣas sprang from him.

6. Diṣṭa's son Nābhāga became a Vaiśya. His son was Bhanandana and Bhanandana's son was Vatsaprīti.

7. Two other sons were Pāṁśu and Khanitra. The latter became a king and his son was Kṣupa. Kṣupa's son was Viṁśa and his son was Viviṁśa.

8. Viviṁśa's son was Khanīnetra. Vibhūti was his son. Vibhūti's son was Karandhama and his son was Avikṣita.

9. Marutta was his son and he begot Nariṣyanta. Nariṣyanta's son was Tamas and his son was Rājavardhana.

10. Rājavardhana's son was Sudhṛti and Nara was Sudhṛti's son. Nara's son was Kevala whose son was Dhundhumān.

11. Vegavān was Dhundhumān's son and his son was Budha. Budha had a son named Tṛṇabindu and a daughter Ailavilā.

12. Tṛṇabindu begot of Alambuṣā a son named Viśāla; his son was Hemacandra; his son was Chandraka.

13. Dhūmrāśva was the son of Candra and Sṛñjaya was born of Dhūmrāśva. Sahadeva was the son of Sṛñjaya and his son was Kṛśāśva.

14. Somadatta was the son of Kṛśāśva and his son was

Janamejaya whose son was Sumantri. These kings are known as Vaiśālakas (because Viśālā was their city).

15. Śaryāti (Manu's son) had a daughter Sukanyā who married the sage Cyavana, and a son Ananta who had a son named Revata. Revata had a son Raivata and a daughter Revatī.

16. Dhṛṣṭa (another son of Manu) had a line of descendants who became Vaiśyas.

17. Nābhāga (another son of Manu) had two sons Nediṣṭa and Ambarīṣa. Ambarīṣa had a son Virūpa whose son was Pṛṣadaśva.

18. His son Rathīnara was a great devotee of Vāsudeva.

19. Ikṣvāku (another son of Manu) had three sons Vikukṣi, Nimi and Daṇḍaka. Vikukṣi became known as Śaśāda because he ate a rabbit.

20. Śaśāda's son was Purañjaya and his son was Kakutstha. His son was Anenas. Pṛthu was the son of Anenas.

21. Viśvarāta was the son of Pṛthu and Ārdra was Viśvarāta's son. His son was Yuvanāśva. His son was Śrāvasta.

22. Bṛhadaśva was his son and his son was Kuvalāśva. His son Dṛḍhāśva became famous as Dhundhumāra.

23. He had three sons named Candrāśva, Kapilāśva and Haryaśva. Nikumbha was the son of Haryaśva and his son Hitāśva.

24. Hitāśva's son was Pūjāśva and his son was Yuvanāśva. Māndhātā was his son whose son was Bindumahya.

25. He had three sons Mucukunda, Ambarīṣa and Purukutsa. He had fifty daughters whom the sage Saubhari married. Yuvanāśva was Ambarīṣa's son and his son was Harita.

26. Purukutsa begot of his wife Narmadā the son Trasdasyu. Anaraṇya was his son and he begot Haryaśva.

27-28. His son was Vasumanas whose son was Tridhanvā. Trayyāruṇa was his son whose son Satyarata became famous as Triśaṅku who begot Hariścandra. Rohitāśva was the son of Hariścandra.

29. Harita was his son. His son was Cañcu and Cañcu's

son was Vijaya. Ruru was born of Vijaya and Vṛka was his son.

30. The successor and son of Vṛka was Bāhu whose son was Sagara.

31. Sagara begot of his first wife Sumati sixty thousand sons and of Keśinī the second wife the only son Asamañjasa.

32. Aṁśumān the scholar was his son and Dilīpa was his son. His son was Bhagīratha who brought Gaṅgā to the earth.

33. Śruta was Bhagīratha's son and Nābhāga was his son. His son was Ambarīṣa and Sindhudvīpa was his son.

34. Ayutāyu was the son of Sindhudvīpa and Ṛtuparṇa was his son. Sarvakāma was Ṛtuparṇa's son and his son was Sudās.

35. Sudās's son became famous as Mitrasaha who begot of his wife Damayantī the son Kalmāṣapāda.

36. His son was Aśvaka whose son was Mūlaka. His son was the king Daśaratha whose son was Ailavila.

37. His son was Viśvasaha whose son was Khaṭvāṅga. His son was Dīrghabāhu whose son was Aja.

38. Aja's son was Daśaratha who had four sons the valiant Rāma, Lakṣmaṇa Bharata and Śatrughna.

39. Rāma's sons were Kuśa and Lava. Bharata's sons were Tārkṣa and Puṣkara. Lakṣmaṇa's sons were Citrāṅgada. and Candraketu.

40. Śatrughna's sons were Subāhu and Śūrasena. Kuśa's son was Atithi and his son was Niṣadha.

41. Nala was the son of Niṣadha and Nabhas was the son of Nala. Puṇḍarīka was the son of Nabhas and his son was Kṣemadhanvā.

42. His son was Devānīka whose son was Ahīnaka. Ruru was his son whose son was Pāriyātra.

43. Dala was the son of Pāriyātra and his son was Chhala. Vuktha was the son of Chhala and his son was Vajranābha. Gaṇa was his son.

44. Uṣitāśva was the son of Gaṇa and Viśvasaha was his son. Hiraṇyanābha was his son. His son was Puṣpaka.

45. Dhruvasandhi was his son and Sudarśana was born of Dhruvasandhi. Sudarśana's son was Agnivarṇa whose son was Padmavarṇa.

46. His son was Śīghra whose son was Maru. Prasuśruta was the son of Maru and his son was Udāvasu.

47. Udāvasu's son was Nandivardhana whose son was Suketu. His son was Devarāta whose son was Bṛhaduktha.

48. Bṛhaduktha begot Mahāvīrya whose son was Sudhṛti. His son was Dhṛṣṭaketu who begot Haryaśva.

49. Haryaśva's son was Maru whose son was Pratīndhaka. His son was Kṛti whose son was Devamīḍha.

50. His son was Vibudha whose son was Mahādhṛti. Kṛtirāta was his son and his son was Mahāromā.

51. Svarṇaromā was his son and his son was Hrasvaromā. Sīradhvaja was the son of Hrasvaromā and his daughter was Sītā.

52. Her brother was Kuśadhvaja. His son was Bhānumān. Śatadyumna was his son whose son was Śuci.

53. Ūrjanāmā was Śuci's son and Sanadvāja was his son. Kuli was born of Sanadvāja and Kuli's son was Anañjana.

54. Kulajit was his son whose son was Adhinemika. His son was Śrutāyu and his son was Supārśva.

55. Sṛñjaya was born of him and Kṣemāri was his son. Anenas was his son whose son was Rāmaratha.

56. Satyaratha was born of Rāmaratha and Upaguru was his son. His son was Upagupta whose son was Svāgata.

57. Svanara was born of him and his son was Suvarcas. His son was Supārśva and Suśruta was Supārśva's son.

58. Jaya was born of Suśruta and Vijaya was his son. His son was Ṛta and Sunaya was the son of Ṛta.

59-60. Vītahavya was his son and Dhṛti was born of Vītahavya. Bahulāśva was his son and Ākṛti was his son. Two different lines started from Janaka who were said to be devoted to Yoga.

CHAPTER ONE HUNDRED AND THIRTYNINE

The Lunar Dynasty

Hari said :

1. I have narrated the names of kings of the solar race. Now listen to the names of kings of the lunar race. Lord Nārāyaṇa's son was Brahmā and the sage Atri was born of him.

2. Soma the moon-god was born of Atri. The beloved of Bṛhaspati named Tārā became his wife.

3. Tārā bore the moon-god the son Budha (Mercury). Budha's son was Purūravas who begot of the celestial damsel Ūrvaśī six sons—Śrutātmaka, Viśvāvasu, Śatāyu, Āyu, Dhīmān and Amāvasu.

4. Amāvasu's son was Bhīma and his son was Kāñcana. His son was Suhotra and Jahnu was Suhotra's son.

5. Sumantu was Jahnu's son and Apajāpaka was Sumantu's son. His son was Balākāśva whose son was Kuśa.

6. He had four sons—Kuśāśva, Kuśanābha, Amūrtaraya and Vasu. Gādhi was born of Kuśāśva and Viśvāmitra was Gādhi's son.

7. His daughter Satyavatī was given in marriage to the brahmin sage Ṛcīka whose son was Jamadagni, father of Rāma (Paraśurāma).

8-9. Viśvāmitra had many sons Devarāta, Madhucchandas, etc. Āyu son of Purūravas begot Nahuṣa who had four sons—Anenas, Raji, Rambhaka and Kṣatravṛddha. The last one, Kṣatravṛddha's son, was Suhotra who became a king. He had three sons—Kāśya, Kāśa and Gṛtsamada.

10. His son was Śaunaka. Kāśya begot Dīrghatamas whose son Dhanvantari was a great physician. Ketumān was born of him.

11. His son was Bhīmaratha whose son was Divodāsa. His son Pratardana became famous as Śatrujit (Conqueror of enemies).

12. His son was Ṛtadhvaja whose son was Alarka. Sannati was born of him. His son was Sunīta.

13. Satyaketu was born of Sunīta and his son was Vibhu. His son was Suvibhu whose son was Sukumāraka.

14. Dhṛṣṭaketu was born of him and his son was Vītihotra whose son was Bharga. His son was Bhargabhūmi.

15. All these descendants of Kāśya were great devotees of Viṣṇu. Raji had five hundred sons, all of whom were killed by Indra.

16. Kṣatravṛddha (son of Nahuṣa) had another son named Pratikṣatra whose son was Sañjaya. His son was Vijaya whose son was Kṛta.

17. Vṛṣaghna was born of Kṛta and his son was Sahadeva whose son was Adīna. His son was Jayatsena.

18. Saṅkṛti was born of Jayatsena and Kṣatradharmā was his son. Nahuṣa had five more sons—Yati, Yayāti, Saṁyāti, Ayāti and Kṛti. Yayāti's sons were as follows:

19. His first wife Devayānī gave birth to Yadu and Turvasu. His second wife Śarmiṣṭhā, daughter of Vṛṣaparvā, bore him three sons—Druhyu, Anu and Pūru.

20. Yadu had three sons—Sahasrajit, Kroṣṭumanas, and Raghu. The eldest Sahasrajit had a son Śatajit who had two sons : Haya and Haihaya.

21-23. Haya's son was Anaraṇya and Dharma was Haihaya's son. He had a son named Dharmanetra whose son was Kunti. His son Sāhañji was the father of Mahiṣmān whose son was Bhadraśreṇya. His son was Durdama.

24. Dhanaka was his son. He had four sons—Kṛtavīrya, Kṛtāgni, Kṛtakarma and Kṛtauja, all of whom were strong.

25. Arjuna was born of Kṛtavīrya and Śūrasena was born of him along with four brothers—Jayadhvaja, Madhu, Śūra and Vṛṣaṇa. All these five were devoted to sacred rites.

26. Tālajaṅgha was born of Jayadhvaja and Bharata was his son. Madhu was Vṛṣaṇa's son and the Vṛṣṇi race flourished after him.

27. Āhi was born of Kroṣṭu and Uśaṅku was the son of the noble-souled Ahi. Citraratha was his son.

28. Śaśabindu was born of Citraratha and he had two wives. The first wife bore him one hundred thousand sons and the second wife a million sons: They were Pṛthukīrti, etc.

29. Pṛthukīrti had three sons ; Pṛthujaya, Pṛthudāna and Pṛthuśravas. The last one Pṛthuśravas had a son named Tamas whose son was Uśanas.

30-31. His son's name was Śitagu whose son Śrī Rukmakavaca had five sons—Rukma, Pṛthurukma, Jyāmagha, Pālita and Hari. Of these Jyāmagha begot of his wife Śaibyā a son named Vidarbha. His sons were Kratha and Kauśika.

32. Romapāda (son of Vidarbha) had a son Babhru whose son was Dhṛti. Kauśika begot Ṛci whose son was king Caidya.

33. His son was Kunti whose son was Vṛṣṇi. His son was Nivṛti and he had Daśārha for his son.

34. Vyomā was his son and Jīmūta was his son. Vikṛti was born of him and had Bhīmaratha for his son.

35. Madhuratha was his son and his son was Śakuni. Karambhi was Śakuni's son and his son was Devamata.

36. Devakṣatra was his son and he begot Devakṣatra whose son was Madhu. Madhu's son was Kuruvaṁśa whose son was Anu.

37. His son was Puruhotra whose son Aṁśu begot Satvaśruta. Sāttvata who became a king was his son.

38. Sāttvata had these sons—Bhajina, Bhajamāna, Andhaka, Mahābhoja, Vṛṣṇi, Divya and Devāvṛdha.

39. Bhajamāna's sons were—Nimi, Vṛṣṇi, Ayutājit, Śatajit, Sahasrājit, Babhru, Deva and Bṛhaspati.

40. Mahābhoja's son was Bhoja and Sumitraka was Vṛṣṇi's son. He had three sons—Svadhājit, Anamitra and Śini.

41. Anamitra had two sons: Nighna and Śibi. Nighna had two sons: Satrājit and Prasena.

42. Śibi's son was Satyaka whose son was Sātyaki. Sañjaya was his son and Kuli was born of Sañjaya. Yugantara was the son of Kuli. Thus I have narrated to you about Śaibeyas.

43. Vṛṣṇi, Śvaphalka and Citraka were born in the family of Anamitra. Born of Śvaphalka in his wife Gāndinī, Akrūra was a great devotee of Viṣṇu.

44. Upamadgu was the son of Akrūra and his son was Devadyota. Akrūra had two other sons—Devavān and Upadeva.

45. Citra had two sons: Pṛthu and Vipṛthu. Andhaka (a son of Sātvata) had a son Śuci. Kukura and Kambalabarhiṣa were the sons of Bhajamāna.

46. Kukura's son was Dhṛṣṭa whose son was Kāpotaromaka. His son was Vilomā whose son was Tumburu.

47-49. Dundubhi was his son and his son was Punarvasu who had a daughter Āhukī and a son Āhuka. Devaka and Ugrasena were the sons of Āhuka. Devaka had seven daughters—Devakī, Vṛkadevā, Upadevā, Sahadevā, Surakṣitā, Śrīdevī, and Śāntidevī. All of them married Vasudeva. Sahadevā gave birth to Deva and Anūpadeva.

50. Ugrasena had many sons—Kaṁsa, Sunāmā, Vaṭa and others. Bhajamāna's son was Vidūratha whose son was Śūra.

51. Śamin was the son of Śūra and his son was Pratikṣatra who was father of Svayambhoja.

52-55. Hṛdika was his son whose son was Kṛtavarmā. Śūra's sons were Deva, Śatadhanus and Devamīḍhuṣ; and in Māriṣā he had ten sons : Vasudeva and others as well as five daughters—Pṛthā, Śrutadevī, Śrutakīrti, Śrutaśravas and Rājādhidevī. Pṛthā was adopted as daughter by Kunti who gave her in marriage to Pāṇḍu. Kunti gave birth to Karṇa, Yudhiṣṭhira, Bhīma, and Pārtha, and Nakula and Sahadeva were the sons of Mādrī through divine contact with Dharma, Anila, Indra and the Aśvinidevas.

56. Dantavaktra the indefatigable was born of Śrutadevī. Śrutakīrti bore Kaikaya five sons: Antardhāna and others.

57. Vinda and Anuvinda were born of Rājādhidevī. Śrutaśravas bore a son Śiśupāla of Damaghoṣa.

58. Ānakadundubhi (i.e. Vasudeva) had many other wives besides Devakī and others mentioned before, viz:—Pauravī, Rohiṇī and Madirā. Rohiṇī gave birth to Balabhadra.

59. Balabhadra begot of Revatī Śaṭha, Niśaṭha, Ulmuka, Sāraṇa and others. Devakī gave birth to six sons:

60. Kīrtimān, Suṣeṇa, Udārya, Bhadrasena, Ṛjudāsa and Bhadradeva and all of them were killed by Kaṁsa.

61. Her seventh son was Saṁkarṣaṇa and the eighth was Kṛṣṇa. He had sixteen thousand wives.

62. Of these the most excellent ones were Rukmiṇī, Satyabhāmā, Lakṣmaṇā, Cāruhāsinī and Jāmbavatī. Each of these wives gave birth to eight sons and the family thus became very vast.

63. Pradyumna, Cārudeṣṇa and Sāmba were the principal ones. Pradyumna begot of Kakudminī the powerful son Aniruddha.

64. Aniruddha begot of his wife Subhadrā the son Vajra who became a king. Pratibāhu was his son and his son was Cāru.

65. In the line of Turvasu (son of Devayānī) Vahni was an illustrious member whose son was Bharga. His son Bhānu had a son Karandhama by name.

66. Maruta was the son of Karandhama. Now listen to the lineage of Druhyu. His son Setu begot Āraddha whose son was Gāndhāra and Dharma was born of Gāndhāra.

67. Dhṛta was Dharma's son and his son was Durgama whose son was Pracetas. Now listen to Anu's lineage.

68. Anu's son was Sabhānara whose son was Kālañjaya. His son Sṛñjaya had Purañjaya for his son.

69. Janamejaya was his son whose son was Mahāśāla. His son was Mahāmanas better known as Uśīnara.

70. Śibi was his son whose son was Vṛṣadarbha. Another son of Mahāmanas named Titikṣu had a son Ruṣadratha.

71. His son was Hema whose son was Sutapas who begot Bali whose sons were Aṅga, Vaṅga and Kaliṅga.

72. Andhra, and Pauṇḍra (along with the three mentioned before) were Bali's sons.

73. Aṅgapāḷa was the son of Aṅga. His son was Diviratha whose son was Dharmaratha.

74. Romapāda was the son of Dharmaratha and his son was Caturaṅga. His son Pṛthulākṣa had Campā for his son.

75. Campā's son was Haryaṅga whose son was Bhadraratha. His son Bṛhatkarmā begot Bṛhadbhānu.

76. Bṛhanmanas was the son of Bṛhadbhānu and his son was Jayadratha. Vijaya was his son and his son was Dhṛti. Dhṛtavrata was the son of Dhṛti and Satyadharmā was the son of Dhṛtavrata.

77-78. His son was Adhiratha who adopted Karṇa as his son. Vṛṣasena was the son of Karṇa. Now, listen to the lineage of Puru.

CHAPTER ONE HUNDRED AND FORTY

Genealogy of the Pauravas

Hari said :

1. Janamejaya was the son of Puru and his son was Namasyu whose son was Abhayada and his son was Sudyu.

2. Bahugati was the son of Sudyu and his son Saṁjāti had a son Vatsajāti by name who begot Raudrāśva.

3. Raudrāśva had six sons—Ṛteyu, Sthaṇḍileyu, Kakṣeyu, Kṛteyu, Jaleyu and Santateyu.

4. Ratināra was Ṛteyu's son and his son was Pratiratha whose son Medhātithi begot Ainila.

5. His son Duṣmanta (Duṣyanta) married Śakuntalā and begot Bharata whose son was Vitatha.

6. Vitatha's son was Manyu whose son Nara begot Saṅkṛti whose son was Garga.

7. Garga's son Amanyu was the father of Śini. Manyu had another son named Mahāvīrya whose son was Urukṣaya.

8. Trayyāruṇi was born of Urukṣaya. Another son of Manyu named Vyūhakṣatra had a son Suhotra who had three sons—Hastin, Ajamīḍha and Dvimīḍha.

9. Hastin had the son Purumīḍha. Ajamīḍha's eldest son was Kaṇva whose son Medhātithi and other descendants became brahmins known as Kāṇvāyanas.

10. Another son of Ajamīḍha was Bṛhadiṣu and his son was Bṛhaddhanuṣ. His son was Bṛhatkarman whose son was Jayadratha.

11. Viśvajit was his son whose son Senajit begot Ruciräśva whose son was Pṛthusena.

12. Pāra was the son of Pṛthusena and his son was Dvīpa whose son was Samara. Pṛthu had a son named Sukṛti.

13. Vibhrāja was Sukṛti's son who had a son named Aśvaha who begot of his wife Kṛti a son Brahmadatta whose son was Viṣvaksena.

14. Dvimīḍha's son was Yavīnara whose son was Dhṛtimān whose son Satyadhṛti was the father of Dṛḍhanemi.

15. Dṛḍhanemi's son was Supārśva who was the father of Sannati whose son Kṛta begot Ugrāyudha.

16. Kṣemya was his son whose son Sudhīra begot Purañjaya father of Vidūratha.

17. Ajamīḍha begot of Nalinī a son named Nīla who became a king. Nīla's son was Śānti who was father of Suśānti.

18. His son Puru was father of Arka who begot Haryaśva whose son was Mukula.

19-20. Mukula king of Pāñcāla had five sons—Yavīnara, Bṛhadbhānu, Kampilla, Sṛñjaya and Śaradvān a great devotee of Viṣṇu who begot of Ahalyā Divodāsa the second, whose son was Śatānanda whose son was Satyadhṛti.

21. Satyadhṛti's semen coming out on seeing Urvaśī the celestial damsel took shape of a son Kṛpa and a daughter Kṛpī who married Droṇa and gave birth to the excellent Aśvatthāman.

22. Divodāsa's son was Mitrayu whose son Cyavana begot Sudās father of Saudāsa.

23. His son was Sahadeva who begot Somaka who had two sons Jantu and Pṛṣata the great.

24. Pṛṣata's son was Drupada whose son Dhṛṣṭadyumna begot Dhṛṣṭaketu. Ajamīḍha had another son Ṛkṣa.

25. His son was Saṁvaraṇa who begot Kuru who had threesons Sudhanus, Parīkṣit and Jahnu.

26. Sudhanus begot Suhotra whose son Cyavana had three sons: Kṛtaka, Uparicara and Vasu.

27. Vasu's sons were Bṛhadratha, Pratyagra, Satya and others. The eldest of them Bṛhadratha begot Kuśāgra father of Ṛṣabha.

28. His son was Puṣpavān, father of Satyahita who begot Sudhanvā father of Jahnu.

29. Bṛhadratha had another son named Jarāsandha whose son Sahadeva begot Somāpi father of Śrutavān.

30. He had many sons Bhīmasena, Ugrasena, Śrutasena, Aparājita, Janamejaya, etc. Jahnu's son was Suratha.

31. His son Vidūratha begot Sārvabhauma father of Jayasena whose son was Āvadhīta.

32. His son Ayutāyu begot Akrodhana, father of Atithi whose son was Ṛkṣa.

33. His son Bhīmasena begot Dilīpa, father of Pratīpa whose son was Devāpi.

34-35. Śantanu Vāhlīka were the brothers of Devāpi. Vāhlīka begot four sons Somadatta, Bhūri, Bhūriśravas and Śāla. Śantanu begot of Gaṅgā the most virtuous Bhīṣma and of Satyavatī two sons: Citrāṅgada and Vicitravīrya.

36-37. Vicitravīrya had two wives : Ambikā and Ambālikā. Vyāsa begot of Ambikā Dhṛtarāṣṭra and of Ambālikā Pāṇḍu and of their maid servant Vidura. Gāndhārī bore Dhṛtarāṣṭra one hundred sons : Duryodhana and others while Pāṇḍu had five sons.

38. The five brothers married Draupadī and begot of her respectively Prativindhya, Śrutasoma, Śrutakīrti, Śatānīka and Śrutakarman.

39-41. The ladies Yaudheyī, Hidimbā, Subhadrā (sister of Kṛṣṇa), Vijayī and Reṇumatī bore the Pāṇḍava brothers these sons respectively—Devaka, Ghaṭotkaca, Abhimanyu (who was quick of movement) Suhotra and Niramitra. Abhimanyu's son was Parīkṣit whose son was Janamejaya. Now listen to the names of the future kings.

CHAPTER ONE HUNDRED AND FORTYONE

Genealogy of the Pauravas and others

Harī said :

1. The future kings will be these in order: Śatānīka, Aśvamedhadatta, Adhisomaka, Kṛṣṇa, Aniruddha, Uṣṇa, and Citraratha.

2-4. (The other kings in the line will be:) Śuciratha, Vṛṣṇimān, Suṣeṇa, Sunītha, Nṛcakṣu, Mukhābāṇa, Medhāvī, Nṛpañjaya, Pāriplava, Sunaya, Medhāvī, Nṛpañjaya, Hari, Tigma, Bṛhadratha, Śatānīka, Sudāna, Udāna, Ahīnara, Daṇḍapāṇi, Nimittaka, Kṣemaka and a line of Śūdra kings, thereafter.

5-8. The future line of kings in the Ikṣvāku race will be :—Bṛhadbala, Urukṣaya, Vatsavyūha, Sūrya, Sahadeva,

Bṛhadaśva, Bhānuratha, Pratīcya, Pratītaka, Manudeva, Sunakṣatra, Kinnara, Antarikṣaka, Suparṇa, Kṛtajit, the virtuous Bṛhadbhrāja, Kṛtañjaya, Dhanañjaya, Sañjaya, Śākya, Śuddhodana, Bāhula, Senajit, Kṣudraka, Samitra, Kuḍava and Sumitra. Now listen to the kings of Magadha.

9-11. Jarāsandha, Sahadeva, Somāpi, Śrutaśravas, Ayutāyu, Niramitra, Svakṣatra, Bahukarmaka, Śrutañjaya, Senajit, Bhūri, Śuci, Kṣemya, Suvrata, Dharma, Śmaśrula, Dṛḍhasenaka, Sumati, Subala, Nīta, Asatyajit, Viśvajit and Iṣuñjaya. These kings will be the descendants of Bṛhadratha.

12. Thereafter all the kings will be Śūdras of evil and impious deeds. Nārāyaṇa the imperishable Lord is the creator of heaven, etc.

13-14. There are three different types of dissolution of the world—1) Naimittika i.e. the conditional dissolution 2) Prākṛtika (the natural or cosmic dissolution) and 3) Ātyantika or the final and absolute dissolution. The Earth will dissolve into water. The water will dissolve into Tejas (Heat). The heat will dissolve into the Air, the Air into Ether and the Ether into the Cosmic ego or Ahaṅkāra, the cosmic ego into the cosmic Intellect, the cosmic Intellect into Jīva (the Cosmic Self) which will dissolve into Avyakta which will dissolve into the Ātman.

15-16. The Ātman is the Supreme Lord Viṣṇu, Nārāyaṇa and Nara which is Imperishable. All the other things are perishable. All the kings have been destroyed. Hence avoid Sin. One shall always be virtuous so that by casting off sins one could attain Hari.

CHAPTER ONE HUNDRED AND FORTYTWO

Greatness of Sītā

Brahmā said :

1. For the destruction of the impious way of living of the demons and the protection of the Vedic Religion, Lord Hari incarnated in the world and saved the pious lines of kings.

2-3. The lord incarnated in the form of Fish, etc. Taking the form of Fish he fought with the demon Hayagrīva in battle, killed him, redeemed the Vedas and saved Manu and others. Taking the form of a Tortoise he lifted the mountain Mandara on his back for the benefit of all.

4-5. At the time of churning the milky ocean, he took the form of the first physician Dhanvantari and holding the vessel full of Nectar rose up from the ocean. He taught the science of medicine and health with its eightfold sub-divisions to Suśruta. Hari took the form of a lady and made devas drink nectar.

6. Incarnating as a Boar he killed Hiraṇyākṣa, extricated the Earth from his clutches and saved the deities.

7. Incarnating as Nṛsiṁha (manlion) he killed the demon Hiraṇyakaśipu and preserved the Vedic religion and its principles.

8. Then Hari incarnated as the son of Jamadagni, Paraśurâma by name and freed the Earth of Kṣatriyas thrice seven (twentyone) times.

9. The Lord then killed Kārttavīrya and gifted away land to Kaśyapa. After performing a sacrifice the powerful lord made a permanent stay on the mountain Mahendra.

10-11. Desirous of incarnating as Rāma, the suppressor of the wicked, he divided himself into four and Daśaratha's four sons were born, viz. Rāma, Bharata, Lakṣmaṇa and Śatrughna. Rāma's wife was Jānakī.

12. To do a good turn to his step-mother and to preserve the truthfulness of his father he came to Daṇḍaka forest passing through Śṛṅgavera and Citrakūṭa.

13-15. He chopped off the nose of Śūrpaṇakhā, killed the demons Khara, Dūṣaṇa, and Rāvaṇa who abducted Sītā along with his brother (Kumbhakarṇa). After installing his other brother Vibhīṣaṇa in the kingdom of Laṅkā he returned to Ayodhyā in the celestial car Puṣpaka accompanied by Sugrīva, Hanumān and others and his chaste wife Sītā of great fidelity.

16. He ruled over the kingdom, protected subjects, saved devas, performed Aśvamedha (horse sacrifice) and other sacrifices and preserved righteousness.

17-18. Rāma lived happily with his loyal wife. Although she stayed in the premises of Rāvaṇa she never went over to him in mind, speech or action. She never thought of anyone except Rāma. She was as good a chaste woman as the celebrated Anasūyā.

19. I shall tell you about the greatness of Sītā by narrating the greatness of chastity. Once, in the city of Pratiṣṭhāna, there lived a brahmin named Kauśika who suffered from leprosy.

20. In spite of his loathsome disease his wife worshipped him like a god. Even when rebuked by him she never ceased to venerate him.

21-22. Ordered by her husband she took him to a prostitute's house, taking with her plenty of money. The sage Māṇḍavya who had been impaled on being suspected as a thief unjustifiably and who was pining in darkness was inadvertently kicked by the brahmin Kauśika who was seated on his wife's shoulders.

23. Māṇḍavya became furious on being kicked with the foot and said, "He who tossed me with his foot shall die at sunrise."

24. On hearing that, the wife of Kauśika said, "The sun will never rise." Since the sun did not rise there was perpetual night.

25. Many years went by like this. The gods became afraid. They went to Brahmā for help. Brahmā told them.

26-28. The splendour of asceticism is being subdued by this splendour of chastity, since the greatness of the chaste lady prevents the sun from rising. If the sun does not rise the loss is yours as well as men's. Hence, go to the chaste wife of Atri, Anasūyā, the holy woman and propitiate her for making the sun rise." The gods went to the chaste lady Anasūyā and entreated her.

29. Making the sun rise she resuscitated Kauśika too. It is said that Sītā was superior to even Anasūyā in chastity.

CHAPTER ONE HUNDRED AND FORTYTHREE

The Story of Rāma

Brahmā said :

1. Now, I shall narrate Rāmāyaṇa (Rāma's story) which mitigates sins on being heard. Brahmā was born of the lotus from the navel of Viṣṇu and Marīci was his son.

2. Kaśyapa was born of Marīci; Sun was born of Kaśyapa; Manu was born of Sun and Ikṣvāku was Manu's son. The king Raghu was a scion of this family.

3. Raghu's son was Aja whose son was the mighty Daśaratha. He had four valiant sons.

4. Rāma was born of Kausalyā. Bharata was the son of Kaikeyī. The two brothers, Lakṣmaṇa, and Śatrughna were born of Sumitrā.

5. Rāma was devotedly attached to his father and mother. He learned the use of many miraculous weapons from Viśvāmitra. Then he killed the ogress Tāḍakā.

6. The powerful Rāma killed Subāhu at the sacrificial altar of Viśvāmitra. Visiting the holy sacrifice of Janaka, he married Sītā.

7. Lakṣmaṇa married Ūrmilā. Bharata married Māṇḍavī and Śatrughna married Śrutakīrti, both of whom were the daughters of Kuśadhvaja.

8. Rāma and his brothers returned to Ayodhyā accompanied by their parents. Then Bharata and Śatrughna went to the former's uncle Yudhājit.

9. While they were away, the king wanted to give his kingdom to Rāma, the best of his sons. Kaikeyī wanted that for her son and also desired that Rāma should go to stay in the forest for fourteen years.

10. For the benefit of his father Rāma forsook his kingdom like a blade of grass and went to Śṛṅgaverapura accompanied by Lakṣmaṇa and Sītā.

11. Abandoning the chariot he passed through Prayāga reaching the mountain Citrakūṭa. Unable to bear the pangs of separation from Rāma the king Daśaratha passed away.

12. After the obsequies of his father, Bharata accom-

panied by the armed forces came to Rāma and said—"Please come back to Ayodhyā to rule over kingdom, noble brother dear."

13-14. But Rāma did not like the idea. As a symbol for ruling kingdom he gave Bharata his sandals. Thus dismissed, Bharata protected Rāma's kingdom stationing himself in Nandigrāma and never entering Ayodhyā. Rāma left Citrakūṭa and went over to Atri's hermitage.

15-16. After paying due respects to Sutīkṣṇa and Agastya he went to Daṇḍaka forest. There the ogress named Śūrpaṇakhā came to devour them. Rāma cut off her ears and nose. Inimically disposed she induced her brothers Khara, Triśiras and Dūṣaṇa who came over there.

17. By means of his arrows Rāma sent them to Yama's abode along with the fourteen thousand Rākṣasa soldiers.

18. Induced by the ogress, Rāvaṇa assumed the form of an anchorite in order to abduct Sītā and came there preceded by Mārīca in the guise of a deer.

19. Requested by Sītā, Rāma went out to beg the deer but killed Mārīca who cried out "Alas ! Sītā Alas Lakṣmaṇa" while dying.

20. When Sītā asked him to go, Lakṣmaṇa too went out and on seeing him Rāma said, "This is only a deceptive trick of the ogress ! Surely Sītā has been abducted."

21. Getting a suitable opportunity Rāvaṇa abducted Sītā and went back to Laṅkā striking Jaṭāyu on the way.

22. He kept Sītā in the Aśoka grove. (Here in the forest) Rāma returned to the hut only to see it empty.

23-25. Grief-stricken Rāma sought Sītā here and there. He cremated Jaṭāyu and as directed by him went southwards and made alliance with Sugrīva. With a single arrow, with a hooked point he cut off seven huge trees and killed Bāli. He made Sugrīva the Lord of monkeys in Kiṣkindhā while he himself remained in Ṛṣyamūka.

26. Sugrīva sent brawny monkeys huge like mountains in search of Sītā to all quarters.

27-28. Those who went to West, North and East came back. Those who went to South in search of Sītā roamed in forests, mountains, islands and on river banks but could not see her. Hence, they decided on self-immolation.

29. On knowing the whereabouts of Sītā from Sampāti's words, Hanumān the elephantine monkey, leapt across the abode of sharks (the ocean) one thousand two hundred kilometres wide.

30-31. There he saw Sītā sitting in the Aśoka grove, rebuked by the ogresses, tormented by the demon king Rāvaṇa with the importunities "Be my wife" and engrossed in thoughts about Rāma. He gave her the signet ring and consoled Sītā by telling her about the welfare of Rāma.

32. "I am the messenger of Rāma, O noble daughter of Mithilā, do not be grief-stricken. Give me a token that could be recognised by Rāma."

33. On hearing that, Sītā gave her crest-jewel to Hanumān saying — "Please tell him everything in such a manner as to make Rāma take me away quickly."

34. "So shall I", said Hanumān and immediately set about uprooting the various trees in the beautiful garden nearby. After killing Prince Akṣa and other demons he voluntarily let them bind him.

35. Bound by Indrajit's miraculous weapons he was led to Rāvaṇa on seeing whom he said, "I am Hanumān the messenger of Rāma. Surrender Sītā to him."

36. On hearing this, the infuriated demon set fire to his tail. The powerful monkey with his blazing tail burnt the city of Laṅkā.

37. After burning the city and feasting himself and his friends on the delicious fruits of Madhuvana, the monkey came back to Rāma, saying "my Lord, Sītā has been found."

38. He then handed over the crest-jewel to Rāma. Accompanied by Lakṣmaṇa, Sugrīva, Hanumān, Aṅgada and others, Rāma marched to Laṅkā.

39. Vibhīṣaṇa, the younger brother of Rāvaṇa, sought refuge in Rāma who readily crowned him as the king of Laṅkā in anticipation.

40. Rāma got the bridge constructed through Nala and crossed the sea to the mountain Suvela from the summit of which he surveyed the city of Laṅkā.

41-46. The leaders of the monkey host were Nīla, Aṅgada, Nala, Dhūmra, Dhūmrākṣa, Vīrendra, Jāmbavān, Mainda,

Dvivida and many others. They attacked and demolished the various parts of the city of Laṅkā. Rāma and Lakṣmaṇa accompanied by the monkey leaders fought with the Rākṣasas of huge bodies dark like mountains of collyrium. The leaders among the demons were Vidyujjihva, Dhūmrākṣa, Devāntaka, Narāntaka, Mahodara, Mahāpārśva, Atikāya, Mahābala, Kumbha, Nikumbha, Matta, Makarākṣa, Akampana, Prahasta, Vīra, Unmatta and the powerful Kumbhakarṇa. Rāma killed them all. Lakṣmaṇa killed Indrajit, son of Rāvaṇa. After chopping off his hands Rāma killed Rāvaṇa.

47. After Sītā had proved her chastity by passing through the blazing pyre she was accepted by Rāma and all of them returned to the city of Ayodhyā in the celestial chariot Puṣpaka.

48-49. Rāma ruled over the kingdom protecting the subjects like his own children. He performed ten horse sacrifices, Piṇḍadāna and other rites in Gayāśīrṣa and charitable gifts too. He crowned his sons Kuśa and Lava in the kingdom.

50-51. Rāma ruled the kingdom for eleven thousand years. Śatrughna killed the demon Lavaṇa. Bharata presided over dramaturgy. Agastya and other sages were worshipped. They told Rāma about the origin and antecedents of the Rākṣasas. Finally, with all the people of Ayodhyā Rāma ascended Heaven.

CHAPTER ONE HUNDRED AND FORTY FOUR

Incarnation of Kṛṣṇa

Brahmā said :

1-2. I shall narrate the story of Viṣṇu where Śrīkṛṣṇa's greatness is explicit. Vāsudeva begot of Devakī Vāsudeva (Lord Kṛṣṇa) and Bala, for the preservation of virtue and the annihilation of evil. Kṛṣṇa sucked the breasts of the ogress Pūtanā and killed her.

3. The Śakaṭa (Cart) demon was upset, and the twin Arjuna trees were uprooted, the serpent Kāliya was humiliated and the demon Dhenuka (Cow) was thrown off.

4-5. The mountain Govardhana was lifted up by Kṛṣṇa and he was honoured by Indra. He freed the Earth of its burden and promised protection for Arjuna and others. The demons Ariṣṭa and others were killed; the demon Keśin was slain and the cowherds were blessed and delighted.

6-7. The wrestlers Cāṇūra and Muṣṭika were killed and Kaṁsa was thrown off his couch and killed. Lord Hari had eight principal wives Rukmiṇī, Satyabhāmā and others, besides sixteen thousand other women. Their sons and grandsons were hundreds of thousands in number.

8 He begot of Rukmiṇi a son Pradyumna who killed Śambara. His son was Aniruddha who became the husband of Uṣā, the daughter of Bāṇa.

9. (In the context of Aniruddha's love-affairs with Uṣā) a great battle between Lord Hari and Lord Śaṅkara ensued wherein thousand hands of Bāṇa were chopped off, leaving him with only two hands.

10. By the Lord, Naraka too was killed and the celestial tree Pārijāta was brought on earth. The asuras Bala, Śiśupāla and the monkey Dvivida were killed by him.

11. Aniruddha's son was Vajra who became king when Lord Hari passed away. He made Sāndīpani his preceptor and reunited him with his son. He installed Ugrasena in the city of Mathurā and set about the task of protecting the deities.

CHAPTER ONE HUNDRED AND FORTYFIVE

The Story of the Mahābhārata

Brahmā said :

1. I shall narrate briefly the story of the Mahābhārata. Fighting for the sake of Pāṇḍavas and others Lord Kṛṣṇa relieved the Earth of its burden.

2. Brahmā was born of the lotus from the navel of Viṣṇu. Atri was Brahmā's son. Soma (moon) was born of Atri. Budha (Mercury) was his son. He begot Purūravas of Ūrvaśī.

3-4. His son was Āyu. In his line the kings Yayāti, Bharata, Kuru and Śantanu were born. Bhīṣma was born of Śantanu and Gaṅgā. He was endowed with all good qualities and he became a master of the Purāṇa called Brahmavaivarta.

5. Śantanu had two sons of his wife Satyavatī. The first son Citrāṅgada was killed by a Gandharva of the same name.

6-8. The other son Vicitravīrya married the two daughters of the king of Kāśī. When he passed away Vyāsa begot of Ambikā his wife Dhṛtarāṣṭra and of Ambālikā the son Pāṇḍu and another son Vidura of the maid-servant. Dhṛtarāṣṭra begot of Gāndhārī one hundred sons of great prowess, the chief of whom was Duryodhana. Pāṇḍu was blessed with five sons in his wives Kuntī and Mādrī.

9. The five sons were: Yudhiṣṭhira, Bhīmasena, Arjuna, Nakula and Sahadeva. All of them were very valiant.

10. Due to the working of Fate an enmity and mutual struggle ensued between the Kauravas and Pāṇḍavas. The frightened and nervous Duryodhana began to harass the Pāṇḍavas.

11-12. After setting fire to the house of lac, the Pāṇḍavas saved themselves by their shrewd intelligence. The pure-hearted noble-souled Pāṇḍavas took the guise of brahmins and stayed in the house of a brahmin in the village of Ekacakrā and killed the demon Baka.

13. They heard of the Svayaṁvara (voluntary self-choice of husband) of Draupadī in the Pāñcāla territory. Prowess and valour being the condition for marrying her they won her hand.

14. With the permission of Droṇa and Bhīṣma, Dhṛtarāṣṭra brought them back and gave them half the kingdom with the capital at Indraprastha, the excellent city.

15. They built a fine Assembly Hall and performed the sacrifice Rājasūya after due performance of sacred rites. Arjuna married Subhadrā, the sister of Vasudeva at Dvārakā and Kṛṣṇa became his lifelong friend.

16. From Agni (fire-god) he got the divine chariot Nandighoṣa, the bow of great renown in the three worlds named Gāṇḍīva, inexhaustible supply of arrows and a coat of mail that could not be pierced through.

17. That bow held in his hand, with Kṛṣṇa for his help Bībhatsu (Arjuna) propitiated the fire god in the forest of Khāṇḍava.

18. He defeated many kings in his campaign of conquest and won precious gems and jewels. He gave gladly all these to his brother, the noble Yudhiṣṭhira, a master of statesmanship.

19. Unfortunately the righteous Yudhiṣṭhira along with his brothers was defeated in a deceitful fraudulent game of dice by the wicked Duryodhana.

20. The wicked Duryodhana followed the counsel of Karṇa, Duśśāsana and Śakuni. The Pāṇḍavas thereafter underwent great hardships for twelve years in the forest.

21-22. In the forests they were accompanied by the sage Dhaumya, their wife Draupadī, and many other brahmins and sages. For one year they stayed in the city of Virāṭa in disguise. They saved a herd of cows and thus being recognised they put forward their claim to their kingdom.

23. In the absence of their full share they wanted only half the kingdom and if that were not given they wanted only five villages. They did not get any of these. Hence, they fought a battle in Kurukṣetra with their vast hosts.

24. They had seven Akṣauhiṇīs (great divisions) of armies and the Kauravas had eleven Akṣauhiṇīs.

25. In the beginning Bhīṣma was the commander-in-chief of Duryodhana's army. A terrific battle not inferior to the battle of gods and demons ensued thereafter.

26. At the head of the army of Pāṇḍavas was Śikhaṇḍin. In the battle, weapons were met with weapons and arrows were split with arrows. It went on thus for ten days.

27-28. Bhīṣma was pierced with hundreds of arrows by Śikhaṇḍin and Arjuna and thrown down. He awaited Uttarāyaṇa (for his final death). He meditated on Lord Gadādhara. He taught Yudhiṣṭhira many religious precepts. He performed Tarpaṇa for the manes. Finally, he merged himself in the pure

Bliss of Supreme God freed of all sins.

29. The battle continued for five days between Droṇa and Dhṛṣṭadyumna in a great terrific manner.

30. Many kings perished in that Vast ocean of arrows, After sinking in the ocean of sorrow, Droṇa finally passed away and attained heaven.

31. Then Karṇa took up the leadership, and fought Arjuna. After two days' battle he sank in the ocean of Arjuna's arrows and attained the Solar region.

32. Then Śalya fought with Yudhiṣṭhira but by midday he was killed by arrows blazing like fire.

33. The powerful Duryodhana seized his club and rushed at Bhīma as terrible as God of death.

34-35. He was killed by the powerful Bhīma with his mace. Aśvatthāmā, the son of Droṇa, infuriated by the death of his father went to the battle-field at night and killed hundreds of sleeping soldiers. He killed Dhṛṣṭadyumna as well as the sons of Draupadī.

36. When Draupadī began to bewail, Arjuna caught hold of Aśvatthāmā and severed his crest-jewel with an Aiṣikāstra (a grass blade arrow). [He being a brahmin and the son of preceptor was not killed by Arjuna. The severance of the crest-jewel was symbolical of slaughter].

37-38. He consoled Yudhiṣṭhira as well as the hundreds of widows plunged in misery. On being consoled by Bhīma, Yudhiṣṭhira took bath, performed Tarpaṇa to the pitṛs, devas and grandfathers. He ruled over the kingdom and performed a horse sacrifice with due gifts.

39. On hearing the destruction of Yādavas in the civil war due to the fight with threshing rods, the king repeated one thousand names of Viṣṇu, crowned Parīkṣit in the kingdom and ascended Heaven in the company of his brothers.

40-43. Vāsudeva will incarnate as Buddha to delude demons, to protect gods, to wipe off evil, and to kill the wicked. In the twentieth Manvantara at the time of churning the milk ocean he incarnated as Dhanvantari and taught Suśruta, son of Viśvāmitra, the whole of Āyurveda, to enliven gods. A man who hears the story of the Mahābhārata and the incarnations of Viṣṇu shall attain Heaven.

CHAPTER ONE HUNDRED AND FORTYSIX

Description of Diseases

Dhanvantari said:

1. O Suśruta,[1] I shall now mention the pathology of all diseases correctly as narrated before by the sages Ātreya and others.

2. The words Roga, Pāpmā, Jvara, Vyādhi, Vikāra, Duṣṭam, Āmaya, Yakṣmā, Ātaṅka, Gada and Bādhā are all synonyms (meaning sickness).

3. The diagnosis of diseases consists of five essential categories, i.e.

Nidāna (Pathology)
Pūrvarūpas (Preliminary stages)
Rūpas (Indications)
Upaśaya (amelioration)
Samprāpti (Localisation and cure)

4. Nidāna or Pathology is mentioned by these words as well—Nimitta (cause), Hetu (Reason), Āyatana (Pathology), Pratyaya (belief), Utthāna Kāraṇa (exciting factor). It is from this that Pūrvarūpa (preliminary stage) is inferred.

5. The preliminary stage is that wherein the sickness about to set in but not excited by all Doṣas exhibits uncertain symptoms.

6. When the same manifests itself in various indications it is called Rūpa (Indications). Other words synonymous with this are Saṁsthāna (fixation), Vyañjana (manifestation), Liṅga (symptom), Lakṣaṇa (characteristic trait), Cihna (sign) and Ākṛti (shape).

7-8. The alleviative employment of medicines, diet and general conduct of the patient antagonistic to the disease or its causes, or capable of producing such antidotes, is called Upaśaya (Amelioration). Another term is Sātmya (identity).

1. Author and compiler of the famous Suśruta-Saṁhitā. He is the earliest writer to deal with surgery. He is later than Caraka. His work was translated in Arabic before the end of the eighth century. There is a Latin translation by Hepler and one in German by Vullers. (*CSL* p. 100; *CDHM* p. 312).

The opposite of this is called Anupaśaya (non amelioration) or Vyādhi-Asātmya (non-identity with the sickness).

9. The removal of sickness by the eradication of the Doṣas, the three principles of Vāyu[1], Pitta[2] and Kapha[3] not being in their normal proportion) is called Samprāpti (localisation and cure. Other terms are Yāti and Āgati.

10. Sickness and its pathology differ due to the change of seasons, force of their attack, time of the day, their importance, and the number of varieties. As for example, now we are going to say that fevers are of eight varieties.

11. What is mentioned as Vikalpa (doubt or suspense) which differentiates one disease from another is preponderance or deficiency of the morbid principles of vāyu, pitta and kapha. Importance as the differentiating character in various diseases means independence or dependence of the different principles in acting as exciting factors of sickness.

12. Differentiation due to potency is to be based on the full complement of the various exciting factors. Differentiation due to the time factor is the various units of time as night, day, season, or the period that lapses between one meal and the next.

13. Thus the meaning of the word Nidāna has been explained briefly now. It will be explained in detail later on. To say, in brief, therefore the cause of all illnesses is the upsetting of the equilibrium of the three Doṣas.

14. The cause of the upset of the doṣas is resorting to Ahita (unwholesome) things which are of three types (i.e. in diet medication and conduct) as mentioned before.

15-16. The Vāyu (the principle connected with nerve forces, vital airs, etc.) becomes upset usually in summer, towards the close of the night or the day or at the end of a meal. It is also caused by gluttonous eating or taking in bitter, sour, astringent, hot and coarse parchifying articles of food. Running, lifting up heavy objects, keeping awake at night too long, loud shouting, sudden onslaught, shock of fear and sorrow, anxious brooding, exercises and excited sexual intercourse also cause the upset of the Vāyu principle.

17. The principle of Pittam (i.e. bile causing defective metabolism) is usually upset in the season of autumn, midday

or midnight or in the course of digestion or acidification of food taken in. Taking in articles of food too hot, pungent sour, and creating a burning sensation in the body is also a cause for such an upset. Getting angry may also cause the upset of Pitta.

18-19. The principle of Kapha or Śleṣmā (i.e. phlegm controlling secretions or excretory process) usually gets upset in the forenoon, early parts of the nights, in the season of spring and immediately after taking food when vomiting, belching etc. accompanies it. Foodstuffs sweet, sour, too saltish, oily and greasy, very heavy, (indigestible), too cold and fluid and soup like in nature too cause the upset of Kapha. Other causes are sedentary habits, sleeplessness, indigestion, sleeping during the day and eructation.

20. The Sannipāta or a combination of these deranged humours takes place due to various causes. Taking in a miscellaneous assortment of food, irregular and incompatible meals, and indigestion cause Sannipāta.

21. Stale beverages and wine, dry vegetables and green, raw radish, etc., asafoetida, oilcakes, putrefying or dry meat—all these cause a jumbled upset of four humours.

22. Sudden change of diet inducing the upset of all humours, exposure to a gust of wind from front affecting the seven vital elements of the body (i.e. the Dhātus viz., secretions, blood, flesh, fat, bones, marrows and semen) and other disorders cause Sannipāta.

23-24. If the food is ill cooked or spoiled in various ways, if bile-producing stuffs are eaten indiscriminately, if the treatment is untimely and ill directed, if various sinful deeds are committed, if the stars are malignant, a sannipāta or combination of deranged humours results. In the case of woman post-parturition disorders not properly remedied may cause this. Sometimes taking in of Aphrodisiacs also upsets this. Various illnesses result therefrom with chemical changes in the blood based on the nature of the disease.